RETAILING IN EMERGING MARKETS

RETAILING

IN

EMERGING

MARKETS

2ND EDITION

EDITED BY

SHUBHAPRIYA BENNUR

JAYA HALAPETE

FAIRCHILD BOOKS
AN IMPRINT OF BLOOMSBURY PUBLISHING INC

BLOOMSBURY
NEW YORK · LONDON · OXFORD · NEW DELHI · SYDNEY

Fairchild Books

An imprint of Bloomsbury Publishing Inc

1385 Broadway	50 Bedford Square
New York	London
NY 10018	WC1B 3DP
USA	UK

www.bloomsbury.com

First edition published 2011
This edition published 2018

Library of Congress Cataloging-in-Publication Data

Names: Bennur, Shubhapriya, editor. | Halepete, Jaya, 1974- editor.
Title: Retailing in emerging markets / edited by Shubhapriya Bennur, Jaya Halepete.
Description: Second Edition. | New York, NY : Fairchild Books, 2017. |
Revised edition of Retailing in emerging markets, 2011.
Identifiers: LCCN 2017013662 | ISBN 9781501319068 (paperback) |
ISBN 9781501319075 (ePDF)
Subjects: LCSH: Retail trade—Developing countries. | BISAC: BUSINESS &
ECONOMICS / Industries / Fashion & Textile Industry. | BUSINESS &
ECONOMICS / Industries / Retailing.
Classification: LCC HF5429.6.D44 R487 2017 | DDC 381/.1091724—dc23 LC record
available at https://lccn.loc.gov/2017013662

ISBN: PB: 978–1–5013–1906–8
        ePDF: 978–1–5013–1907–5

Cover design by Eleanor Rose
Cover images © Getty Images

Typeset by RefineCatch Limited, Bungay, Suffolk
Printed and bound in the United States of America

To find out more about our authors and books visit www.bloomsbury.com. Here you will find extracts, author interviews, details of forthcoming event, and the option to sign up for our newsletters.

CONTENTS

EXTENDED CONTENTS

PREFACE

As domestic retailers outgrow their native markets, many begin to make plans for international expansion. In the past, they targeted mainly developed countries with cultures similar to their own. For example, many American retailers operate successfully in Canada and the United Kingdom. But the market has become saturated in the developed world, and the focus has shifted to developing countries in Asia, the Middle East, and South America. These markets offer great opportunities. But, they come with inherent complexities in terms of how to conduct business. It is important to understand each of these markets from a multidimensional perspective. Students who will be a part of this new trend after they join the workforce as well as retailers need to have a complete understanding of these emerging markets in order to succeed. This book covers aspects such as retailing formats and cultural influences that distinguish selected emerging markets. The main theme of this book is to understand retail as it exists in the emerging markets and various cultural and other factors that influence the retail setup.

Although many books cover some aspect of emerging markets, such as local retail formats or how to behave while doing business, there is no single book that is comprehensive in terms of providing a complete understanding of retail in emerging markets. While teaching courses on the global marketplace for retail industry, we felt a need for a text that would look at emerging markets and provide an understanding of how these markets are different from developed nations. That is what prompted us to write this book. It is designed for courses in international retailing and retailing in emerging markets, and can be used as a supplement for any other apparel-retail courses that require a global perspective. It is also designed for people in retail business who are interested in international markets or retail expansion in these countries.

This text covers the most important aspects of conducting business in nine emerging markets that are consistently ranked in the top 20 in industry reports. The book is designed to help the reader understand the complexities of these markets and provide a detailed understanding of key attributes for conducting business. With emerging markets becoming crucial for international retail expansion, and with many retailers looking to set up offices in multiple countries, it is essential to be knowledgeable about emerging markets. The core chapters in this book are written by experts in retailing from the country being covered. Each contributor provides an understanding of the various concepts from a local perspective.

FEATURES

This is the only book that covers every topic regarding retailing in the top emerging markets specific to the apparel retail industry, including the unique characteristics of consumers in a particular country, common retail formats, and regulations for foreign direct investment. To aid in student understanding of these topics, the book includes the following features:

▶ Objectives at the beginning of every chapter help students understand what they can expect to learn.

▶ Key terms are in bold and appear in the glossary for ready reference. Illustrations are provided to give the reader a better feel for foreign retail formats.

▶ A section in each chapter on retail careers will help students learn what it takes to work in these countries.

▶ Case studies at the end of each chapter show how retailers have succeeded or failed due to certain characteristics of the concerned country.

NEW TO THIS EDITION

Because the world is rapidly changing and new markets are emerging daily, we've updated the text to include new research and pedagogy:

▶ New to this edition are two new chapters—on South Korea and Qatar—investigating the current marketplace opportunities and challenges.

▶ All chapters provide increased coverage of the legislative landscapes and long-term economic outlooks for each country.

▶ Updated and new chapter case studies analyze the expansion strategies of international retailers, including Natura (Brazil), Stylenanda (Korea), LC Waikiki (Turkey), Gap (Thailand) and Grupo Sanborns (Mexico).

▶ New *Chapter Summaries* and *Critical Thinking Questions* offer additional learning tools.

INSTRUCTOR RESOURCES

▶ Instructor's Guide provides suggestions for planning the course and using the text in the classroom, supplemental assignments, and lecture notes

► PowerPoint® presentations include images from the book in full color and provide a framework for lecture and discussion

Instructor's Resources may be accessed through Bloomsbury Fashion Central (www.BloomsburyFashionCentral.com).

ACKNOWLEDGMENTS

Writing this book has been a dream come true, and this would definitely not have been possible without the contribution and support from various people. Some of them helped us start it, whereas others were with us throughout the process.

First of all, Jaya Iyer and Shubhapriya Bennur would like to thank all the contributing authors of each chapter of this book. They were tremendously knowledgeable, supportive, and very enthusiastic about the book and contributing to it. Without their help, this book would not have been possible. We are thankful to Amanda Breccia, Kiley Kudrna, and Corey Kahn at Fairchild Books, who helped us streamline the contents of the book and gave us very useful feedback for the first set of reviews. We would like to thank Edie Weinberg of Fairchild Books for helping with the art work of this edition. We would also like to thank Jennifer Crane and Alexandra Rossomando for their feedback and inputs. We also appreciate the reviewers who gave us their feedback: Leo Archambault, Mount Ida College; Vertica Bhardwaj, Texas State University; Catherine Campbell, Art Institute of Tampa; Barbara Stewart, University of Houston; Tammy Tavassoli, The Illinois Institute of Art-Schaumburg; Catharine Weiss, Lasell College.

There are some people who have made a major difference in Jaya Iyer's life and always inspire her to strive to be the best. She would like to thank her brother, Sameer Halepete, and her major professor Dr. Mary Littrell for being her inspiration. She would like to thank her mom for giving her all the love, her dad for pushing her to do her best, and all her family for always being so supportive. Lastly, tremendous love, support, and encouragement from her husband, Sesh Iyer, made this book possible. Her children Sohum and Swaha, who are wonderful in every way and make it possible to work on projects such as this book.

Likewise, Shubhapriya Bennur would like to thank her grandfather who was an educator and a role model in her life. She would also like to thank her parents and family for being supportive especially her husband Deepak Rudrappa and sister Shweta Gavai for their encouragement and support. Her children Aarav and Ava were curious helpers throughout the process. Thank you everyone for making the second edition possible.

The Publisher wishes to gratefully acknowledge and thank the editorial team involved in the publication of this book:
Acquisitions Editor: Amanda Breccia
Development Editor: Corey Kahn
Assistant Editor: Kiley Kudrna
Art Development Editor: Edie Weinberg
In-House Designer: Eleanor Rose
Production Manager: Claire Cooper
Project Manager: RefineCatch Ltd.

EMERGING MARKETS

Shubhapriya Bennur

Jaya Halepete

OBJECTIVES

After reading this chapter, you will

- ▶ Be able to define "emerging market"
- ▶ Understand the basic terminology of retailing formats
- ▶ Know the terms used for market-entry strategy
- ▶ Grasp the importance of understanding consumers in emerging markets

The term **emerging market** was coined in the 1980s, by Antoine van Agtmael. A developing market economy is an economy with a low-to-middle per capita income. Such countries constitute approximately 80 percent of the global population and represent about 20 percent of the world's economy. From developing economies, countries transition into emerging markets. Emerging markets are marked by following characteristics that include:

- ▶ *Transitional Economy*—Emerging markets are often in the process of moving from a closed economy to an open market economy.
- ▶ *Young and Growing Population*—Emerging markets often have younger populations with spurring strong long-term growth rates. Often a younger population is replacing aging workers; they are affluent consumers.
- ▶ *Underdeveloped Infrastructure*—Emerging markets are often in the early stages of building infrastructure. While this means there is often demand

for government spending, it can also mean higher costs and less efficiency for businesses.

▶ *Increasing Foreign Investment*—Emerging markets usually have lenient regulations for foreign direct investments. However, too much capital can quickly lead to overheated market saturation (Kuepper 2016).

As apparel markets of developed countries have become saturated, their retailers have begun to focus on emerging markets for expansion. Even retailers that have not reached high levels of saturation at home are looking to expand into these emerging markets to gain **first-movers advantage**, a sometimes insurmountable advantage gained by the first significant company to move into a new market.

It is important to note that the first-mover advantage refers to the first *significant* company to move into a market, not merely the first company. For example, Amazon.com may not have been the first online bookseller, but Amazon.com was the first significant company to make an entrance into the online book market.

Many research firms have been conducting analysis to understand emerging countries such as India, Russia, China, the Middle East, and Latin America These economies may have the best potential for apparel retailing; they have an expanding consumer base with higher disposable income.

A.T. Kearney is a Chicago-based global management consulting company founded in 1926. It focuses on the strategic and operational concerns of a CEO's agenda. The retail-apparel index (including all the important drivers that make a market attractive to foreign investors) indicates the rank of a country as an emerging market attractive to foreign investors. A.T. Kearney calculates the retail apparel index using three metrices: clothing market attractiveness (60 percent), retail development (20 percent), and country risk (20 percent). The growth prospects number includes clothing sales, imports, clothing sales per capita, GDP per capita, and population growth. Based on the A.T. Kearney report and other research reports, this book covers Brazil, China, India, Russia, Turkey, Thailand, South Korea, Qatar and Mexico (Table 1.1). Some markets remain as important emerging markets and attractive to investors for a longer time as compared to some others that mature and saturate very quickly. Based on a thorough research of important emerging markets in the current times and owing to space constraints, this book is restricted to these nine emerging markets.

Many large retail chains, such as Tesco (United Kingdom), Metro (Germany), Walmart (United States), and Carrefour (France), have already

TABLE 1.1 2013 Apparel Retail Index A.T. Kearney

Rank	Country	Market Attractiveness	Retail Development	Country Risk	Score
1	China	40.2	10.8	11.8	62.8
2	UAE	39.1	7.2	16.0	62.4
3	Chile	32.8	7.8	17.4	57.9
4	Kuwait	38.8	5.5	12.8	57.2
5	Brazil	33.5	9.9	12.1	55.5
6	Saudi Arabia	36.2	5.6	13.2	55
7	Russia	36.5	9.3	8.6	54.4
8	Malaysia	30.4	6.0	15.7	52.1
9	Mexico	26.9	11.8	11.7	50.4
10	Turkey	28.4	9.3	12.6	50.3

Source: A.T. Kearney, 2013

established themselves in developing countries in various ways. Although these markets may not offer immediate profits due to problems such as poor infrastructure, widespread corruption, and a very diverse customer base driven by strong local culture, traditions, habits, and values, there is the potential for rewards in the long term.

According to International Monetary Fund (IMF) data, the gross domestic product (GDP) based on purchasing-power-parity (PPP) share of world total for emerging markets' is about 57.5 percent as of June 2016. Since 2007, consumers in emerging markets have been spending more money than Americans. The potential growth rate of revenue, return on investment, and low cost of investment make emerging markets attractive to investors. But with increasing competition from many domestic as well as international players, the cost of investment in these emerging markets is increasing. Hence, it is becoming more and more important to make an entry and gain first-mover advantage.

Understanding the apparel retail market in emerging markets is a challenge that most international retailers face. In general, these developing countries have a large geographical spread, cultural diversity, and more than one language, which makes retailing extremely challenging for foreign companies. Other factors such as political situation, economic stability, real estate issues, market size, government regulations for entry, technical advancement, and consumer behavior all affect foreign retailers, who should grasp these challenges fully before making a decision to enter a foreign market. Due to the high level of risk involved in investing in an emerging market, retailers look for acquisitions (buying an existing company) rather than greenfield investments (a foreign company investing in a country by starting the construction from ground up).

This chapter covers some basic concepts that are essential for an understanding of these emerging markets.

EMERGING MARKETS FOR APPAREL RETAIL: WHAT MAKES THEM IMPORTANT?

Certain characteristics unique to emerging markets make them attractive to foreign investors. All these factors have to be thoroughly analyzed before investing in the market. Timing is very important in making the investment in these markets for various reasons:

▶ *Growing economy:* Emerging markets grow at a very fast pace. Taking advantage of increasing **gross domestic product** (GDP, which is the total value of all the goods and services produced in a country) and incomes in a country helps retailers become established and profitable quickly.

▶ *Reduced legislative burden*: To attract foreign investors, emerging markets are reducing regulations associated with starting a business. Many markets are changing their foreign direct investment policies to make entry easier for foreign investors.

▶ *Market saturation*: Some emerging markets were identified a decade or more ago, and many foreign investors have long since invested in them to have the first-mover advantage. Although some markets may be getting saturated, it is important to identify gaps in the market so that foreign companies can still consider investing to cover those gaps. So it is important to keep a lookout for the right markets to invest in at the right time.

▶ *Domestic competition*: Domestic retailers know their consumers much better than foreign retailers, making them the biggest threat. Domestic companies learn best practices from international retailers and combine them with knowledge of the local culture to become formidable competition for foreign retailers; however, the retailing environment in emerging markets is not as highly sophisticated in terms of technological excellence and high level of customer service as it is in developed nations like the United States.

CONSUMERS IN EMERGING MARKETS: A COMPLEX LOT

In 2015, the GDP for emerging markets such as India, China, and Russia was over 7 percent. In these parts of the world, less than 10 percent of the retail sector is organized and consumption is growing. These factors make for compelling retail opportunities. The spending power of consumers is rapidly changing the retail industry in most of these emerging economies. Multinational retailers seeking new sources of growth are watching the mass markets of Brazil, China, and India. Consumption is also on the rise in Mexico, Turkey, and Russia. As consumers in these nations have greater disposable income, they increasingly spend their money on items beyond the basic necessities. Huge populations and strong economic growth have made them places of high interest in terms of market expansion.

Throughout the 1980s, most multinationals were reluctant to invest in low-income economies because they assumed that people with low incomes spent all their money on basic needs like food and shelter, with nothing left for goods and services. They also assumed that barriers to commerce such as corruption, illiteracy, inadequate infrastructure, currency fluctuations, and bureaucratic red tape made it impossible to do profitable business in these regions. For example, liberalization of trade policies in India began only around 1991. But today, many multinationals run successful businesses in developing economies due to improving conditions; these developing economies are no longer considered as low-income economies. Increasing income levels of the large middle-class population in these economies has fueled the retail market in the developing countries.

Due to the economic growth in sectors such as manufacturing and information technology, many families that fell under the low-income group now have jobs and are a part of the middle-class population. Thus, the middle-income segment has expanded and can represent up to 70 percent of the total population in some emerging markets (Heyde & Sundjaja, 2008). For example, in the large southern and eastern cities of China, consumer spending in the middle income segment has more than doubled since the mid–1990s and is growing rapidly (Moriarity, 2008).

Consumers in emerging markets are intensely interested in branded products. Products that have been customized for local customers attract intense interest. For example, brands such as L'Oreal have introduced fairness products (such as skin-lightening face creams) especially for the Indian market due to high demand for these products in the country. Brands must not be afraid to evolve. Consumers love brands that adapt and commit to emerging markets (Gilpin, 2009). Brands that seek a lasting commitment from consumers need to offer more than just the superficial excitement of their otherness. Brands that do not consider consumers' preference for their local culture will surely fail. Some brands also change their image (from high-end stores to low-end stores or the other way around) in emerging markets. For example, H&M is a mass-market retailer in the West. However, prices that are cheap in Europe and the United States are expensive for the average Chinese consumer; but with increased income levels, Chinese consumers today have higher disposable incomes. To acquire Chinese consumers, H&M has reinvented itself as a profitable player by offering clothes, shoes, and accessories unmatched in terms of style and (lower) pricing by local competitors (Gilpin, 2009).

It is important for foreign investors as well as domestic retailers to classify consumers into groups in order to understand them better and cater to their specific needs. In most emerging economies, consumers fall into four distinct groups:

- ▸ At the apex is the **global tier**, which consists of consumers who want products and goods to have the same attributes and quality as products in developed countries. For example, they shop for the same products at Louis Vuitton as consumers in developed countries do. They are well educated and well informed about global markets (Khanna & Palepu, 2005). Most companies that enter foreign markets try to cater to consumers in the global tier.
- ▸ The next set of consumers falls under the **glocal tier**, which consists of consumers who demand customized products of near-global standard and are willing to pay a shade less than global consumers do (Khanna & Palepu, 2005). In this group the competition between domestic and foreign companies intensifies. The domestic company understands the needs of the local consumers and can easily tailor the global product to suit. Foreign retailers need to spend time understanding the local consumers to meet their requirements. For example, in Mexico, McDonalds

has a McMolletes, which are refried beans, cheese, and pico de gallo served on an English muffin.

- The set of consumers who follow the glocal consumers falls under the **local tier**. These consumers are happy with products of local quality, at local prices (Khanna & Palepu, 2005). The local retailers of the emerging markets cater to consumers in this group because they understand the consumers and offer them local products at local prices.

- At the lowest tier lie consumers who can afford only the least expensive products. This tier is referred to as bottom of the pyramid (Khanna and Palepu, 2005).

A proper understanding of consumer types in the country where a retailer is interested in investing helps yield the right product and the right price, which in turn helps achieve success in the foreign market.

RETAIL FORMATS FOR ENTERING EMERGING MARKETS: DEPENDENT ON REGULATORY ENVIRONMENT

Availability of real estate in a country is one of the most important factors in attracting foreign investors. Procuring real estate is important for retailers who want to build new stores rather than acquire existing ones. If a retailer cannot find a format that they are comfortable with due to unavailability or difficulty in obtaining prime location for a store, they are less likely to enter the market. There are many different formats to suit different retailers. Some formats are specific to a country (see individual chapters), but most modern formats are common in all the emerging markets. Some of the most common retail formats are:

Hypermarket: Hypermarkets are supermarkets and department stores combined together. Walmart is a great American example. These very large stores sell a wide range of products under grocery, household merchandise, apparel, and general merchandise, and usually have a selling area of at least 50,000 square feet (4,645 square meters) and ample parking. Able to buy in bulk, hypermarkets offer very good prices. They are often adjacent to towns and base their attraction on these prices and convenience to car-owning consumers, who can make many of their purchases in one place. Hypermarkets are widespread, especially in grocery retailing (Law, 2010).

Supermarket: A large, self-service store that carries a wide variety of food, household products, and other goods, which it sells in high volumes at relatively low prices (Law, 2010).

Cooperative store (consumer cooperative store): A store that is owned and controlled by members of the cooperative who use the products and not an individual owner. In this retail outlet format, members enjoy not only the benefits of good-quality products at fair prices but also a share of the profits (a dividend) based on the amount of each member's purchases (Law, 2010). Cooperatives vary in store type and number of members. These stores are beneficial for promoting products of small business owners or other less-powerful people (What is a cooperative, 2010).

Warehouse club (wholesale club; membership warehouse): A cut-price retailer that sells a limited selection of brand-name grocery items, appliances, clothing, and other goods at substantial discounts to members, who pay an annual membership fee (Law, 2010). These stores are normally established in warehouse-type buildings where merchandise is displayed without any frills. Sam's Club, a division of Walmart Stores, Inc., is an example of a warehouse club.

Main street store: A store that is located on the primary street of a town. This street is where most of its shops, banks, and other businesses are located (Law, 2010).

Mom-and-pop store: A small retail business, such as a grocery store, owned and operated by members of a family and often located on a main street. In developing countries, mom-and-pop stores don't congregate on any specific street; they can be located anywhere, such as in regional markets, markets in residential areas, or markets in suburban areas (The Oxford American Dictionary of Current English, 1999).

Cash-and-carry store: A wholesaler that sells to retailers and other businesses at discounted prices on condition that they pay in cash, collect the goods themselves, and buy in bulk (Smullen & Jonathan, 2008). One needs to be a member of the store in order to make purchases. These stores sell products in bulk and the main customers are other business owners. For example, Metro (Germany) is an example of a cash-and-carry store where only business owners that are members can shop.

ENTRY MODES FOR EMERGING MARKETS: DEPENDENT ON REGULATORY ENVIRONMENT

A retailer chooses its entry format based on a country's regulations for venturing into new markets. The options include the following.

Franchising: A license given to a manufacturer, distributor, or trader that enables them to manufacture or sell a named product or service in a particular area for a stated period. The holder of the license (**franchisee**) usually pays the grantor of the license (**franchisor**) a royalty on sales, often with a lump sum as an advance against royalties (Law, 2009). The franchisor may supply the franchisee with a brand identity as well as financial and technical expertise. Common franchises are fast-food restaurants, gas stations, and travel agencies.

Joint venture: A joint venture is a contract between two companies to conduct business for an agreed upon duration of time. Companies get together in a joint venture to share each other's strengths, reduce risks, and be more competitive by using each other's skills in a marketplace. Joint venturers often carry on their principal businesses independently at the same time as the joint venture is functioning (Smullen & Jonathan, 2008).

Licensing: An agreement by which a company (the **licensor**) permits a foreign company (the **licensee**) to set up a business in a foreign market using the licensor's manufacturing processes, patents, trademarks, and trade secrets in exchange for payment of a fee or royalty (Black, 2003).

Direct investment: In this method of entry, the foreign company owns 100 percent of the company. Direct investments are made in different ways:

- *Wholly owned subsidiary*: A parent company holds a majority or all of the shares of a **subsidiary** and controls all of its functions. In a wholly owned subsidiary, the parent holding company owns virtually 100 percent of the common stock. There is no minority interest in the subsidiary (Downes & Goodman, 2006; Smullen & Jonathan, 2008).
- *Acquisition*: An acquisition is the purchase of a company or asset. A foreign company may acquire a small or a large domestic company to enter the market depending on the size of the foreign company. The foreign investor does not have to worry about buying real estate and building from the ground up (Moles & Nicholas, 2005).

> ▸ *Greenfield investment*: A form of foreign direct investment in which a parent company starts a new venture in a foreign country by constructing new operational facilities from the ground up. In addition to building facilities, most parent companies also create long-term jobs in the foreign country by hiring local employees (Clark, 1999).

REGULATIONS FOR FOREIGN DIRECT INVESTMENT: OPENING UP FOR TRADE

Foreign direct investment, in its classic definition, is defined as a company from a country making a physical investment into building a factory or setting up a business in another country. Smart investors consider a country's regulations for foreign direct investment (FDI) very carefully before investing in an emerging market. Most emerging markets are interested in attracting foreign investment and are working to make their FDI regulations simple and ensuring that their policies create a friendly business environment. The governments in emerging markets are also working to control corruption, eliminate unnecessary paperwork, and encourage transparency (where all laws and regulations are clearly defined and understood easily) (Foreign Direct, 2010).

TOP GLOBAL RETAILERS: MARKET LEADERS

There are many successful retailers in the world. Some are successful in their home country and only present there. Some others are successful not only in their home country (for example, El Corte Inglés in Spain) but also in all the countries where they are present (for example, Walmart, Metro). In this section, the top four global retailers, based on their domestic and international revenues, will be discussed.

WALMART

Walmart is the largest retailer in the United States. It operates over 6,300 retail facilities globally. Walmart provides general merchandise that includes family apparel, health and beauty aids, household needs, electronics, toys, pet supplies, fabrics, crafts, lawn and garden, jewelry, and shoes. It also runs a pharmacy department, tire and lube express, and a photo processing center (Wal-Mart, 2016). Walmart is largely a discount retailer, and it sells products at the lowest possible prices. Its strategy is to expand by selling goods at low prices, thus outselling its competitors. The company's competitive strategy is to dominate every sector the company enters into. Walmart measures success in terms of sales and dominance over competitors. Internationally, the company's strategy has been to acquire companies and convert them into Walmart stores (Walmart, 2016). The company first expanded into Mexico, Brazil, Argentina, and Canada. In 1996, Walmart moved to China. It subsequently tapped European markets such as Germany and the UK, as well as other Asian markets such as South Korea. Japan was the next stop. As of 2016, Walmart has 11,535 stores in 27 countries. The retail giant has succeeded everywhere but Russia, Germany, and South Korea. The failures were mainly due to tough competition in the low-price segment and lack of understanding of the local culture in these countries.

CARREFOUR

France's Carrefour is the largest retailer in Europe and second largest in the world. The company operates through four formats: hypermarket, supermarket, hard discount, and convenience stores. The group has over 11,935 stores in more than 30 countries; these are either operated by Carrefour or are franchise operations. Carrefour is looking to grow into China, Brazil, Indonesia, Poland, and Turkey. Depending on the country of operation, almost 90 to 95 percent of the merchandise sold in the store is sourced locally. Carrefour's main strategy is to gain customer trust in the company, the product quality, price, and service. Carrefour pioneered the hypermarket model, selling everything from household electronic items to fresh produce (Carrefour, 2016).

Carrefour has opened stores in many countries and has eventually pulled out of many in a strategy to close down poorly performing stores to invest in more profitable countries. The countries where they pulled out include Japan, Mexico, Russia, Switzerland, the United States, the UK, and China. In 2010, the company opened several new stores in China and Romania, and its first cash-and-carry (where only business owners that are members can shop) in India.

METRO

Metro group has over 2,100 stores in 34 countries in Europe, Africa, and Asia. Metro is Europe's third-largest retail chain after Carrefour and the UK's Tesco and the world's third-largest trade and retail group in terms of sales. This German retail giant's guiding principle is "as decentrally as possible, as centrally as necessary." The group started as a wholesale store in Dusseldorf in 1964, and transformed itself into Germany's largest retailer (Metro group, 2016). Though the company generated the majority of its sales from its home market, retail sales in Germany began to show a decline during the early twenty-first century due to a high unemployment rate, the country's wavering economy, a rise in inflation, and an increase in taxes. This led Metro group to operate in a high-cost environment with a low profit margin, which in turn had an adverse effect on the company's profits in Germany. To compensate for the declining sales in its domestic market, Metro pursued a strategy of expansion and internationalization through its cash-and-carry business model, and started focusing on emerging markets in Asia and Eastern Europe. Metro's focus on international markets has been an important factor in driving its growth in the light of the slowed growth in its home country. In its expansion, the company has a long-term focus on growing economies and consumers with high purchasing power. On March 30, 2016 Metro Group announced that it would be splitting into two independent companies: a leading international wholesale and food specialist, comprising Metro, Makro and Real, as well as a corresponding division and service companies and a leader in consumer electronics products and services, comprising Media Markt and Saturn and its portfolio including strong formats and brands (Metro Group, 2016).

TESCO

Jack Cohen, who sold groceries in London's East End markets, founded Tesco in 1924. It is the UK's largest retailer with 3,529 stores including all its formats Express, One Stop, Super Stores etc. worldwide (Tesco.com, 2016).

There are two primary reasons for Tesco's success: first is the company's tremendous market penetration in the UK (95 percent) and European markets. The second is Tesco's commitment to supply its online visitors with a continuous stream of new, compelling offers and editorial information every time they visit the Tesco.com site (Tesco.com, 2003).

Tesco.com was initially launched in 1999 with a major relaunch in 2005. Tesco is the world's largest online grocery retailer and recognizes that product images and packet information are essential for online shoppers. Customers must be able to visualize products and have access to full label information to allow them to make more informed purchases (Tesco.com, 2003). Tesco has expanded into Central Europe and Asia. It operates in 12 markets. By the beginning of the 1990s, Tesco had 371 stores in England, Scotland, and Wales— 150 of which were superstores—and the company had become one of the United Kingdom's top three food retailers. On the international front, Tesco entered Thailand in 1998, South Korea in 1999, Taiwan in 2000, Malaysia in 2002, and China in 2004. The company's existing operations abroad were bolstered by several acquisitions, including the 2002 purchase of Poland-based hypermarkets HIT, the 2003 purchase of Kipa, a four-store hypermarket chain in Turkey, and the 2003 acquisition of the C, a chain of 78 food stores in Japan (Tesco Plc, n.d.). On 27 January 2017 it was announced that Tesco had reached an agreement to merge with Britain's biggest wholesaler Booker Group to create the UK's largest food group.

THE FUTURE OF EMERGING MARKETS: CHALLENGING MARKETS

More than a dozen of the United States' top 20 retailers have focused their attention on emerging markets in their expansion plans. Retailers that invested early on in these markets are at a definite advantage over latecomers. Many factors, such as cultural differences, consumer behavior, local competition, and a business environment very different from home, make these markets challenging. But a proper understanding of the market and alterations that meet the market requirements can make a retail investment very profitable. Economists expect emerging markets to yield the world's biggest growth between 2010–2020. These emerging markets are at various levels of maturity. Foreign retailers have just begun to enter some markets and have already established themselves in others. A foreign retailer needs to analyze each emerging market separately to determine the right moment to invest in it.

Case Study

Emerging markets or emerging economies are those lower-income but rapid-growth countries that use economic liberalization as their primary engine of growth and are participating in a more industrious capacity. They are moving away from their traditional economies which were depend on agriculture and the export of raw materials. In order to create a better quality of life for their people, leaders of developing countries want to rapidly industrialize and adopt a free market or mixed economy. Emerging markets are important because they drive growth in the global economy. Furthermore, their financial systems have become more sophisticated.

Emerging markets have few agreed-upon characteristics. First, they have a lower-than-average per capita income. They have either low or lower middle per capita income of less than $4,035 as per World Bank estimates. Second, they have Rapid Growth. Emerging markets are willing to accept the rapid change to a more industrialized economy. For example, in 2016, the economic growth of most developed countries, such as the United States, Germany, the United Kingdom and Japan, was less than 3 percent. In contrast, growth in Egypt, Turkey, and the United Arab Emirates was 4 percent or more. China and India both saw their economies grow by around 7 percent. Third, the emerging markets are highly volatile due to rapid social change that can come from natural disasters, external price shocks, and domestic policy instability. Emerging markets are more susceptible to volatile currency swings and changes in the price of commodities, such as oil or food. Fourth, the rapid growth requires a lot of investment capital. But the capital markets are less mature in these countries than the developed markets. However, if investors take risk, there is the promise of a higher-than-average return for investors, as many of these countries focus on an export-driven strategy. They don't have the demand at home, so they produce lower-cost consumer goods and commodities for developed markets. The companies that fuel this growth will profit more, which translates into higher stock prices for investors. This characteristic makes emerging markets attractive to investors.

While each market has its own unique characteristics, multiple challenges distinct from those facing the developed world are common factors. These include:

- ▸ Severe financial and digital divides between more wealthy urban centers and rural districts
- ▸ Less developed or poor infrastructure

- ▸ Growing labor costs
- ▸ Bureaucratic and corrupt government.

REFERENCE

Amadeo Kimberly (2016). What Are Emerging Markets? Five Defining Characteristics. Retrieved January 26, 2017 from, https://www.thebalance.com/what-are-emerging-markets-3305927

Discussion Questions

1. List the characteristics of emerging markets. Why it is important for foreign investors to understand these markets?
2. What are some of the challenges of emerging markets?

REFERENCES

Anonymous (2003). Retrieved from www.rjmintz.com/general-partnerships.html

Anonymous (2009). Marketing Terms Glossary. Retrieved August 31, 2010 from www.marketingterms.com/dictionary/first_mover_advantage/

Black, J. (2003). *A Dictionary of Economics.* Oxford Reference Online. Oxford: Oxford University Press.

Carrefour (2016). Retrieved January 20, 2017 from www.carrefour.com/cdc/group/our-group/

Clark, J. (1999). *International Dictionary of Banking and Finance.* Glenlake Publishing Company: Chicago.

Downes, J. & Goodman, J. E. (2006). *Dictionary of Finance and Investment Terms.* Barron's, Hauppauge, NY: Expanding chains target emerging markets (2008). *SCTWeek, 13* (37), p. 4.

Foreign direct investment policies (2010). Retrieved March 4, 2010 from www.economywatch.com/policywatch/fdi-policy.htm

Gilpan, G. (2009, June 17). Insight is Everything. *Harvard Business Review.*

"High Street Noun" *The Oxford Dictionary of English* (revised edition). Ed. Catherine Soanes and Angus Stevenson. Oxford University Press, 2005. Oxford Reference Online. Oxford University Press.

Heyde, R. A. & Sundjaja, K. (2008). Busting the Myths about Emerging Markets. Retrieved March 5, 2010 from www.oliverwyman.com/ow/pdf_files/OWJ25–4-Busting_Emerging_Market_Myths.pdf

Khanna, T. & Palepu, K. G. (2005). Emerging Giants: Building World Class Companies in Developing Economies. Retrieved March 4, 2010 from www.hbr.org

Kuepper, J. (2016). What are Emerging Markets? Finding and Investing in Emerging Markets. Retrieved January 24, 2017 from, www.thebalance.com/what-are-emerging-markets–1978974

Law, J. (2009). *A Dictionary of Business and Management.* Oxford Reference Online Premium. Oxford: Oxford University Press.

Mangalorkar, R., Kuppuswamy, R. & Groeber, M. (2007). The BRIC promise.

Metro Group (2016). Retrieved January 21, 2017, from www.metrogroup.de/servlet/PB/menu/1000083_l2/ index.html

Mexico "Breaks the BRIC" to Appear in the Top Four Emerging Economies (2008). Retrieved November 8, 2010 from www.gti.org/ Press-room/Mexico-breaks-the-BRIC.asp

Moles, P. & Nicholas T. (2005). *The Handbook of International Financial Terms.* Oxford Reference Online Premium, Oxford University Press: New York

Moriarity, M. (2008). Emerging Opportunities for Global Retailers. Retrieved February 24, 2010 from www.atkearney.de/.../pdf_atkearney_bip_grdi_2008_1212762749d09c.pdf

Russo, J. (2008, December 5). Times Are Not as Tough for Some: Consumers in Emerging Markets are Likely to Perceive the Recession will be Short. Retrieved March 18, 2010 from http://blog.nielsen.com/nielsenwire/consumer/times-are-not-as-tough-for-some-consumers-in-emerging-markets-are-likely-to-perceive-the-recession-will-be-short/

Smullen, J. & Jonathan, L. (2008). *A Dictionary of Finance and Banking*. Oxford Reference Online. Oxford: Oxford University Press

Tesco Plc (n.d.). Retrieved November 9, 2010 from www.fundinguniverse.com/company-histories/ Tesco-plc-Company-History.html

Tesco.com (2003). Tesco.com Ensures Online Offer are as Fresh as Produce with Interwoven. Retrieved November 9, 2010 from www.interwoven.com.cn/documents/casestudies/tesco_august.pdf

Thailand's Investment Market Retains its Attractiveness (2008, May 9). Retrieved November 8, 2010 from www.nationmultimedia.com/2008/05/09/business/business_30072622.php

Walmart (2016). Retrieved January 20, 2017 from http://walmartstores.com/AboutUs/

Walmart Seeks Re-entry into Indonesia (2010, November 4). Retrieved November 18, 2010 from www.thejakartaglobe.com/business/wal-mart-seeks-re-entry-into-indonesian-market/404947

What is a Cooperative? (2010). Retrieved November 16, 2010 from http://sfp.ucdavis.edu/cooperatives/whatis.html

Wooldridge, A. (2010, April 17). The World Turned Upside Down. *The Economist*. Retrieved May 19, 2010 from http://www.economist.com/specialreports/displayStory.cfm?story_id=15879369

BRAZIL

Silvio Abrahao Laban Neto
Jaya Halepete
Luciana de Araujo Gil
Youssef Youssef
Flavia Silveira Cardoso
Wlamir Xavier

OBJECTIVES

After reading this chapter, you will

▶ Understand why Brazil is considered to be an emerging market
▶ Learn about unique characteristics of Brazilian consumers
▶ Gain knowledge about various traditional and nontraditional retail formats in the country
▶ Understand government regulations for foreign direct investment in Brazil

Many people have agreed with Jeffrey Simpson, Canadian journalist and national affairs columnist for *The Globe and Mail,* when he wrote in 2010, "For a country with a tumultuous economic history, the first decade of the twenty-first century has been remarkably good: low inflation by Brazilian standards (4 to 5 percent), steady growth (4 to 5 percent), shrinking national debt, an economy lifted by high commodities prices, and success in selected industrial sectors. Who would have thought a decade ago that Brazil would actually be lending money to the International Monetary Fund? Best of all, studies show a slow but steady diminution in income inequality. Poverty rates have fallen from 35 percent to 25 percent in a decade." However once again six years later, Brazil has been struggling with unemployment rates, inflation is on the rise and it has impeached its second president in the last 25 years. Additionally, part of the social and economic gains are being diluted and for some economists, Brazil has gone back 10 years in terms of economic development. Even so, given its geographical and market size, the country may still be considered a potential market with huge untapped potential. Is Brazil still the country of the future? How far in the future will this be?

Slightly smaller in area than the United States, Brazil has the fifth-largest population in the world and the largest in Latin America. According to the World Bank, Brazil is the world's seventh-largest economy (2014). By 2020, the majority of its population will be between the ages of 15 and 44, making Brazil one of the most important job and consumer markets in the American continent (Table 2.1).

Brazil has a wide range of natural resources. About 40 percent of the world's biodiversity is located in Brazil. Its continental dimension holds five important biomes: the Amazon (rain forest), the Cerrado (savanna), the Atlantic Forest, the caatinga (dryland), and the Pantanal (swamplands). The Brazilian Amazon is the most important biological reserve in the world and holds 10 percent of the world's total freshwater reserves. Mineral deposits are also abundant in the country.

The Portuguese, who claimed Brazil in 1500 and ruled for more than three centuries, first brought the region into the global economy. Throughout the eighteenth and early nineteenth centuries, the Portuguese crown grew wealthy on the gold and diamonds they forced Native Americans and African slaves to mine. The colony became a constitutional monarchy in its own right in 1822. In 1889, a military coup established a constitutional democracy, which was destabilized by additional coups in 1930 and 1964. In 1985, the military returned power to civilian rulers, and a democratic regime was implemented. However, the international oil crisis in the 1970s plus a noncompetitive state-driven and somewhat closed economy have created a high inflationary business environment. In 1985, the indirectly elected president Tancredo Neves never took office. He was rushed to the hospital on his inauguration day where he died 39 days later. His vice president, José Sarney, took office definitively and tried through many different economic plans to control one of the world's highest inflation rates. Fernando Collor, the first directly elected president, took office in 1990. In an attempt to improve Brazil's competitiveness, he tried

TABLE 2.1 Fast Facts about Brazil	
Capital	Brasilia
Population	204.3 million (2015 est.)
Type of government	Federal Republic
GDP: purchasing power parity in US$	$3.166 trillion (2015)
Age structure	0–14 yrs: 23.27 percent 15–24 yrs: 16.47 percent 25–54 years: 43.80 percent 55 yrs plus: 16.46 percent
Religion	Catholic: 65.0 percent Protestant: 22.3 percent None: 8.0 percent Others: 4.3 percent Unspecified: 0.4 percent
Ethnicity	White: 47.7 percent Mixed Black and White: 43.1 percent Black: 7.6 percent Other: 1.6 percent

Source: CIA factbook.gov

to implement drastic economic measures to control inflation, reduce government weight in the economy, and eliminate many legal restrictions to import goods such as cars and computers. Collor was impeached in 1992, accused of political corruption; his vice president, Itamar Franco, then took office. Under Itamar Franco, a set of economic measures, known as Plano Real, was implemented, and finally inflation started to be controlled and a stable foundation for economic growth was set. Itamar Franco was succeeded by Fernando Henrique Cardoso, his Finance Minister under whose guidance Plano Real was created. Fernando Henrique's first term was characterized by the continuation of inflation control and the launch of some relevant social programs.

Although re-election was not allowed then, changes were implemented to the Constitution in order to allow presidents to be re-elected. Fernando

Henrique was easily re-elected; however, his second term was tainted by accusations of maneuvering to approve the re-election legislation and an enormous electricity and power crisis. Accused of being too liberal, Fernando Henrique's candidate for succession was defeated by Luiz Inacio Lula da Silva. The early days of Lula were very complicated: there was a big devaluation of the Real, and characteristic of Lula's historical position as a union and workers' leader, a hard and strong speech against the private sector and the markets. However, to everybody's surprise, Lula integrated the business community into his government and maintained the gains from the economic stability created by his predecessors. Lula improved the existing social programs and increased their scope and reach; however, corruption scandals started to pop up which led to important changes in his government team, including the fall of Antonio Palocci his Finance Minister, who had been very well accepted by the business community. Lula succeeded in being re-elected but, during his second term, despite social progress and inclusion, corruption was still a major issue. This culminated in the fall of José Dirceu, one of the most visible members of the Workers' Party and a virtual candidate to replace Lula.

During Lula's terms, Brazil was elected to host the World Cup in 2014 and the Olympics in Rio in 2016. Lula nominated Dilma Roussef to succeed him and with a speech against the privatization of Petrobras and other state and mixed ownership companies as well as the maintenance of the social programs, she was elected. However, Dilma Roussef was not as savvy as Lula as a politician and has faced many different issues with Congress. Her government was still tainted by corruption issues and by a lack of dialogue with politicians and society. During her first term, a lot of attention was given to the World Cup preparation and the infrastructure legacy that such an event would entail. In mid–2013, Brazilians started protesting in the streets since a lot of funds were being invested in the World Cup while other critical areas, such as healthcare, security and education were neglected. Economic indicators were already deteriorating but, once again, Lula helped Dilma and she was re-elected in a very close election with Aécio Neves. This dispute really divided the country and Dilma took office under a cloud of suspicion related to another huge corruption scandal involving Petrobras, the largest Brazilian company and one of the top oil companies in the world. In September 2016, Dilma was impeached by Congress due to fiscal malpractice. Michel Temer, the Vice-president took office and inherited a country with high inflation and high unemployment rates. The dream of transforming Brazil into a developed economy and country was, once again, postponed: GDP hasn't grown since 2014 and was down 3.8 percent in 2015. FMI's projections indicated another contraction of almost 4 percent in 2016, followed by zero growth in 2017. Unemployment rates and inflation are on the rise. Since 2003, Brazil's economy has grown steadily at 5 percent per year (Brazil takes off, 2009) but recent years' results will delay development for some time.

Highly unequal income distribution is a critical challenge. Since 2003, the government's social policies have helped increase the minimum wage and boost retail sales, but these gains are at risk given the present economic outlook. Brazil has a predominantly urban population (81 percent live in urban areas) and a very young population with increasing disposable income. Additionally, the country has no ethnic or religion conflicts and its localization and relevance in Latin America represents a very attractive gate to the region. These characteristics still make Brazil a very up-and-coming market for foreign investors. The private sector and the government have both been encouraging foreign investment by expanding and restructuring various sectors. Brazil is consid-

▲ FIGURE 2.1 The commercial zone of Saara, in the central region of Rio de Janeiro, Brazil. Stores sell nonbranded apparel, either from China or locally produced. These stores still dominate the market targeting new and growing lower classes of consumers.

ered a very promising economy and its internal market makes it very attractive and resilient as the recovery following the 2008/2009 crisis has demonstrated. The familiar quote says it all: "Brazil is the country of the future—and always will be." It seems, however, that with many recent political and economic changes, the strengthening of the country's democracy and an ideal customer base for retailers, the future seems to have finally arrived. Brazil is still an emerging and relevant market that has caught the attention of foreign retailers.

RETAIL INDUSTRY IN BRAZIL: GIANTS AND DWARFS

Even with a large number of consolidations among retail businesses, small, independent outlets still dominate Brazil's retail landscape. Modern retail formats such as hypermarkets, supermarkets, and shopping centers have expanded very quickly in recent years due to mergers, acquisitions, and foreign investment. Food retailing is by far the most developed retail segment in Brazil, and the French-Brazilian Grupo Pão de Açúcar, French-based Carrefour, and the U.S.-based Walmart dominate some Brazilian markets. However, in some capitals, and mainly in the interior of the country, small and medium independent players and retail networks are dominant.

In an August 2010 article, Sara Andrade, fashion editor of *Vogue Portugal*, wrote, "Unlike [in] Europe or the U.S., where there are many high-street options like Zara and Mango, in Brazil most brands fall into two extremes: They have very low-profile brands like C&A, where you can get things of rather low quality at a really cheap price and, on the other end, designer brands like Maria Bonita and smaller independent labels that offer good quality and design at a high price point." Six years later, C&A is still in the market in Brazil, while Maria Bonita has closed all its stores. This example reflects the dynamics of retail apparel in Brazil.

Although multinational retailers, such as Timberland and Zara, serve the country's richer consumers, few global retailers, except for C&A, compete in its mass market, which is served mainly by small and medium independent stores, and large local single-format retailers accounting for more than 60 percent of the country's apparel sales (Artigas & Calicchio, 2007). "Brazil is the most attractive apparel market for reasons of demographics and demand: there is great potential for global apparel retailers," says Hana Ben-Shabat, a partner with global management consulting company A.T. Kearney. It seems some global companies have discovered such potential: TopShop opened in Brazil in 2012, followed by GAP in 2013 and Forever 21 in 2014. Recently, TopShop has already ended its operations in the country alleging difficulties with taxes and exchange rates (Duarte, 2015).

With a per capita apparel consumption of US$210 per year, Brazilian consumers are extremely fond of shopping for clothes. The importance of individual identity among Brazilian consumers makes clothing retail an essential for them. Consumers are highly fashion conscious and celebrities tend to influence fashion trends in a country where more than 60 percent of the population is under the age of 39. Given income restrictions, Brazilian consumers look for good-quality products at the lowest possible prices, with credit playing a major role in the apparel market.

The apparel industry in Brazil is very competitive and has a significant number of local brands. The highly fragmented retail industry in Brazil provides an interesting opportunity for consolidation by retailers willing to understand and explore the idiosyncrasies of such a large and complex market ("Opportunities in Brazil," 2007). A study conducted by A.T. Kearney in 2009 ("Emerging markets," 2009) ranked Brazil as the most attractive market for apparel retailing. This ranking considers, among other factors, the size of the market as well as the country demographics and economic perspectives. The 2015 Global Retail Development Index from A.T. Kearney still presents Brazil as the eighth most attractive market for retailing despite its stagnant GDP growth with inflation on the rise and consumer confidence low.

Financial experts consider Brazil to be an extremely attractive market for retail expansion, and the most dynamic emerging market for the luxury retail sector. A better understanding of the Brazilian market requires an understanding of Brazilian consumers and the various formats in which the retail industry operates in Brazil.

CONSUMERS: DIVERSITY AND COMPLEXITY

Brazil has a vast territory, a diverse culture, and nearly 205 million inhabitants. Although the common Portuguese language and an excellent communications system (in both TV and radio) have created some homogeneous tastes and behavior, local consumer habits are still very relevant. A closed economy and a low per capita income used to limit consumers' access to imported goods and brands, but the 1990s witnessed economic stabilization and inflation reduction. In the 2000s, the gross domestic product (GDP) started to grow at a low but steady rate, prices were reduced on some imported goods (through import-taxes reduction), and consumer credit became cheaper. As a result, the Brazilian middle class boomed.

Saving is not a common practice in Brazil. On the contrary, a substantial part of people's income is used to reduce debt. Financial institutions profit from anxious customers who may pay interest rates of 6.5 percent per month on average to own a new appliance or fashion apparel. Big retail stores use credit as a marketing tool to boost sales, and small ones need to offer credit services through credit card companies in order to compete.

Due to the presence of many informal businesses that do not pay taxes in total or partially, it is not easy to assess the Brazilian apparel industry, but Brazilian Textile and Apparel Industry Association (ABIT) reports that for 2015, 5.5 billion items were produced, there was a $36.2 billion revenue, and 1.5 million jobs, of which 75 percent are female in 33,000 formal companies. Unlike Asian countries, Brazil is not recognized as a cheap clothing exporter, and products such as Havianas (the rubber flip-flop) and Osklen (beachwear) are sold in all continents at premium prices.

Brazilians are living longer and the middle class is growing. The United Nations' *Centro Latinoamericano y Caribeño de Demografia* (CELADE) classifies Brazil as a country where the elderly population is increasing (ONU, 2008). In the 2000s, a 100 percent increase in the minimum wage and the acceleration of income-oriented social programs have reduced income inequality and given millions of consumers access to basic products for the first time. Those emerging consumers are not looking for exclusivity; they are looking for inclusion and belonging. As a result, several industries, including apparel, have had to increase production and reshape their product lines.

These new middle-class consumers have different preferences and priorities: sustainability issues, for instance, alter upper-class consumer behavior in many industries, but "the (emerging) C class [middle class] is not concerned about the environment, if they buy a low-energy-consumption home appliance, they are more concerned about their wallet, not the world," states Fabio Mariano, professor and partner of Insearch, a consulting firm which focuses on consumer behavior (Folha de Sao Paulo, 2010a).

Apparel stores in Brazil may benefit from the population's preference for similar fashions. Apart from designs and materials influenced by weather and cultural differences, a store in the northeastern region may carry a stock very similar to a store in the south, 2,000 miles away. Heloisa Omine, professor and former president of the Brazilian chapter of The Global Association for Marketing at Retail (POPAI), alerts her colleagues that "stores need to adapt to drag the attention of consumers from the emerging middle class, product displays must be accessible and enable self-service" (Portal Exame, 2010). Traditional regional apparel is usually restricted to special occasions.

Brazilian consumers' favorite place to buy apparel is the shopping center. In Brazil, in 2015, 19 percent of all retail revenue is through malls. This industry's revenue in 2015 was approximately US$50 billion, distributed among 549 malls, over 100,413 stores, with 1,056,055 employees (www.portaldoshopping. com/br/). For Brazilians, the shopping experience is a social event. Shopping does not necessarily mean buying, as a visit to the mall encompasses meeting people (and even flirting), going to the cinema, and sharing meals. In big and violent cities, malls are safe islands where middle-class parents can leave their children for some leisure time. Usually people go to the malls in small groups: family, couples, or with friends. But teenagers sometimes gather in parties of a dozen people or more, with no intention of buying. In many cities, small downtown shopping centers with a limited number of stores continue to thrive.

Through fashion, Brazilian people achieve group identity, social conformity, and distinction. Fashion is a means to show creativity and express sexuality (Mello et al., 2003). A 2007 survey (Garcia & Miranda, 2007) identified the following motivations among Brazilian shoppers:

- ► Communication. Even fashion denial is a way to reject society's standards.
- ► Integration. Fashion style denotes the group someone belongs to.
- ► Individuality. Clothing distinguishes members of a specific group.
- ► Self-esteem. Clothing reinforces the buyer's self-regard.
- ► Transformation. People dress to be different.

Brazilian consumers differ significantly from consumers in most developed and many emerging markets. Some important differences for foreign retailers interested in entering the Brazilian retail market to keep in mind are (Artigas & Calicchio, 2007):

- ► About 80 percent of Brazilian consumers are very fond of shopping for clothes and they look forward to it. The wear these clothes mainly for going out with family and friends.
- ► They are very fashion conscious, and local celebrities dictate fashion trends. Local retailers in Brazil offer local fashion trends in clothing to their consumers.

- Brazilian consumers like to have a full range of merchandise to choose from, even if they don't intend to buy the high-end products. They want to treat themselves occasionally.
- Consumers trust local brands. The current multinationals have established a local identity by using local models in their advertising campaigns.
- Brazilians are more comfortable using credit than consumers in other emerging markets.
- They are very brand loyal to the brands associated with designers.
- They have special fondness for cotton apparel such as denim and T-shirts.
- Foreign brands are associated with wealth.
- Brazilian consumers are addicted to promotions. They look for promotions with attractive credit offerings, such as installment payments. These promotions are year-round, not seasonal as in other countries.
- Brazilian consumers demand good customer service in the stores. They prefer being known by salespeople, and like being extended credit without any formalities.

▲ FIGURE 2.2 Buzios, Brazil. People browse and window shop in a shopping arcade.

- ▸ They are known for comparison shopping. Brazilian consumers know the prices of twice as many products as consumers in other emerging markets. They visit several stores to compare prices before making a decision to buy.

WOMEN

Through fashion, human beings demonstrate their basic desires and instincts, and most fashion activity is related to social integration (Garcia & Miranda, 2007). Brazilian women in particular express their personalities not only with clothes but also with accessories and jewelry. Fashion also may indicate social status, professional activity, and style (Leao et al., 2007). In Brazil, women generally have an important role in apparel buying by shopping alone, without other family members. Teenagers and young adults usually rely on friends and fashion trends for their shopping decisions (Rubens, 2003).

Since the mid–1980s, Brazilian women's participation in historically male-dominated professions such as law, medicine, and engineering has increased. Their new incomes combined with their fashion consciousness have created a huge market for women's clothing. This market grew considerably in the first decade of the twenty-first century.

Soap opera stars and other TV celebrities are a powerful influence on the fashion choices Brazilian women make. Many Brazilian women stay abreast of fashion trends by reading magazines such as *Vogue, Caras, Manequim,* or *Nova* (the Brazilian version of *Cosmopolitan*) and when they go shopping, they are not shy. Sônia Hess de Souza, former CEO of Dudalina, a Brazilian apparel manufacturer with stores in six different countries, observed that "(Brazilian) women do not buy a single shirt, they buy two or three at a time" (Folha de Sao Paulo, 2010b).

MEN

Many Brazilian men don't own a suit, blazer, or jacket because they will never have the need to wear one. Casual business wear is the most common clothing worn by Brazilian men in both formal and social settings. Brazilian men dress casually in their tropical climate. In many places, a shirt and slacks are acceptable business attire.

There are signs that Brazilian men are increasingly concerned about personal aesthetics. For example, Brazil is the fifth-highest consumer of men's cosmetics in the world and the highest in Latin America. According to industry reports, men's cosmetics consumption is expected to grow by 9 percent in the Latin American region. Advertising and social expectations are changing the way men's cosmetic purchases are made. Instead of their wives, men are making these purchases for themselves. Most of these purchases are made in supermarkets.

CHILDREN

Children's apparel accounts for 15 percent of the industry's market share (IEMI, 2015) in Brazil. The mother, who used to make all decisions regarding her children's apparel, is starting to share the process with their other parent and the children themselves. Clothing is an opportunity for children and their parents to express themselves and leads to social integration (Frederico & Robic, 2006). Buying behavior has four primary drivers when it comes to children's apparel:

- ► Product quality
- ► Point of sale (store)
- ► Appearance
- ► Fashion

Appearance and fashion affect both children and parents, but quality and shopping convenience mainly concerns parents. Brazilian retail and apparel brands devote significant advertising efforts to attracting children's attention, although there are several legal restrictions on advertising for children.

The children's clothing market has been growing at a steady pace in Brazil, generating revenue of US$6 billion in 2014. Small stores with sole proprietors dominate the children's wear market. The market does have a few large retail chains that account for a significant portion of the business. But a lack of brand loyalty in this sector leaves space for more retail chains in Brazil (Childrenswear in Brazil, 2009). An investor could very easily enter this sector through small-scale investment and healthy growth is attracting foreign retailers. However, entrants should study the market carefully to avoid issues experienced by companies such as Petit Bateau, DPAM and JC Penney (a tentative joint venture with Brazilian department store chain Lojas Renner). Unable to adjust their processes and products to local business practices, tastes, taxes, and income levels, these companies exited the market.

THE ELDERLY

The number of people over 60 is significantly high in Brazil (Ibge, 2008). Increased life expectancy is such a recent change that the fashion industry has not yet responded with products or services, but changes are already visible in other industries, such as tourism and hospitality. The elderly have slightly different motivations from younger generations for buying apparel in Brazil (Slongo et al., 2009):

- Comfort
- Self-esteem and vanity
- Emotional security
- Fitness to age and physical conditions
- Self-expression

For the elderly, clothing is symbolic and socially important. Health concerns may also drive apparel choices, not only because of attendant constraints on finances and mobility constraints but also because health issues change people's motivation. Key elements that influence elderly people in their apparel-buying behavior are also different from young adults:

- Social group, friends, and family
- Fit to a special occasion or event
- Willingness to please someone
- Worries about their appearance and presentation

THE BEAUTY INDUSTRY IN BRAZIL

Brazil's youth culture is obsessed with beauty and celebrity. The country has two salons for every bakery, making beauty seem more important than bread (Research, 2005). Brazil is the third major consumer of cosmetics in the world and represents 9.4 percent of the global consumption (ABIHPEC, 2015). The Brazilian beauty fair, Hair Brasil, has more than 500 exhibitors and nearly 148,000 visitors. Natura, a domestic cosmetic company, is one of the most successful brands in Brazil. They sell through direct sales (like Avon in the United States), and have more than 1.3 million representatives in Brazil.

▶ Beauty Industry and Women

The average Brazilian woman devotes much of her time and money to her appearance. This behavior is not limited to wealthy people; even in poor income areas, including slums and shantytowns, beauty salons are easily found. An average middle-class Brazilian woman has a manicure at least once a week, usually along with another body or hair treatment. The majority (65 percent) of Brazilian women have either wavy or curly hair, and fashion dictates straight hair. Hence, there is a huge market for hair treatments. A single hair treatment in a luxury salon, for a bride for instance, can cost thousands of dollars.

Beauty products for black women, both services and cosmetics, represent another fast-growing market in Brazil. Several cosmetic lines have been released to fulfill the demand created by racial pride and consciousness. Beleza Natural (belezanatural.com.br) is a very interesting example of entrepreneurship focusing on the black women's market, particularly for haircare. From a humble start in a community in Rio de Janeiro, the company accounts for 40 stores dedicated to curly-haired people and has been the subject of one book and a case study from Harvard Business School. Other interesting examples are O Boticario, a Brazilian franchise, which offers beauty products through over 2,700 stores and is already present in 15 countries and L'Occitane au Brésil a branch from the French company that leverages Brazil's biodiversity in its offering and accounts for 70 stores across the country.

▸ Beauty Industry and Men

Previous generations linked pride in appearance to homosexual behavior. That attitude is gone. Men's health and beauty represents a promising new market. Men who until recently limited their grooming activities to a haircut and shave at the barber now have at their disposal professional treatments and dedicated salons, such as Garagem (http://www.garagemestetica.com.br/), a franchise with customers who spend 15 percent of their net income on beauty products or Barbearia Cavalera (https://www.facebook.com/Barbeariacavalera/). It is not hard to find men in beauty salons, taking care of their nails, beard or hair, or even in depilation sessions.

Young men in Brazil are leading important changes, and new beauty products for men have come into play. As men usually do not set aside as much time as women for their home beauty care, cosmetics for men are developed to consider not only gender and biological differences but also ease of application.

All of these factors make the beauty industry in Brazil a lucrative market for international investors.

LUXURY RETAIL IN BRAZIL

Brazil's GDP expansion in the first decade of the 2000s created an affluent customer base, reducing income-distribution inequality to bring the country closer to international standards.

In general, Brazilians also spend more of their disposable income on fashion products than consumers in many other countries. Brazilians spend more money on designer clothing, luxury cars, and cruises than consumers from other nations. This hedonistic consumption is one of the main reasons so many international luxury retailers want to enter the Brazilian retail market.

Many foreign luxury retailers are entering the market on their own, but some are partnering with Brazilian companies, a smart move given the country's complexity in terms of income distribution, taxes, and logistics (Brazil: The Allure, 2009).

It seems that Joãosinho Trinta, producer of Brazil's most spectacular Carnival, was right when he said "only intellectuals like misery; what poor people go for is luxury." Luxury stores such as Tiffany & Co. and Louis Vuitton stores in São Paulo are among their most profitable. Lack of cash does not deter Brazilians from purchasing luxuries (A Better Today, 2009), however, the economic downturn in 2015 has affected all retail segments, including luxury goods.

▲ FIGURE 2.3 A man walks past a showcase of Brazilian luxury store Daslu for men on sale at the high-class Cidade Jardim shopping center. Luxury shopping centers are expanding fast in Brazil and particularly in São Paulo. Cidade Jardim hosts Tiffany, Hermès, Chanel, and Furla stores.

São Paulo is not the only market for luxury products, and many other cities have emerged for luxury retailers to consider, such as Rio de Janeiro, Belo Horizonte, Campinas, Brasília, and Recife. One of the most significant barriers to the luxury retail market is the escalated price of products with high import and local taxes and duties. Many products cost twice or three times their retail prices in the United States.

APPAREL RETAIL FORMATS: OLD AND NEW WITH A LOCAL TWIST

Similar to most emerging markets, Brazil has a wide range of retail formats, and Brazilian consumers tend to shop in many of them, regardless of their social or economic status. There are specialty retailers in urban markets, along with boutiques, discount stores, department stores, and street markets. Even as more organized retail formats enter the market, the unorganized sector is not affected much. Tax evasion and lean overheads may give traditional retail formats a relevant advantage in operating margins over organized modern retailers.

TRADITIONAL RETAIL FORMATS

Some traditional retail formats are still common in Brazil. They create competition for some of the large format stores by undercutting them on prices and selling right on their doorstep. The traditional classification approach, through store and nonstore-based retail, can be used to classify retailing in Brazil.

▸ *Store-based Retail*

A physical store is the primary characteristic of store-based retail, which is further classified according to the following criteria.

Specialized small stores: Small and medium-sized family-owned businesses that are mainly located on city streets and in shopping centers. According to the Brazilian Development Bank (BNDES) this type of store is predominant in the Brazilian apparel retail market.

Specialized retail network: A network of stores controlled by a central headquarters with very little flexibility on price and promotion policies. Franchising is also an alternative to develop specialized retail networks. Such a network may be local, regional, or national and classified as small, medium, or large according to the number of stores in it. Examples of big Brazilian retail networks include C&A, Hering, Marissol, Casas Pernambucanas, Riachuelo and Marisa. This type of retail is mainly present in commercial galleries, malls, and shopping centers.

Non-specialized stores: Stores that carry a diverse mix of products, including:

▶ **Department stores:** Traditional American brands like Sears, Dillard's, and Mappin (a Brazilian company) have been replaced by specialized networks, such as Lojas Renner, carrying only apparel, accessories, bed and bath apparel, and health and beauty products. Casas Pernambucanas is the closest example of a traditional department store by carrying some electronics.

▶ **Discount stores:** Medium-sized stores offering a limited mix of products including groceries, music, basic electronics, and basic apparel. Decor and service are very simple and prices are very aggressive. An example is Lojas Americanas.

Outlet stores: Big retail stores, far from urban centers, offering good deals and value to consumers.

Off-price stores: Stores that specialize in off-stock apparel, with big discounts to the consumers. This type of store can be located in or outside big urban centers.

Popular markets: Small, popular street shopping centers are present in almost every Brazilian city. Most products are low quality, very inexpensive compared to similar products, and sourced from China. Although popular and targeted to the low-income population, these markets are frequented by medium- and even high-income classes looking for replicas and cheaper imported goods.

Camelôs: Unregistered street traders who are part of many Brazilian neighborhoods. Camelôs are part of the "informal economy," a consequence of the complex tax system, high taxes, and weak fiscal controls. Camelôs present a great challenge to Brazilian policymakers; some studies demonstrate that informality impedes economic development and reduces competitiveness (Kenyon and Kapaz, 2005; Elstrod and Bebb, 2005).

►Non-store-based Retail

This format focuses on consumers who have little time for shopping or who live far from urban centers.

Personal sales: Sales made through direct contact between vendor and buyer. Sellers include:

- ▸ Registered street traders: Individuals who sell their products legally. They work mainly on streets with high pedestrian traffic or near office buildings.
- ▸ Door-to-door sales: This traditional approach is still very popular in Brazil, mainly in low-income areas: a door-to-door salesperson offers goods from his mobile showroom, which may be a van, a small truck, a motorcycle, or even a peddler's cart.

▲ FIGURE 2.4 The commercial zone of Saara, in the central region of Rio de Janeiro. Mainly tailored to low- to medium-income consumers, these popular commercial areas include specialized small and even retail network stores. Abundance of low-price merchandise and credit are the most used sales tactics. They are very common in the majority of Brazilian large cities and attract customers from Latin America and Africa.

- In-home store: An individual transforms part of his or her home into a showroom and regularly invites customers for coffee or tea parties that are followed by sales events.
- Network marketing: Consultants visit their customers' homes selling directly from manufacturers' catalogs. Similar to Avon or Mary Kay in the United States, the most well-known Brazilian equivalent is the local cosmetic and health and beauty aids brand, Natura.

Sales through direct marketing action (without personal contact): Sellers include:

- Catalogs: The twentieth century's high inflation rates prevented the development of catalog sales in Brazil. In any case, this sales format is decreasing in importance with the advent of the Internet and e-commerce.
- Teleshopping: This sales alternative is becoming popular in Brazil with some dedicated TV stations, as well as slots on regular TV stations. Many players use the infomercial approach, in which products are presented within an informative context. Some television retailers include Shoptime, Medalhão Persa, Shop Tour, and Polishop.
- Telemarketing: Telemarketing is very common in Brazil, mainly for magazine subscriptions and mobile phone services. When product images are mandatory, this format loses relevance.

MODERN FORMATS

Brazil has retail formats that are very similar to those in developed nations. In the food distribution sector modern retail formats like supermarkets and hypermarkets dominate. In the apparel industry the classic department store is not present: it was practically eliminated by high inflation and hypermarket competition. Some additional modern formats worth mentioning that reflect the structure of the market as well as changes in consumer behavior are as follows.

▸Hypermarkets

These are large stores covering more than 52,000 square feet (5,000 m²) dedicated to a one-stop shopping experience. Hypermarkets are mainly located in big urban and suburban centers, easily accessed by car and public transportation, and require a significant parking area. Brazilian examples include Extra and Bourbon alongside international players such as Carrefour and Walmart.

▶ Buyers Clubs

Buyers clubs are members-only stores similar to Costco in the United States. Examples include Dutch cash-and-carry operator Makro and Sam's Club.

▶ Atacarejo

Atacarejo is a typical Brazilian format, blending wholesaling and retailing under the same roof with little or no service to customers. Whenever apparel is sold, the products are cheap and very basic. Brazilian retailers Atacadão and Assaí are some examples.

▶ Convenience Stores

Convenience stores are a very popular format in Brazil, with stores located near or inside gas stations. The convenience store format has been modified to a hybrid format with stores becoming more like small supermarkets and fast-food restaurants.

▶ Category Killers

The fragmented bookselling industry was the first retail sector to be impacted by the category-killer format. Atica, a publishing house, launched Brazil's first book megastores and sent a clear sign of the industry's consolidation. When Atica was bought by the French FNAC, other bookstores, like Saraiva and Livraria Cultura, got the message and started revamping their networks by replacing small stores with larger ones that included other categories in their offerings, like computers and videogames. The category-killer format is being developed in other categories like pet shops, furniture, and home decor.

▶ Hard/Soft Discount

Europe's very popular hard-discount format is noteworthy for its absence in Brazil. The value proposition is based upon low prices, small stores with almost no service, and an assortment of 700 basic and high-quality private label grocery and housekeeping items with no national brands. The closest representative of this no-frills, value-driven approach in Brazil is Dia percent, part of France's Carrefour Group. Dia percent carries a very limited assortment with some national brands and a strong presence of private labels.

► *Neighborhood Stores*

The advent of the supermarket and hypermarket has reduced the mom-and-pop stores, mainly in big cities; however, time and convenience have become essential for many consumers pressed by busy schedules in the biggest cities. Additionally, the threat posed by hard and soft discounters has triggered actions from some retailers like Pão de Açúcar Group (Minuto Pão de Açúcar) and Carrefour (Carrefour Express), which has revamped the old mom-and-pop grocery store with a new **neighborhood store** format—a small, conveniently located supermarket that carries an assortment customized for its location, which includes grocery, perishables, cleaning, and health and beauty products.

► *E-Commerce*

As access to computers and the Internet increases for Brazil's middle and lower classes, e-commerce is gaining momentum. However, the lack of standard sizes represents a strong barrier to apparel sales. This scenario seems to be changing thanks to companies such as Netshoes.com and Dafiti.com who are helping shape the apparel e-commerce landscape. According to Webshoppers Report 2015, Apparel Fashion & Accessories accounts for 14 percent in the transactional volume of e-commerce. As general trends in e-commerce, mobile shopping and omnichannel initiatives promoted by consolidated "brick and mortar" retailers are on the rise.

STORE OWNERSHIP: THE CHANGING LANDSCAPE

As in most emerging markets, individual families dominate the retail business, from small, traditional formats to very large retail chains. Recent economic and political stability has led to the rapid expansion of capital markets. In 2016, only seven apparel retail companies had gone public. In other words, the industry is very fragmented. The publicly traded are all Brazilian apparel companies: Arezzo, Grazziotin, Riachuelo (Guararapes), Hering, Renner, Marisa, and Restoque. Casas Pernambucanas, another large Brazilian apparel retailer, is an example of a private, family-owned business.

Many local, regional, and national family-owned brands and their respective stores are respected for their creativity and design; however, a clear opportunity for process, productivity, and distribution improvement exists and is being explored by private equity funds and stronger brands through acquisition and consolidation. Companies like InBrands (encompassing Brazilian brands 2nd Floor, Bintang, Ellus, Fashion Rio, Herchcovitch: Alexandre, Isabela Capeto,

Richards, Salinas, and SPFW) and BRLabels (Calvin Klein and Brazilian brands VR and Mandi) are acting as consolidators in this market by bringing technology, controls, and professional management to the companies while keeping the founders and creators at the product end. When this process is concluded, these companies are likely to go public.

FDI REGULATIONS: CHALLENGING BUT IMPROVING

Brazil offers a challenging environment for foreign direct investment (FDI). In 2015, Brazil had the second highest FDI in Latin America with an investment of $17 billion. Heavy taxation and regulatory requirements in Brazil are major deterrents for FDI by international retailers. Brazil has investment agreements with Belgium and Luxembourg, Chile, Cuba, Denmark, Finland, France, Germany, Italy, the Republic of Korea, the Netherlands, Portugal, Switzerland, the United Kingdom, and Venezuela (Doing Business, 2009).

To sustain high growth rates, Brazil needs FDI. There are no restrictions on FDI in the apparel retail sector. To attract more FDI, the government is working on domestic infrastructure. A company that is properly registered in Brazil is allowed to acquire real estate without any limitations. The retail stores are allowed to set their own hours for opening and closing. The government also has simple repatriation rules. A foreign company can take all the money earned in Brazil back to its country of origin as long as it is registered with Central Bank of Brazil and all taxes are paid (Legal Guide, 2007).

Some problems that foreign investors may face are the implicit costs of owning a business in Brazil, commonly known as "Custo Brasil." Distribution, logistics, government procedures, and employee benefits all involve implicit costs. In addition to these expenses, complex customs regulations, an ineffective legal system, and a tax burden that increases the prices of imported products to 200 percent (Doing Business, 2009) create problems for foreign investors. Brazil is a relational country, a characteristic that is ingrained in the country's business culture. Successful companies build relationships with potential partners before entering the market.

INTERNATIONAL BRANDS: RISKS AND REWARDS

Songwriter Tom Jobim, who wrote "The Girl from Ipanema," liked to say, "Brazil is not for rookies." Many retailers successful in their country of origin have had to rethink and eventually abandon plans after entering the Brazilian market. Economic and political instability as well as a competitive market with many institutional voids have led to many of these aborted attempts. Companies that have quit the Brazilian market include the likes of Sears, JC Penney, Portuguese retail group Sonae, Topshop and Dutch food retailer Ahold. Since the implementation of the economic measures known as Real Plan in 1994, the scenario has dramatically improved, and Brazil has become a destination for foreign investment in many areas, including retail. International retailers have entered the market using different methods, but still need to better assess and understand the market before deciding upon entry.

WHOLLY OWNED SUBSIDIARIES

Several successful companies have entered the market without any partnerships through wholly owned subsidiaries. Such companies, including Dutch wholesaler Makro, French home improvement chain Leroy Merlin, Spanish fast fashion apparel retailer Zara, Tiffany & Co., Forever 21 and Dutch popular apparel retail chain C&A, have started Brazilian operations from scratch and are growing organically. Other companies such as Carrefour have entered the market through this format and later accelerated their expansion through acquisitions.

ACQUISITIONS

This method is also a common way to enter the market. The French retailer FNAC bought Brazilian publishing house Atica store and the Chilean retailer CENCOSUD bought Brazilian companies G. Barbosa and Irmãos Bretas. Through such acquisitions, the foreign company does not have to spend time acquiring real estate or store space because they already have that from the existing stores of the companies they buy.

JOINT VENTURES (JVS)

These are less frequent in Brazil. Walmart initially attempted a joint venture with Lojas Americanas but then decided on a wholly owned subsidiary with a mix of organic growth and acquisitions. Other recent examples are the JV between Sodimac from Chile and Di Cicco, both home improvement retailers and between GAP and Grupo Empresarial Pasmanik controller of brands such as Cori, Emme and Luigi Bertolli. Perhaps the most successful joint venture in Brazil is between French retail group Casino and Brazilian Grupo Pão de Açúcar, who have formed the largest Brazilian retailer operating supermarkets, hypermarkets, and electronics stores. Casino is an interesting example, since Grupo Pao de Açúcar is now a 100 percent subsidiary of the group, demonstrating that JVs may serve very well for entry purposes followed by other alternatives, once the relationship and the business mature.

Except for the fast-food industry, there are no records of franchising as an entry strategy for retailing.

INFLUENCES ON APPAREL RETAILING: TV AND MUCH MORE

Two factors are key influencers in the apparel retailing industry in Brazil: the shopping mall culture and fashion.

SHOPPING MALL CULTURE

The development of the shopping mall industry in Brazil goes hand in hand with the development of the apparel industry. When shopping malls in São Paulo and Rio sponsored fashion shows in the 1990s, Brazilian fashion saw its biggest boom. Whereas shopping malls in most Western countries cater to blue-collar and middle-class consumers, this is not necessarily the case in Brazil. Several corporations are transforming sites in upper-class neighborhoods of major cities into upscale malls with apparent success. In São Paulo, for example, three luxury malls coexist within a 15-mile (25 km) radius. These malls serve as entertainment centers as well as fashion outlets for most luxury brands. For instance, of the six Louis Vuitton stores in Brazil, four are in shopping malls.

FASHION INFLUENCES

Until the 1930s, Brazilians followed European fashion, with Paris setting the standard for women and London for men. Fashion magazines were mostly translations of top European publications. In the 1930s, Flavio Carvalho, a Brazilian architect and artist in Recife, led a movement to rescue native values and reinforce Brazil's tropical identity. Stylists slowly started to adapt global trends to the lifestyles and climate in Brazil. Clothes became more informal and more colorful.

Since the 1970s, the major laboratory for trendsetting has been the soap opera world, mainly the primetime shows on Brazil's main TV channel, Rede Globo. Whatever the lead character in a soap wears is what the middle class will want to wear. The 1980s saw the arrival of the local editions of major global publications such as *Elle, Marie Claire*, and *Vogue*.

In 1994, Brazil's first group fashion show was organized. It featured most of the top brands in Brazilian fashion and was sponsored by a cosmetic company named Phytoervas. Phytoervas Fashion ran for two years until, under the sponsorship of a major shopping mall, it converted into Morumbi Fashion. By 2000, it had evolved into São Paulo Fashion Week and left the mall for the Bienal Pavilion, the site of Latin America's most important contemporary art exposition. The leaders of Brazil's fashion industry selected the location to raise the show to the level of a world-class event, with attendant international press coverage (Souza Lopez, 2007).

Two fashion shows in Brazil draw attention from international media: São Paulo Fashion Week (SPFW) and Fashion Rio, both run by the domestic conglomerate Inbrands.

OTHER INFLUENTIAL FACTORS

Other factors influencing the development of the apparel industry in Brazil are:

- The strengthening of the Brazilian real, which favors:
  - The entry of global brands into the Brazilian market
  - International travel by members of the middle and upper classes, which raises their awareness of global brands
  - Discretionary income, which allows for more expenditure on fashion and apparel
- Young Brazilian designers finding their way into the international fashion community (Ocimar Versolatto, Francisco Costa, Isabella Capetto, Tufi Duek, and Alexandre Herchcovitch, among others)
- Top Brazilian models becoming international fashion icons (Gianne Albertone, Shirley Malmmann, and Gisele Bundchen)

GETTING TO KNOW DOMESTIC COMPETITORS: LEARNING FROM THEIR SUCCESSES AND FAILURES

Savvy foreign retailers wanting to enter the Brazilian retail industry will investigate the competition and try to understand the reasons for their success. The following sections present the companies that must be part of such a study.

GRUPO PÃO DE AÇÚCAR (GPA)

GPA is the largest retail chain in South America. It reported sales of about $15 billion in 2015. GPA has continued to be successful even in the face of tough

▲ FIGURE 2.5 Isabeli Fontana walks the runway during the Agua de Coco show at Sao Paulo Fashion Week Fall/Winter 2017 on October 26, 2016 in Sao Paulo, Brazil.

competition from foreign retailers entering the Brazilian market. The company operates different retail formats (hypermarkets, supermarkets, convenience stores) and acquires competitors to remain in the forefront. Excellent customer service and broad geographic coverage make GPA highly successful.

LOJAS AMERICANAS

This retailer defies categorization; the chain sells confectionery, personal care, lingerie, and music CDs. It offers low prices at high-end locations. The stores are mainly located in shopping malls. They have many promotions on seasonal products and offer credit, making expensive products accessible to a larger consumer base.

RIACHUELO

The company was founded in 1947 and operates more than 289 apparel department stores in five regions of Brazil. It is also Latin America's largest apparel manufacturer, selling women's, men's, and children's apparel.

Riachuelo is investing in integrating production and retail towards a fast fashion strategy.

Again, the credit card has been important to their success. Many Brazilians thought of Riachuelo as the place their mother shopped until the store decided to revamp the brand to attract younger customers. Middle and lower middle classes dominate their customer base.

RENNER

Founded in 1922, the company has more than 120 stores with 94 percent located in premium shopping malls. The company targets customers on the medium to higher income strata. They sell private label apparel brands, private label cosmetics, accessories, and footwear. Their mission is customer "enchantment" to gain a competitive edge over their competitors. Recently the company announced the intention to start operating in Uruguay.

MARISA

This retailer has 401 stores in all Brazilian states. The chain differentiates itself by catering to lower- and middle-class women. Credit draws many customers, along with the lingerie and underwear. They mainly sell their own private label with a few exceptions. They have a fully automated distribution center and operate on a much higher profit margin than their competition.

HERING

Founded in 1880, with apparel retail activity since 1993, this retail chain operates more than 823 stores serving middle to upper-middle class with brands such as Hering Store, PUC, Hering Kids, Hering for You and Dzarm. Most stores are franchised and their private apparel brand is available in more than 15,000 multibrand stores. Additionally, as at the end of 2015, the company had 17 franchisees in Uruguay, Paraguay and Bolivia. They produce a wide assortment of premium-quality basic items, particularly T-shirts.

HOW MATURE IS THE RETAIL INDUSTRY? EVOLVING FAST

Although the Brazilian retail industry is highly fragmented, and 60 percent of it is made up of small local retailers, modern retail is well developed due to the entry of many modern retail formats in the late 1990s. Many statistical reports show that hypermarket sales are the highest in all retail categories. Nevertheless, these figures may arise from unreported sales by independent retailers seeking to evade taxes. Government interference makes entering the Brazilian market cumbersome. Registering a business takes 83 days compared to 6.3 days in Mexico. Street stores are still popular. A complex regulatory and tax environment increases the cost of doing business, and many people choose the informal method of retailing. Many high-end products, such as electronics, jewelry, and apparel, are made in China and enter Brazil illegally by way of Paraguay. Informal retailers purchase these products and sell them throughout the country. Because these retailers do not pay import tariffs and taxes, it is difficult for formal retailers to compete with them on prices (Treewater & Price, 2007).

The apparel sector is Brazil is still largely untapped by foreign investors because the demand for products is very different from the home market of many retailers. Brazilian consumers have a strong preference for local brands and fashions. Even low-income consumers are trendy and fashion conscious. Although the market is not mature yet it has plenty of opportunities to explore, a foreign retailer interested in entering Brazil must understand consumer preferences, behavior, and regional differences; develop skills to compete against local retailers; learn promotional techniques that are season specific; and offer special credit terms like the local retailers. The success of some local retailers relies on a good understanding of the local consumers' preferences, strong brands, and modern manufacturing technology, as well as appropriate distribution.

BUYING FOR APPAREL RETAIL STORES: LOCAL SOURCING STILL DOMINANT

A foreign retailer who wants to import products into Brazil must pay import duty, industrialized product tax (federal tax), and merchandise and service circulation tax (state government value added tax), as well as a number of smaller taxes and fees (Doing Business, 2016). These costs make it difficult for foreign retailers to compete with locally sourced products in terms of pricing.

Retailers in Brazil buy from manufacturers and wholesalers. Both industries are highly fragmented in Brazil. More than 33,000 retailers generating 1.5 million direct jobs form the links in the textile production chain, including yarn manufacturers, fiber producers, weaving mills, and apparel industries (ABIT, 2016). With the liberalization of import regulations, more retailers are buying from countries with low labor costs, such as China. Because apparel production is labor intensive, low labor costs significantly reduce the overall price of the final product (Apparel Retail, 2009).

RETAIL CAREERS: FLEXIBILITY AND CULTURAL BLENDING

Brazil is open to skilled and knowledgeable executives from all over the world joining the workforce in the country. A number of publications, websites, and recruiting companies have been established to help expatriates get jobs in Brazil. Many immigrants are coming to Brazil to look for jobs because the country has a well-organized work structure, high salaries, and standardized working hours (Brazil Jobs, 2010).

Personal relationships are important in Brazil and personal recommendations make it much easier to land a job. Jobseekers can attend various career fairs posting jobs in different sectors of the retail industry.

According to recruiting company Michael Page International (a U.S.-based recruitment consultancy) a temporary residence visa will be required to live and work in Brazil. A temporary visa for employment purposes requires a job offer from a company based in Brazil. The company will apply to the Immigration Division of the Ministry of Labor on behalf of the candidate. Educational qualifications or work experience, an employment contract, adequate means of subsistence, no criminal record, and a satisfactory medical examination are the main criteria for approval of an employment visa and all documents required must be translated into Portuguese. The application-processing period is around two to three months, and the visa is issued for a specific job and is not transferable between employers.

Knowledge of Portuguese is essential for communication. Some websites that post job offerings in retailing are www.careerjet.com.br, www.zap.com.br/empregos, www.olx.com.br, and www.jobzing.com/brazil.

THE FUTURE OF APPAREL RETAIL: GROWTH, REWARDS, AND RISKS

Brazil is a popular destination for foreign investors. In 2015, FDI into Latin America dropped to US$70.2 billion, but Brazil has kept its capital investment levels with a decline of 0.2 percent against a much higher decline in the region. In all, Brazil has increased its market share from 19 to 25 percent. Despite the economic and political issues, the country is still attractive and given the Real devaluation, Brazilian assets have become cheaper and, therefore, more interesting.

Consumers have brand loyalty largely toward designer brands. However, there is a large market for discount apparel retail with private labels. Discount stores can capture that market by developing private labels to follow local fashion trends. European and U.S. apparel retailers and manufacturers must consider seasonality and fashion cycles because Brazil is located in a different hemisphere. The apparel industry is highly fragmented, leaving room for several small retailers (Apparel Retail, 2009).

Foreign retailers that first began entering the Brazilian market in the 1980s operated with an imperialist mind-set that considered Brazil a new market for their old products. They relied on incremental sales for their existing products. They did not see this emerging market as a source of technical and managerial talent for their global operations. Such blindness has been one of the main reasons for their limited success in the market.

Economic instability, high inflation, and exchange volatility also contributed to the failure of many foreign investments. Now that the market has become more predictable, success is more likely. Foreign companies also have to understand some local cultural norms, such as the art of *jeitinho,* the Brazilian way of getting around problems in business and in life (Arrivals, 2009).

The Brazilian retail market presents various challenges to a new entrant.

- New entrants often have to fight price wars initiated by existing retailers who lower their prices to compete with the new entrant.
- Despite the evolution of the democratic system, corruption is still a part of Brazilian life.
- Infrastructure is a work in progress. Many small, unpaved roads, an almost irrelevant railroad, and airports and air traffic control all require improvement.
- A huge amount of investment is required to complete the infrastructure and development projects under way (airports, roads, public transportation, and deep-sea oil exploration, among others). A slowdown in FDI will slow the infrastructure development.
- Brazil has a high crime rate. Security is a state-government responsibility, and dealing with organized crime represents a major challenge to some cities. Some big cities have high crime and murder rates (Brazil, 2009).
- Brazil has a highly regulated labor market, making the cost of employment high and leading to a high level of unemployment in the formal sector.
- Taxes are high and not wisely spent or invested by the government. Such waste increases the cost of labor, services, and consumer goods.

The biggest challenge that a foreign retailer will face in Brazil is a need to develop new products or alter its current offerings to suit the local market. Brazil is a large country with considerable differences among regions. A preference for local fashion and the heavy use of credit in an underdeveloped market also pose problems for foreign retailers. The high level of trust for local brands among local consumers is another hurdle that foreign retailers will have to clear. Providing consumers with fashion that is associated with their local celebrities may help develop loyalty among Brazilian consumers. Hiring local staff to interpret the wants and needs of the local population will also lead to a strong foothold in the local market.

SUMMARY

Famous Brazilian songwriter and maestro Tom Jobim, who wrote "The Girl from Ipanema," used to say, "Brazil is not for rookies." Many retailers, no matter how successful in their country of origin, learned this lesson the hard way, by rethinking and, eventually abandoning their plans after entering the Brazilian market.

Economic issues associated with a young democracy as well as a competitive market with many institutional voids have led to many of these aborted attempts.

However, a country that represents roughly 50 percent of Latin America population, GDP and surface cannot be ignored.

Until 2013, it seemed that Brazil would finally achieve a new status by becoming a global and relevant player. However, once again, the country and its government were not capable of anticipating global economic challenges and movements that, in addition, to poor political, economic and social decisions have put the country to a questionable position with high inflation, unemployment and low consumer confidence index as well amidst major corruption scandals.

The covers of *The Economist* magazine may properly illustrate Brazil's challenges. In 2009, the cover stated "Brazil's Take Off". Just four years later the same magazine asked "Has Brazil Blown It?". Finally, in 2015, the headlines was: "Brazil's Fall".

Regardless, the Brazilian retail market still represents an interesting opportunity and according to the Global Retail Development Index, the country is ranked as the twentieth most attractive market.

Challenges and opportunities abound and many authors have written about Brazil being the country of the future. In the recent past, it seemed this future has arrived, however Brazilians will have to wait a little more to see this prophecy being fulfilled.

In 2004, a campaign launched by the Brazilian Advertisers Association portraying different famous Brazilians that had come back from unfortunate experiences, intended to improve the country's self-esteem with the slogan: "I am Brazilian: I never give up". This phrase synthetizes what is required from individuals and companies in Brazil in the coming years.

CRITICAL THINKING QUESTIONS

1. How do you compare Brazil and other emerging markets? What are the main differences and commonalities?
2. Given the existing social demographic characteristics which segments seem to be more promising for retailers?
3. How can one explain the performance of luxury goods in a country like Brazil?
4. You were invited to prepare a presentation to a retailer willing to enter the Brazilian market, what would be your three top recommendations?
5. Many retailers are investing in multiformat/multibrand strategies. How can this strategy be justified by the marketing dynamics in Brazil?
6. Famous Brazilian songwriter and maestro Tom Jobim, who wrote "The Girl from Ipanema," used to say, "Brazil is not for rookies." Discuss this phrase in the context of retailing.

Case Study

NATURA: GOING BACK TO NATURA

Natura has been succeeding in making its business dealings as attractive as the faces of its Latin American customers since 1974. The company's business acumen is impressive, and its commitment to corporate social responsibility sets it apart from its global competitors. Its programs for social and environmental change and the products themselves set high standards.

Natura's Ekos line of products, available since 2005, uses sustainable ingredients from special reserves in rain forests and savannas, maintained by small local communities. The products contain Brazilian berries and plants, such as guarana, Brazil nuts, mate verde, and cocoa. Independent bodies such as the nongovernmental organization Imaflora monitor the nature reserves.

Natura is also careful not to let any community become reliant on producing any single ingredient, in case it is no longer needed. It tries to aid other forms of development in the area, such as handicrafts and ecotourism. "We have a concept called 'bem estar bem'—'well being well,'" explains Guttilla. "Well-being is about the harmonious relationship with oneself. But it is also about having empathetic, successful, and gratifying relationships with others and nature." Natura is also tackling other environmental issues. Some initiatives, such as its Rainforest Education and Recovery Project, have taken on the mammoth job of regenerating the damaged rain forest ecosystem. Others, such as the Rio de Janeiro Botanical Gardens initiative, have smaller aims. The company intends simply to help the gardens maintain and improve their medicinal plant beds.

Bia Saldanha, co-founder and marketing director of the Brazilian fair trade fashion brand AmazonLife, says she admires the Natura brand for its business practices. She believes that Natura is one of only a few Latin American brands that genuinely makes a positive difference for both its consumers and communities.

Natura's commitment to the environment resonates with consumers throughout the continent. Natura's Mexican operations opened in August 2005, and it is already present throughout Argentina, Chile, Peru, and Colombia.

Natura acquired Australian company Aesop and through this acquisition has improved its global presence to 16 countries, including the USA, the UK, Germany and France. International operations account for 27 percent of total sales. Natura counts an army of more than 1.3 million beauty consultants in Brazil in addition to roughly other 400,000 in Latin America.

Discussion Questions

1. What does Natura's success tell you about Brazilian consumers?
2. What makes Natura stand out from other cosmetic brands?
3. Can Natura go global (beyond Latin America) with their current strategy?
4. What role may Aesop play in Natura's internationalization strategy?

REFERENCES

A better today (2009, November 14). *Economist, 393* (8657), 9.

ABIT—Brazilian Textile and Apparel Industry Association Statistical Data Brazil. Retrieved November 6, 2010 from www.abit.org.br/site/ navegacao.asp?id_menu=13&IDIOMA=EN

ABIT—"Agenda de Prioridades—Têxtil e Confecção 2015 a 2018". Retrieved May 29, 2016 from www.abit.org.br/conteudo/links/publicacoes/agenda_ site.pdf

Andrade, Sara. "Inside Brazil's Booming Fashion Industry—The Business of Fashion," *Vogue Portugal,* August 5, 2010.

Arrivals and departures (2009, November 14). *The Economist, 393* (8657), 9.

Artigas, M. & Calicchio, N. (2007). Brazil: Fashion Conscious, Credit Ready. *McKinsey Quarterly,* 4, 76–79.

Bouças, Cibele. "NA MODA, VOLUME DE VENDAS CRESCE 2,5 percent". Retrieved May, 29, 2916 from: www.sbvc.com.br/2014/1906079-na-moda-volume-de-vendas-cresce–2–5/

Brazil (2009). Datamonitor

Brazil & Columbia: Apparel Attitudes (2008). Retrieved January 7, 2010, from www. cottoninc.com/SupplyChainInsights/Brazil-and-Columbia-Apparel-Attitudes/ Brazil-and-Columbia-Apparel-Attitudes.pdf?CFID=2363940&CFTOKEN= 72793671

Brazil: The Allure of the Underdog (2010). Retrieved May 20, 2010, from http://beta. luxurysociety.com/articles/2009/10/brazil-the-allure-of-the-underdog

Brazil jobs (2010). Retrieved February 23, 2010 from www.jobzing.com/brazil/

Brazil Retail: Time to e-shop (2009, September 28). *Business Latin America.* The Economist Intelligence Unit Brazil takes off (November 14, 2009). *The Economist, 393* (8657), 15.

Capp, J., Elstrod, H. & Bebb Jones Jr., W. (2005). Reining in Brazil's Informal Economy. *McKinsey Quarterly,* 1, 9–11.

Doing Business in Brazil (2009). Retrieved January 7, 2010, from www.buyusainfo.net/ docs/x_7220198.pdf

Duarte, M. "Depois de fechar lojas do Iguatemi e do Market Place, Topshop encerra atividades no Japão" Retrieved May 29, 2016 from http://ffw.com.br/noticias/ business/depois-de-fechar-lojas-do-iguatemi-e-do-market-place-topshop-encerra-atividade-no-japao–357/

"Emerging Markets Offer Growth Opportunities for Apparel Retailers Battling Declines in Domestic Consumer Spending." Retrieved December 4, 2009 from www.atkearney.com/index.php/News-media/emerging-markets-offer-growth-opportunities-for-apparel-retailers-battling-declines-in-domestic-consumer-spending.html

Financial Times—"The FDI Report 2016: Global Greenfield Investment Trends" Retrieved May 29, 2016 from http://forms.fdiintelligence.com/report2016/files/The_fDi_Report_2016.pdf

Folha de São Paulo Newspaper (March 16, 2005). Retrieved October 21, 2010, from www1.folha.uol.com.br/fsp/dinheiro/fi1603200502.htm

Folha de São Paulo Newspaper (January 1, 2010a). Retrieved September 16, 2010, from www1.folha.uol.com.br/folha/ambiente/ult10007u673513.shtml

Folha de São Paulo Newspaper (August 30, 2010b). Retrieved September 16, 2010, from www1.folha.uol.com.br/fsp/mercado/me3008201023.htm

Hall, C. (2009). WWD List: Windows of Opportunity. Retrieved November 2, 2009, from www.wwd.com/retail-news/wwd-list-windows-of-opportunity–2199757/print/

Kearney, A.T. "The 2015 Global Retail Development Index—Global Retail: an Unstoppable Force". Retrieved, May, 29, 2016 from: www.atkearney.com/documents/10192/5972342/Global+Retail+Expansion-An+Unstoppable+Force+-+2015+GRDI.pdf/22c67371–43ec–4c27-b130–5c7c63c296fc

Kenyon, T. & Kapaz, E. (2005). The Informality Trap. *Public Policy for the Private Sector—The World Bank Group*, Note Number 301, December.

Legal guide for the foreign investor in Brazil (2007). Retrieved January 7, 2010, from www.brasilemb.org/docs/Trade%20and%20Investment/guide_investors.pdf

Portal Exame. Retrieved September 16, 2010, from http://portalexame.abril.com.br/gestao/noticias/lojas-classe-c-devem-ter-estetica-propria–596591.html/

Prahalad, C. & Lieberthal, K. (2003, August) The End of Corporate Imperialism. *Harvard Business Review. 81*(8), 109.

Research: Reaching Brazilian Consumers (2005). *Brand Strategy,* p. 48.

Treewater, E. & Price, J. (September 2007). Navigating Latin American Distribution Channels. *Logistics Today, 48*(9), 1.

Webshoppers 2015—Edition—Retrieved January 29, 2016 from www.ebit.com.br/webshoppers

SOUTH KOREA

3

Ji Hye Kang
Shubhapriya Bennur
Sowon Hahn
Junghwa Son
Sung Ha Jang
Youngsoo Ha

OBJECTIVES

After reading this chapter, you will

- ▸ Understand why South Korea is an important emerging market
- ▸ Grasp various aspects of retailing in the country
- ▸ Recognize the unique characteristics of a Korean consumer
- ▸ Know about foreign direct investment regulations for investing in South Korea

South Korea is a highly urbanized nation located in the southern part of the Korean peninsula in East Asia. Its capital, Seoul, has a population of around 9.79 million. The entire population of the nation is estimated at around 48.58 million, 82.5 percent of which is comprised of urban residents. A few urban areas other than Seoul include Busan (Pusan) 3.216 million; Incheon (Inch'on) 2.685 million; Daegu (Taegu) 2.244 million; Daejon (Taejon) 1.564 million; Gwangju (Kwangju) 1.536 million (CIA World Factbook, 2015). South Korea is one of the most ethnically homogeneous societies in the world, with more than 99 percent of inhabitants having Korean ethnicity.

As per CIA World Fact book 2015 South Korea has a per capita income of around $36,500 (PPP) per annum. It is the fourth-largest economy in Asia and eleventh-largest in the world. The US–Korea Free Trade Agreement was approved by both governments in 2011 and came into effect in March 2012. However, between 2012 and 2015, the economy experienced slow growth of about 2–3 percent per year due to slow domestic consumption and lower investment. In 2015, the administration faced the challenge of balancing heavy reliance on exports with developing domestic-oriented sectors, such as services.

TABLE 3.1 Fast Facts about South Korea

Capital	Seoul
Population	50,924,172 (July 2016 est.)
Type of government	Presidential Republic
GDP: purchasing power parity: in US$	$1.929 trillion (2016 est.)
Export commodities	semiconductors, petrochemicals, automobile/ auto parts, ships, wireless communication equipment, flat display displays, steel, electronics, plastics, computers
Age structure	0–14 years: 13.45 percent 15–24 years: 13.08 percent 25–54 years: 45.93 percent 55–64 years: 14.01 percent 65 years and over: 13.53 percent 3,972,796) (2016 est.)
Religion	Christian 31.6 percent (Protestant 24.0 percent, Catholic 7.6 percent), Buddhist 24.2 percent, other or unknown 43.3 percent
Ethnicity	Homogeneous

Source: CIA factbook.gov

TABLE 3.2 Transaction Value

By commodity groups	By the type of management	2015
Total	Total	53,888,271
	Online mall	34,205,569
	On/Offline mall	19,682,702
Fashion and related goods	Total	8,467,279
	Online mall	5,448,409
	On/Offline mall	3,018,869
Clothing	Total	5,845,043
	Online mall	3,799,035
	On/Offline mall	2,046,008
Luggage	Total	940,128
	Online mall	627,182
	On/Offline mall	312,947
Footwear	Total	785,125
	Online mall	465,932
	On/Offline mall	319,193
Fashion goods and accessories	Total	896,983
	Online mall	556,262
	On/Offline mall	340,722
Cosmetics	Total	3,519,503
	Online mall	1,257,788
	On/Offline mall	2,261,716

Other long-term challenges of the South Korean economy include a rapidly aging population, an inflexible labor market, the dominance of large conglomerates (chaebols), and a heavy reliance on exports (which comprise about half of GDP). The current government, in an effort to address the long-term challenges and sustain economic growth, has prioritized structural reforms, deregulation, promotion of entrepreneurship and creative industries,

TABLE 3.3 Consumption Ratio of Revenue (Statistics Korea, 2015)

By industry	2014 Total	shop sales	visiting sales	internet sales	TV home shopping, telephone, post	Others
Wholesale and retail trade: Whole country	100.0	62.9	10.4	3.9	2.4	20.4
Wholesale and retail trade: Seoul	100.0	40.5	10.2	6.2	3.2	39.9

and the competitiveness of small- and medium-sized enterprises. All of this has made Korea an ideal place for foreign companies and investors.

South Korea is currently ranked seventh among the most attractive countries of South and East Asia for foreign companies, according to the UNCTAD 2015 World Investment Report. The FDI flows into South Korea have been more or less constant in recent years—averaging around USD 10 billion. In the first half of 2015, FDI reached USD 8.87 billion (South Korea Foreign Investment, 2016)

Apart from the country's rapid economic development, some of the reasons South Korea appeals to foreign direct investors are its highly skilled workforce, advanced R&D capabilities, high-quality infrastructure, brand-savvy consumers willing to spend on quality products, high level of disposable household income, strong shipping and air cargo infrastructure. All these reasons make the country a great hub for expansion into other markets.

KOREAN CONSUMERS

These days, the lifestyle of Korean consumers can be described in three key-words: individualism, rationalism, and digital.

INDIVIDUALISM

Korean consumers focus on themselves and seek self-enhancement value. Individualistic trends can be found in various aspects of the current market including marriage, married life, and the lifestle of elderly people. According to the Cheil Annual Consumer Report (2014), 66 percent of participants aged 60 or older wanted to live by themselves rather than living with their children. Such a result is remarkable: the lifestyle of current Korean consumers is contrary to Korea's traditional, communal culture.

LG Economic Research Institute (2011) showed that single-person households accounted for about 27 percent of the total Korean population in 2015, and it is still on the increase. Consumers in single-person households in Korea reported that they had already experienced or used products or services designed for single-person households such as daily supplies (30 percent), home appliances (23 percent), movie/cultural events (20 percent), and housing (15 percent). They also reported a positive purchase intention for single-person households' products and services; daily supplies (28 percent), home appliances (34 percent), movie/cultural event (30 percent), and housing (26 percent) (Park, 2011).

Due to individualism, the power of the male consumer has strengthened. Traditionally, Korean male consumers left shopping decisions up to their parents or partners. However, because of the the increase of single-person households, most male Korean consumers purchase products or services themselves.

Korean consumers also spare no expense on their health. Health is the first priority of current Korean consumers. According to the 2014 OECD

TABLE 3.4 The percentage of male shoppers in Korea (Lim & Park, 2016)

Age/Year	1999	2004	2009	2014
20	9.6	14.5	18.0	21.3
30	18.7	23.5	26.1	33.9
40	14.3	19.9	26.0	29.4
50	8.2	11.6	16.2	20.6
60	7.4	11.0	13.0	15.6

survey, Koreans' self-evaluation of their health was ranked the lowest among OECD member countries, even though their average life expectancy was higher than the OECD average. Over the past 15 years, the time that Korean consumers spend on activities such as working, housekeeping or study has been decreasing, whereas the time spent on activities such as sleeping, eating, appearance management and health management has been increasing (Lim & Park, 2016).

RATIONALISM

Korean consumers today place a high value on actual benefits and results. There has been a protracted economic recession in Korea. The recession affects all ages of Korean consumers in various ways, so they show rational consumption behaviors by seeking inexpensive and efficient products and services.

Rational consumption behaviors are especially prevalent among consumers in their twenties because of financial constraints (Hwang, 2015). These consumers regard use value as more important than possession value. In 2014, the top three major convenience stores in Korea reported that the sales record of their PB products exceeded the sales record of national brands (Hwang, 2014). The price of PB products is 10 to 20 percent lower and satisfies the young Korean consumers who seek inexpensive and efficient products. The success of IKEA, an international furniture company who launched their business in Korea for the first time in 2015, is also evidence of the utility-seeking tendency of current Korean consumers (Hwang, 2015).

Consumer needs in financially constrained situations have resulted in a new consumption behavior known as "the little luxury". Consumers are drawn to products that provide a sense of luxury, in an affordable price range (Hwang, 2014). "The little luxury" provides an escape from restrained consumption situations. Since Korean consumers find it difficult to achieve satisfaction from major purchases, such as buying a house, they try to purchase products or services in an affordable price range which provide the best value for them. The consumption phenomenon of "the little luxury" reflects Korean consumers' need to enjoy life today, rather than saving for the future, in an unexpected and extended recession. "The little luxury" phenomenon is found in various product categories. For example, although the sales growth rate of department stores in Korea has slowed down during the past few years, that of luxury dessert stores has increased (Hwang, 2014). A store that sold a $4 French macaroon recorded $40,000 sales on the first day of opening, even though its price was three times higher than normal macaroons. A store selling German luxury desserts recorded a 15 percent jump in sales during the six months from its opening, and recorded $2.9 million in sales (Hwang, 2014).

DIGITAL CONSUMER

Korean consumers are living in the digital age. The penetration rate of cell phones is 98 percent in Korea; the number of smartphone users surpassed 10 million in 2015 (Statistics Korea, 2015). Resistance to smartphone usage has disappeared, and the SNS (social network service) has become a daily routine for current Korean consumers. In infinitely changing circumstances, Korean consumers are provided with endless opportunities and uncertainty at the same time.

Korean consumers use SNS in their everyday life. Korean consumers prefer to communicate with others using SNS, rather than communicating face-to-face, and believe that those activities enhance the quality of life. The younger

▲ FIGURE 3.1 South Korean rescue members wearing chemical protective suits walk past a monster character during an anti-terror drill as part of a disaster management exercise at the COEX shopping and exhibition center in Seoul where South Korea held its 2016 Safe Korea anti-disaster exercise against terrorist threats and natural disasters.

age group shows more prevalent usage of SNS as a communication channel. They also regard SNS as a more reliable, comfortable communication channel, compared to traditional communication channels such as phone calls or text messages. Korean consumers use SNS for various reasons: information gathering (38 percent), rapid information (19 percent), timely communication (13 percent), relationship building and management (11 percent), and fun and enjoyment (6 percent) (Park, 2011). The widespread diffusion of SNS influences various aspects of Korean consumers and their consumption behaviors. Social consumers gather together using the SNS and share consumption-related information. Korean social consumers are sensitive to social issues (Park, 2011). They try to contribute to the progress of the society through their consumption. They emphasize a company's social responsibility and engage in altruistic consumption behaviors.

CONSUMER BEHAVIOR IN THE KOREAN FASHION INDUSTRY

The current lifestyles of Korean consumers (e.g., individualism, rationalism, and digital) influence the Korean fashion industry.

INDIVIDUALISM AND FASHION CONSUMERS

Korean consumers spend a lot on their physical appearance (Shin, 2014). Due to their collectivistic culture, Korean consumers regard the opinions of others as important. Due to the collectivistic culture and the current individualistic consumer tendency that regards health and the body as the most important value, Korean consumers seek "Lookism" in consumption. Korean consumers consider their body as an object of improvement. In the 2011 LG Consumer Report (Park, 2011), Korean consumers answered that: "If I don't have a good appearance, I will have a disadvantage" (64.9 percent), "I can have plastic surgery to have better appearance and body" (36.5 percent, female only), "I prefer a fashion style that makes me look younger than my actual age" (42 percent, female only), "Even though I am old, I should invest time and money in appearance management" (50.9 percent).

Single-person households in Korea spend more on themselves than consumers in a regular household (Park, 2011). They are less concerned with price than regular household consumers, and enthusiastic in expressing themselves through the consumption of fashion brands. In the 2011 LG Consumer Report (Park, 2011), single-person household consumers answered that: "fashion reveals my status" (45 percent, regular household consumers 34 percent),

"I willingly pay a higher price for the fashion brand that I want" (45 percent, regular household consumers 26 percent).

RATIONALISM AND FASHION CONSUMERS

The rational consumption tendency of Korean consumers influences the Korean fashion industry. A department store has been a representative retail channel for fashion products, especially for luxury fashion products, in Korea for a long time. However, the sales growth rate of department stores has slowed since 2012 (Bang & Kim, 2016). Because Korean fashion consumers seek utilitarian value through the consumption of "the little luxury", retailers have stopped opening new department stores and started to expand outlet stores which sell cut-price merchandise. The number of outlet stores has increased from four in 2009 to 22 in 2015 (Bang & Kim, 2016).

DIGITAL CONSUMER AND FASHION CONSUMERS

Korean consumers use the internet and digital technologies for the consumption of fashion products (63 percent of Korean consumers immediately search

▲ FIGURE 3.2 A woman walks through an alleyway in the popular Myeongdong shopping district of Seoul.

for information when they are in need). Among all of the information searched by using a smartphone, 0.3 percent is shopping-related (Park, 2011). Cross-border online shopping is one of the newest consumption phenomena in the Korean market, where consumers directly purchase foreign products from foreign online retailers. Cross-border online shopping has risen from the combination of rational consumption and the digital environment (Han, 2014). Lee and Choo (2015) reported that cross-border online shopping in Korea exceeded $0.8 billion in 2012, and had risen to $1.6 billion in 2014. Among the top 10 product categories of cross-border online shopping, fashion and beauty products are reported as the most frequently purchased product category. Although cross-border online shopping was originally started by consumers who had experience living abroad, it has become the normal way of purchasing foreign products for Korean digital fashion consumers (Lee & Choo, 2015).

SOCIAL FACTORS THAT INFLUENCE THE KOREAN RETAIL INDUSTRY

Korea's drastic social changes began with the modernization process at the beginning of the twentieth century, and have continued through the globalization of the twenty-first century. The following is a discussion of four social factors that influence the Korean retailing industry: culture, government policy and regulation, technology, and demographics.

CULTURE

Compared to other countries, Korea is one of the purest and most homogeneous cultures in the world (Gannon, 2004). Korea has a low tolerance of deviant behavior and there are many strong norms with which Koreans are expected to comply, which creates a tight culture. Korea was ranked fifth among 33 countries in terms of tightness; in comparison, Korea's score was almost twice that of the U.S. (Gelfand et al., 2011). The Korean fashion industry is a direct reflection of this tight culture. In any one season, Korean fashion markets are dominated by a few styles and colors. Since the styles are introduced as the fashion for the season, fashionable Koreans feel an urge to possess these styles; the styles then become the fashion. In a tight culture, social consensus is very important as people make decisions about what should or should not be worn, especially in public. Low tolerance of diversity in a tight culture is one reason for only a few dominant fashion styles per season, and it is rare that subculture fashions are seen in the fashion market.

Korea is also known as the most Confucian nation in the world (Gannon, 2004). It is a high-power distance society; an individual in this type of society has his/her rightful place, there is respect for old age, and status is important to demonstrate power (Hofstede, 1991; De Mooij & Hofstede, 2002). In this culture, "face" is a very important concept to determine an individual's behavior, including fashion purchases. "Face" refers to a person's place in his/her social network; it is the most important measure of one's social worth in Confucian collectivism (Jin, Gavin, & Kang, 2012). Even though the concept of face is universal, the significance is greater in a Confucian culture such as Korea. Face can be saved when something makes others look up to or be envious of the individual, such as wealth, intelligence, attractiveness, skills, rank, etc. (Seligman, 1999). Since luxury brands can signify the wearer's wealth and enhance his/her attractiveness, they serve as an important face booster; this is an important motivation to buy well-known luxury branded products and provides one reason why the Korean luxury market ranked eighth in the global luxury market (La, 2015) even though the Korean population is 27th in the world.

Admittedly, the Korean culture is transitioning and becoming more individualized and westernized, especially among the younger generation. However, the traditional Korean culture continues to fundamentally affect fashion purchase behavior.

GOVERNMENT POLICY AND REGULATION

In 1996, the Korean retail market was fundamentally changed when the Korean government opened it up to foreign countries; which is referred to as "the liberalization of the Korean retailing market". This policy brought revolutionary changes to the Korean retailing market, especially during the first 10 years.

The most noticeable change was the emergence and predominance of discount retailers. At the same time that the liberalization was taking place, the top three world discounters entered the Korean market: Walmart from the U.S., Carrefour from France, and Macro from the Netherlands. In response to these foreign companies, Korean domestic discounters such as E-Mart and Homeplus began trading. Before liberalization, there were no Western-type discount retailers in Korea with large stores selling a variety of goods. However, after the Korean economic crisis in 1996, consumers became more price-sensitive; the discount market kept growing and emerged as a place for fashion item shopping (Park, 2012). The discount market in Korea grew by 60.8 percent during 1996–2006 and settled as a main retailing outlet (Park, 2006). Contrary to the concerns of the Korean domestic discounters at the beginning of the liberalization, the domestic discounters won the game and all three of the top world discounters withdrew from Korea within about 10 years (Kim, 2016).

The second important change that the liberalization brought was diversification of retailing outlets. The liberalization allowed more than one retailer to import the same brands. Hence, it became popular for many different types of retail stores to buy the same imported brand products and offer them at various prices (Park, 2012). The concept of the convenience store was introduced after the liberation; it emerged as a retail outlet and showed the fastest growth rate (Kim, 2016). TV shopping was also introduced and became a new fashion shopping place. Recently, major TV shopping channels have increased fashion items to about 50 percent of their total revenue and now carry high-end brands and private labels to differentiate from their competitors (Lee, 2014). Another impact of the liberalization has the growth in popularity of premium outlets. In 2007, a U.S.-type premium fashion outlet located in suburban areas began carrying imported luxury brands at discounted prices. Since then, the premium outlet market has grown by double digits (Korean Fashion Association, 2014). Because Korea is now in a phase of sluggish development, consumer demand for good value for their money will be stable and a driving force to the success of the outlets.

Before the retailing liberalization, another government policy greatly influenced the Korean consumer market: the liberalization of overseas travel in 1989. This allowed all Koreans to travel overseas. Previously, special permission was required from the government to have passports issued. Those desiring to travel overseas needed to have a very clear purpose (e.g. travel, for either government duties or business or study abroad). Recreational travel (e.g. backpacking and honeymooning) was not permitted. Since liberalization, the number of Korean outbound travelers has increased from 720,000 in 1988 to 15 million in 2013 (Son & Choi, 2014). This increase in overseas travel has changed people's experiences, which has, in turn, influenced their shopping behavior. Overseas travel has become a part of ordinary Koreans' lives; 18 percent of the total shopping consumption of a Korean individual now occurs in the overseas market (Korea Chamber of Commerce & Industry [KCCI], October 24, 2014). The most popular shopping item in the overseas market are fashion items such as clothing (26 percent of male consumption) and cosmetics (26 percent of female consumption) (KCCI, October 24, 2014).

With the experience of foreign fashion products plus internet shopping malls serving as agents through which to buy foreign products, direct purchase from foreign retailers has become increasingly popular. These shopping malls provide very detailed guidelines for ordering the products consumers want from the foreign online retailers, provide post office boxes in the foreign countries for domestic deliveries, and then deliver the products to consumers and charge extra delivery fees. Using this system, Korean consumers purchase various products from around the world that are available only for domestic delivery in the foreign country. In a survey asking why consumers prefer direct shopping from foreign online retailers, respondents indicated a less expensive price for the same product (67 percent), brands unavailable in Korea (37.8 percent), and a variety of products (35 percent) (as cited in Samsung Economic Research Institute, 2014). Another reason for the increase in direct shopping is lower tariffs. In 2012, Korea and the U.S. government agreed to raise the free purchase amount from $130 to $200, as long as the products were purchased directly from the U.S.; this agreement encouraged Korean consumers to be more interested in and use U.S. online retailers.

TECHNOLOGY

Korea is well known as a leading information technology (IT) nation of the twenty-first century. According to *The Wall Street Journal*, Korea ranked first in the world for high-speed internet penetration (Fitzgerald, 2014). Another survey reported that, as of March 2015, 83 percent of Koreans possessed a smart phone (Park, 2015). This highly technology-oriented consumer behavior is reflected in retailing; as Korea entered its slow economic development phase, the retail industry saw a slow down in growth: 1.6 percent for 2013, 2.2 percent for 2014 and 2.4 percent for 2015 (KCCI, December 1, 2014), but online shopping increased by 19.1 percent in 2016 (Fashion Channel, 2016). Of purchases made from online shopping malls, about 50 percent were made through mobile shopping; online shopping is forecast to be the most promising market in the future.

The trend is the same regarding fashion items. Over 50 percent of online shopping mall revenues were made using mobile shopping. Therefore, Korean retailers provide the best omni-channel environments to satisfy Korean consumer technology-friendly shopping behavior (Fashion Channel, 2016). Nielsen's research on the use of mobile phones also evidenced that more Koreans use mobile phones for commercial purposes such as mobile shopping, mobile banking, location-based services, and barcode/QR code scanning than individuals in the U.S., the U.K., Italy, Russia, and Brazil (China is at a level similar to Korea) (Nielsen, 2013).

▲ FIGURE 3.3 Shoppers at Starfield Hanam Shopping Mall. South Korea.

DEMOGRAPHICS AND VALUE CHANGES

Korea is currently experiencing two significant demographic changes: the growth of both single-person households and the senior population. The number of single-person households in Korea has drastically increased. Termed the "solo economy", as of 2016, one in four Koreans is in this category; by 2030 this group will account for 20 percent of the total domestic consumer market, (Information & Cultural Contents Technology, 2016). Individuals in this market are known to have the highest disposable monthly income (33 percent), almost twice that of households with three to four people (17.2 percent) (Lee, 2016). For these reasons, this group is expected to lead the future Korean consumer market and has already created many phenomena. Among Korean retailing outlets, convenience stores are the most successful in terms of sales volume and number of stores because they provide small amounts of food for single people and provide a 24-hour service. These stores are also investing in products and services such as fashion, cosmetics, travel, and habit items (Ahn, 2012). Online retailers providing self-related products and services and subscription services, such as regular delivery of staple items, are expected to continue to grow in concert with this population.

The second demographic change influencing Korean retailing is the senior population, which includes baby boomers. A Korean baby boomer was born between 1955 (after the Korean War) and 1963. Because this generation comprises the largest portion of the Korean population (14.5 percent), it has a significant impact on the Korean market (Park, 2013). Baby boomers are also called active seniors or new seniors because they are very interested in fashion and trends and want to stay young. Due to the purchasing power and interest in fashion of this generation, businesses targeting this demographic do well; purchases in luxury cosmetics and outdoor wear have greatly increased. For example, Lotte, one of the largest department chains in Korea, reported a two-digit sales volume increase by the new senior segment, and fashion brands with young taste and style are very successful in this market (Hong, 2016). Even though not all seniors have resources such as time and money, they have distinctive lifestyles and more resources than previous seniors. Therefore, the senior markets with young tastes are expected to grow substantially.

RETAIL FORMATS IN KOREA

The Korean retail industry accounts for 31.6 percent of employment as of 2014 (Samjong KPMG, 2014). The employment rate in the manufacturing sector has continuously reduced because of increased production outside the country; however, employment rates in the retail sector have grown consistently over the last few decades.

The market liberalization of the Korean economy in 1996 had a noteworthy effect and has restructured the retail industry to be more efficient. Giant international retailers, such as Makro, Carrefour, Costco Wholesale Club, Wal-Mart, Tesco, DAISO, and IKEA entered the Korean markets after the full market liberalization in 1996. The speedy expansion and growth of the retail industry led to significant diversification and evolvement during the last few decades. Currently, the influence of the economic recession has negatively influenced the retail industry in terms of a slow growth rate, the shrinkage of consumers' consumption rate, and the reinforcement of regulation on the retail sector.

Today, the co-existence of traditional and modern retail formats in Korea has created intense competition between retail formats, highly concentrated major players, dull and slow growth of sales, and the diversification of retail formats and structures (Park, 2001). In other words, significant characteristics of

TABLE 3.5 The growth rate of retail formats percent current value growth]

	2011	2012	2013	2014
Total	8.4	4.4	1.4	1.4
Department stores	11.4	5.4	2.6	−1.6
Discount stores*	10.9	6.3	2.4	3.4
Supermarkets	8.5	4.8	3.1	0.8
Convenience stores	17.9	18.3	7.8	8.7
Non-store based retailing	10.6	11.1	7.2	7.0
Specialty stores	5.2	0.0	−2.5	−1.3

Source: Korea Chamber of Commerce & Industry

Note: * indicates that the growth rate of discount stores include duty-free stores and outlet Malls

the Korean retail industry can be summarized as: high competition between players, polarized size of stores and number of employees, and low productivity.

From the 1960s, the Korean government focused mainly on exports to develop and expand the domestic economy. In line with supporting the export sector, the Korean government primarily supported the manufacturing sector. This gave huge power to the manufacturing sector compared to the retail sector, and led to unique retail features in terms of the consignment system and the intensive use of manufacturer's franchised sales outlets (Sternquist, 2008). Since manufacturers had the power, they took on the role of retailers, such as planning, buying and presenting merchandise and handling unsold merchandise. Retailers' roles were limited.

From the early 2000s, the power between retailers and manufacturers has moved from manufacturers to retailers due to the increasing buying power of retailers, intense competition, and the dominance of giant retailers—the three key players in Korean department stores (Lotte, Shinsegae, and Hyundai) and in Korean discount stores (E-mart, Home Plus, and Lotte Mart) (Sternquist, 2008). Those three giant department stores shared more than 75 percent of sales; about 60 percent were accounted for by the three key discount stores (Sternquist, 2008).

Lately, the economic downturn and consumers' restriction on spending has led to a drastically low growth rate in the retail sector. The growth rate of entire retail formats was 1.4 percent in 2014 (Korea Chamber of Commerce & Industry, 2015). Department stores and specialty stores reached negative growth rates; however, convenience stores and non-store based retailers (i.e., e/m-retailing and TV home shopping) recorded respectively 8.7 and 7 percent growth rates in 2014 (Korea Chamber of Commerce & Industry, 2015). Table 3.5 presents the growth rate by retail formats from 2011 to 2014.

TRADITIONAL MARKETS

Traditional markets were the most popular and concentrated retail format until the 1960s in Korea. The main characteristics of traditional markets are small size, self-employed, limited merchandise, unorganized retailers, low quality of products and services, and backwardness of facilities and environments (Yoo, 2015). There were 1,660 traditional market stores in 2005; by 2013, this had fallen to 1,502 (see Table 3.6; Korea Chamber of Commerce & Industry, 2015). This indicates that the number of stores in traditional markets has gradually reduced. In 2013, the number of stores in traditional markets was 210,437 and currently, the number of stores in traditional markets is 186,636 (Korea Chamber of Commerce & Industry, 2015). In general, traditional markets focus heavily on agricultural and aquatic products (26 percent) followed by apparel and shoes (24.3 percent) (Small Enterprise and Market Service, 2013). Most traditional markets accept credit cards, but retailers still prefer cash payment.

Traditional markets have changed to compete with other retail formats such as supermarkets and discount stores. They have rebuilt and restructured buildings, provided parking spaces, accepted credit cards, and offered

TABLE 3.6 Number of stores within traditional markets

Year	2005	2006	2008	2010	2012	2013
Number of stores within traditional markets	1,660	1,610	1,550	1,517	1,511	1,502

Source: Small Enterprise and Market Service

advanced customer services (Small Enterprise and Market Service, 2013). Additionally, the support from the Korean government has helped to promote consumers' consumption in traditional markets. The regulations and laws help and protect retailers in traditional markets, yet there are still some challenges for them. To compete with other types of retail formats, they need to adopt new and modern technology, improve the quality of merchandise and services, and diversify and differentiate merchandise assortments.

SUPERMARKETS

Supermarkets primarily sell fresh foods (e.g. fruit, vegetables, fish, meats, etc) and are self-service. The first supermarket, Korea Supermarket, opened in 1964, but only foreigners were allowed to purchase merchandise from the store (Park & Suh, 2015). Korea Supermarket purchased merchandise from overseas and only accepted foreign currency (Park & Suh, 2015). The first modern supermarket was New Seoul Supermarket, which opened in 1970 to improve and change the distribution structure in the domestic market. It was opened and operated with support from the Korean government (Park & Suh, 2015).

Since the 2000s, the number of medium- and large-sized supermarkets has slowly increased with an average five years' growth rate of 2.0 percent in 2013 (Korea Chamber of Commerce & Industry, 2015). In contrast, the number of small and medium-sized supermarkets has continuously decreased, but the sales volume of small and medium-sized supermarkets increased by 6.8 percent over the previous five years (Korea Chamber of Commerce & Industry, 2015). The government restricts regulations for medium and large-sized supermarkets in terms of operating hours, closing days, and opening stores, and protects and supports small and medium sized supermarkets, so it causes the dissimilar growth rate between the two different-sized supermarkets. Table 3.7 shows the size of supermarkets.

Recently, the patterns of consumers' consumption have changed. Consumers prefer to shop at neighborhood stores, rather than traveling to discount stores. In addition, the increase of the smaller and single-person households which need frequent small purchases will lead to growth in supermarket sales. However, intense competition between convenience stores and non-store-based retailers is also expected because of the penetration of convenience stores on every corner and diverse promotions, including free shipping, buy one get one free, bundling products, etc., from non-store based retailers.

TABLE 3.7 The size of supermarkets

Type		2006	2008	2010	2011	2012	2013	Average Growth Rate[1) percent
Small-Medium Supermarkets	Number of stores	96,922	87,271	79,193	76,043	73,101	72,391	-3.4
	Number of employees	163,477	146,507	135,581	132,989	128,604	132,862	-1.9
	Sales volume (Billion, KRW)	6,639	7,715	8,982	9,421	9,961	10,325	6.8
Medium-Large Supermarkets	Number of stores	7,122	8,060	8,341	8,277	9,047	8,865	2.0
	Number of employees	52,981	63,824	69,348	73,361	79,806	80,369	5.2
	Sales volume (Billion, KRW)	12,279	15,636	19,828	22,315	23,765	24,401	11.2

Source: Korea Chamber of Commerce & Industry

Note: [1)] Indicates the average annual growth rate of last five years.

DEPARTMENT STORES

Department stores have traditionally led the retail industry and are one of the key players in the retail sector in Korea. The first department store in Korea, which opened in 1906, was the Japanese-owned Mitsukoshi department store (Chae, 2012). The first department store owned by Koreans was the Hwa Shin Department store, which opened in 1931.

After the economic boom in the 1980s, many department stores opened and growth was fast. They mainly focused on women's, men's, and children's apparel, home furnishings, cosmetics, kitchenware, and small appliances (Levy, Weitz, & Grewal, 2014). The increased number of department stores led to intense competition: Lotte, Shinsegae, and Midopa were key players during the 1980s (Chae, 2012).

Currently, the main players are Lotte, Shinsegae, and Hyundai. Their growth rate stayed in double digits until 2011, but dramatically dropped to 5.4 percent in 2012, and reached a negative growth rate of 1.6 percent in 2014

▲ FIGURE 3.4 Style Nanda Cosmetic store.

(Korea Chamber of Commerce & Industry, 2015). This is not only because of the slow economy, but also because the main target consumers in their twenties and thirties shop at and move to other retail formats, such as outlet shopping, direct foreign purchases, and online shopping. In addition, the sales volume of women's, men's and children's apparel and accessories in terms of the main merchandise of department stores has dropped sharply (Korea Chamber of Commerce & Industry, 2015). In order to recover this sales volume and growth rate, department stores have adopted diverse approaches. They now promote sales to more affluent customers in their forties and fifties, by adopting private label brands and have developed omni-channel retailing, special sales and discount promotions. They are also focusing on food and groceries, targeting international tourists, especially the Chinese (Korea Chamber of Commerce & Industry, 2015; M2 Presswire, 2016).

SPECIALTY STORES

Specialty stores (e.g. apparel and footwear stores and fashion brand stores) focus on a limited number of merchandise categories and provide a high level of service (Levy et al., 2014). They offer very deep but narrow assortments and sales associate expertise. According to Euromonitor International, the total value sales of specialty stores accounted for KRW 85,403.7 billion in 2015 (Euromonitor International, 2016). Currently, health and beauty specialty stores targeting women in their twenties are booming (Korea Distribution Association, 2013). In particular, low and medium-priced health and beauty specialty stores like Aritaum, Etude House, Innisfree, Nature Republic, etc. have received more attention from younger consumers in their late teens to women in their twenties (See Image 5 to 8). Even though low- and medium-priced health and beauty specialty stores are growing, they have some barriers. It takes a huge initial investment to open a store, as most health and beauty specialty stores are required to be located in the central business districts, main streets, or shopping centers where there is a high level of pedestrian traffic and shopping flow (Korea Distribution Association, 2013). Thus, the growth of specialty stores is anticipated to be slow.

CONVENIENCE STORES

Convenience stores offer a limited variety and assortment of merchandise at a convenient location with a speedy checkout (Levy et al., 2014). The first convenience store in Korea was a 7-Eleven located in Seoul in 1989. The growth of convenience stores has been incredible since 2004. From 2008 to 2012, the average annual growth rate of convenience stores was about 15.6 percent and it refers to the highest growth rates among off-line retail formats (Korea Chamber of Commerce & Industry, 2015). However, the growth rates and sales volume have begun to slow since 2013. This indicates that the life cycle of convenience stores in Korea is approaching the stage of maturity (Korea Chamber of Commerce & Industry, 2015). However, their growth is expected to remain positive due to consumers' preference for shopping in their neighborhoods, value-focused shopping trends, and increasing numbers of single-person households (Korea Distribution Association, 2013).

Unlike in other countries, convenience stores in Korea provide a courier service, so consumers can easily send and pick up packages at their local stores. Recently, convenience stores have focused heavily on private brands (PB) to increase their sales volume. Lunch boxes, ice cream, noodles, and fast foods are the main PB of convenience stores. In addition, aggressive promotions, such as buy one get one free, buy two get one free, etc., threaten other retail formats, including supermarkets and discount stores (Korea Chamber of Commerce & Industry, 2015). CU, GS25, and 7-Eleven are the main competitors in the convenience store market.

DISCOUNT STORES

Discount stores were introduced after the full market liberalization of the Korean economy in 1996. Discount stores have led the retail industry in Korea in terms of the growth rate and sales volume. Between 1999 and 2002, it showed an incredible growth rate (about 32 percent) and was a significant player in the retail sector (Lee, 2003). However, the growth rate of discount stores has shown a negative growth rate since 2012, and it reached a negative growth rate of 3.4 percent in 2014 due to the economic recession, the change in consumers' consumption trends, the success of online shopping, and regulations and restrictions from the government (Korea Chamber of Commerce & Industry, 2015) (see Table 3.8).

TABLE 3.8 Sales volume of discount stores

	2011	2012	2013	2014
Increasing rate	2.9 percent	–3.3 percent	–5.0 percent	–3.4 percent

Source: Ministry of Trade, Industry and Energy (2015).

E-mart, Lotte Mart, and Homeplus are the major players in Korea. The main key players are discount stores owned by Chaebol and large family-controlled business groups (Sternquist, 2008). Shinsegae owns E-mart, Lotte owns Lotte Mart, and Homeplus is owned by Samsung. As with department stores, discount stores are owned and operated by Chaebol, so they can use their buying power to take advantage of the size and scale of stores.

Previously consumers used to bulk-buy at discount stores once a week; however, consumers' shopping trends have changed due to the increase of single-person households. Consumers are willing to purchase frequently in a smaller quantity. Additionally, consumers tend to purchase groceries in non-store retailers (e.g online and mobile retailers and TV home shopping). These trends have guided the extension of online shopping channels and supermarkets of discount stores (Korea Chamber of Commerce & Industry, 2015). In order to keep maintaining sales growth, discount stores have tried to provide value products (i.e., PB), hold price competitiveness or use the multiple channels approach (Korea Chamber of Commerce & Industry, 2015).

CATEGORY SPECIALISTS

Category specialists are discount stores that provide a narrow and deep assortment of merchandise (Levy et al., 2014). Category specialists are frequently called "category killers." Category specialists are very similar to specialty stores in terms of assortments of merchandise and level of service; however, prices of merchandise are dissimilar: category killers offer less expensive prices for merchandise than specialty stores. For example, Hi-Mart carries only small home appliances and less expensive electronics than its competitors, such as washers and dryers, refrigerators, televisions, vacuums, etc., but all different kinds of brands, sizes, styles, and prices. ABC Mart (a shoe store) is another example of this category. However, category killers have not much grown in the Korean market compared to other countries as the rapid growth of discount stores and e-retailing has hindered their growth (Korea Distribution Association, 2013).

DRUG STORES

Drug stores refer to "specialty stores that concentrate on health and beauty care products" (Levy et al., 2014, p. 54). Drug stores carry mainly pharmaceuticals but are expanding into foods, cosmetics, etc. (Levy et al., 2014). Olive

Young and other drug stores which operate in Korea focus mostly on cosmetics and beauty products rather than pharmaceuticals. Olive Young is a leading retailer and is followed by Watsons and Lohb. Drug stores have recently received attention from consumers, but they take up a small part of the retail sector in Korea. It is expected that the growth rate and sales volume of drug stores will increase as the consumption of cosmetics and beauty products steadily rises (Korea Chamber of Commerce & Industry, 2016).

OUTLET STORES

Outlet stores have gradually increased their sales volume and growth of sale since 2010. Its growth rate reached double digits in 2014 (Korea Chamber of Commerce & Industry, 2015). In the beginning, outlet stores were located in the suburban areas near Seoul, but nowadays they are found in shopping malls and lifestyle centers in cities (Korea Distribution Association, 2013). In addition, premium outlet malls, such as Shinsegae-Simon Premium Outlet and Lotte Premium Out, are also booming. Consumers tend to save money, but tend to spend it on valuable merchandise. Many middle and upper middle class consumers now try to find and look for value, rather than just spending on expensive new arrivals. This explains why sales of department stores have dropped. This consumption trend has led to the growth of outlet stores and outlet malls in Korea. The growth rates and sales volume of outlet stores are expected to continuously grow over the next few years, and it is anticipated that major department stores will actively extend their retail format to outlet malls (Nam, 2014).

NON-STORE BASED RETAILING

TV home shopping started its business with two companies in 1995, and it now has six players (i.e., CJO shopping, GS Shop, NS home shopping, Lotte home shopping, Hyundai home shopping, and home & shopping) with 9 trillion and 290 billion Korean won of the market value in 2014 (Korea Chamber of Commerce & Industry, 2015). The rise in the market value of TV home shopping has been expected because of the increased number of cable TV, IPTV and satellite TV subscribers, and the approach of a variety of retail channels (i.e., PC-based internet and mobile retailing) (Korea On-Line Shopping Association, 2014).

Ubiquity of high-speed internet access and dominance of mobile devices has been fueling the growth of sales through internet and mobile shopping (M2 Presswire, 2016). In 2011, the market growth rate of online shopping accounted for 15.6 percent compared to the previous year (Korea Chamber of Commerce & Industry, 2015). The sales volume of online shopping reached almost KRW53 trillion in 2015 (Euromonitor International, 2016).

Between 2005 to 2010 online marketplaces, for example, Auction, Gmarket, and 11th street, led online shopping. An online marketplace refers to a type of e-commerce site where product or service information is provided by multiple third parties, whereas transactions are processed by the marketplace operator (Buettner, 2006). Even though online marketplaces led online shopping, the growth rate of online marketplaces has been slow since 2013. At that time, mobile shopping showed unbelievable growth due to the dominance of mobile devices and the exponential growth of the smartphone users. The popularization of mobile devices has guided the growth of mobile retailing and the shift from PC-based internet retailing to mobile retailing. Mobile retailing is anticipated to continuously grow because of the convenience of access, easy pay system, low initial investment cost compared to PC-based internet retailing, and the growth of mobile social commerce (Korea Chamber of Commerce & Industry, 2015). Table 3.9 indicates the sales in non-store based retailing.

TABLE 3.9 Sales volume in non-store based retailing (KRW billion)

	2010	2011	2012	2013	2014	2015
TV home shopping	6,015.5	6,917.8	8,322.1	9,595.4	10,622.1	11,170.7
PC-based internet retailing	21,675.6	24,645.2	27,479.3	30,776.9	33,825.0	37,207.5
Mobile retailing	–	1,456.5	2,283.5	4,702.7	10,621.1	16,743.4

Source: Euromonitor International (2016).

KEY RETAILING TRENDS IN KOREA

Overall, retailing showed a positive performance in 2015 and is expected to witness healthy growth over the next five years due to improving economic conditions and government efforts (Euromonitor International, 2016). The most significant retail trend in Korea is the increase of non-store retailing (i.e. PC-based internet retailing and mobile retailing). The convenience of shopping, price comparison, cheap prices for the same product, and the increasing adoption of mobile devices has boosted the growth of non-store retailing in Korea.

Recently, "malling" culture has become popular in Korea. "Malling is a trend in which consumers enjoy diverse activities such as dining, gaming or watching films or concerts during shopping trips in a one-stop location" (Euromonitor International, 2016, p. 1). Even though the "malling" culture has existed from 2000, it has become more popular since the opening of the COEX mall and IKEA in Korea. Since the "malling" culture lately prevails in Korea, it is expected that many other types of retailer, such as department stores, hypermarkets, and outlet malls, will extend and create more shopping complexes (Korea Chamber of Commerce & Industry, 2015). In line with this, many luxury brands, specialty retailers, or newly launched brands will be expected to find locations in shopping complexes since more consumers visit and spend time as a culture of malling.

The latest information technology development has affected payment systems in retailing and non-store retailing since 2015 (Euromonitor International, 2016). Kakao pay owned by Daum was launched in 2014 and has become popular as a payment system in retailing. Kakao Talk is the most popular instant messaging application in Korea: 97 percent of smart device users have this app (Euromonitor International, 2016). Once Kakao talk users have the app in their devices, they do not need to download Kakao pay. Consumers can add up to 20 credit cards to the Kakao pay application, and they do not need to carry cash or credit cards when purchasing merchandise at various retail stores in Korea if they have the app. Naver, a leading portal site in Korea, also launched Naver pay in 2015 (The Korea Herald, 2015). Users can link their Naver ID with their credit card or bank account information and manage their purchase history with the Naver ID. With the popularity of the payment systems of Kakao pay and Naver pay, shopping at internet shopping malls or mobile shopping malls has become much easier and more convenient. Given this, more consumers are ready to enjoy shopping using e-retailing or mobile-retailing, which will lead to strong growth over the next few years.

EMERGING RETAIL IN SOUTH KOREA

COSMETIC RETAIL

South Korea is one of the world's most exciting and fast-paced beauty markets, introducing industry-leading innovations and setting trends globally. Until the 1990s, the best gift for Korean women had been imported cosmetics from the United States, France or Japan. However, as interest in Korean cosmetics increased after the 2000s, the Korean cosmetic industry has been growing rapidly. In addition to the proliferation of exports for electronics and cars, cosmetics have become one of Korea's biggest exports. In 2014, for the first time, Korea exported more beauty products than it imported. In 2015, the total export value of cosmetics recorded up to USD 2.9 billion, a 53.33 percent growth from the previous year and largely surpasses imports amounts of USD 1.4 billion. China is the biggest buyer of South Korean beauty products, accounting

▲ FIGURE 3.5 The Shilla Duty free shop that carries luxury end brands.

for 40.3 percent of the country's entire cosmetics exports. Hong Kong comes in second, followed by the United States (KCII, 2015). In its 2016 economic policies outlook announcement, the Korean government selected cosmetics as one of its export promotion items (KHIDI, 2015). Korean cosmetic brands are rapidly growing in the global beauty market due to innovative products, beauty trends, quality and reasonable prices (J. Walter Thompson Intelligence, 2014).

DISTRIBUTION CHANNEL

The retail formats such as sales at a department store or at a single brand shop, door-to-door sales, sales at a hypermarket or at a specialty store, home shopping, online sales and so forth are used for cosmetics sales channels in Korea. In the past, cosmetic sales were heavily dependent on door-to-door sales. However, various forms of distribution channels are beginning to appear in the Korean market. After 2010, the market share of department stores began to shrink. However the numbers of tourists from China increased. They had a notable preference for Korean cosmetics, so duty free shops were becoming a key sales channel. The proportion of tourists who purchased cosmetics increased from 36.9 percent in 2014 to 59.6 percent in 2015. Among Chinese tourists, 84.4 percent purchased perfumes and cosmetics in Korea (KTC, 2015).

Online retailing has also registered the fastest growth among all distribution channels for cosmetic retail in South Korea. In 2015, retail sales through online shopping reached KRW 3.5 trillion, a 32 percent increase over the previous year. In particular, within these sales of online shopping, retail sales through mobile shopping were KRW 1.9 trillion, an 82 percent increase over the previous year (KOSIS, 2015).

Multi-brand cosmetic shops are expanding their presence in Korea. Korean law bans corporate bodies from operating drugstores in the domestic market, so drugstores in Korea concentrate on "H&B (Health and Beauty)" products. After the CJ Group first opened its "Olive Young" in Shinsa-dong, Seoul, in 1999, drugstores continued to attract Koreans due to and in pace with the changes in their lifestyles. In 2004, GS Retail opened "Watsons" after forming an alliance with global drugstore, A.S Watsons. Lotte Shopping started "LOHB's" in 2013.

In Korean H&B retail, beauty care products' sales ratio is around 55 percent, with a ratio of 61 percent in "LOHBS". Cosmetic brands usually only available at department stores are also expanding into drugstores which is helpful in drawing in even more customers. Furthermore, drugstores have developed PB products in the beauty and personal care sector in order to improve price competitiveness and secure the differentiated products (Kim, 2013).

The form of cosmetics shops where various brands are sold under one roof has steadily expanded, giving sophisticated customers more options. AmorePacific Co. operates about 1,350 multi-brand stores, called "Aritaum", nationwide, which offer a wide selection of its products, including mass brands. LG Household & Health Care Ltd, the nation's second-largest cosmetic maker, launched a multi-brand cosmetic shop called "Nature Collection" in 2016. These multi-brand shops improve customer convenience, brand management, promotion, and provide easier access to new brands for customers (Yonhap News, 2016).

INNOVATIVE PRODUCTS

South Korean consumers traditionally are strongly image-consciousness and are willing to invest in beauty products to maintain their appearance. This is stimulating the performance of beauty and personal care. Domestic manufacturers, in particular, are renowned for creating new beauty trends through novel benefits and creative application methods/packaging; those strategies are always stirring the consumer interest of both local consumers and tourists. AmorePacific Corp and LG Household & Health Care Ltd are the two leaders in beauty and personal care. Both offer comprehensive product portfolios across the category as well as a spectrum of brands whose prices range from mass-market to premium (Euromonitor, 2016).

Key drivers of the growth of the Korean cosmetics industry are the innovation of product development and consistent investment into R&D over the last few decades. A number of new innovations such as BB/CC creams and foundations with other advanced products, have made their way to the rest of the world market. Air Cushion, the most successful product in the cosmetics industry, refers to a makeup compact built with specially-designed urethane foam that safely contains and preserves liquid makeup comprised of foundation, sunscreen and skincare formula. Amore Pacific's IOPE launched Air Cushion in 2008 to develop a multi-functional sun protection product that is easier to carry and apply than conventional tube or pump-type products. Air Cushion totaled KRW 3.8 billion in the first year it launched, and surpassed KRW 200 billion in 2014 alone, becoming one of the best-selling items in the Korean cosmetics market (AmorePacific, 2015).

▲ FIGURE 3.6 Style Nanda Cosmetic store.

ONLINE RETAIL

South Korea has the third largest online retail market in Asia Pacific, after China and Japan. Online retail sales have grown significantly over the years in South Korea. With broadband speeds which are among the highest in the world, a high percentage of online consumers shop via the web.

While retail sales of department stores, hypermarkets and specialty stores, which are Korea's major distribution channels, are showing a slower growth rate, online retail transaction value increased by 16.1 times in 2015 compared with 2001 and online transactions have grown by an annual average rate of 22.0 percent during the last 15 years. Since mobile shopping increased faster than internet retailing, the mobile transaction value increased strongly to account for a 45.4 percent share within overall internet retailing in 2015.

In comparison with 2001, online shopping transaction volume for apparel and accessories increased by 4,714.3 percent. Moreover, mobile shopping transaction volume for apparel and accessories amounted to 57.3 percent of all online retail in 2015 (Statistics Korea, 2016a).

OPEN MARKET

Open market, one of the online retail forms in Korea absorbs small and medium-sized on/off-line retailers. Equipped with an open structure where anyone who is interested in selling is allowed to participate, the open market establishes a virtuous circle in terms of pricing. In other words, the open market provides the same opportunities to all sellers and is producing a large number of sellers at the same time. This open structure creates an environment where numerous sellers compete by selling homogenous products at a stiffer price competition. This competition leads to a decline in product prices while attracting more clients and bringing in more sellers (ShinHyung-Won, 2008). "G Market" and "Auction" owned by eBay Korea, "11ST" owned by SK planet, and "Interpark" are four major occupants in Korea's open market.

SOCIAL COMMERCE

Korea's online distribution market which has been centered on a "C2C (Consumer to Consumer)" open market has become fiercely competitive as social commerce becomes a major player in the market. Social commerce refers to e-commerce transactions delivered via social media. More specifically, social commerce is a combination of e-commerce, e-marketing, the supporting technologies, and social media content (TurbanEfraim, StraussJudy, LaiLinda,

2015). In Korea, social commerce was started by "TMON" in 2010 followed by the participation of "Coupang" and "Wemakeprice" in the same year. There is no dominant player in the market since most of the social commerce players sell similar products and operate in a similar way, focusing on pre-planned sale in the form of special deals (ParkJack H., 2014).

As e-commerce transaction switches its platform from PCs to mobile phones, the boundaries between open markets and social commerce have become blurred. In 2016, "Coupang" expanded its platform to an open market by establishing direct sales and purchase channels between consumers and suppliers. This may show that as a social commerce player, "Coupang" attempts to make up for its weakness in product assortment. "11ST", one of the biggest open markets in Korea has taken different approaches by expanding its platform to direct purchases. "11ST" has focused on mediating transactions between buyers and sellers, but it is now directly purchasing products sorted by merchandisers and selling them back to consumers (ShinJoseph, 2016).

CROSS-BORDER COMMERCE

Cross-border online shopping by Korean consumers continues to grow rapidly as such online shopping has been supported by the Korean government's policy of stabilizing consumer prices by facilitating direct purchases from overseas merchants (ParkSangchul, 2015). Making direct purchases from foreign businesses has become a new pattern of consumption in Korea. The amount of direct overseas purchases has grown from USD 270 million in 2010 to USD 1.55 billion as of 2014—an annual growth rate of 54.5 percent. This new market has been constructed through the development of information and communication technology. Driven by IT technology, online and mobile shopping has allowed consumers worldwide to purchase quality goods at reasonable prices without the restrictions of national boundaries. Young, tech-savvy Korean shoppers compare product prices and quality before making direct purchases from US online sites; they take advantage of optimized shopping even during Black Friday in the US (KimGwang-Suk, 2015; KBS, 2015).

As Koreans make direct purchases at foreign online shopping malls, foreigners around the world are also encouraged to visit Korean online malls. Benefiting from the growth of retail businesses without off-line shops, simplified payment systems, and the widespread popularity of K-Pop, Korean TV dramas and Korean movies, namely "Korean wave", the reverse direct purchase market is growing at rapid pace. Reverse direct purchase means that consumers in foreign countries purchase Korean products directly from

Korean shopping malls. From Korea's perspective, direct purchases from foreign countries are imports, and direct overseas reverse purchases are exports. In 2014, the volume of reverse direct purchase remained at 40 percent. However, in 2015, the volume reached 79 percent and in the first quarter of 2016, the volume of reverse direct purchase exceeded that of direct purchase from overseas for the first time (Statistics Korea, 2016b).

Online retailers in Korea are providing services for reverse direct purchase. "CJ O Shopping" started the reverse direct purchase business in China by opening an online store at the largest B2C site in China, "Tmall" which is operated by Alibaba. "Lotte.com" sells more than 70,000 kinds of locally made products to 20 countries in partnership with "Alipay", the largest online payment service provider in China. In 2016, "Gmarket", which was the first online auction and shopping mall website to provide instructions in English and deliver overseas, has created a Chinese version of its website. Reverse direct purchases are mostly made in Chinese-speaking countries, but an increasing number of people in Russia, the Middle East, and Latin America are buying Korean products directly from Korean websites (ChoJin-young, 2014).

OMNI-CHANNEL

With the spread of mobile devices, more and more people are purchasing items online, where they can shop anytime and anywhere they want. Customers collect information about a product online, check out the actual product at an offline store, and then purchase the product online at a discounted price. As the retail industry evolves into a seamless "omni-channel" environment, consumers are now getting the most satisfactory shopping experiences regardless of the channels or devices they are using (ShonJi-young, 2014).

Offline retailers are making all-out efforts to attract consumers who are migrating to online shopping. In Korea, department store sales which once led the retail industry, turned negative in 2013 for the first time in history. The "Lotte" department store focused on expanding its omni-channel service including "Smart coupon book", "Beacon" and "Smart Pick" to recapture customer support. In 2014, the "Smart Coupon Book" app replaced the hard copy DM (Direct Mail) allowing customers to have access to events and free gift information. With "Beacon", various shopping information is provided based on the current location of the customer. Customers who order via the online store can visit the offline outlet, Lotte Department Store, to try out the product and request a refund if necessary. These are prime examples of efforts to combine the advantages of online and offline shopping, which in turn leads to greater sales in online stores and more visitors to offline stores (Lotte Shopping, 2015). Hypermarket "Emart" has a virtual-store application that displays products using the same layout as its physical stores to provide an easy, consistent, shopping experience.

"Naver", Korea's biggest internet search portal with the largest number of domestic users, launched a mobile platform "Shopping Window" as its first service in the "O2O (Online to Offline)" area. "Shopping Window" is a new O2O service that introduces products from small and mid-sized offline stores including fashion, living, food, kids, beauty and department products. "Naver" is setting up a one-stop shopping ecosystem where "Shopping Window", "Naver Pay", a convenient payment service and "Naver Talk Talk", which is a business chatting platform are combined and jointly operating. "Naver Pay" allows users to purchase multiple products from various distributors in a single window. "Naver Talk Talk" is a chat platform exclusively for "Naver" shopping users, which brings the online shopping experience closer to that of shopping in a bricks-and-mortar store by facilitating real-time Q&A between shoppers and sellers (Park E.-j., 2014).

SUMMARY

The Korean retail industry accounts for 13.05 percent of GDP and 31.6 percent of employment as of 2014. The retail industry and employment in the retail sector has continuously grown over the last few decades. After the full market liberalization of the Korean economy in 1996, there has been speedy expansion and growth in the retail industry. For example, giant international retailers, such as Makro, Carrefour, Costco Wholesale Club, Wal-Mart, Tesco, DAISO, and IKEA entered Korean markets, and many retailers started to extend their stores on a large scale. Currently, however, the economic recession has negatively influenced the retail industry in terms of a slow growth rate, the shrinkage of consumers' consumption rate, and the reinforcement of regulation on the retail sector. Thus, the downturn of the economy has led to intense competition between retail formats, the diversification of retail formats and structures, and highly concentrated major players.

From the 1960s, the Korean government focused mainly on exporting to develop and expand the domestic economy. In order to support the export sector, the Korean government primarily supported the manufacturing sector. This gave a huge power to the manufacturing sector, and let the manufacturing sector take the retailer's role. However, since the early 2000s, the power has moved from manufacturers to retailers due to the increased buying power of retailers, intense competition, and the dominance of giant retailers.

Overall, retailing showed a positive performance in 2015 and is expected to witness healthy growth over the next five years due to improving economic conditions and government efforts. The most significant retailing trend in Korea is the increase of non-store retailing (i.e. PC-based internet retailing and mobile retailing). The convenience of shopping, price comparison, cheaper prices for the same product, and the increasing adoption of mobile devices has boosted the growth of non-store retailing in Korea. In addition, convenience stores and outlet stores are expected keep growing due to the change of consumption trends such as the increase of single-person households, people shopping in their neighborhoods, purchasing frequently but in smaller quantities, and value-for-money shopping, all of which have influenced the retail sector in Korea.

Korea's four social factors (i.e., culture, government policy and regulation, technology, and demographics) were discussed as critical factors influencing the Korean retailing industry. *First*, Korea's culture has low tolerance to deviation and values social approval from others. This social background makes the majority of Koreans pursue dominant trendy fashion styles rather than differentiating from the mainstream. Also, status and face saving are very important in Confucian cultures such as Korea and play a role in boosting the success of luxury brands. *Second*, the liberalization of individual travel brought drastic changes to the Korean retailing industry. As Koreans were allowed to travel overseas without the government's permission, Korean consumers became familiar with products, brands, and retailers outside of Korea. They bought more products during their overseas travel, resulting in changes in Koreans' shopping behaviors and preferences. The *third* factor is technology. Korean consumers are highly technology savvy and more people use new technology such as smart phones for commercial purposes such as shopping. This technology-oriented shopping behavior accelerates mobile and internet retailers' vitalization in Korea and consumers' omni-channel experience. *Lastly*, the growth of the single-person household and senior population were discussed as demographic changes. For example, an increase of the single-person household directly led to the success of convenience stores which provide smaller portion sizes and 24-hour service. A new type of senior population contributes to the growth of fashion brands with younger tastes and styles. Due to growth in these two market segments, Korean retailers are expecting to see continued growth in the retail market.

The lifestyle of Korean consumers can be described in three key terms: individualism, rationalism, and the digital consumer. Korean consumers spend a lot of money on their physical appearance and health. Due to the collectivistic culture and the current individualistic consumer tendency that regards health and body as the most important value, Korean consumers seek "Lookism" in their consumption.

Korean consumers set a high value on actual benefits and results and show rational consumption behaviors by seeking inexpensive and efficient products and services. Because Korean fashion consumers seek utilitarian value through the consumption of "the little luxury," retailers have stopped opening new department stores and have started to expand outlet stores that sell reduced-price merchandise.

The widespread diffusion of SNS influences various aspects of Korean consumers. Cross-border online shopping has risen due to a combination of rational consumption and the digital environment. Among the top 10 product categories of cross-border online shopping, fashion and beauty products are reported as the largest and most frequently purchased product category.

CRITICAL THINKING QUESTIONS

1. Considering Korean culture, do you think U.S. fashion retailers should adjust their marketing strategies such as products and advertising when they expand their businesses to the Korean market?
2. Explain the consumption and consumer dynamics in the current Korean market using the three keywords presented in the chapter.
3. How will this help the foreign retailers decide on their retail offerings?
4. What trends in retailing in Korea do you see in the near future?
5. How would you suggest revitalizing traditional markets in Korea?
6. What are the pros and cons of the concentrated major players in each retail format in the Korean retail industry?

Case Study

STYLENANDA.COM

INTRODUCTION

Since the rise of the Internet, many small online fashion shops operated by only one or two persons have opened. Stylenanda (http://en.stylenanda.com) began as one of these shops, but it is now the largest online fashion shop with offline shops in Korea. The CEO, So-Hee Kim, started her business in 2004. She bought clothes in the Dongdaemoon market, the largest clothing wholesale market in Korea, and sold them through an open market website. In 2005, she opened her own online women's clothing shop and incorporated it in 2007 (Kim, 2015).

Stylenanda's sales growth has been remarkable. Sales were $35.8 million in 2012, $67.7 million in 2013, $115.5 million in 2014, and $120 million (estimated) in 2015. Notably, 35 percent of the sales come from international markets including Hong Kong, China, and Singapore. The profits in 2014 were 24 percent of sales, which is higher than competitors (Park, 2015). In this case study, we focus on Stylenanda's product, promotion, and distribution strategies as its main success keys.

PRODUCT STRATEGY

The brand identity of Stylenanda is "Playing Sisters' Sexy Vintage" (Hong & Lee, 2013). To keep this brand identity, the CEO still leads new product selections. The competitive advantage of Stylenanda is "distinct and colorful design products at medium-end prices," says Changyoung Cha, senior buyer of Women's Fashion at Lotte Department Store (Lee, 2015).

The popularity of Stylenanda's unique and trendy clothes eventually resulted in brand extension (Song, 2014). Stylenanda launched Nandagirl (the accessory brand) in 2006, Seminanda (the lingerie and loungewear brand) in 2007, 3 Concept Eyes (the makeup brand, hereafter 3CE) in 2009, and KKXX (the Kitsch style brand) in 2012. The company has also extended its product assortments to include designer brands, imported brands (e.g., Jeffrey Campbell, Paislee, Adeen, and Greycity), and vintage items (Stylenanda, 2016).

Among its product lines, Stylenanda brands account for 70 percent of sales and contribute to a high margin. Recently, the sales of the cosmetic brand, 3CE, were as high as the main brand, Stylenanda, and yielded a high mark-up. Because customers are interested in makeup methods after clothes shopping, clothing customers are also willing to purchase makeup lines (Hong & Lee, 2013).

PROMOTION STRATEGY

Stylenanda uniquely promotes its products on its website. It hires professional fitting models and provides a lot of high-quality pictures of those models as advertisements (Choi, 2015). Detailed product information and text/picture reviews help potential customers make purchase decisions.

One unique promotion on this website is that customers are called "Sister,"an expression to show friendliness and connectedness between Stylenanda and its customers. In addition, the website is similar to blog pages on which customers can share fashion information and female customers form their own online communities (Choi, 2015). Another unique promotion method began in 2011 when the CEO published a style guidebook to share her styling, business knowledge, and passion. The book was recommended by top stylists and internationally published. The royalties from this book are donated to Stellar's House, an organization that helps poor single mothers (Hong & Lee, 2013). The effectiveness of these unique promotion methods has resulted in a high repurchase rate (80 percent of sales come from repurchase), strong brand loyalty, and online word of mouth.

DISTRIBUTION STRATEGY

The success of Stylenanda was so outstanding that it opened its first offline store in Hongdae, a popular hangout for the young and stylish, in September 2012. This flagship store is unique not only because of its exterior design, an enormous three-storey glass building, but also because of various items inside. The store carries clothing and cosmetics (Stylenanda's traditional assortments), books, interior items, and living items. It features various sales promotions, art performances, and entertainment facilities (e.g., free photo booths). This store attracts current and potential customers who are interested in fashion, new trends, and culture. This store is a hot place to visit near Hongdae (Hong & Lee, 2013).

Stylenanda also opened an offline store at Lotte Department Store, the largest department store in Korea, in Myeong-dong in 2012, which is the first instance of an online fashion shop opening in a department store (the department store is the symbol of offline stores). Myeong-dong is one of the attractions that Chinese tourists prefer to visit. Stylenanda is one of the leading Hallyu (Korean Wave) fashion brands in China and was the most sought after Korean brand by Chinese tourists in 2014, according to Lotte Department Store (Kim, 2013).

As of 2016, Stylenanda had 12 branches in department stores and 14 branches in duty-free shops. Combined with the global stores in Hong Kong, China, Singapore, and Thailand, Stylenanda has a total of 51 offline stores. Due to the popularity of Hallyu and this brand, growth within these countries is expected. Offline stores are a key to the growth of Stylenanda (Stylenanda, 2016).

It has been only 12 years since this one-person company was founded, but with distinct clothing and makeup lines, Stylenanda has expanded its business in Korea and many Asian countries, including China. Stylenanda has shown a new business model for online fashion shops, and the value of the firm has been estimated at US$1 billion (Kim, 2015). However, the potential is much higher based on its strengths so far.

Discussion Questions

1. Stylenanda carries only two major product categories: women's clothing and makeup categories. What other product categories would be appropriate for its growth considering its current brand image?
2. Stylenanda has opened many offline stores in Korea and other Asian countries. Do you think that opening more offline stores keeps Stylenanda competitive over other online fashion shops? Explain your reasons.
3. Do you think that Stylenanda needs to advertise on TV to reach more customer segments and build a strong brand image? Explain your reasons.

REFERENCES

Ah, S. (2012). Busanghaneun 1in gaguui 4dae sobi teurendeu [Four Consumption Trends of Single-person Households]. *Samsung Economic Research Institute.* Retrieved from www.seri.org/db/dbReptV.html?g_menu=02&s_menu=0212& pubkey=db20120802002

AmorePacific. (2015). Korea's 'Cushion Boom' Changes Global Beauty Trends. Retrieved from www.amorepacific.com: www.amorepacific.com/content/ company/global/footer/amorepacificnews/group-news/2015–01–21.html

Bang, E., & Kim, D. (2016). Off-price Shopping of Fashion Consumers. KB Financial Group Report. Retrieved from www.kbfg.com/kbresearch/index.do?alias=vita min&viewFunc=default_details&categoryId=3&subCtgId=&boardId=308& articleId=1003233&menuId=&tSearch=T

Buettner, R. (2006). A Classification Structure for Automated Negotiations. 2006 IEEE/WIC/ACM International Conference on Web Intelligent Agent Technology, May 27–June 1, 2012. Hong Kong, pp. 523–530. http://ieeexplore. ieee.org/xpl/articleDetails.jsp?arnumber=4053306

Chae, S. (2012). The History of Korean Department Stores. Joongangilbo. Retrieved from http://news.joins.com/article/7245097

Cho, J.-y. (2014). Overseas Direct Purchase Craze. Retrieved from http://businesskorea. co.kr/english/news/ict/7566-overseas-direct-purchase-craze-korean-small- mid-sized-manufacturers-hit-direct

Choi, G. (2015). Online shopping mallui shinwha! Stylenandaui hyuckshin yiyagi [Online Shopping Mall Myth! The Innovation Story of Stylenanda] [Web log post]. Retrieved from http://comm20.tistory.com/260.

De Mooji, M. & Hofstede, G. (2002). Convergence and Divergence in Consumer Behavior: Implications for International Retailing. *Journal of Retailing, 78*(1), 61–69.

Dongdaemum Market (n.d.). Google image. Retrieved, April 5, from https://a2.muscache. com/locations/uploads/photo/image/36230/0_4200_84_2716_two_Seoul__ Dongdaemun_manchul_034.jpg

Euromonitor. (2016). *Beauty and Personal Care in South Korea.* Euromonitor International.

Euromonitor. (2016). *Retailing in South Korea.* Euromonitor International.

Fashion Channel. (2016). Mobaili yutongjidoreul bakkunda [Mobile Changes the Retailing Map]. *Fashion Channel, 4,* 30–35.

Fitzgerald, B. R. (2014). Data point: U.S. Ranks behind Latvia in Offering Top-speed Broadband Connections. *The Wall Street Journal.* Retrieved from http://blogs.

wsj.com/digits/2014/06/27/data-point-u-s-ranks-behind-latvia-in-offering-top-speed-broadband-connections/?mod=ST1

Garak Market. (n.d.). Google image. http://cfs12.tistory.com/image/31/tistory/2009/07/13/16/43/4a5ae58dafddb

Gannon, M. J. (2004). *Understanding Global Cultures: Metaphorical Journeys through 28 Nations, Clusters of Nations and continents* (3rd Edn). Thousand Oaks, CA: Sage Publications.

Gelfand, M. J., Raver, J. L., Nishii, L., Leslie, L. M., Lun, J., Lim, B. C., & Yamaguchi, S. (2011). Differences between Tight and Loose Cultures: A 33-nation Study. *Science, 332*(6033), 1100–1104.

Han, K. H. (2014). Promotion Strategy for Domestic Internet Shopping Malls in the Foreign Consumer Market. *The Korean-Japanese Journal of Economics & Management Studies, 65*, 139–165.

Hofstede, G (1991). *Culture and Organization: Software of the Mind.* Maidenhead, UK: McGraw-Hill.

Hong, S. (2015). Lebeige, RO&DE noir deung sinieo jeogyeok item inki [Senior target items' hit]. *Fashionbiz.* Retrieved from www.fashionbiz.co.kr/TN/?cate=2&recom=2&idx=153512

Hong, J., & Lee, J. (2013). Mumchuji annun shinhwa, global Stylenandaui Kum [Unstoppable myth, the dream of global Stylenanda]. *International BNT NEWS.* Retrieved from http://bntnews.hankyung.com/apps/news?mode=sub_view&popup=0&nid=02&c1=02&c2=06&c3&nkey=201306201328093.

Hwang, H. (2014). 'A Little Luxury' as an Exit of Restrained Consumption. LG Business Insight. Retrieved from www.lgeri.com/uploadFiles/ko/pdf/man/LGBI1321-30_20140930132839.pdf.

Hwang, H. (2015). Consumers Turn to a 'Light Consumption' from a Heavy Possession. LG Business Insight. Retrieved from www.lgeri.com/uploadFiles/ko/pdf/man/LGBI1341-17_20150216091335.pdf.

Information & Cultural Contents Technology. (2016). *1in gagu—solo iconomy sijang ddeunda [Single-person Household—Solo Economy is Booming].* Retrieved from http://blog.naver.com/2icct/220729734797

J. Walter Thompson Intelligence. (2014). *The Future 100: Trends and Change to Watch in 2015.* JWTintelligence.

Jin, B., Gavin, M., & Kang, J. H. (2012). Similarities and Differences in Forming Purchase Intention Toward a US Apparel Brand: A Comparison of Chinese and Indian Consumers. *Journal of the Textile Institute, 103*(10), 1042–1054.

KBS. (2015). *The Development of Overseas Direct Purchase Market and its Implications.* Retrieved June 20, 2016 from world.kbs.co.kr: http://world.kbs.co.kr/english/program/program_economyplus_detail.htm?no=5248

KCII. (2015). *Import/Export Trade Statistics of Cosmetics.* Retrieved Jume 1, 2016, from Korea Cosmetic Industry Institute: www.kcii.re.kr/_Document/Center/TRADE_30L.asp?menucode=01

KHIDI. (2015). *Cosmetic Industry Analysis Report.* Korean Health Industry Development Institute.

Kim, G.-S. (2015). *Direct Purchase Market Prospects and Implications.* Seoul: Hyundai Research Institute.

Kim, J.-y. (2013). Korean Drugstores Prosper on Lifestyle Trends. *The Korea Herald.* www.koreaherald.com.

Kim, N. (2015). Surun dosal ownerui Stylenanda kiup gachi 1cho [32-year-old Owner's Stylenanda Firm Valued at $1 billion]. *Money Today.* Retrieved from http://news.mt.co.kr/mtview.php?no=2015102512054331802.

Kim, V. (2013). 10 hot South Korean fashion brands and where to buy them. *CNN.* Retrieved from www.cnn.com/2013/07/17/travel/top-korean-designers/.

KOSIS. (2015). *Online Shopping Retail Sales.* Retrieved 1 June, 2016, from Korean Statistical Information Service: http://kosis.kr/statHtml/statHtml.do?orgId=101&tblId=DT_1KE1007&conn_path=I2

KTC. (2015). *2014 Analysis on Tourism Market in Korea.* Wonju-si: Korea Tourism Organization.

Kim, J. (2016). Yutong gaebang 20nyeon, gyeongjaenggwa yanggeukwa simhwa [Retail Liberalization 20 years, Competition and Polarization Intensified]. *Nexteconomy.* Retrieved from www.nexteconomy.co.kr/news/quickViewArticleView.html?idxno=9583

Korea Chamber of Commerce and Industry. (2014). *Naegukin haeyoe syoping siltae josa [Research on Koreans' overseas shopping].* Retrieved from http://retaildb.korcham.net/file/Document/(10%EC%9B%94%2024%EC%9D%BC%EC%9E%90%20%EC%A1%B0%EA%B0%84)%20%ED%95%B4%EC%99%B8%EC%87%BC%ED%95%91.pdf

Korea Chamber of Commerce and Industry. (2014). *2015nyeon somae yutongeom jungmangjosa [2015 retailing prospect].* Retrieved from http://retaildb.korcham.net/Service/Report/appl/ActualResearchList.asp

Korean Fashion Association. (2014). Guknaeoe paesyeon aulletui tansaenggwa hyeonhwang *[Domestic and Foreign Outlets' Advent and Status].* Retrieved from www.koreafashion.org/info/info_content_view.asp?flag=2&cataIdx=803&boardId=story&clientIdx=860&num=811.

Korea Chamber of Commerce & Industry. (2015). Retail Industry Report 2015.

Korea Chamber of Commerce & Industry. (2016). Monthly Trends in the Retail Industry.

Korea Distribution Association. (2013). A Study on the Improvement Suggestions of the Classification of Retail Formats.

Korea Herald. (2015). Naver Launches Mobile Payment Tool. Retrieved from www. koreaherald.com/view.php?ud=20150625000430

Korea On-Line Shopping Association (2014). Understanding and Anticipation of Online Shopping.

La, J. (2015). Mi myeongpum sijang naholrohohwang jaknyeon 733eokdalreo segyelwi [Only the U.S. Luxury Market is Booming . . . $ 73 billion world's No. 1]. *Hankook-Ilbo*. Retrieved from www.hankookilbo.com/v/ a2e71df15081424db950c342018cb410.

Lee, H. (2015). Stylenanda, annual sales 1000 uk . . . tuinun design tonghatda [Stylenanda, Annual Sales 100 million dollars . . . Unique Design Succeeded]. *The Korea Economic Daily*. Retrieved from www.hankyung.com/news/app/ newsview.php?aid=2015020156961.

Lee, J. (2016, May). Daehanmingukeseo 1ingaguro sandaneun geot [Living as a Single-person Household in Korea]. *Naver Magazinecast*. Magazinecast retrieved from http://navercast.naver.com/magazine_contents.nhn?rid=2867&contents_ id=115752.

Lee, S. (2014). Lotte homsyoping, pasyeon sijang jabneunda [Lotte TV Shopping, Push Fashion Markets]. *Fashion Insight*. Retrieved from http://fi.co.kr/main/view. asp?idx=47931

Lee, Y. (2003). A Study on the Development of Innovative Retail Sector and the Change of Retailing Structure. Korean Scholars of Marketing Sciences, Proceedings of Annual Conference, pp. 363–382.

Lee, J., Choo, H., & Lee, H. (2015). Fashion Consumers' Purchase Intention on Cross-Border Online Shopping, *Fashion & Textile Research Journal, 17*(5), 741–753.

Levy, M., Weitz, B. A., & Grewal, D. (2014). *Retailing Management* (9th Edn). New York, NY: McGraw Hill Education.

Lim, J., & Park, J. (2016). 24 hours of Koreans after 2000. LG Business Insight. Retrieved from www.lgeri.com/uploadFiles/ko/pdf/man/LGBI1391-17_20160203131424.pdf.

Lotte Shopping (2015). *Lotte Shopping Strengthens Omni-channel Strategy*. Retrieved from www.lotteshopping.com.

Ministry of Trade, Industry and Energy. (2015). Trends of major retail formats.

M2 Presswire. (2016). Retailing in South Korea—Market Summary and Forecasts. Retrieved from http://search.t.com.argo.library.okstate.edu/docview/1756022119? rfr_id=infor%3Axri%2Fsid%3Aprimo

Nam, S. H. (2014). A Report on the Expectation of Retail Industry. Heungkuk
  Securities.

Namdaemun Market. (n.d.). Google image. Retrieved from http://dimg.donga.com/
  egc/CDB/WOMAN/Article/20/11/10/17/201110170500036_2.jpg

Nielsen. (2013). *The Mobile Consumer*. Retrieved from www.nielsen.com/
  content/dam/corporate/uk/en/documents/Mobile-Consumer-Report–2013.pdf

Norangjin Fisheries Market. (n.d.). Google image. Retrieved from http://cfile215.uf.
  daum.net/image/186324154B531EBB8271B7

Organization for Economic Co-operation and Development. (2014). OECD Economic
  Surveys Korea. Retrieved from www.oecd.org/eco/surveys/Overview_
  Korea_2014.pdf.

Park, E.-j. (2014). *Naver to Launch Shopping site for Offline Retailers*. Retrieved from
  http://koreajoongangdaily.joins.com/news/article/Article.aspx?aid=2997629

Park, I. (2015). 'Stylenanda' Kim So-Hee daepyo, olhaeui fashion kyungyoungin
  sunjung [Stylenanda CEO Kim, So-Hee, Fashion CEO of the Year]. *Maeil
  Business News Korea*. Retrieved from http://news.mk.co.kr/newsRead.
  php?no=1172804&year=2015.

Park, I. (2006). Yutong gaebang 10nyeon sungjeokpyo & 5nyeonhu sinyutong jido
  [Report of 10 Years after the Retail Liberalization and a New Retail Map of Next
  5 Years]. *Economy Chosun*. Retrieved from http://economyplus.chosun.com/
  special/special_view_past.php?boardName=%BD%BA%C6%E4%BC%C8%B8
  %AE%C6%F7%C6%AE&t_num= 1314&myscrap=&img_ho=17

Park, J. (2011). The Seven Lifestyles of Korean Consumers. LG Business Insight.
  Retrieved from www.lgeri.com/uploadFiles/ko/pdf/man/LGBI1149–02_
  20110613084913.pdf

Park, J. (2013). Beibi bumeo 50daero jeobeodeulda [Baby Boomers enter Fifties]. *Naeil
  News*. Retrieved from http://news.naver.com/main/read.nhn?mode=LSD&mid=
  sec&sid1=102&oid=086&aid=0002143452

Park, J. (2015). Hanguk seumateupon bogeubyul segye 4wi . . . 1wineun Arab Emirates
  Korea Ranks the Fourth in Possessing Smartphones . . . the First Rank is the
  United Arab]. *Chosun.com*. Retrieved from http://news.chosun.com/site/data/
  html_dir/2015/07/08/2015070800759.html

Park, J. (2014). *Social Commerce Companies Fiercely Fighting For Market Share*.
  Retrieved 15 June, 2016, from www.businesskorea.co.kr/english/news/
  industry/7817-e-commerce-competition-social-commerce-companies-fiercely-
  fighting-market-share

Park, M. (2001). Challenges of a Retail Industry in the 21st Century. *Excellence
  Marketing for Customer, 35*(1), 20–26.

Park, S., & Suh, D. (2015). *Korea's Supermarkets*. Seoul: Korea eBook Publishing Company.

Park, S. (2015). Legal Issues in Cross-Border e-Commerce and Policy Implications. *Distribuation Law Review*, 161.

Park, W. (2012). Eopaereol nyuseuro bon paesyeonsaneob 20nyeon [Fashion industry 20 years by Apparelnews]. *Apprelnews*. Retrieved from http://m.apparelnews. co.kr/m/mpnews.php?table=paper_news&query= view&uid=65217

Samsung Economic Research Institute. (2014). *Haeooejikguga saeroun syoping daeani doen iyu [Reasons Why Direct Shopping becomes a New Alternative]*. Retrieved from www.seri.org/ic/icDBRV.html?s_menu=0608&pubkey=ic20140716002& menu_gbn=6&menucd=0600&tabGbn=SBJT

Samjong KPMG. (2015). Samjong insight, Issue 40.

Santander (2016). South Korea Foreign Investment. Retrieved from https://en.portal. santandertrade.com/establish-overseas/south-korea/foreign-investment

Seligman, S. D. (1999). *Chinese Business Etiquette*. New York: Warner Business Books.

Shin, J. (2014). Cheil Annual Consumer Report, 456, 10–11. Retreived from www.cheil. com/web/magazine/download.jsp?file=00_201401_all.pdf&path=magazine/ kor/201401.

Shin, H.-W. (2008). *Online Shopping Market in Korea Rising Fast*. Seoul: Samsung Economic Research Institute.

Shin, J. (2016). *Korea's Online Shopping Malls Embrace Open Markets*. Retrieved 1 July, 2016, from http://koreabizwire.com/koreas-online-shopping-malls-embrace-open-markets/54500.

Shon, J.-y. (August 2014). Omni-channel stores offer seamless offline and online retail experiences. *Cheil's Up*, Retrieved from www.cheil.com/web/magazine/ download.jsp?file=02_201408.pdf&path=magazine/eng/201408.

Small Enterprise and Market Service. (2013). Report on Traditional Markets and Store Management

Son, M., & Choi, S. (2014). Jay uwa 25nyeon . . . haeoeyeohaeng eojewa oneul [Liberralization 25 Years . . . Overseas Travel Past and Present]. *JoongAng Daily*. Retrieved from http://news.joins.com/article/13548604

Song, I. (2015). Oneseo offkaji 'Nanda' gogong hangjin! [From Online to Offline 'Stylenanda' Riding High]. *Fashionbiz*. Retrieved from www.fashionbiz.co. kr/BR/?cate=2&idx=138618.

Statistics Korea. (2016a). *20 Years' Online Shopping Statistics*. Daejeon: Statistics Korea.

Statistics Korea. (2016b). *Foreign Online Direct Selling and Buying Trends*. Daejeon: Statistics Korea.

Sternquist, B. (2008). *International Retailing* (2nd Edn). New York, NY: Fairchild Publications.

Statistics Korea. (2015). Retrieved from http://kostat.go.kr/portal/eng/index.action.

Stylenanda. (2016). About NANDA. Retrieved from http://en.stylenanda.com/shopinfo/company.html.

Turban, E., Strauss, J., & Lai, L. (2015). *Social Commerce: Marketing, Technology and Management.* Springer International Publishing AG.

Yonhap News. (2016). Multi-brand Cosmetic Shops Expand Presence in S. Korea. Retrieved from http://english.yonhapnews.co.kr.

Yoo, D. K. (2015). Distribution and Marketing. Retrieved from http://dept.woosuk.ac.kr/cbus/2015/inner.php?sMenu=F1000&pno=5&mode=view&no=43

CHINA

4

Shubhapriya Bennur
Yiyue Fan
Md. Rashaduzzaman
Laubie Li
Jun Ying Yu
Jaya Halepete

OBJECTIVES

After reading this chapter, you will:

► Understand why China is considered an emerging market
► Comprehend the unique characteristics of Chinese consumers
► Understand the market structure of Chinese markets
► Know the regulations for foreign direct investment

In just 35 short years, the world has witnessed the transformation of China from an underdeveloped, agriculture-based economy into a global manufacturing hub. The capacity of the People's Republic of China to cope with rapid change is astonishing. A powerful central government is said to be the reason for this communist nation's effective and systematic collateral transformations. The irony is that, in spite of a strong central government, intense competition exists among provinces and cities. The competitive nature of the provincial or city relationships in turn has fostered a culture of competition at the firm level. Chinese firms are always prepared to compete with local and international competitors;

this is reflected in a booming retailing industry that is riding on the wave of an expanding middle class.

Over the course of two millennia, China was home to many of the world's great emperors. Its transition to modernity was exceedingly difficult. In the nineteenth and early twentieth centuries, its people endured civil unrest, famines, and foreign occupations. After World War II, Mao Zedong's communist government imposed strict regulations on people's everyday lives, and millions died due to poor economic planning. Mao's regime ended with his death in 1976, and by 1978 Deng Xiaoping was at the helm. He and others leaders reset China's course toward market-oriented economic development. Living standards improved dramatically. For the first time, Chinese people congregated around the televisions and other modern conveniences that began to appear in their villages.

Since the 1980s, China has transformed from an economy that was largely closed to international trade to a more open market. The Chinese economy experienced astonishing growth in the last few decades that catapulted the country to become the world's second largest economy. In 1978, when China started the program of economic reforms, the country ranked ninth in nominal gross domestic product (GDP) with USD 214 billion; 35 years later it jumped up to second place with a nominal GDP of USD 9.2 trillion (Focus Economics, 2017).

China's population of 1.373 billion people excites and attracts many investors, as does their gross national savings rate of 46 percent of their GDP (Table 4.1). China in 2015 stood as the largest economy in the world, surpassing the US in 2014 for the first time in modern history. Still, China's per capita income is below the world average (CIA Factbook, 2017). China still remains a developing country (its per capita income is still a fraction of that in advanced countries) and its market reforms are incomplete. However, rapid economic ascendance has brought on many challenges as well, including high inequality; rapid urbanization; challenges to environmental sustainability; and external imbalances. China also faces demographic pressures related to an aging population and the internal migration of labor.

Significant policy adjustments are required in order for China's growth to be sustainable. Experience shows that transitioning from middle-income to high-income status can be more difficult than moving up from low to middle income. China's 12th Five-Year Plan (2011–2015) and the newly approved 13th Five-Year Plan (2016–2020) forcefully address these issues. They highlight the development of services and measures to address environmental and social imbalances, setting targets to reduce pollution, to increase energy efficiency, to improve access to education and healthcare, and to expand social protection.

TABLE 4.1 Fast Facts about China

Capital	Beijing
Population	1.373 billion
Type of government	Communist state
GDP: PPP US$	$21.27 trillion
Age structure	0–14 yrs: 17.1 percent
	15–24 yrs: 13.27 percent
	25–54 yrs: 48.42 percent
	55–64 yrs:10.87 percent
	65 yrs plus: 10.35 percent
Religion	Folk religion: 21.9 percent
	Buddhist: 18.2 percent
	Christian: 5.1 percent
	Muslim: 1.8 percent
	Unaffliated: 52.2 percent
Ethnicity	Han Chinese: 91.6 percent
	Zhuang 1.3 percent
	Manchu, Hui, Miao,Uighur, Tujia, Yi,
	Mongol, Tibetan, Buyi, Dong, Yao,
	Korean, and others: 7.1 percent

Source: CIA Factbook.gov

The annual growth target in the 12th Five-Year Plan was 7 percent and the growth target in the 13th Five-Year Plan is 6.5 percent, reflecting the rebalancing of the economy and the focus on the quality of growth while still maintaining the objective of achieving a "moderately prosperous society" by 2020 (World Bank Data, 2016).

THE RETAIL LANDSCAPE: A LUCRATIVE MARKET FOR INVESTMENT

Retail sales in China rose 10.9 percent year-on-year in December of 2016, following a 10.8 percent increase in November and beating market expectations of a 10.7 percent rise. It was the strongest growth since December 2015, boosted by sales of office supplies, personal care, automobiles, cosmetics and garments (Trading economics, 2017) According to forecast made by Euromonitor, China will exceed the United States and become the world's largest apparel market by 2019. Specifically, annual apparel sales in China will reach $333,312 million in 2019, an increase of 25 percent from $267,246 million in 2014. However, despite its overall market size, as a developing country, dollar spending on apparel per capita will remain much lower in China than many developed economies around the world. On average, consumers spent $240 annually on apparel versus consumers in US spent $815, even though apparel spending accounted for a larger share in household income in China (around 10 percent) compared with the United States (less than 3 percent) (Lu, 2015).

CONSUMERS: IMPROVING QUALITY OF LIFE

As economic conditions in China continue to improve, consumption of textile, apparel, and beauty products increases correspondingly. Understanding Chinese consumers helps foreign investors to provide them with the right product mix. As quality of life improves among Chinese consumers as a whole, their expenditure on apparel is on the rise.

Consumers of apparel and beauty products today tend to be in their twenties and thirties. Although younger consumers are more sensitive to price than older consumers, younger consumers do purchase high-end clothing, brand-name beauty products, or even luxury items. In addition to an improved material life, the Internet has helped to lower the consumer's age. Chinese consumers in the 25–45 years age range are more likely to do non-shop shopping than those who are in their fifties.

Since the 2000s, quality has become a more important factor, which is affecting the purchasing behavior of Chinese consumers. A large number of people prefer to buy clothing made in France, Italy, or the United States instead of locally, and they want to buy products with foreign brand names. Consumers prefer foreign brands not only because they like the quality and styles but also because the lifestyle indicated by the labeled country of origin appeals to them. Therefore, the influence of country of origin or brand is significant.

The consumption of garments and beauty products via multiple channels is becoming popular. Consumers choose traditional retailers when they need to buy social or work clothes, but also buy basics, fad, and fast fashion from non-shop retailers for convenience, wide selection, and low prices.

Some unique features of Chinese consumers that a foreign retailer needs to know in order to cater to them are:

- The middle class, which will be the main customer group in the 2010s and 2020s, is becoming highly brand conscious.
- Sporty fashion has emerged as a key trend among young people. Fast fashion companies have also actively launched sporty series to exploit the trend while sportswear players have also extended fashion sporty product lines to meet the demand.
- Consumers are looking for trendy clothing that is fashion forward. As in many developed nations, apparel sold in China has a short life cycle.
- Function (such as protection from the environment) is becoming as important as factors like color and comfort to Chinese consumers. Chinese consumers consider innovative fabrics in their apparel purchase decisions (anti-perspirant finish on fabrics for running clothes).
- As China became a rising fashion hub with consumers willing to pay for products with the latest designs, more international brands, such as Tom Tailor and GU, looked to enter the Chinese market in 2015.

Fast fashion brands focus more on the internet retailing channel rather than rapidly offline store expansion. For some premium brands, such as Gate G1 One and Beanpole, they took initial steps to collaborate with high-end department stores to establish brand image and enhance consumers' shopping experience (Euromonitor, 2016).

WOMEN

Retailers interested in investing in China need to understand the emotional and rational behavior of Chinese women and cater to their needs to be successful in the market (Silverstein & Sayre, 2009). In general, Chinese women are optimistic and enthusiastic about their personal lives, communities, and the world. China's one-child policy, implemented in 1979, has allowed these women an opportunity to pursue higher education and to do well in life. However, on January 1, 2016, China has updated its "one-child" policy because of the ageing population; and couples are now allowed two children. Nevertheless, Chinese women have learned from their parents how to live frugally. They do not like to spend too much money on shopping, take out loans, or spend on unnecessary purchases. They prefer to invest and save their money. However, the savings pattern is changing, with women spending a bigger portion of their salaries than before. Almost 78 percent of married women make grocery and apparel purchases for the family and 65 percent of women spend 60 percent of their salary (The rise of female consumerism, 2007).

Chinese women like to spend on products that lessen their workloads and free up their time. They are also unsatisfied with the type of lingerie available in the market and are willing to spend more on it. The purchasing power of Chinese women is on the rise, with highly educated women earning and spending more and empty nesters having more disposable income than before.

MEN

"A total of 80 percent of wealthy male Chinese consumers are aged between 18 and 44, have an annual household income of more than 250,000 yuan ($37,550), are well educated and are open to the acquisition of luxury products," says Kunal Sinha, Regional Cultural Insights Director for Ogilvy & Mather's Asia Pacific office (Yip & Chang, 2010).

Chinese men spend money to splurge as well as to express their masculinity. Spending money is another way for Chinese men to display power. They do not like shopping around for deals, are repeat purchasers, and stick to brands that they like. Hence, it is important for retailers to build a brand image. Chinese men are also very quality conscious and look at every aspect of a garment from fabric to craftsmanship. Men also like to mix and match pieces, which has encouraged the growth of the accessories market (Performance of China's, 2006). Menswear in China is an untapped market, hence it is a very important market for retailers to focus on.

CHILDREN

China has the largest population of children in the world, which makes them an important customer base for retailers to target. Chinese children also have higher economic power than children in other developing economies (Cheng 1993, Shao & Herbig, 1994). In addition, as the abandonment of the "one-child" policy will lead to as many as 2 million newborns from when the policy change was first announced in 2016 (Jiang, Armstrong, & Cullinane, 2015), they have more discretionary income than children of any other country (McNeal & Yeh, 2003).

THE BEAUTY INDUSTRY IN CHINA

After tourism, automobiles, and real estate, beauty is the fourth-largest industry in China. Skincare products are the most popular beauty product sold in

China, accounting for almost 71 percent of the total sales in this category, followed by makeup and fragrances. Anti-aging and skin-whitening products make skincare the most popular category. It is very different from the American beauty industry, in which skincare products represent only one third of sales. The aging Chinese population is ready to spend extra money on anti-aging skincare products, so high-end brands do well in China.

Historically, Chinese women have not worn makeup, and so they are not well educated regarding its usage. With growing Western influence, Chinese women are showing greater interest in learning how to wear makeup. The Chinese beauty and personal care market continued to record strong current value growth in 2015, driven by steady demand for hair care and oral care products as well as rising interest in color cosmetics and skin care. This can be attributed to increasing awareness of personal hygiene and rising disposable incomes. To remain competitive, online distribution via different online platforms is increasingly evident in the Chinese market. For example, Lancôme opened an online store on Tmall.com in January 2015; Sephora followed suit on JD.com in May 2015 to complement its own online store (Euromonitor, 2016).

▲ FIGURE 4.1 China, Hunan Province, Fenghuang County, Open air Market.

Beauty retailers focus on traditional services such as whitening, breast enlargement, weight loss, hair dyeing, and hairdressing. The women's beauty market is already intensely competitive. Demand for the men's beauty market is expected to increase as there is a developing interest in beauty and nutrition. With the Chinese economy growing at a fast pace, the beauty industry is expected to continue to grow.

LUXURY RETAIL IN CHINA

In 2015, China offered more luxury retail selling space than Japan and is fast catching up on the US. The Chinese accounted for over a third of all global luxury spending. However, China will not overtake Japan to become the world's second largest luxury goods market in the world in the next five years; it is expected to maintain its third position ahead of France and the UK (Robert, 2016). Luxury drivers in China include wealthy consumers. Between 2015 and 2030, China is expected to add in excess of 3.4 million additional individuals to this wealthy population,

Bain & Company's 2015 China Luxury Market Study notes that a younger and more sophisticated generation of shoppers with markedly different tastes, aspirations and consumption habits is reshaping the landscape of luxury in China. Educated, well-traveled and tech-savvy consumers are emerging as the new target market. In the past, luxury goods were seen as a symbol of wealth and status for Chinese consumers; today, they buy luxury goods for their own enjoyment (Horton, 2016) A number of niche luxury brands and designer labels have won great popularity among Chinese consumers. Brands like Acne Studios, 3.1 Phillip Lim and Jil Sander have emerged as aspirational brands, focusing on individuality and posing a real challenge to competitors in luxury goods (Euromonitor, 2016).

APPAREL RETAIL FORMATS: BEING REVOLUTIONIZED BY MODERN FORMATS

According to a study conducted by soupu.com, there were more than 100 foreign brands across different retail, consumer products to food and beverages markets entering China for the first time in 2015. In general, these brands entered the Chinese market by:

- ► opening physical stores;
- ► launching a Chinese language website;

- ▶ partnering with China's third-party e-commerce or mobile- commerce platforms such as Tmall, JD.com, Yihaodian and Mengdian to launch flagship stores; and
- ▶ adopting a multi-sales channel approach.

Multiple retail formats, such as big department stores, exclusive stores, mail order, discount stores, warehouse stores, and shopping centers, co-exist in China. The success of a retail format depends partly on region. Apparel companies are experimenting with different approaches to selling and marketing their products. New retail formats are leading a quiet revolution.

Department stores have the largest share of clothing retail sales because such store formats sell high-end and middle-high-end apparel merchandise to consumers who have higher incomes than most Chinese consumers. Chain stores tend to concentrate on middle-high and middle-end clothing. General merchandise stores, warehouse stores, and supermarkets are popular outlets for middle- and low-end clothing. They form the fastest-developing retail sector, due to lower operating costs. Convenience and price advantage have made online, telephone, mail order, and other nonstore sales another integral part of China's retail formats. Wholesale and retail outlets operated by garment manufacturers or low-end suppliers from the cities primarily service the rural markets. Unlike the past decade, establishing an online store is now a crucial step for foreign brands to kick-start their business in China. China is the world leader in e-commerce with the largest number of online shoppers, reaching 413 million (60 percent of the Internet population) as of December 2015 (Fung Business Intelligence, 2016).

TRADITIONAL FORMATS

Open-air markets and street stores pre-date modern formats in China and continue to be popular.

▶ Open-Air Markets

Open-air markets can be found along major commercial streets and trade centers, or in shopping centers. Open public places or parts of major streets convert to open-air markets at specific times of day, some of which are seasonal. There are morning and evening open-air markets. Morning open-air markets usually start around 6 a.m. and finish by 9 a.m., attracting people who participate in morning exercises (which many Chinese do in large groups) and then shop early for the day's groceries. Such open-air-markets are restricted to neighborhood residents. Vendors sell basic apparel merchandise at low prices at such markets. Evening open-air markets usually start after regular office hours, and close around midnight or even later depending on whether there are still customers around. There are many booths selling produce, meat, spices, canned goods, clothing, and hardware. Open-air markets are good places to find last season's or contractor's over-run clothes at discount prices. Besides local consumers, they also attract tourists.

▶ Street Stores

Urban and small-town consumers alike shop in street stores, which may be present on any street. They sell many different categories of products, but mainly grocery or other convenience items. Most stores are part of renovated residential apartments. Owners of these ground-floor apartments renovate their apartments to be street stores, and either run the stores themselves or rent them out for others to run. Sometimes a street store is just a window on the side of a building. Some street vendors sell clothing or other products from

▲ FIGURE 4.2 A vendor demonstrates a toy ox for the upcoming Chinese New Year in Shanghai, China.

small temporary stalls or stands. Apparel is mainly sold through stores lined along the streets.

MODERN FORMATS

Modern retail formats such as department stores, supermarkets, convenience stores, and warehouses are emerging and becoming popular in China.

▸Department Stores

From the Chinese consumer's perspective, shopping at department stores means buying high-quality products (Zhu, 2008). Large department stores are popular venues for shopping in China. Urban residents normally do not have large living spaces. They like to shop in department stores as a leisure activity or a brief break from home when it's too crowded. In China, department stores sell general merchandise including both soft lines such as apparel and hard lines such as furniture. Some department stores even include a supermarket selling

▲ FIGURE 4.3 A view of a five-floor-tall steel slide under construction in a department store in Shanghai, China. The swirling structure opened to the public in March 2016.

groceries. Most department stores allocate a large space for selling apparel merchandise. Apparel merchandise retail sales through department stores seem to be the main contributor to total apparel sales, accounting for 30 to 40 percent of total store sales.

Department stores are ideal outlets for famous fashion brands, geared to customers who are looking for high-quality products. Foreign-owned department stores in China usually possess a good image and marketing experience, and are, therefore, popular product outlets for apparel companies. Department stores that originate from Asian countries, such as the Japanese Yohan, Isetan, and Seiyu, the Malaysian Parkson, and the Taiwanese Pacific, are good examples, as is the French Printemps. Printemps has claimed the consumer base of luxury goods in China by opening an up-market version of its international department store format. However, in order to adapt to local supply conditions, it deviates from its normal practice and in China it relies on licensees operating their own areas in the stores.

For department stores, the main revenue comes from "joint operation," which means that department stores provide premises to brand agents to set up and operate counters or showrooms, while collecting payments through the storewide cash register. Joint operation constitutes 80 to 90 percent of total department store sales. Sales generated directly from other divisions of department stores are secondary to joint operation. In addition, department stores work with vendors on consignment (where a retailer pays the vendor only after the goods are sold and can return unsold merchandise) and on general sale (where a retailer pays the vendor before the merchandise is sold, based on payment terms agreed upon by both).

▶ *Supermarkets, Convenience Stores, and Warehouses*
(Membership Clubs)

Supermarket-style outlets have a much shorter history than department stores in China. The first supermarket or "free-to-choose market" in China was established in 1981 at the Guangdong Friendship Store in Guangzhou. When China started "open-door" reform, the coastal province of Guangdong, home to one of the world's major ports, as well as the country's most populous and prosperous province, was the guinea pig for testing a market economy. The initial supermarket took only foreign exchange certificates; therefore, normal local residents could not shop at supermarkets. The first renminbi-based supermarket was subsequently opened in 1982, also in Guangzhou, and others began to appear in Beijing, Hangzhou, Shanghai, and other parts of China.

▲ FIGURE 4.4 Customers shopping at a Chinese apparel store March 2016.

Nearly all of the supermarkets in those days were operated as subsections of local department stores. The success of the trial in Guangdong province laid the foundation for free market retailing in the world's most populous country. Apparel sales in China as a result have been a direct beneficiary of this development.

In China, supermarket-style outlets can be divided into three groups according to size. Each group has specific market positioning when it comes to apparel sales. Large-scale comprehensive supermarkets sell low-grade underwear, shoes, coats, and other essentials. They are price-driven markets for consumers with little concern for brands. Good examples of such comprehensive supermarkets include French-based Carrefour, American-based Wal-mart and Sam's Club, Germany's Metro Cash & Carry, and the Dutch company Makro. However, it is worth noting that exclusive brand outlets selling apparel merchandise are joining this group of supermarket stores. The second group of supermarket-style outlet stores is medium-sized domestic supermarkets, such as Lianhua and Nonggongshang, Hualian-Lawson, and Kedi, which are mainly franchised convenience stores selling a very limited stock of cheap apparel, such as socks, underwear, and pajamas. The third group of supermarkets is warehouse clubs or membership clubs. They are usually small in size and specialize in specific types or styles of apparel, such as sports or casual.

▶ Specialty Stores, Company-Owned and Franchised Chain Outlets

Many Chinese garment companies have replicated European formats directly. Company-owned chain stores and franchises are common in China. Chinese firms have also picked up the vertical integration concept developed by the Spanish fashion brand Zara. For instance, YiShion, the well-known casual wear brand, is operated as a vertical integrated apparel business. YiShion's parent company started as a manufacturer, taking contract orders from foreign manufacturers or retailers. In 1997, the company launched its own brand YiShion to be in charge of the whole market chain to increase its profitability.

The Hong Kong–based Giordano operates a large chain of small apparel stores in the former colony. In China, it has developed a new store concept. Its stores are much bigger, offering more varied assortments of apparel merchandise. In addition, whereas it owns its Hong Kong stores, its Chinese stores are operated by franchisees. The new format has become the base for its Asian expansion.

Stores that specialize in casual wear are very popular in China. This format was initially introduced to mainland China by Hong Kong–based retailers. The first groups of specialty store retailers opening stores in first-tier cities such as Guangzhou, Shanghai, and Beijing included Giordano, Bossini, and Jeans West. A few years later, Chinese domestic entrepreneurs established their own brands and opened stores across other cities. Specialty stores are mainly privately owned and located in major commercial streets or inside department stores, shopping malls, or shopping plazas. Most specialty store retailers use franchising to expand their market and earn more market share. In addition, both domestic and foreign specialty stores sell online.

▸ Fashion Boutiques

Fashion boutiques specialize in selling higher-priced items in small quantities. Since 1990 high-end fashion boutiques have become increasingly popular in major cities. Boutiques are mainly located on major commercial streets in first-tier cities such as Beijing, Shanghai, and Guangzhou. Boutiques are all privately owned businesses. Domestic fashion boutique retailers are increasingly investing in developing and promoting brand names to differentiate themselves from competitors.

▸ Designer Stores

In the early 1980s, French designer Pierre Cardin introduced the **designer store**—the format of a store carrying products of one single well-known brand to China (Mitchell, 2002). Several years later, many well-known international labels, including luxury brands, started entering the Chinese market. Louis Vuitton opened its first store in a Beijing hotel in 1992. With increasing sales of foreign luxury goods in China, many luxury brands have opened stores in China. Giorgio Armani, Chanel, Givenchy, Bentley, Hermès, Maserati, Kenzo, and many other clothing designers all have boutiques in China ("Louis Vuitton opens Beijing flagship store" 2005).

▸ Hypermarkets

French retailer Carrefour introduced the format of hypermarkets, which has been well received by Chinese consumers. Since 1995, Carrefour has kept the lead position among foreign retail companies in China. In 2010 it operated 156 stores in 45 major cities of the Chinese mainland, with over 50,000 employees. Hypermarkets are taking hold in China thanks to the lure of low prices, convenient one-stop shopping, accessible locations, and the integration of other

▲ FIGURE 4.5 Menswear section in a Chinese department store.

retail facilities such as restaurants, cinemas, and coffeehouses that can turn a shopping trip into a day out. Among the companies, leading this industry growth are Walmart/Trust-Mart (US), Carrefour (France), Tesco (UK), and RT-Mart (Taiwan). Domestic retailers adopted this format very quickly. In 2010, the largest hypermarket retailer in China was Shanghai-based Lianhua Supermarket Holdings Co. Ltd. Hypermarkets are privately owned or public corporate ("Hypermarket culture booms in China," 2010). In China, supermarkets mainly sell low-price and basic apparel products. The majority of hypermarket shoppers buy necessities, except for clothes. Even though all hypermarkets have a clothing department, product assortments are mainly the basics, therefore not very attractive to customers who are looking for fashion merchandise. In addition, Chinese consumers are not used to buying apparel products from hypermarkets or supermarkets ("Hypermarket apparel sales are struggling," 2004).

▶ Manufacturer's Outlet

The joint-venture retailer, Yansha department store, opened its first manufacturer's outlet in China, Yansha Outlet, in Beijing in 2002. Yansha Outlets feature over 200 brands like Versace, Prada, and CK, and they offer mostly new but off-season products. Urban Chinese who prefer brand products have embraced this format. Chinese consumers favor outlets because they offer authentic brands and products, discount prices, easy accessibility, and convenient parking. Outlets are only located in major cities, such as Beijing, Shanghai, and Chongqing, and provincial capitals such as Hangzhou, Suzhou, Harbin, and Hefei.

▶ Apparel Wholesale Market

The **apparel wholesale market** format is a hybrid retail format combining the functions of manufacturer's showroom, wholesaler, and retailer. Such markets are located at commercial sites with low rent. Wholesale-market customers include retailers and individual consumers. Wholesale markets carry a wide range of different categories of apparel merchandise, including high-end, moderate price, and low-end products. Vendors from all over the country not only sell products to retail buyers and individual consumers but also take production orders and look for franchisees to expand their businesses. Many foreign retailers' Chinese contractors sell their overrun or returned merchandise in wholesale markets. Chinese consumers, especially middle- or lower-class consumers, favor this retail format. They can find the latest styles at relatively low prices through bargaining or buying more items. For instance, Qipu Lu Wholesale market is the largest wholesale market in Shanghai. The market is actually a cluster of small vendors offering the latest styles of all categories of apparel products at low prices. Both retail buyers and consumers can buy merchandise at wholesale prices based on the amount of purchase. Retail buyers and consumers negotiate with vendors. Such markets attract the most apparel shoppers not only from local areas but also visitors.

▶ Secondhand Luxury Brand Boutique

Retailers started selling secondhand apparel products in the late 1980s. By 2010 many boutique stores selling secondhand luxury brands saw increasing sales. **Secondhand luxury brand boutiques** target savvy consumers who desire luxury brands but cannot afford or are not willing to pay full price. Such

▲ FIGURE 4.6 Hanfu, also called Han clothing, is the Han dynasty's traditional dress. It consisted of a yi, a narrow-cuffed, knee-length tunic tied with a sash, and a narrow, ankle-length skirt, called chang, worn with a bixi, a length of fabric that reached the knees. Vivid primary colors and green were used, due to the degree of technology at the time.

retailers obtain inventory by buying from different distribution channels. They also sell products for individuals on commission. Sometimes celebrities send their used luxury items to secondhand luxury brand boutique stores. Retailers carefully select every item based on brand, style, and quality. All the used items have to be in good condition. The prices are set by owners and are priced at 40 percent to 60 percent of original prices. The normal commission rate is 15 to 20 percent of sales. If the item cannot be sold, owners pay 5 percent of the prices as a display fee. Some celebrities even open such stores to sell not only their own used items, but also second-hand luxury items collected from their social network. The normal commission rate is 15 percent of sales.

▶ Online Retail

Online retailing has developed rapidly in China. According to China Internet Network Information Center (CNNIC) reports, up to June 2016, China had around 450 million online shoppers with an increase of 8.3 percent over the

▲ FIGURE 4.7 Luxury outlet carrying a variety of brands in Shanghai, China.

end of 2015. In addition, the usage rate of mobile shopping increased from 54.8 to 61 percent from 2015 to 2016 and mobile online shoppers grew rapidly to over 400 million. Jonathan Lu, president of Taobao, a popular Chinese online auction site, says, "We are excited about the prospect of growing China's online fashion market through a partnership with world-leading casual wear brand UNIQLO. UNIQLO's decision to join the lineup of global companies already operating online stores on Taobao underscores the continued growing strength of online retailing in China, as nearly 100 million people have elected to purchase goods, such as apparel, via the Internet rather than through traditional brick-and-mortar retail."

STORE OWNERSHIP: CONSOLIDATION AND INVESTMENT

Given the difficulty in separating apparel retailing from general retailing in China, any discussion of ownership of apparel enterprises has to spring from ownership in the retail industry.

DOMESTIC ENTERPRISES

To modernize China's retail industry in response to foreign competition, large domestic retailers (especially those located in the same cities) have consolidated among themselves or taken over small operators to form retail chains. These actions have received strong support from the Chinese government as a means to promote the development of indigenous retail chains. Both Lianhua (United China) and Hualian (China United), the two largest retail chains in China, have pursued this growth approach by providing management to franchised stores and supplying merchandise thereto through their corporate distribution networks. To fend off foreign competition, two of Beijing's largest retailers—Wangfujing Co. Ltd. and Dong'an Group—merged in 2000 to form the capital's first super-retailing group, Beijing Wangfujing-Dong'an Group Co. Ltd. (China Economic Review, 2000; Fang, 2006).

Retailers originating from Hong Kong, Macao, and Taiwan have mainly invested in exclusive or franchised specialty stores, which require low investment and, hence, involve low risks. Examples are Jeans West, Giordano, Crocodile, and Goldlion, all of which are owned by Hong Kong interests. With their familiarity with the social environment in China and knowledge of the local culture and cost-effective ways of operating in China, these enterprises have made big investments in department stores and supermarkets.

FDI REGULATIONS: OPEN WITH DEEP COMMITMENT

China's retail sector totally opened up to foreign direct investment in December 2004. With these new regulations, foreign retailers do not have restrictions on the number of stores or their locations in China.

When China joined the World Trade Organization (WTO) in 2001, the Chinese government began to lift restrictions on foreign direct investment gradually, and this greater level of liberalization has enabled international retailers to pursue expansion in China. In turn, these retailers have strongly influenced modern retailing techniques and have introduced new formats into the Chinese market. By 2006, the distribution sector opened up further. Most strikingly, China opened up the entire market of logistical chain and related services to foreign enterprises, including inventory management; assembly, sorting, and grading of bulk lots; breaking bulk lots and redistributing into smaller lots; delivery services; refrigeration, storage, warehousing, and garage services; sales promotion, marketing, and advertising; and installation and after services including maintenance and repair and training service. No other WTO member has made such deep commitments in this sector.

Despite substantial fluctuations in the Asian and global economies China has attracted more FDI than any other developing country (Lu Yi, Sophie Han, 2014). The Chinese government is focused on high-quality investment projects that generate long-term economic value and that increase employment. Data from the Ministry of Commerce's (MOC) 2013 statistics on FDI in China indicates that the key sectors attracting FDI include manufacturing, real estate, leasing and business services, and retail. In 2015 India replaced China as leading recipient of capital investment in Asia-Pacific while China suffered a 23 percent decline in capital investment and a 16 percent drop in FDI projects. The US was the highest ranked destination by FDI projects, recording 1,517 FDI projects in 2015 (The FDI Report, 2016).

However, Ministry of Commerce data showed foreign direct investment in China increased 4.1 percent amounting to 813.22 billion yuan in 2016. Foreign direct investment in China reached an all-time high in 2016 and a record low in January of 2000 (Trading Economics, 2016).

▶ *Amendments of China Foreign-Investment Laws*

On October 8, 2016, the Ministry of Commerce of China issued provisional measures on the Administration of Record Filing for the establishment of and changes to Foreign Invested Enterprises (FIEs). These interim measures implement reforms in the government approval process and filing system for most FIEs that were announced in September, 2016 by the Standing Committee of the People's Republic of China. On September 3, 2016, the Standing Committee amended four regulations on foreign direct investment and investment from Taiwan (FDI), which marks a new, more lenient FDI regulatory regime. These amended regulations took effect on October 1, 2016, and apply to FIEs, including wholly foreign owned enterprises (WFOEs), equity joint ventures (EJVs) and cooperative joint ventures (CJVs) (Oberlies and Lu, 2016).

> ► *Shift from Current "Approval System" to "Filing-for-Records System"*

Under the Existing Approval System, which was first laid down when China started opening up to foreign investment in the early 1980s, foreign investors must apply for the prior approval from China's foreign investment approval authority, the Ministry of Commerce (together with its local offices and counterparts) for the establishment of any wholly-foreign-owned subsidiaries and/or Chinese-foreign joint ventures in China (such wholly-foreign-owned subsidiaries and/or Chinese-foreign joint ventures established by foreign investors in China are customarily referred to as "foreign-invested enterprises" or "FIEs"), and for any subsequent changes in and to such FIEs (including changes to such FIEs' charter documents) on a case-by-case basis (Zhang and Yang, 2016).

Under the "negative list plus filing-for-records" system, the State Council is expected to soon issue the national catalog of sectors into which foreign investments are restricted or prohibited, also known as the "negative list". The establishment of and subsequent changes to an FIE that intends to carry on or carries on businesses outside the sectors listed in the applicable "negative list" will no longer be subject to the prior approval; instead, a filing-for-records for the establishment and changes will be required. The Existing Approval System, however, would remain applicable if the foreign investment is made into sectors that fall within the "negative list" to be issued by the State Council (Zhang and Yang, 2016).

INTERNATIONAL BRANDS: PROVIDING RESPITE FROM DAY-TO-DAY WAY OF LIVING

Foreign retailers in China do business in a variety of formats. Those from Asian countries have mostly adopted a department store format, which provides the much-needed psychological escape from crowded living conditions in China. The Japanese Yohan, Jusco, Sogo, Isetan, and Seiyu, and the Malaysian Parkson are good examples. European and North American retailers came after these Asian retailers and introduced hypermarkets (Carrefour), cash-and-carry warehouse retail stores (Metro, Makro, Ikea), discount department stores (Walmart), and membership clubs (Sam's Club, Pricesmart, Metro, and Makro), all of which also provide a respite from cramped housing (Dawson et al., 2003).

INFLUENCES ON APPAREL RETAILING: A NEW GENERATION AND A NEW WAY OF LIFE

The retail industry in China has some unique features that one must understand to be successful in this country. Culture, technology, fashion, apparel exhibitions, and fashion magazines are the major factors that influence apparel retailing in China.

CULTURAL INFLUENCES

As people around the world worried about the financial crisis and its economic effects, luxury consumption in China reached new heights, thanks to the government policy to boost domestic consumption. A March 2009 *New York Times* article declared China the world's fastest-growing luxury consumption market. It is hard for many people to understand how a developing country has become the world's second-largest luxury consumption market. It's cultural. The prosperity of China's market economy has brought dramatic changes in urban consumers. For one thing, they have become more eager to "keep up with the Joneses." The new generation is tempering traditional attitudes about consumption. "The philosophy is 'enjoy life today' against the old Chinese custom of saving, saving, saving," notes Lawrence Lau, management controlling director of L'Oreal, China. New ways and old together constitute the unique Chinese apparel consumption concept. Consumers choose particular products or brands not only for function or performance but also as expressions of specific personality and social status.

Chinese consumers regard "face" (*mianzi*) highly. They transmit social status through dress. Luxury products are a way to strengthen one's identification with a high class, which is attractive to Chinese consumers. The rich use luxury to express themselves and the rest use whatever luxury they can afford to give the appearance of wealth.

TECHNOLOGICAL FACTORS

The Chinese government has realized the importance of advancing its technology for economic development. Although information technology has not been widely applied in China's brick-and-mortar retail market, some apparel retailers have adopted systems such as online electronic cash registers (ECRs), electronic point of sales (EPOS), cash-free payments, and electronic security. Foreign retailers can use their sophisticated technology in China to gain an upper hand in this area.

FASHION INFLUENCES

The influences of fashion on apparel retailing are huge. The mass media has emerged as one of the most powerful forces shaping consumer attitudes in China. Consumers acquire information about fashion through many channels, such as fashion exhibitions, fashion shows, and fashion magazines. Movie stars or celebrities are often featured in the advertisements of domestic brands. Regarded as fashion innovators, consumers look to them for correct ways to wear apparel. Understanding and catering to this group of consumers can increase the rate of adoption of a particular fashion style and thereby increase sales (Muzinich et al., 2003).

APPAREL EXHIBITIONS

Apparel and fashion shows and fairs have significant influence on fashion trends. Since 2000, more and more international apparel and fashion shows have been held in China, significantly broadening the perspectives of Chinese consumers. Shanghai is gaining a reputation as a global fashion center, and a fair share of China's television programming consists of local models striding down catwalks. The Annual China Fashion Awards organized by trendy Shanghai broadcaster Channel Young is starting to gain international clout. But not all broadcasts are up to global standards. Shanghai has plans to develop its fashion business and aims to join the ranks of Paris, New York, and Milan. To achieve that goal, Shanghai must improve its ability to host international fashion exhibitions and communicate effectively.

FASHION MAGAZINES

Fashion magazines are important channels through which fashion information is transmitted to the public. Since *Vogue* hit Chinese newsstands in 2005, a lot of other high-end fashion magazines, such as *Cosmopolitan* and *Elle*, have arrived. The Chinese fashion magazine market has become highly competitive, which is very good for spreading fashion information.

GETTING TO KNOW DOMESTIC COMPETITORS: GEARING UP FOR COMPETITION

The major competition for foreign investors in China's retail market are domestic privately owned companies, other wholly owned foreign companies, and state-owned enterprises. Bailian Group, a state-owned retail company, is the second-largest retailer in China. The parent company of this group operates department stores, grocery stores, hypermarkets, and convenience stores. The company has adopted foreign retail formats and hires managers from foreign competitors in order to remain competitive. Such state-owned retailers have been catering to Chinese consumers since long before foreign competitors entered the market, which strengthens their position.

METERSBONWE

Metersbonwe is one of several successful domestic apparel brands that may be major competition for foreign retailers entering the Chinese market. As a domestic casual clothing brand that responds to market changes with innovative approaches, Metersbonwe saw an enormously successful first decade in the new century. Positioning itself as a "young and energetic" purveyor of casual wear, the company has established itself as the top domestic brand with a target market of young consumers from 18 to 25 years old, mostly high school and college students. It offers fashionable products at affordable prices. Among its many pioneering moves, the most important has been the adoption of a franchising business model. Metersbonwe strategically focuses on design, marketing, and distribution, and outsources manufacturing and most of its retail sales through franchising. During the first five years after its establishment in 1995, they expanded gradually, growing by approximately 50 franchising stores annually. Metersbonwe had over 5,000 stores in 2012 however, as the development of the electronic business, Metwesbonwe closed around 1,500 stores in total within three years and now retains around 3,500 stores in 2016. Among all the stores, around 87 percent were franchising stores. Its annual sales reached 7 billion (RMB) ($1.05 billion). Metersbonwe owns the largest market share of casual apparel in China (Metersbonwe.com).

After the first five years, several domestic brands started duplicating Metersbonwe's success by using its business model, benchmarking its marketing strategy as well as positioning their brands to compete in the same target market. At the same time, foreign brands such as Zara and H&M have been competing for this corner of the Chinese apparel market. Under attack on two fronts, Metersbonwe has taken a series of actions to strengthen its brand and market competitiveness.

Metersbonwe has been focusing on distribution channel development. The franchising business model helped the retailer in two ways. Using franchising to expand its market saved the cost of opening new stores. Metersbonwe supplies the products, and franchises keep 25 percent of sales. All the franchisees work hard to increase sales, helping this retailer to develop and maintain market share. In addition, outsourced manufacturing has saved them money.

JNBY

Established in Hangzhou, China in 1994 by JNBY group, JNBY is another successful private apparel business in China. It carries apparel, shoes, and accessories for women, men, and kids. In general, JNBY is targeting middle- and upper-income customers, who pursue high-quality apparel products that can represent them on a personal level. JNBY has more than 700 stores over the world, mostly in China but they also expanded to Europe, Japan, America, and Canada. The first official expansion of JNBY in the USA was the Seattle store in 2015, and it also has an online JNBY store on Amazon. The annual sales were expected to reach €410 MM ($437 MM) in 2014.

LA CHAPELLE GROUP

La Chapelle is a Chinese clothing and accessories retailer based in China. The company was founded in 1998. The fashion group also owns brands such as "La Chapelle SPORT", "Candies", and "La Chapelle Homme" selling menswear, womenswear, and childrenswear targeting different types of consumers in different age ranges. In 2016, there were more than 7,000 stores across all 34 provinces in China.

La Chapelle opened its first official online store in Tmall in August 2014. According to its 2015 annual report, at the end of 2015, the company had increased about 16.4 percent compared with 2014, and profited 9 hundred million Chinese Yuan (over 13 hundred million dollars). The company is expecting to operate 10,000 stores in China at the end of 2016.

YISHION

YiShion has established itself as a nationally famous casual clothing brand. Targeting the same groups of consumers as Semir and Metersbonwe, YiShion produces and sells menswear, womenswear, and childrenswear. It relies on high-quality garments, an advanced computer-aided design production system, and well-established distribution channels. In 2010, there were more than 3,000 franchised stores across all 23 provinces in China.

Unlike other casual apparel brands, YiShion is a vertically integrated enterprise. They do product design and development and have their own production facility and distribution channel. Their headquarters are at Donguan in Guangdong province, which is one of the country's largest apparel production and distribution clusters. YiShion hires employees to open stores in different provinces as well as recruit franchisees. They are also expanding internationally into countries such as Iran, Jordan, Kuwait, Malaysia, and Oman, as well as other emerging markets in Asia and Africa.

HOW MATURE IS THE RETAIL INDUSTRY? STIFF COMPETITION YET OPEN MARKET FOR INVESTMENT

Ever since the Chinese retail opened up to foreign investors, domestic retailers have undergone major restructuring to get ready for the intense competition expected from the international retail chains. Some domestic retail chains also hope to improve their valuation in case an international retailer is interested in acquiring them. The domestic retailers' strong relationship with their suppliers makes them stiff competition. Successful international retailers find a niche in the Chinese market. An international retailer interested in entering the Chinese market needs to find the right strategy and investment vehicle if they are to prosper.

International brands are becoming popular in China. Whereas only a small proportion of the Chinese population can afford expensive, imported brand apparel items, consumers with increased exposure to foreign fashion through the media are becoming more receptive to international fashion styles and trends (China's beauty market, 2005). Demand for imported brand products is growing also due to changes in buying behavior and increasing purchasing power. Although Chinese registered local brands have also developed quickly (there are at least 100,000), only 0.3 percent of them are considered well known among Chinese consumers (China National Commercial Information Centre, 2006). Typical examples are Yonger, Firs, and Li Ning. It is generally agreed that foreign apparel brands occupy the high end and middle end of the market.

International brands set the pace of the contemporary Chinese apparel business. It wasn't until 2001 that brand name products started to become household words, and by 2006 the luxury brands had gained Chinese consumers' attention. China's premier cities are beginning to mature in terms of retail stores, so retailers are focusing on second-tier cities, that is the provincial capital cities with populations of less than two million, such as Changchun, Shijiazhuan, Ulumqi, and third-tier cities, which are those coastal cities with better developed economies and relatively higher consumer purchasing power, such as Qinhuangdao, Weihai, and Beihai. For international retailers that are interested in expanding into the Chinese market, it would be wise to consider second- and third-tier cities for expansion.

BUYING FOR APPAREL RETAIL CHAINS: IT'S ALL AT HOME

Since 1960, the internationalization of markets, competitive advances in product, process, and business technologies, and changing consumer requirements have brought about radical and continuous change in the textile and apparel industries. A few of the transformations over this period have included the emergence of large, powerful retail groups; widespread integration and then de-integration in textile manufacturing; the emergence of diversified apparel companies without factories; and the development of new channels to market, such as the Internet (Kilduff, 2000). All of this has made the Chinese apparel manufacturing an important part of the retail industry.

China is an important international hub of sourcing for apparel retailers. Its role is becoming increasingly important because of its ability to gauge its products to apparel consumption trends. Retail chains in China use the Chinese manufacturing industry for their low-end products, and luxury brands import from their own manufacturing setups abroad. Country of origin plays a very important role in luxury brands among Chinese consumers. Many of the international retailers (such as Walmart) in China source their products from within the country, which helps reduce the costs associated with importing.

RETAIL CAREERS: REGULATED ENVIRONMENT

Despite the country's opening up since 1978, China still has a relatively centralized manpower planning system that regulates the labor market. In general, a worker has to obtain an employment permit to enter the job market. Jobs are classified into 66 directory entries by the Ministry of Labor and Social Security, and one must undergo training and obtain professional qualification certificates under the Chinese Labor Law and Vocational Education Law to get an employment permit. In China, individuals have the opportunity to pursue careers in the retailing industry as vendors, store employees, and buyers.

For a foreigner interested in working in China, the employer has to apply for approval and for a People's Republic of China Employment License. The company may hire a foreigner only in case of special needs and only if a domestic candidate cannot fill the position. The foreigner has to also meet some basic regulations, such as be older than 18 years of age, have professional skills, have no criminal record, and have a valid passport. The regulations for foreigner's employment in China promulgated jointly by the Ministry of Labor, Ministry of Public Security, Ministry of Foreign Affairs, and the Ministry of Foreign Trade and Economic Cooperation of the People's Republic of China can be found at the government website at http://www.gov.cn/english/2005–08/29/content_27366.htm.

THE FUTURE OF APPAREL RETAIL: ON THE WAY TO BECOMING A FASHION CAPITAL OF THE WORLD

The apparel retailing industry in China has experienced a significant transformation since the country opened its doors to the world in 1978. In step with China's economic growth and integration with a globalized economy, and in response to rising expectations of the "newly rich" consumers, the industry underwent changes in terms of firm ownership structure, retailing format, and distribution channels. However, given the disparity of income between cities and the countryside and between different classes of people in the country, the development of apparel retailing in China will follow a hybrid model reflecting a combination of price-sensitive, fashion-sensitive, and brand-sensitive approaches.

Most Chinese believe in moderation. They are usually fashion followers, not innovators. Traditional Chinese culture frowns on full self-expression, but a new generation has started to develop its own ideas. They have the courage to express themselves in public and transmit their style and personality through their dress. Personalized consumption is replacing blind following. In a campaign to showcase Shanghai's creativity in the lead-up to its 2010 Expo, this "Sin City" declared its aspiration to become the Fashion Capital of Asia. Because Shanghai is already a popular venue for fashion shows and apparel exhibitions, the declaration signals the coming of age of China's proactive stance on the apparel industry, including retailing. The government support given to local designers in Beijing, Shanghai, and Guangzhou may pave the way for China to become a fashion capital in the years to come.

SUMMARY

In just the past few years, China has transformed from an underdeveloped nation to the world's second largest global manufacturing hub. However, China still remains a developing country (its per capita income is still a fraction of that in advanced countries) and its market reforms are inadequate. Fast economic growth has also brought many challenges, including: high inequality; rapid urbanization; challenges to environmental sustainability; and external imbalances. China also faces demographic pressures related to an aging population and the internal migration of labor.

As economic conditions in China continue to improve, consumption of textile, apparel, and beauty products is increasing. Consumers prefer foreign brands not only because they like the quality and styles but also because the lifestyle indicated by the labeled country of origin appeals to them. Since the influence of country of origin or brand is significant in China, understanding Chinese consumers helps foreign investors to provide them with the right product mix. Although younger consumers are more sensitive to price than older consumers, younger consumers do purchase high-end clothing, brand-name beauty products, or even luxury items. In addition to an improved material life, the Internet has helped to lower the consumer's age. Chinese consumers in the 25–45 age range are more likely to do non-shop shopping than those who are in their fifties.

In the past, luxury goods were seen as a symbol of wealth and status for Chinese consumers and today they buy luxury goods for their own enjoyment (Horton, 2016). A number of niche luxury brands and designer labels have won great popularity among Chinese consumers. Bain & Company's 2015 China Luxury Market Study notes that a younger and more sophisticated generation of shoppers with markedly different tastes, aspirations and consumption habits is reshaping the landscape of luxury in China. Educated, well-traveled and tech-savvy consumers are emerging as the new target market.

Open-air markets and street stores found along major commercial streets, around major trade centers, or in shopping centers pre-date modern formats in China and continue to be popular.

Modern retail formats such as department stores, supermarkets, convenience stores, and warehouses are emerging and becoming popular in China. Many Chinese garment companies have replicated European formats directly. Company-owned chain stores and franchises are common in China. Chinese firms have also picked up the vertical integration concept developed by the

Spanish fashion brand Zara. Since 1990, high-end fashion boutiques have become increasingly popular in major cities. Boutiques are mainly located on major commercial streets in first-tier cities such as Beijing, Shanghai, and Guangzhou. Boutiques are all privately owned businesses.

To modernize China's retail industry in response to foreign competition, large domestic retailers (especially those located in the same cities) have consolidated among themselves or taken over small operators to form retail chains. These actions have received strong support from the Chinese government as a means of promoting the development of indigenous retail chains.

The Chinese government has realized the importance of advancing its technology for economic development. The influences of fashion on apparel retailing are huge. The mass media has emerged as one of the most powerful forces shaping consumer attitudes in China.

CRITICAL THINKING QUESTIONS

1. Discuss Chinese consumerism. How is this favorable for foreign retailers?
2. Discuss retail formats available in China and why is online retailing becoming increasingly popular in China?
3. Discuss FDI regulations in China and in what way do they help foreign retailers?
4. What are some of the challenges faced by apparel retailers in China?

ONLINE SHOPPING TREND IN CHINA

In the recent past Chinese consumers have been shifting from brick-and-mortar shopping to online shopping. E-commerce now represents a high-growth sector. Though relatively new to online shopping, Chinese consumers already make up almost half of global online retail sales, and are only growing in numbers. Online retail sales amounted to $581.61 billion in 2015, surging 33.3 percent from the previous year. The volume of online sales in China now exceeds that in the US; online sales are expected to grow 20 percent annually by 2020. The Chinese online shopping sector is not just replacing traditional retail transactions but also stimulating consumption that would not otherwise take place. Finally, online shopping may catalyze a "leapfrog" move by the broader retail sector, putting it on a fast track to a more digital future. Online shoppers tend to be young, urban, and highly educated. They have a different attitude toward shopping than the older generation; young shoppers are more willing to spend. E-tailing is enabling China's shift from an investment-oriented society to one that's more consumption driven.

Some 90 percent of Chinese electronic retailing occurs in virtual marketplaces. E-commerce platforms include manufacturers, large and small retailers, and individuals offering products and services to consumers through online storefronts on Mega sites similar to eBay or Amazon Marketplace. The mega sites include PaiPai, Taobao, and Tmall, which in turn are owned by bigger e-commerce groups. A large and growing network of third-party service providers offers sellers marketing and site-design services, payment fulfillment, delivery and logistics, customer service, and IT support. By contrast, in the United States, Europe, and Japan, the dominant model involves brick-and-mortar retailers (such as Best Buy, Carrefour, Darty, Dixons, and Wal-mart) or pure-play online merchants (such as Amazon), which run their own sites and handle the details of commerce.

Although still in the early stages of growth, China's online shopping sector is profitable, logging margins of around 8 to 10 percent of earnings before interest, taxes, and amortization comparatively higher than those of average physical retailers. According to Boston Consulting and Ali Research, e-commerce sales often experience fewer licensing requirements and quicker customs clearance than brick-and-mortar retailing in China. As a result, e-commerce is to some extent replacing shopping in physical marketplaces, and will comprise 42 percent of growth in private consumption by 2020. Online shopping also allows consumers to access products that are not available in stores, including organic foods and some luxury products from overseas. To keep up with increasing demand from smaller urban and rural areas, online retailers are seeking to expand logistics infrastructure and services. For example, Alibaba's logistics arm, Cainiao, now owns 180,000 express delivery stations for the shipment of products and has recently expanded its fresh food distribution centers across China. The firm recently completed its first external funding round and is expected to spend $16 billion over the next five to eight years to expand its network. Growth in China's underdeveloped logistics sector can certainly be expected to accompany the expansion of e-commerce. China's stifling growth in online shopping reflects increasing incomes, higher education, and more sophisticated consumption patterns of the typical consumer. Due to the expansion of online retail shopping and the necessary logistical services, e-commerce is at the frontier of consumption growth in China.

E-tailing's impact is more pronounced in China's underdeveloped small and midsize cities. While incomes in these urban areas are lower, their online shoppers spend almost as much money online as do people in some larger, more prosperous cities and also spend a larger portion of their disposable income online. The online purchasing may be higher for small & midsize cities since consumers in smaller cities have access to products and brands previously not available to them, in locations where many retailers have yet to establish footholds.

Further boosting online can be attributed to lower prices. Depending on the category, online products are on average, 6 to 16 percent lower than in China's stores. Apparel, household products, recreation and education are the categories where price discounts are greatest. They are also the three largest online retail segments.

REFERENCES

China Eclipses the US to Become the World's Largest Retail Market (2016). Retrieved from www.emarketer.com/Article/China-Eclipses-US-Become-Worlds-Largest-Retail-Market/1014364

Sara Hsu (2016). China's E-Commerce Addiction Has Serious Market Potential. Retrieved from www.forbes.com/sites/sarahsu/2016/07/16/chinas-growing-e-commerce-addiction/#299005083b01

Richard Dobbs, Yougang Chen, Gordon Orr, James Manyika, Michael Chui, Elsie Chang (2013). China's e-tail revolution. Retrieved from www.mckinsey.com/global-themes/asia-pacific/china-e-tailing

Discussion Questions
1. Why has online shopping increased in China?
2. Is there anything you would recommend the company should do differently to fulfill the needs of the Chinese online consumer market?
3. Why is online shopping increasing in small and middle cities in China?
4. Describe the profile of the typical Chinese online consumer. What strategies should companies formulate in order to attract these consumers?

REFERENCES

About Li Ning (2010). Retrieved October 10, 2010 from www.lining.com/EN/company/
inside-1_1.html

Au, K.F. (2000), 'Market wide open,' *Textile Asia*, August, 73–6.

Balfour, F. (2008, May 1). China's Li Ning Toe-to-Toe against Nike and Adidas.
Retrieved October 10, 2010 from www.businessweek.com/magazine/
content/08_19/b4083051446468.htm

Bruce, M., Daly, L. & Towers, N. (2004). Lean or agile—A solution for supply chain
management in the textiles and clothing industry? *International Journal of
Operations and Production Management, 24*(2), 151–170.

Cheng, C. (1993). Little Emperors Make Big Consumers. *China Today,* 42 (April), 47–49.

China Economic Review (2000). Beijing Stores Announce Merger. *China Economic
Review,* October.

China National Commercial Information Centre (2006), *Industry Series on China's
Apparel Market 2006,* Li & Fung Research Centre, Li & Fung Group, Hong Kong.

China's Beauty Market (2005, August 4). Retrieved October 6, 2010 from www.hktdc.
com/info/vp/a/cepa/en/1/3/1/1X009S7H/Closer-Economic-Partnership-
Arrangement—CEPA—Obsolete-/China-s-Beauty-
Market.htm

Chuang, Y. (2009). The Rise of China and Its Implications for the World Economy.
38th Taiwan U.S. Conference on Contemporary China, Session IV, pp. 2–33.

Christopher, M. (2007). 'New directions in logistics'. In *Global Logistics—New
Directions in Supply Chain Management,* 5th Edn, Kogan Page.

Dawson J., Mukovama M., Choi, S. C. & Larke, R. (2003). *The Internationalisation of
Retailing in Asia.* London: RoutledgeCurzon, p. 117.

Euromonitor International (2016). Apparel and Foorwear in China. Retrieved January
24, 2017 from www.euromonitor.com/apparel-and-footwear-in-china/report

Fang, H. (2006) Comparative Study and Optimization in the Field of Clothing Retail in
Direct Selling Model, Southwest Jiao Tong University.

Fung Business Intelligence (2016). Foreign Brands Continue to Foray into China's
Retail and Consumer Products Sector in the New Normal—Recent Trends and
Implications. *Asia Distribution and Retail.*

Focus Economics (2017). Retrieved January 24, 2017 from www.focus-economics.com/
countries/china

Hayes, S. G. & Jones, N. (2006). 'Fast Fashion: A Financial Snapshot'. *Journal of Fashion
Marketing and Management, 10*(3), 282–300.

Horton Christopher (2016). 'When It Comes to Luxury, China Still Leads.' Retrieved January 15, 2017, from www.nytimes.com/2016/04/05/fashion/china-luxury-goods-retail.html

Hypermarket apparel sales are struggling: More window shoppers than purchasers (2004). Retrieved April 15, 2010, from http://sports.eastday.com/eastday/2004qsy/node7342/userobject1ai723147.html

Hypermarket culture booms in China (2010). Retrieved February 15, 2010, from www.talkingretail.com/news/industry-news/7164-hypermarket-culture-booms-in-china.html

Jiang, S., Armstrong, P., & Cullinane, S. (2015). 'China Unveils Two-child Policy.' *CNN*. Retrieved January 5, 2017, from www.cnn.com/2015/12/27/asia/china-two-child-policy/

Kilduff, P. (2000). Evolving Strategies, Structures and Relationships in Complex and Turbulent Business Environments: The Textile and Apparel Industries of the New Millennium. *Journal of Textile and Apparel, Technology and Management* *1*(1), 1–10.

Kwan, C. Y., Yeung, K. W. & Au, K. F. (2003). A Statistical Investigation of the Changing Apparel Retailing Environment in China. *Journal of Fashion Marketing and Management*, *7*(1), 87–100.

Louis Vuitton Opens Beijing flagship Store (2005). Retrieved April 1, 2010, from www.chinadaily.com.cn/english/livechina/2005–11/21/content_496633.htm

Lu Yi, Sophie Han (2014), Retrieved January 20, 2017 from www.iflr.com/Article/3306883/2014-FDI-Report-China.html

Lu Sheng (2015). China to Become the World's Largest Apparel Market in 2019. Retrieved January 20, 2017 from, https://shenglufashion.wordpress.com/2015/08/28/china-to-become-the-worlds-largest-apparel-market-in–2019/

Mattoo, A. (2003). China's Accession to the WTO: The Services Dimension. *Journal of International Economic 6*(2), 299–339.

McNeal, J. U. & Yeh, C. H. (2003). Consumer Behavior of Chinese Children: 1995–2002. *Journal of Consumer Marketing*, *20*(6), 542–554.

Mitchell, S. (2002). All about Pierre Cardin: An brief biography of Pierre Cardin, his life, his work, and his business empire, from www.essortment.com/lifestyle/pierrecardinfa_solw.htm

Muzinich, N., Pecotich, A. & Putrevu, S. (2003). A Model of the Antecedents and Consequents of Female Fashion Innovativeness. *Journal of Retailing and Consumer Services*, *10*(5), 297–310.

Oberlies, R M. and Lu, J. (2016), New Regime for China Foreign Direct Investment. Retrieved January 22, 2017 from www.fredlaw.com/news__media/2016/10/13/1353/new_regime_for_china_foreign_direct_investment

Performance of China's Apparel Product Sectors (2006). Retrieved October 25, 2010 from www.idsgroup.com/profile/pdf/industry_series/ISissue7.pdf

Roberts Fflur (2016), The Latest Facts and Figures about the Chinese Luxury Market. Retrieved 25 January 2017 from, www.luxurysociety.com/en/articles/2016/08/the-latest-facts-and-figures-about-the-chinese-luxury-market/

Shao, A. & Herbig, P. (1994). Marketing Implications of China's Little Emperors. *Review of Business*, 16 (Summer/Fall), 16–20.

Silverstein, M. J. & Sayre, K. (2009). *Women Want More*. HarperCollins Publishers, NY.

The Rise of Female Consumerism in China (2007, August 7). Retrieved October 25, 2010, from www.womenofchina.cn/Data_Research/Latest_Statistics/18158.jsp

The FDI report (2016), Global Greenfield Investment Trends, Retrieved January 20, 2017 from www.fdiintelligence.com/Utility-Nav/Highlights-Bar/The-fDi-Report–2016

Trading Economics (2016), China Foreign Direct Investment. Retrieved January 21, 2017 from www.tradingeconomics.com/china/foreign-direct-investment

Trading Economics (2017), China Retail Sales YoY, retrieved January 21, 2017 from www.tradingeconomics.com/china/retail-sales-annual

World Bank Data (2016). Retrieved 25 January 2017 from, www.worldbank.org/en/country/china/overview

Yip, K. & Chang, B. (2010, August, 12). Male Big Spenders Splash Their Cash in China. Retrieved October 25, 2010, from www.asianewsnet.net/home/news.php?id=13079

Zhang, J. and Yang, K. (2016), China Amends Its Foreign-Investment Laws, Officially Reforming Its More Than Three-Decade-Old Foreign-Investment Approval Regime, retrieved January 23, 2017 from www.reedsmith.com/China-Amends-Its-Foreign-Investment-Laws-Officially-Reforming-Its-More-Than-Three-Decade-Old-Foreign-Investment-Approval-Regime–09–22–2016/

Zhu, J. (2008). A Comparative Study on Apparel Marketing Channels between China and South Korea. Beijing Institute of Fashion Technology, Masters Thesis.

INDIA

Shubhapriya Bennur
Jaya Halepete Iyer

OBJECTIVES

After reading this chapter, you will

▶ Understand the characteristics of the unorganized (traditional) and organized (nontraditional) retailing sectors of the Indian retail industry

▶ Grasp the role of foreign direct investment policies in establishing retail setups in India

▶ Understand the in-depth profile of the Indian consumers

▶ Recognize the factors that influence apparel retailing in India

▶ Understand career opportunities in the Indian retail industry

As one of the oldest civilizations in the world, India has a strong culture that makes it a complex country in terms of understanding the market and consumers. India has taken a place of pride in international trade since at least the fourth century BCE, when the Mauryan emperors who unified the subcontinent built and maintained roads throughout the country to form trade routes. They minted coins for trade, which was done in a very organized and corporate manner. During the first to eleventh centuries BCE, India had 32.9 percent share of world gross domestic product (GDP), making it the world's greatest economy (Madison, 2003). In the sixteenth century, Portuguese, Dutch, English, and French interests began to establish trade stations in India. The British East India Company was the most successful venture. By the middle of the nineteenth century, it controlled all of what is today India, Pakistan, and Bangladesh. In 1858, the British government took over. India's GDP plummeted from 24.4 percent in 1700 to 3.8 percent in 1952. India had been known for its wealth until it became a British colony. On August 15, 1947, India won its independence. The British influence on the country remains in the education system, infrastructure, and English-speaking population, all of which have facilitated international investment and brought employment to countless telephone customer service representatives.

India is the world's largest democracy and has emerged as the fastest growing major economy in the world as per the Central Statistics Organisation (CSO) and International Monetary Fund (IMF). As per the global consumer confidence index created by Nielsen, India was ranked the highest globally in terms of consumer confidence during the October–December quarter of 2015. The Indian economy is expected to grow at 7–7.75 percent during FY 2017–2018, despite the uncertainties in the global market according to IMF's world economic outlook January 2016. Due to numerous government initiatives like Make in India and Digital India, many foreign companies are setting up their facilities in India. These initiatives are expected to increase the purchasing power of the average Indian consumer (Indian economy overview). The Digital India initiative focuses on three core components: creation of digital infrastructure, delivering services digitally and to increase the digital literacy. The initiatives in recent times have shown positive results as India's gross domestic product (GDP) increased to a growth rate of 7.6 percent (Table 5.1).

The retail industry in India has emerged as one of the fastest growing industries which accounts for 10 percent of the total GDP of the nation and 8 percent of total employment in India. There are 12 million retail outlets employing more than 33 million people. India ranks seventh in market potential after the United States, China, Canada, the UK, Brazil and Germany. (India Chamber of Commerce, 2015). The organized sector includes licensed retailers operating in hypermarkets, supermarkets, malls, departmental stores, etc., and the unorganized sector is dominated by a large number of small retailers comprising of local shops, general stores, chemists, apparel shops, pavement vendors, hand cart hawkers, etc. In addition online retaling or e-commerce is a major area for retail growth in India. Retail e-commerce sales in India are expected to reach $17.5 billion by 2018, from $5.3 billion in 2014 (Indian Chamber of Commerce, 2015). The key drivers of retail growth in India are

TABLE 5.1 Fast Facts about India

Capital	New Delhi
Population	1.266 billion (July 2016 est.)
Type of government	Federal Republic
GDP: purchasing power parity: in US$	$3.57 trillion
Export commodities	Petroleum products, precious stones, machinery, iron and steel, chemicals, vehicles, and apparel
Age structure	0–14 yrs: 27.71 percent 15–64 yrs: 66.2 percent 65 yrs plus: 6.09 percent
Religion	Hindu: 79.8 percent Muslim: 14.2 percent Christian: 2.3 percent Sikh: 1.7 percent Other & Unspecified: 2 percent
Ethnicity	Indo-Aryan: 72 percent Dravidian: 25 percent Mongoloid and other: 3 percent

Source: CIA factbook.gov

increasing disposable income, urbanization, rising internet penetration, higher brand consciousness, liberalization of FDI policies and attitudinal shifts of consumers.

THE RETAIL LANDSCAPE: AS ATTRACTIVE AS IT CAN GET

India is the world's second largest exporter of textiles and clothing. Readymade garments remain the largest contributor to total textile and apparel exports from India. The domestic textile and apparel industry in India is estimated to reach US$141 billion by 2021 from US$67 billion in 2014. Rising government interest and favorable policies have led to growth in the textiles and clothing industry. Foreign direct investment (FDI) in the textiles sector increased to US$1,587.8 million in FY15 from US$1,424.9 million in FY14 (India Brand Equity Foundation, 2016). India is a complex market in many different ways. Its multicultural, multilingual, and multiethnic consumers make it a unique and interesting challenge as an emerging market for foreign retailers.

An understanding of Indian cities is fundamental for a retailer to establish the best possible areas in which to enter and grow their business. Economists categorize Indian cities into three tiers, based on factors such as infrastructure, skill availability, and quality of life (Table 5.2).

Tier I cities are major metropolitan areas with the best infrastructure. These cities have the biggest organized retail markets. This tier has a large concentrated segment of upper-class consumers. The cost of real estate is very high and so is the standard of living. These cities account for about 60 percent of the total real estate space and global consumers. Retailers interested in expansion start with Tier I cities, then slowly acquire real estate in other tiered cities (Images Yearbook, 2009). As Tier I cities become saturated with organized retail formats, retailers move to the next tier cities. For luxury retailers, Tier I cities are the main markets followed by some cities of Tier I-I such as

TABLE 5.2 India's Major Cities

Tier number	Cities included
Tier I	Bengaluru, Mumbai, and New Delhi
Tier I-I	Hyderabad, Chennai, Pune, NOIDA, Gurgaon, and Navi Mumbai
Tier II	Kolkata, Mangalore, Ludhiana, Chandigarh/Mohali, and Bhopal
Tier III	Ahmedabad, Thiruvananthapuram, Coimbatore, Mysore, Nasik, Kochi, Nagpur, Jaipur, Indore, Shimla, Lucknow, Kanpur, Panaji, Srinigar, Patna, and Bhubaneshwar

Source: "Growth Potential: Tier II and Tier III Cities in India," India Reports. Retrieved from www.india-reports.com/Products/try/ IR-tier-2-3-011208-Try.pdf. Also INRnews. com.

NOIDA and Gurgaon, where there are many upper-class people who would buy from high-end luxury stores. The consumers in different tiers differ based on income levels and expenditure due to standards of living in different tiers. For example, Tier I cities are home to large multinational corporations that pay more.

Tier I-I cities are very much like Tier I cities except that they fall a little behind in areas such as infrastructure development, concentration of population, and number of organized retail setups. However, because of high rentals, market saturation and low footfalls, one-third of retailers at shopping malls in large Tier I cities like Mumbai, Delhi-NCR, Chennai, Bengaluru and Kolkata are shifting to Tier-II and -III cities. With promising opportunities, brands are planning new retail strategies well to move into these markets. Urban India accounts for 30 percent of the population, which currently accounts for 64 percent of its consumption. Tier II and Tier III cities are showing strong momentum with consumers changing behavioral patterns with increased earnings, western influences, increased number of working women and a growing desire for luxury items. In terms of market size, it is anticipated that the retail market will grow from US$5.7 billion today to over US$80 billion in value by 2026. (India Retailing, 2014)

CONSUMERS: CONFLUENCE OF CULTURES

Every one of India's 29 states is different in terms of language or dialect; some of them differ in terms of dress and food, making India an extraordinarily diverse country in terms of culture. For example, in the northern states, roti (a flat wheat bread) is eaten with vegetables; in the south, rice is the staple part of a meal. Northern Indians are known for their ostentatious clothing and displays of wealth, whereas southern Indians have simpler tastes. Northern Indians have fairer skin tones and like to use a lot of makeup. Southern Indians are darker in complexion and like to use skin-lightening creams and generally tend to use less makeup. This diversity poses a big challenge for the retail industry.

Another big influence of Indian fashion is the movie industry in India, which produces a large number of movies each year (about 1,969 in 2015 as compared to an average of 600 in Hollywood) in various languages. Although Bollywood (a word created by combining Bombay and Hollywood) is a major influence on fashion all over India, there are local movie industries that make movies in regional languages and dictate fashion in those regions. In addition, many budding designers across India are bringing an interesting dimension to the clothing and apparel needs of Indian consumers.

Buyers must also consider India's many seasonal variations. For example, the capital city of Delhi experiences winter between November and March, with temperatures ranging from 40 to 50 degrees Fahrenheit; however, Mumbai, the financial capital, does not really have a winter, with the lowest temperatures hovering around 70 degrees Fahrenheit. It is important for retailers to buy appropriate assortments for these two major cities. As the vice president of an international brand in India noted, "Zara launched in Delhi and Mumbai with the same winter merchandise. Who will buy trench coats in Mumbai? This is the most common mistake made by many international retailers."

Store layout and decor are critical for attracting Indian consumers. A browser visiting the store frequently likes to see changes in the layout; otherwise, he may get the impression that stock is not moving. Buyers ensure that the same item that has been in store for a season is not carried again and that it is replaced with a different design, style, and color.

India is also a culturally sensitive market. Converse once made shoes with pictures of a god on them. In India, to put a god on a dirty shoe is sacrilege. This would not be acceptable to an Indian. In a similar instance, a software company created a map of India on their product showing the northern state of Kashmir as a disputed state between India and Pakistan. Although the rest of the world may consider Kashmir to be a disputed state, Indians do not. The company had to withdraw the product. A foreign retailer needs to understand the cultural sensitivities of the consumers before launching a product for the citizens of that country.

Retailers in most countries need to micro market their products for stores in different regions due to variations in weather, ethnicity, and major industries. In India, apparel retailers must also attend to cultural differences. The prevalent culture of a state dictates unique behavioral characteristics. There are even cultural differences between Tier I, Tier II, and Tier III cities within the same state. For example, in Tier I cities, there are more nuclear families as compared to other tiers (only husband and wife living with their children), whereas in Tier II and Tier III cities, one can still find extended families (where more than one family—usually two brothers along with their wives, children, and parents—live under one roof). People living in Tier I cities are more global consumers because they travel abroad, dress in Western clothing (a larger percentage than other tiers), and buy international brands. Tier I cities will continue to witness emergence of new malls and lifestyle stores to cater to the needs of their consumers. However, the consumers in Tier II and Tier III cities are becoming more global consumers, expecting global quality at local prices and yet dressing more conservatively in Indian clothing (which may be due to the fact that they live in joint families and need to be more modest, as a mark of respect for their elders, compared to those living in nuclear families). However, new developments are happening in the Tier-II and -III cities. For example, greater emphasis on visual displays, staff training and modern ambiance can be seen in smaller towns. This vast difference in the population makes it very difficult for retail chains to employ the same selling techniques across the country, as in the United States.

Big Bazaar is a department store chain on the lines of a Wal-Mart supercenter. The stores sell groceries along with household items and clothing.

▲ FIGURE 5.1 Indian wholesale customers browse the newly-opened Wal-Mart outlet in northwestern Punjab state's Jalandhar. The store sells groceries along with household items and clothing. It caters to the middle-class and lower-middle-class population. Being a foreign group, Wal-Mart can currently only be wholesalers to sell in India.

The store chain is known for aggressive advertising and for catering to the middle-class and lower-middle-class population.

Indian consumers once believed in saving rather than spending but this mind-set is changing, especially among the younger generation, Indians like to compare pricing in different stores before making any big purchase and they like to bargain. It allows them to feel that they have gotten a good deal. They believe that bigger stores are expensive. This aspect of their personality is also changing with organized retail becoming a regular part of their lives. The economic growth has resulted in Indians willing to invest in a life of luxury. This is the major reason behind India's growing consumerism and retail trends. India is the fifth largest retail industry in the world, and the trends of the retail industry are quite remarkable. Consumer groups can be divided into three clear groups: the first group includes consumers who are extremely brand conscious and shop at the high-end retail stores; the second group shops at outlets that do not hold popular brands and are also much cheaper; the third group, follows the middle path— they satisfy their consumer needs either from high-end retail outlets or the less popular retail outlets, as and when necessary. (Consumerism & Retail Trends) The advent of international and national brands and easy accessibility to designer wear has changed the face of the retail clothing industry in India. Consumers' urge to be smart and fashionable has revolutionized this industry. Major shopping for clothing is done during the wedding season (May and December) and festival season (October and November). Festivals may be different for different regions of India (Sheth & Vittal, 2007).

One characteristic that sets Indian consumers apart from other Asian nations is that English is a commonly used language because of the British influence on Indian culture. The education system in most schools in India is in English, and it is also the common language of conversation in big cities. This makes communication with Indian consumers a lot easier for foreign retailers.

Some of the factors that contribute to the changing consumer profile of Indian consumers are:

► **The growing middle class.** The growth of the Indian economy has led to the creation of employment and business opportunities, which in turn has resulted in a substantial rise in the disposable incomes of the people, particularly, the middle class. Indian consumers are ever-evolving with the market—habits, lifestyles, tastes and preferences—especially with the advent of organized retailing malls and multiplexes. According to current estimates, over 50 percent of India's population are under the age of 25; furthermore, the majority of them are educated. This generation that grew up in the post-liberalization era is more receptive and adaptive to lifestyle changes (On device research, 2012).

A survey conducted by Nielsen indicated that Indian consumers continued to lead the global confidence index for the 2015 quarter. Piyush Mathur, President, Nielsen India Region said: "The optimistic trend in consumer sentiment continues. There are signs of a positive growth in consumer spending on consumer packaged goods, mainly because there has been a gradual decrease in concerns on job security, along with interest-rate cuts, and an increase in intention for home loans—thus enhancing the sentiment on the economy and portraying an optimistic picture for the future."

The increasing number of connected consumers. The Internet in India is no longer a limited-reach or primarily an urban phenomenon. The Internet user base is both expanding and diversifying to include rural and lower-income consumers across all age groups, especially internet usage via mobile phones and laptops. Consumers in all segments are using the Internet as their first stop in making their purchase decisions. BCG's Center for Consumer and Customer Insight surveyed users in 25 cities and found that more than half of those who have access to the Internet go online to make informed purchase decisions. This number varies among different categories of products and services, but it is on the rise everywhere. (Bajpai, Jain, & Samtani, 2015)

WOMEN

Indian women generally prefer traditional clothing, more so in Tier II and Tier III cities than Tier I cities. But, with an increasing exposure to "metro" lifestyle and improved level of income, there is a slow shift in the consumers of these tiers (Nielsen, 2012). The slow shift in consumer adoption of Western apparel poses a challenge for international apparel brands and retailers seeking to gain market share in the women's wear segment. Indian ethnic garments and garments mixing ethnic and Western styling have dominated the ready-to-wear market for Indian women since the mid-1990s.

Indian women select apparel by frequently visiting boutiques (Chattaraman, 2009). They like exclusivity and believe that smaller boutiques have better quality products. Many boutiques in India offer tailoring services.

▲ FIGURE 5.2 Picture of Bollywood actress Aishwarya Rai in traditional as well as Western clothing. This picture depicts the prevalence of Indian traditional clothing in the current times in India.

Women visit these boutiques to see their new design range, select the fabrics they like, and have clothes tailored. Many domestic retail chains offer fabric and tailoring services to meet this demand (Chattaraman, 2009). These stores hire a tailor or sign a contract with an external tailoring service to fulfill the tailoring needs.

The population of working women is increasing in India. Today, most women prefer to wear Western clothing to work as they consider it a sign of confidence. College students form one of the largest segment of women in India. Movies have a strong impact on the clothing habits of this population. T-shirts, shorts, skirts, and tops form a major part of their wardrobe. Traditional Indian clothing is kept for special occasions and festivals (Textile value chain, 2015). The women in their forties and fifties have become equally fashion concious and are encouraged to wear jeans and tops instead of traditional attire. The women-empowering socioeconomic paradigm is fast unfolding,

▲ FIGURE 5.3 Two Indian women (mother and daughter) have styled traditional wear with jewelry. They have a bindi (dot in the middle of the forehead). A red bindi is usually worn by a married women. Today, the bindi has been influenced by fashion trends and is available in many different colors and designs.

▲ FIGURE 5.4 Two Indian women in Indo-Western clothing. This type of clothing is very popular among the younger generation who want to wear Western clothing but are still attached to the traditional Indian designs.

especially in urban India. The income of women living and working in cities has increased, doubling the household income. YLR Moorthi, a marketing professor with Indian Institute of Management, Bangalore, believes companies are now on the cusp of building successful brands exclusively for women. Marketers expect this market to keep growing for the next couple of decades (The Economic Times, 2012).

MEN

Menswear in India registered a retail value growth of 15 percent in 2015. Indian male consumers are more concerned about their looks and appearance and are willing to spend more on apparel and accessories especially urban young consumers going to university, men joining the workforce and working men traveling more frequently (Euromonitor International, 2016). Among average income male consumers, brand awareness is moderate, brand loyalty is low, and retailer loyalty is high.

Clothing reflects lifestyle and social status among India's affluent male population. This group of consumers frequently travels overseas and purchases international brands during their travels. There is a high level of awareness of international brands among this consumer group. Although this is an important segment for international retailers to target, these consumers prefer to make their purchases abroad. As Dhiren Desai, vice president of an international brand in India, says, "Due to high import duties in India, many international brands in India are more expensive than many (not all) other countries. Also, for the purchases made in Europe, the consumer gets VAT (value-added-tax) refund making it even cheaper."

THE BEAUTY INDUSTRY IN INDIA

Since ancient times, Indian women have used homemade products for their beauty regimen. Some popular beauty products of the past have been hair oils, kohl pencils, and bindis. But the availability of a large variety of branded products and increasing brand consciousness among the middle class have piqued women's interest in purchasing high-quality, branded beauty products. International retailers have had to modify their offerings to suit the regional requirements of Indian women. For example, in general, Southern Indian women spend more on fairness creams and are more conservative than Northern Indian women in their choice of color cosmetics.

In 2015, the Indian beauty industry saw a rise in demand for natural, herbal and Ayurvedic products mainly due to strong promotional campaigns carried out by top players such as Hindustan Unilever, Colgate-Palmolive India, Dabur India, Marico, Godrej Consumer Products and Patanjali Ayurved (Euromonitor International, 2016). Experts predict that India's retail beauty and cosmetics industry, estimated at $950 million in 2015, is most likely to treble to $2.68 billion by 2020. Annual growth in the Indian beauty and cosmetics markets is estimated to remain in the range of 15–20 percent in the coming years, twice as fast as that of the US and European markets. Massooma, Editor at *New Age Salon & Spa* magazine and knowledge partner for "International Beauty Mart" (IBM) 2014, believes "awareness in India of the latest global beauty trends and the numbers are prompting more international players to set up shop and increase their presence in India" (Cosmoprof, 2015).

Indian men living in Tier I and Tier II cities have also begun spending a considerable amount of time on grooming. Beauty salons that specifically cater to men are cropping up all over the country. Indian men are not shy about frequenting these places anymore due to a general change in attitude toward grooming (Bhattacharya, 2009). Demand for skin whitening products by men as well as women, is driving the trend. Over the last five years, the market for cosmetic products has seen a growth of 60 percent. However, there is

▲ FIGURE 5.5 Luxury mall in Jaipur, India. These malls are a recent phenomenon in India. They house many high-end international brands and have a large clientele in India.

relatively slower growth for products such as anti-wrinkle creams, cleansers and toners compared to facial creams, moisturisers and fairness creams.

CHILDREN

In the past, parents preferred to buy functional clothing for kids over branded clothing. Children's garments were usually purchased from small stores and from street shops, and only very high-status families bought branded garments. This trend is gradually changing and the market for branded kids' clothing is growing, as disposable incomes rise and foreign cultures influence the way people dress. Influenced by mass media and peer pressure, today's kids are more informed and self-conscious and like to have a say in their clothing purchases.

Children's apparel includes clothing for kids between 1 and 14 years of age. Jeans, shorts, and shirts are the evergreen pieces in kids' apparel. It is a growing market in India that has huge untapped potential. Certain brands and apparel makers have tieups with Walt Disney, Warner Bros, etc. They use famous cartoon characters in their designs to appeal to children.

LUXURY RETAIL IN INDIA

The luxury market size in India is expected to increase from the current population of 10 million to 26 million households in 2025. In addition, the household income for this market will also increase by 1.7 times making it really attractive for any luxury retailer (Luxury Daily, 2016). In the past, when some luxury brands tried to enter the Indian market using their previous season's merchandise, they failed. Indian consumers are well aware of what each brand offers. The Internet revolution, and the consequent demand for Indian brainpower, has led to an economic boom that has created a whole new breed of wealthy, cosmopolitan Indians. Luxury buyers in India fall into three categories: the old rich, wealthy professionals, and first-generation entrepreneurs. The old rich buy luxury products to keep up their image; the wealthy professionals (CEOs and non-resident Indians) travel the world and buy luxury products to show off their foreign travels; and the entrepreneurs buy luxury goods to show off their wealth. Luxury products are not new to Indian consumers who have been purchasing them during their frequent trips abroad; however, having luxury stores in India is something new.

Indian consumers are sensitive to price, even in the luxury segment. They compare prices of products sold in India to those sold abroad before making purchases. "We want to bargain; we want to feel we have got a good deal," says Vikram Phadke, co-founder of the Indian retailer Evoluzione. Indian consumers feel uncomfortable making expensive purchases in India, surrounded by poverty. "Indian consumers have tremendous spending power, but also feel great shame in spending exorbitantly on luxury products in their home turf," says Charu Sachdev, head of the luxury retail wing of the Indian Sachdev Group. "But when in London, Paris, or Dubai, they will happily spend. Even NRIs (non-resident Indians) visiting their country of origin suddenly don't feel it is correct to spend so much on a bag or dress," says Vikram Phadke: "He wants to buy, but does not want to be seen as buying" (Sridhar, 2010).

According to a study conducted in 2016 by Assocham, increasing brand awareness and the growing purchasing power of the upper class in Tier II and III cities, the Indian luxury market is expected to cross $18.3 billion by 2016 from the current $14.7 billion growing at a compounded annual growth rate of about 25 percent. "The factors that have fuelled the luxury industry's growth are rising disposable incomes, brand awareness amongst the youth and purchasing power of the upper class in Tier II & III cities in India," said D.S. Rawat, secretary general, Assocham (The Economic Times, 2016).

▲ FIGURE 5.6 Indian clothing store in North India. This is an example of a mom-and-pop store. Such stores are owned by individuals and are seen all over the country. These are a part of the unorganized market, which is the majority of the retail market in India.

Indian consumers like to mix shopping for various product categories, such as luxury products such as designer handbags and other nonluxury items such as regular-priced clothing products. This aspect of Indian consumers makes it essential for luxury malls to have the right mix of stores. Malls in various parts of India that have not taken this factor into consideration suffer slow sales. To meet the demands of Indian consumers, some luxury brands are opening stand-alone stores in regular shopping areas. Luxury retail has tremendous potential in India and it will remain a growing market for years to come.

APPAREL RETAIL FORMATS: CHANGING ON A FAST TRACK

The diversity of retail formats in India is as prevalent as the diversity in its population. Even within the unorganized retail setting, there are many different formats. There are vendors who sell from carts, peddlers who carry baskets of products door to door, salespeople who host at-home parties, vendors who sell in the local weekly markets, and shopkeepers who own small shops selling basic necessities. Some of these formats are unique to India (mainly the traditional formats), whereas others can be found in other developing nations. Retailers are changing their store formats based on market demands and the margins are shrinking due to fierce competition. There is a movement toward smaller organized retail formats for better control over operations.

The retail sector in India is growing at a fast pace. Indian retailers are adopting various retail formats for their business which are best suited to them. For convenience, we can divide the Indian retail market into two formats: Traditional and Modern. The format classification is based on size and location of the store, assortment of merchandise, type and price of the merchandise offered, and the level of customer service.

TRADITIONAL STORES

These formats have been in existence for many centuries. They do not have a defined structure and are family owned. The most common are mom-and-pop stores, street markets, and stores that carry multiple brands or nonbranded merchandise.

▶ Mom-and-Pop Stores

Like mom-and-pop stores in the United States, these stores are family owned. The differentiating factors are that they are not only present in the main market areas but also in residential areas, and they provide a high level of service. So far, the mom-and-pop-store formats have been able to adjust well to the increasing number of organized retail stores because they have been around for a long time and have customer loyalty on their side. In addition, they provide micro credit to their customers making it really convenient for the consumers in small towns. These stores can give products to consumers in any quantity they want as the products are not packaged. Many of the mom and pop stores have been in existence for many decades and don't have to deal with the high rent for newer spaces (Indian Retailer, 2015). Because these stores are also set up near residential neighborhoods in both urban and rural areas, they are convenient. Mom-and-pop stores know their customers much better than any of the new entrants. Being small in size, they are able to make changes to their offerings at a much faster rate than any large retailer. They provide many desirable services such as home delivery, and credit to known customers. A problem that this format may face is price-based competition. With their inability to order in bulk or negotiate based on the size of an order, and no law protecting them from quantity-based pricing, they may eventually be more expensive than non-traditional retailers.

Apparel, textiles, beauty products, grocery, and many other varieties of products are sold through this format of stores. To keep up with the organized retailers taking over the market, some small retailers have been forming their own groups and hiring consulting firms to gain some competitive advantages. So, in the long run, even if this format is not able to survive in the large cities, they might still be able to have a market share in smaller Tier III cities and rural areas.

▶ *Street Markets*

In this format vendors sit along the roadside and sell different products such as clothes, furnishings, flowers, vegetables, and other items. This method of

▲ FIGURE 5.7 Street market on a busy street in Mumbai. These markets are present in all cities in India. They sell locally made, inexpensive, and average-quality merchandise. Among the clothing sold are cheap imitations of the Bollywood fashion or other very basic designs.

▲ FIGURE 5.8 Window display at a mall in India.

selling is not only popular in rural areas but also in Tier I cities such as New Delhi and Mumbai. On "market days" (any chosen day of the week) when the mom-and-pop stores are closed, street markets are flooded with vendors selling a much wider range of products. These street markets are popular by the names of the day of the week they set up shop. For example, if the local mom-and-pop stores are closed on Mondays and the vendors set up their goods on that day, it is called "Monday market." Street-side vendors occupy space outside the closed storefronts. These types of markets are usually found near train stations, bus stations, or main market areas. The vendor lays a piece of fabric on the ground and displays his or her products on it.

The setup with different vendors resembles a bazaar with colorful banners to get the consumer's attention. Usually street vendors occupy the same spot from week to week so that their customers can find them easily. Some street vendors even pay a small amount of money to shop owners to reserve a place. They sell clothing and other goods at highly competitive prices and hence attract the attention of their customers. The major problem with this method of selling is that, as cities take steps to expand roads and clear sidewalks, the street markets have less and less ground. Also, with very limited product offerings, they are not a threat to any other type of retailer. They do sell textile, apparel, and beauty products, but the offerings are mainly geared toward the lower to lower-middle-class populations.

▲ Exclusive Multiple Brand/Nonbrand Stores

A store that carries multiple brands or nonbranded merchandise falls under this category. These stores are not always chains but are privately owned and exist all over the country, usually in the main market area. These stores are more popular in smaller cities where department stores have not yet entered the market. They have a loyal customer base. These stores usually specialize in one category of clothing, for example saris or salwar kameez, and carry a wide range of styles in that category. They understand the local market really well and carry products based on the taste of their local customers. Modern retail formats are a threat to this format of stores. But the ability to change their products easily with new fashions is a big advantage for this format.

These formats are becoming popular in the retail of beauty products. Stores such as the Health and Glow chain carry beauty products of various brands. Consumers prefer shopping at these smaller stores for high-level and personalized customer service. Sephora in the United States would be an example of this kind of format.

MODERN FORMATS

Organized retail formats are a complete contrast to the traditional formats. The emergence of these formats in tandem with large malls has completely transformed the Indian retailing environment. Although the modern retail format is present only in Tier I cities and some Tier II cities, they are expected to grow at a very fast pace across India through 2020. Malls comprise 90 percent of the total future retail development in India. The entry of modern retail formats has revolutionized overall consumer spending, making them a very important segment of the Indian retail industry.

▸ Supermarkets

This format is most prevalent in food retailing. Supermarkets attract consumers looking for convenience, quality, and cleanliness while shopping. Supermarkets are nothing but modern grocery retailing in India and registered current value growth of 17 percent in 2015. This was stronger than the growth observed by traditional grocery retailers, which was 10 percent. The stronger growth was due to the increased footfalls by urban consumers at supermarkets. Young urban consumers prefer to shop for their groceries once a week, and appreciate the convenience to do so at supermarkets, as the offers given by these retailers when buying in bulk translate to lower pricing as compared to that of traditional grocery retailers. However, the size of traditional grocery retailers continues to be much larger than that of modern grocery retailers. Consumers continue to prefer traditional retailers when buying daily goods, as it requires less time, billing processes are much faster and free home delivery is available as well (EuroMonitor International, 2016). Apparel is not sold in these formats in India.

▸ Hypermarkets

In India's retail setup, food and groceries account for 76 percent of consumer expenditure. Hypermarkets typically stock both food and nonfood items (which include apparel and beauty products) at a 60 percent and 40 percent ratio respectively. Examples of such stores, which are similar to Walmart, are Big Bazaar (owned by Pantaloon Retail), Star Indian Bazaar (owned by Tata Trent group) and Reliance Mart (owned by Reliance group). This format is becoming successful in India as a one-stop shop for time-pressed city dwellers. Retailers have managed to maintain lower pricing, which is also attractive to the consumers and works well for building customer loyalty (India, 2009).

▶ Department Stores

Department store formats carry multiple brands and multiple product categories including apparel, textile, and beauty products. Domestic retail chains carry a variety of traditional Indian and Western apparel to cater to the Indian consumers. Due to their large size and need for high customer traffic in order to be profitable, these stores are located in metropolitan cities. Some examples of top apparel deparment stores are Pantaloon Retail (India) Limited, a large Indian retailer, which is part of the Future Group, and operates multiple retail formats in both the value and lifestyle segments. Headquartered in Mumbai, the company has over 1,000 stores across 71 cities in India and employs over 30,000 people. Lifestyle International (P) Ltd. is another retailer, a part of the prestigious Dubai based Landmark Group, which started its operations in India with the launch of the first Lifestyle store in Chennai in 1999. Today Lifestyle has positioned itself as a youthful, stylish and a vibrant brand. Another example is Shoppers Stop which is an Indian department store chain promoted by the K Raheja Corp Group, started in the year 1991 with its first store in Andheri, Mumbai. Shoppers Stop Ltd. has been awarded "the Hall of Fame" and won "the Emerging Market Retailer of the Year Award", by World Retail Congress at Barcelona, on April 10, 2008. With the launch of the Navi Mumbai departmental store, Shoppers Stop has 34 stores in 15 cities in India. Some other examples include Globus (owned by R. Raheja Group), Reliance Trends (owned by Reliance group) and Westside (owned by Trent Limited). Variety, novelty, and cosmopolitan ambience attract customers to these stores.

▶ Specialty Stores

This type of store format carries niche product categories, like Crate and Barrel in the United States. Besides home furnishings, categories include, but are not limited to, clothing, books, music, cosmetics, and medicine. Many retail chains have now established specialty stores that carry one of these categories. Single-branded stores, such as Levi's, Provogue, United Colors of Benetton, and Lee (India, 2009) have been in the Indian retail market since 1991.

▶ Company Owned, Company Operated

Many companies in India own and operate their stores, like Gap and Old Navy in the United States. Such vertically integrated companies own the stores and manufacturing units, and run the stores instead of franchising or licensing their brands to other retailers. In addition to operating their own stores, they also sell their products through other retailers. Companies that produce fabric for men's formal clothing such as dress shirts and suits own these kinds of stores. These stores also sell custom-tailored clothing for customers who would like to select fabrics and have shirts and suits made. Some of the best examples of these stores in India are Reid and Taylor, Park Avenue, and Raymonds. These stores carry the entire range of fabrics produced by the company and tailor formal clothes based on the customer's requirements. Among International retailers, there are Zara and Gap among others.

▶ E-commerce

By 2030, about 1 billion Indian consumers are expected to be online. Although total e-commerce sales amounted to only about $16 billion in 2015, India has become one of the most sought after countries for internet retailers. Amazon is a prime example of one such company; it hopes that India will be its second biggest market in the world.

Between Flipcart, Snapdeal, and Amazon, Indian e-commerce business has surpassed the sales of the top ten "brick and mortar" stores. A third of the Indian population being under 35 years of age and internet savvy, makes e-commerce a more attractive platform for retailers (India online, 2016).

Apparel e-tailing has seen a significant growth in the last few years. Online shopping has really taken off in India, due to lack of time, increased accessibility to fashion trends, and changing lifestyles and access to better internet services. There are multibrand stores such as yebhi.com, single branded stores that have chosen to add an e-commerce platform such as FabIndia, Zodiac, and niche market stores such as Babyoye.com. Although still considered to be in its infancy, the e-commerce industry in India is definitely an attractive market to invest in for an international retailer (Ankur & Aman, 2016).

RETAIL OWNERSHIP: CHANGING WITH TIME

In both the traditional and modern retail sectors in India, most stores are family owned. Among the traditional retail formats, the stores are run by family members and then passed on to the next generation. Depending on the size of the stores, the sales staff may be family members only or additional employees from outside the family.

The organized retail chains that first started in India were also family-run businesses. Many domestic retail chains are still family owned, such as Globus Stores and Ebony, but some, like Reliance and Pantaloon, have gone public, with stocks traded om the Indian stock exchange. There is no clearly established or recognizable ownership trend, be it private limited, public limited, or family owned, in India's apparel retail market. However, various factors, such as government regulations, taxation policies, the need for funding from various sources, and the need for talent, may influence ownership patterns. International retailers have used various ownership formats, including joint venture and franchise.

FDI REGULATIONS

Investment made by foreign companies in India is governed by the government's 1999 Foreign Direct Investment (FDI) Policy and Foreign Exchange Management Act. This defines all the rules and regulations to be followed by a foreign company interested in making an investment in India. In 2012, the Indian Government introduced two key reforms aimed at allowing greater FDI into the Indian retail sector. The delineation between single-brand and multi-brand retail, present for many years, was maintained—the former aimed at businesses that sell only their own goods to consumers whilst the latter was effectively concerned with addressing the opening of foreign-owned supermarkets in India. FDI was liberalized in both sub-sectors but to differing degrees (Wessing. 2015). For the retail sector, India has the following regulations for FDI as of May 2015.

1. For franchisee and cash-and-carry wholesale formats, foreign direct investment can be 100 percent. This means that the foreign retailer can own and operate the company and does not need any Indian partner.
2. For single-brand stores, such as Gap or Ann Taylor, the goverment approves FDI from minimum 51 percent to maximum 100 percent. Although the permitted FDI limit was increased from 51 percent to 100 percent, an investment of more than 51 percent FDI triggers the mandatory requirement to source at least 30 percent of the value of products from Indian cottage industries (businesses that have a total investment in plant and machinery not exceeding USD1 million). To be approved, products should be sold under the same brand internationally and branded during manufacturing. The foreign investor must own the brand. A single brand retail can now also operate as wholesale retail in India which has opened up a significant opportunity for global single brand retailers interested in the mix of retail and wholesale activities in India (Wessing, 2015).

3. The FDI permits 51 percent investment for multibrand store formats. However, introduction of foreign owned supermarket chains is politically sensitive and therefore heavily regulated. FDI of up to 51 percent comes with the following requirements:

- State government discretion: multi-brand retail outlets can only be set up in those states, which agree to allow it. So far, those are Andhra Pradesh, Assam, Haryana, Himachal Pradesh, Jammu & Kashmir, Karnataka, Maharashtra, Manipur, Rajasthan and Uttarakhand and the Union Territories of Delhi, Daman & Diu and Dadra and Nagar Haveli. At present FDI is therefore permitted in Bangalore, Delhi and Mumbai but not in other key cities such as Chennai or Kolkata.
- Minimum investment: the foreign investor must invest a minimum of USD100 million.
- Minimum extent of investment: at least 50 percent of the total FDI must be invested in backend infrastructure within three years. "Backend infrastructure" includes capital expenditure on activities such as manufacturing, packaging, logistics, warehousing and distribution but excluding investment in front-end units, land cost and rentals.
- Greenfield investment: investment in backend infrastructure must be in greenfield assets only (i.e. not through acquisition of supply chain/ backend assets or stakes from an existing entity; or use of backend facilities of any existing wholesale trading/cash and carry wholesale trading arrangement).
- No franchising: stores must be owned and operated by the entity attracting investment and set up as new stores, not through acquisition of existing retail stores.
- Sourcing from small industries: Like the single-brand requirement, at least 30 percent of the value of the manufactured or processed products must be sourced from Indian cottage industries. Note that the procurement of fresh produce is not covered by this condition.
- Minimum population requirement: FDI is only permitted in cities with a population of more than 1 million (determined by the 2011 census). Note, however, that the above requirement to invest in backend infrastructure can be anywhere in India, including in states that have not approved FDI in multi-brand retail.
- No online or wholesale trading: the entity attracting the investment cannot trade online or via a wholesale model. Although FDI is permitted

in cash & carry wholesale trading, any FDI in such a business must be through a different entity.

- ▶ Approval procedure: every application seeking approval for FDI in multi-brand retailing must be approved by two government departments—first by the Department of Industrial Policy and Promotion and then by the Foreign Investment Promotion Board.
- ▶ FDI in multi-brand retail has complex regulations mentioned above meaning entry into the market is unlikely to be straightforward. An example of FDI in multi-brand retail is Tesco, the UK's largest retailer. Tesco's application to invest USD110 million into a joint venture with the Tata Group was approved in December 2013. Trent Hypermarket, the joint-venture entity, operates under the Star Bazaar brand in India.

WHOLESALE CASH AND CARRY

Metro (Germany) started its operation as the first cash-and-carry business in India. Because FDI regulations allow 100 percent ownership for cash-and-carry business, international retailers are the sole owners of this type of format (India, 2009). In 2010, Carrefour opened its first store in the capital city of New Delhi with a cash-and-carry format. Earlier wholesale/cash and carry retailers were restricted from opening retail shops to sell to the consumer directly. However, a single brand can now undertake both Single Brand Retail and wholesale/cash and carry activities, subject to compliance with conditions. The biggest advantage of this format is that the retailers are free to make decisions without worrying about mutual agreement between partners as in a joint venture. One of the disadvantages is that they lack expertise or consumer understanding that an Indian partner would bring.

MANUFACTURING AND LOCAL SOURCING

Companies that set up manufacturing units in India are allowed to sell their products in the country. Among apparel retailers, Tommy Hilfiger, Levi's, and United Colors of Benetton have entered India this way. The government allows these companies to sell their products in India through their own stores, or franchising, local distributors, or existing domestic Indian retailers. The international retailer doesn't have to pay import duties on their products because they are manufactured in India, which means they can price their products competitively. But, they still need to understand the local consumer and provide the right merchandise mix.

FRANCHISING

Franchising is the easiest route by which to enter the Indian market because the international retailer does not need to invest in real estate and other store-related expenses. Most international retailers choose this format. Lacoste, Nike, Mango, and Marks and Spencer are among the retailers that operate in this format in India (India, 2009). By using this method, the international retailer does not need a large capital investment and gets to test the market; but the franchisee does not have a say in the kind of merchandise that should be sold and has to pay high duties on importing the apparel from the franchiser.

DISTRIBUTOR

Foreign retailers that set up distribution centers in India, including Swarovski and Hugo Boss, sell their products through domestic retailers. Distribution centers require less of an investment than opening actual stores. Also, local retailers understand the market.

JOINT VENTURES

Some foreign retailers have entered the India market through Joint Ventures. For example, Walmart joined forces with the Bharati group of India to open stores on the subcontinent. But finding a reliable and long-term partner in India is not always easy. The biggest problem that one can face in a joint venture is that the partnership falls apart after considerable investment. But, for companies where the partnership does work, a joint venture can be very beneficial, as the local partner has a better understanding of the Indian consumer than the international retailer.

INFLUENCES ON APPAREL RETAILING: SAME OLD CONSUMERS, NEW DEMANDS

Since 2000, apparel retail has changed from a made-to-order market to a ready-to-wear market. Increasing use of standard sizing in organized apparel retail may be a big reason for this change, along with the new generation's demand for instant gratification. They want to wear something without waiting for alterations. With increasing customer demand, retailers are improving their offerings in apparel as well as beauty products.

Apparel retailing in India underwent a major revolution in the century's first decade. New shopping avenues, the advent of organized shopping centers, and large shopping malls with food and entertainment under one roof have transformed Indian retail. The way Indian consumers have embraced this sea change is encouraging retailers to continue in the same direction.

MALL CULTURE

When Crossroads, the first mall of Mumbai, opened in 1999, it became a major tourist attraction in the city. Mall culture is something that an Indian consumer was not familiar with until the twenty-first century. Many Indians had never used an escalator, and shoppers suffered accidents as they struggled to get on and off the moving stairs. Today, Indian shoppers hop on and off escalators all the time at malls in every Tier I and many Tier II cities. Indian consumers are becoming accustomed to buying a large variety of products under one roof. Malls have become places to socialize and spend time with friends and family. India is booming as one of the largest shopping destinations in the world by offering a unique shopping experience in the mall. Domestic retail chains, such as Pantaloons, Westside, Lifestyle, and Globus, are part of these malls and also present as standalone stores in some cities, unlike in the United States where stores are usually either only in the malls or in strip malls as stand-alone stores. The shoppers get an international shopping experience in such retail outlets with self-service shopping, air-conditioned stores, and wide-open shopping spaces (Ernst and Young Inc., 2007).

BOUTIQUES

Boutiques have become very popular and operate in malls as well as other shopping areas. These stores may be one of a kind or part of a chain. They sell exclusive, unique or trendy products. The product range is vast, including apparel, jewelry, accessories, footwear, and so on. Satya Paul, Sheetal Design Studio, Ritu Kumar, Manish Malhotra, and Tarun Tahiliani are some top Indian designers that sell through their own boutiques. With an increase in disposable income among Indians, more and more people are buying designer wear (Ernst and Young Inc., 2007).

ART GALLERIES

Art galleries in many of India's Tier I cities display the works of independent designers who can't afford their own stores. The designer rents a gallery for a weekend, or the entire week depending on their budget. The products sold in art galleries are usually unique and cannot be found in regular stores. Many talented housewives develop designer outfits under their own private labels and then sell their lines in gallery exhibitions (Ernst and Young Inc., 2007).

ADVENT OF BRANDS

Brand name has been unimportant to a large percentage of Indians who have had their clothes custom made for a long time. But, as the apparel retail market becomes more popular and associated with good quality, Indian consumers are becoming more and more brand conscious. The first company to sell shirts under a brand name in India was Liberty shirts in the 1950s. Peter England, Park Avenue, Charagh Din, Raymonds, and Arrow are some leading domestic brands. A growing demand for jeans sparked the branding process in the country. Lee, Levi's, Seven Jeans, and Pepe Jeans were the first international denim brands to enter India. Today, some well-established domestic denim brands, such as Flying Machine, Killer, and Numero Uno, are competing fiercely with international brands. Branded apparel has captivated both the menswear and women's wear retail markets and is slowly capturing the children's market (Ernst and Young Inc., 2007).

FASHION WEEK

The Fashion Design Council of India (FDCI) had its first fashion week in India in 2000. India now has multiple fashion weeks in which designers from all over the country display their lines. These events attract buyers from all over the world. Extensive media coverage of these shows is increasing fashion consciousness among Indian consumers. Retail chains copy fashion-week trends to cater to customers who cannot afford the high-end clothing on display at these shows.

GETTING TO KNOW DOMESTIC COMPETITORS: A BOOMING DOMESTIC SECTOR

India has the largest unorganized retail market in the world. Traditionally a retail business in India was a small, family venture with the shop in the front and house in the back. Branded merchandise is becoming increasingly attractive to urban consumers with purchasing power. To compete with foreign brands, Indian retailers must realize the value of building their own stores as brands. It may help reinforce their market positioning, as brands communicate quality as well as value. A sustainable competitive advantage depends on combining products, image, and reputation into a coherent retail brand strategy.

The Indian retail scene is booming. A number of large corporate houses—Tata's, Raheja's, Reliance, Piramals', Goenka's—have already made a foray into this arena, with beauty and health stores, supermarkets, self-service music stores, bookstores, everyday-low-price stores, computers and peripherals stores, office equipment stores, and home/building construction stores. The organized players have attacked every retail category. Too many players in too short a time have crowded several categories without considering their core competencies or developing a well-thought-out branding strategy.

SHOPPER'S STOP

This chain was started by K Raheja group of companies in 1991. Shopper's Stop has the advantage of being among the first retail chains established in India. It is known for its expertise and acumen specific to current practices in the retail industry. For example, Shopper's Stop initiated the accumulate-points-for-discounts program called "First citizen's club" where customers' purchases received points to redeem for merchandise of a certain value. In 2005, Shopper's Stop differentiated itself by including a bookstore and coffee shop in all its stores (Indian Retail Report, 2009). Although the company has changed its image multiple times, it is known for quality of service, product offerings, and a cosmopolitan shopping environment. It has partnered with some international companies such as Mothercare and Allied Industries of Australia to provide unique products to its customers. It also has private labels that provide merchandise at a lower price range to cater to a wider segment of customers.

WESTSIDE

Trent Ltd., a part of Tata group, owns Westside, which was started in 1998. The company acquired Littlewoods, a London-based retail chain, and renamed it Westside. Westside was India's first private-label-only store chain. It carries apparel for all segments, such as footwear, cosmetics, household furnishings, and gifts, and has 49 department stores throughout the country. With its private label, the company offers unique products that draw repeat customers. In 2004, the company launched a hypermarket store format called Star Bazaar. They sell groceries, beauty products, consumer electronics, and household items at very affordable prices. The store also sells apparel. Trent Ltd. also has stake in Landmark, one of India's largest book and music retail chains (About Trent, 2010).

PANTALOON

The Future Group started Pantaloon in 1997. Pantaloon is now acquired by Adithya Birla Fashion & Retail Ltd. This group owns multiple retail formats, all of which have been highly successful and cater to a large segment of the population. Pantaloon is among the largest retail chain stores in India with 76 stores in 44 cities across the country. Pantaloon caters to customers who want good value for their money and are willing to pay extra for an improved lifestyle. It is one among India's largest and fastest growing big box fashion retailers. Pantaloon is constantly innovating designs, concepts and products by infusing the latest trends in fashion and clothing styles, it has a repertoire of lifestyle brands to cater to every consumer's needs across multiple occasions.

LIFESTYLE

Landmark Group, a Dubai-based company, started this chain in 1999. Lifestyle has an extensive footwear department and carries a large selection of both Western and traditional women's and menswear. It carries high-quality children's clothing and toys. The store carries about 250 national and international brands under one roof. Its prices are affordable. There are about 43 Lifestyle stores around the country (Lifestyle Department Stores, 2016).

HOW MATURE IS THE RETAIL INDUSTRY? A LONG WAY HOME

As domestic and international retailers flood the market, the Indian retail industry is rapidly expanding. Still, certain opportunities in apparel retail remain untapped. One of the major problems in the Indian apparel retail industry is the issue of standardized sizing. Retailers use their own size charts, so there is no consistency between a medium size at one store and the medium size at another. Consumers do not feel comfortable buying clothes without trying them on. Most retailers have a tailor on site that makes the alterations while the consumer shops. To avoid having to deal with alterations, some customers also prefer having clothing tailored as they can customize the garment to their needs. International retailers have an opportunity to streamline the shopping experience with the introduction of standardized sizing.

Although the Indian retail market is growing at a rapid pace with many modern retail stores being set up in different parts of the country, the market is still not a mature one. There are issues related to consumer expectations (example: mom-and-pop stores' delivery of groceries), which modern retail formats do not meet. Many grocery stores do not have proper refrigeration systems, so one does not always find fresh vegetables. International retailers can study the market and make changes to fill in such gaps.

BUYING FOR APPAREL RETAIL STORES: BETTER COST AND QUALITY AT HOME

India is rich in raw materials and low-cost labor, both of which are prerequisites for a successful apparel manufacturing business. The domestic textiles and apparel market in India is the fastest-growing market in the world (Ernst and Young, 2009). India has been an important source of apparel for retailers in Europe and the United States. With an increase in demand for apparel manufacturing in the domestic market, many of the manufacturing units that earlier made apparel only for export are shifting gears in order to cater to the domestic market. Exporters such as Gokaldas, Orient Craft, Royal Classic, Creative, and Shahi have either completely shifted to manufacturing for domestic brands or are considering doing so. India has many advantages that keep the domestic apparel manufacturers from looking outside. These are:

- ► Availability of raw materials and processing ability from fiber to apparel
- ► Availability of highly differentiated products with a setup for experimenting with new styles due to possibility of producing lesser quantities
- ► High level of flexibility with respect to order quantity and lead time for production
- ► A large, low-cost, and highly skilled labor population
- ► A large number of manufacturing units with high technology
- ► Removal of certain government restrictions of foreign investment in textile and apparel manufacturing.

Domestic retailers are mainly looking to local apparel manufacturers to provide them with good quality apparel. However, some retailers are going to China to diversify their sourcing. Many international retailers that have set up shops in India want to increase their sourcing from India. For example, in 2009 Marks and Spencer made plans to source 70 percent of its apparel from India as opposed to its then 20 percent (Jain & Dutta, 2009). Although India seems to be the right place for companies with an Indian retail presence to source apparel from, low productivity in factories might be a challenge.

Indian manufacturers are known for producing clothes with the "Indian look," which is achieved through use of embroidery, mirrors, and sequins sewn on the clothing, tunic-style tops, and bright colors (a preference among most Indian women, although color choices may vary based on location). But the manufacturing setup is also capable of producing jeans, undergarments, tailored suits, formal shirts, and many other categories of clothing. Many domestic retailers are sourcing a large number of accessories from China, and apparel from Thailand and Mauritius. But a large number of retailers are having their private label apparel produced within the country. High import duties are another deterrent for retailers. However, to source within the country, a retailer needs to set up an office.

Another problem with importing is the major difference in customer needs for the same season around the world. For example, the fall lines of most international retailers have clothing in dark and dull colors such as grays and blacks. Fall is the beginning of festival season in India where everybody dresses in bright cheerful colors such as red, yellow, and orange. International brands that import clothing from their home countries in the northern hemisphere end up with offerings that are not suitable for the Indian market at that time. Hence, retailers that do have a large number of stores, or have major expansion plans, can consider setting up a local office and sourcing domestically so that they can produce special lines for the Indian market. Retailers that want to set up shop in India can easily do their sourcing domestically (Textile Intelligence Report, 2006).

RETAIL CAREERS: SKILLED PERSONNEL WANTED

Lack of skilled labor is a major problem in the Indian retail industry. To tackle this issue, many educational institutes are offering short-term programs to prepare individuals for careers in retailing. The National Institute of Fashion Design (Delhi) and SNDT Women's University (Mumbai) offer undergraduate and graduate-level programs to prepare students for careers in buying and merchandising. Other private institutes, such as the Pearl Academy of Fashion (New Delhi), offer diploma programs in merchandising, buying, and retailing. Many other institutes offer short-term certification courses for store management positions (Career in Retail, 2009).

Formed in 2004, the Retailers Association of India (RAI) is working with some of the top business schools in the country to offer a master's program in retail management. An educational qualification in retail or a related area would work to one's advantage for a career in retail. A large number of positions are available in the apparel retail business, in different areas such as logistics, store management, sales, marketing, store design, information technology, buying, and merchandising. With an increasing demand for qualified and experienced personnel and lack of talent, the retail industry in India offers job candidates much higher financial gains than its counterpart in the United States.

Retail companies in India are open to international students applying for internships. Many companies get foreign exchange students through student-run AIESEC (Association Internationale des Étudiants en Sciences Économiques et Commerciales, www.aiesec.org) international network. Local chapters of this network place students in internships in many different countries. The companies help students to obtain a temporary work permit and pay them during the internship period. The only positions that are lucrative for foreigners in India are upper-management positions because junior-level positions do not pay very well. Some websites that can be explored to find jobs in Indian retail are www.indiaretailjobs.com, www.naukri.com, and www.monsterindia.com.

FUTURE OF APPAREL RETAIL: LAND OF PROMISE

The Indian retail market is estimated at USD 520 billion and is expected to reach around USD 950 billion by 2018. The current estimation of organized retail penetration is at 7.5 percent, and is expected to reach 10 percent by 2018. The retail growth is fueled by retail penetration in Tier-II and III cities, development in business models and operations, coupled with movement from unorganized to organized trade. Furthermore, the liberalization of FDI policy is expected to push global retailers to expand in the Indian market, further fueling the growth of organized retail in India (Ernst & Young, 2014). However, both domestic and international retailers should be ready to face numerous challenges when trying to expand in India:

- ▶ Lack of proper infrastructure. It causes a major problem with transporting goods from one location to the other. Traffic volume far exceeds capacity. The government is working on building a network of highways, but it will take years to have it in place (India, 2009).
- ▶ Supply chain issues. Inventory management is a top concern for companies, mostly the supply chain management such as low fill rates, long lead times and ordering cycles and lack of process orientation, which in turn results in high inventory holding, low turns and high investment in stock (Ernst & Young, 2014)

- Increasing cost of real estate. Many real estate agencies are developing malls and other retail space as demand increases. But the cost of retail space is rising apace. Along with rising real estate cost the unavailbility of retail space in appropriate locations for retail business is a major challenge (Ernst & Young, 2015).
- Lack of skilled labor. Skilled labor is needed to manage stores at the front as well as back ends. Retailers must bring in trained personnel to manage their stores. Some domestic retailers have teamed up with management schools to train people for retail setups. Other retailers have established their own retail schools. Some retail chains contact local unemployment offices to find people, train them, and hire them to work as sales staff (India, 2009).
- Pilferage in stores. Indian retailers lose up to $1.13 billion a year to shoplifting, employee pilferage, and vendor fraud. Indian retailers use security cameras, thorough checking of sales staff, and security tags on expensive products, but a more sophisticated system needs to be implemented; for example, having security tags sewn into the garment as many American retailers do.
- Transportation. Trains and trucks form the major modes of transportation in India. The operators are members of unions, and every year before peak season, they go on strike with a set of demands. Retailers need to be prepared for delays and plan ahead.
- Uncertainty about the mall culture. A large number of malls are popular and crowded, but there are many malls in India with vacant store spaces due to high rents. With so many malls cropping up all over the country, each one may not be able to generate enough foot traffic to make all its stores profitable. So, it may be wise to wait and watch. However, there may be no space for new entrants in the future.
- Government policies. Corruption at every level of conducting a business makes dealing with the government a challenge because investors need to deal with several people and a lengthy process to get simple approvals for starting a business.

All these factors need to be considered while launching a store in India. The Indian retail industry is growing by leaps and bounds, and every retailer is in a rush to gain first mover's advantage; but retailers in India need to think first. They must ensure that they have the right square footage for the products they want to sell. A large store may be attractive, but it may not provide the required return on investment. In the race to have the maximum number of stores in the country, retailers should not fail to measure the performance of each store on a regular basis. Poorly performing stores need to be monitored and proper action must be taken to fix the issues. It takes time to establish stores and become a leader in the market. Many retailers in the United States (e.g., Walmart, Gap) and Europe (e.g., Carrefour) are very familiar with the advantages of being slow but steady.

Although the Indian market may seem saturated with a large number of traditional and modern retail formats, there is enough scope for many more retailers to enter India. Some opportunities that international retailers can bank on are:

- ► Lack of modern retail setups. The unorganized sector still dominates Indian retail industry. As consumers become more demanding, modern retail facilities will attract them.
- ► Relaxation of FDI regulations opens oppurtunities for foreign companies to enter India and have much control on their choosen format. The regulations on e-tailing also enabled many foreign companies to have multichannel retailing.

SUMMARY

India is the world's largest democracy and has emerged as the fastest-growing major economy in the world. The retail industry in India has emerged as one of the fastest-growing industries which accounts for 10 percent of the total GDP of the nation and 8 percent of total employment in India. There are 12 million retail outlets employing more than 33 million people. India ranks seventh in market potential after the United States, China, Canada, the UK, Brazil and Germany. (Indian Chamber of Commerce, 2015). The organized sector includes licensed retailers operating in hypermarkets, supermarkets, malls, departmental stores etc. and, the unorganized sector dominated by a large number of small retailers comprising of local shops, general stores, chemists, apparel shops, pavement vendors, hand cart hawkers, etc. In addition, online retailing or e-commerce is a major area for retail growth in India. Retail e-commerce sales in India are expected to reach $17.5 billion by 2018, from $5.3 billion in 2014 (Indian Chamber of Commerce, 2015). The key drivers of retail growth in India are increasing disposable income, urbanization, rising internet penetration, higher brand consciousness, liberalization of FDI policies and attitudinal shifts of consumers. The diversity of Indian consumers poses a big challenge for the international retailers operating in India. Store layout and decor are critical for attracting Indian consumers. Consumers visiting the store frequently like to see changes in the layout; otherwise, they may get the impression that stock is not moving. Retailers in most countries need to micro market their products for stores in different regions due to variations in weather, ethnicity, and major industries. In India, apparel retailers must also attend to cultural differences. The prevalent culture of a state dictates unique behavioral characteristics. There are even cultural differences between Tier I, Tier II, and Tier III cities within the same state. Also the economic growth has resulted in Indians willing to invest in a life of luxury. Such a wish is the major cause behind India's growing consumerism and retail trends. The advent of international and national brands and easy accessibility to designer wear has changed the face of the retail clothing industry in India. Consumers' urge to be smart and fashionable has revolutionized this industry. Indian women have generally preferred traditional clothing. But, with an increasing exposure to "metro" lifestyle and improved level of income, there is a slow shift in the consumer's adoption of Western apparel. The population of working women is increasing in India. Most women today prefer to wear Western-style clothing to work as they consider it a sign of confidence. Menswear in India registered a retail value growth of 15 percent in 2015. Indian male consumers are more concerned about their looks and appearance and are willing to spend more on apparel and accessories especially urban young consumers. Children's apparel is a growing market in India that has huge untapped potential. International brands and apparel makers have tie-ups with Walt Disney, Warner Bros, etc. to use famous cartoon characters in their designs that appeal to children. The luxury market size in India is expected to increase from the current population of 10 million to 26 million households in 2025. In addition to that, the household income for this market will also increase by 1.7 times making it really attractive for any luxury retailers.

The diversity of retail formats in India is as prevalent as the diversity in its population. Even within the unorganized retail setting, there are many different formats. There are vendors who sell from carts, peddlers who carry baskets of products door to door, salespeople who host at-home parties, vendors who sell in the local weekly markets, and shopkeepers who own small shops with basic necessities. Some of these formats are unique to India (mainly the traditional formats), whereas others can be found in other developing nations as well. Retailers are changing their store formats based on market demands and the margins are shrinking due to fierce competition. There is a movement toward smaller organized retail formats for better control over operations.

Investment made by foreign companies in India is governed by the government's 1999 Foreign Direct Investment (FDI) Policy and Foreign Exchange Management Act. This governing policy and act defines all the rules and regulations to be followed by a foreign company interested in making an investment in India. In 2012, the Government of India introduced two key reforms aimed at allowing greater foreign direct investment (FDI) into the Indian retail sector. The delineation between single-brand and multi-brand retail, present for many years, was maintained—the former aimed at businesses that sell only their own goods to consumers whilst the latter was effectively concerned with addressing the opening of foreign-owned supermarkets in India. FDI was liberalized in both sub-sectors but to differing degrees.

Brand name has been unimportant to a large percentage of Indians who have had their clothes custom made for a long time. But, as the apparel retail market becomes more popular and associated with good quality, Indian consumers are becoming more and more brand conscious. India has the largest unorganized retail market in the world. Traditionally a retail business in India was a small, family venture with the shop in the front and house in the back. Branded merchandise is becoming increasingly attractive to urban consumers with purchasing power. To compete with foreign brands, Indian retailers must realize the value of building their own stores as brands. It may help reinforce their market positioning, as brands communicate quality as well as value. A sustainable competitive advantage depends on combining products, image, and reputation into a coherent retail brand strategy. As domestic and international retailers flood the market, the Indian retail industry is rapidly expanding. Still, certain opportunities in apparel retail remain untapped. One of the major problems in the Indian apparel retail industry is the issue of standardized sizing. Retailers use their own size charts, so there is no consistency between a medium size at one store and the medium size at another. Consumers do not feel comfortable buying clothes without trying them on. Most retailers have a tailor on site that makes the alterations while the consumer shops. To avoid having to deal with alterations, some customers also prefer having clothing tailored as they can customize the garment to their needs. International retailers have an opportunity to streamline the shopping experience with the introduction of standardized sizing. India is rich in raw materials and low-cost labor, both of which are prerequisites for a successful apparel manufacturing business. The domestic textiles and apparel market in

India is the fastest-growing market in the world (Ernst and Young, 2009). India has been an important source of apparel for retailers in Europe and the United States. With an increase in demand for apparel manufacturing in the domestic market, many of the manufacturing units that earlier made apparel only for export are shifting gears in order to cater to the domestic market.

CRITICAL THINKING QUESTIONS

1. How is Indian consumerism changing? Is this in favor of foreign retailers or domestic retailers?
2. Discuss FDI regulations in India. In what way do the regulations favor foreign companies?
3. Discuss the retail formats available in India and the opportunity for new retail formats in the country.
4. What are some of the main challenges that the apparel companies might face while doing business in the India market?

BUILDING BRANDS IN EMERGING MARKETS

As their spending power increases in emerging markets, consumers are facing a marketing environment where product choices and communication channels are exploding. Consumer empowerment is on the rise. There is a subtle difference in consumer behavior in emerging markets and developed markets. David Court and his coauthors proposed a new approach for understanding consumer behavior. They put forward a framework, which called as *consumer decision journey*, and identified four critical arenas where marketers can win or lose:

1. *Initial consideration* is the first stage when the consumer decides to buy a product or service.
2. *Active evaluation*, when the consumer investigates potential purchases.
3. *Closure*, when the consumer selects a brand at the moment of purchase.
4. *Post purchase*, when the consumer experiences the product or service selected.

It is at these stages companies have to develop marketing strategies to entice the consumers to buy their brand.

In this case study, we highlight the impact of three key differences between emerging- and developed-market consumers. First, harnessing the power of word of mouth is invaluable, as it seems to play a more important role in the decision journeys of emerging-market consumers than developed market consumers. Purchase decisions of emerging-market consumers are heavily influenced by recommendations from friends and family members. Often, word of mouth is a local phenomenon in emerging markets, partly because these consumers generally live close to friends and family. Word of mouth's relatively local nature means that companies in emerging markets are likely to reap higher returns if they pursue a strategy of geographic focus than if they spread marketing resources around thinly (targeting all big cities nationwide, for example). By attaining substantial market share in a cluster of cities in close proximity, a company can unleash a virtuous cycle: once a brand reaches a tipping point—usually at least a 10 to 15 percent market share—word of mouth from additional users quickly boosts its reputation, helping it to win yet more market share, without necessarily requiring higher marketing expenditures.

Second, getting brands into a consumer's initial consideration set is even more important in emerging markets, because that phase of the journey appears to have an outsized impact on purchase decisions. Emerging-market consumers tend to consider smaller sets of brands initially and, compared with consumers elsewhere, are less likely to switch later to a brand that was not in their initial set. To include a brand in the initial consideration set, consumers must be made aware of it. As a first step, visibility can be achieved through advertising on TV and other media. Here again, geographic focus is critical. Emerging-market consumers not only generally live close to friends and family but also tend to view local TV channels and read local newspapers rather than national ones. Gaining a high share of voice through local outlets in targeted geographies can help create a sense that a company's priority brands are in the forefront, which is valuable, because status-conscious, relatively inexperienced emerging-market consumers tend to prefer brands they perceive as leaders.

Finally, companies need to place special emphasis on what happens when products reach the shelves of retailers, because the in-store phase of the consumer decision journey tends to be longer and more important in emerging markets than in developed ones. Emerging-market consumers like to visit multiple stores multiple times mainly for collecting information, especially when they purchase big-ticket items. These consumers like to test products, interact with sales reps to collect product information, and negotiate with retailers to get the best deal. As a result, in emerging markets there is significantly more room to influence and shape consumer decisions at the moment of purchase. It is important to control the in-store experience.

Some of the challenges companies face in emerging markets arise when similar products are sold in tens of thousands of retail outlets. Companies often have limited visibility into what happens at the moment of purchase. Unpredictable merchandising, packaging, and in-store promotions can easily overshadow superior products. Companies therefore should carefully craft their advertising strategies. The first step in avoiding it is gaining a clear vision of the retail landscape as to how it is segmented and where the priority outlets are. Companies must then develop tailored control systems based on incentive schemes, collaboration with distributors, and retail-management programs. For priority outlets, companies must often deploy a heavy-control model using supervisors and mystery shoppers with supporting IT infrastructure to ensure that the performance of stores is visible enough to assess. For example, Unilever deploys massive resources in India to cover 1.5 million stores in tens of thousands of villages. Many of the salespeople carry a handheld device so that they can book replenishment orders anywhere, anytime, and sync their data with distributors.

Although these principles of harnessing word of mouth, getting brands into a consumer's initial consideration set, and emphasizing in-store execution may sound obvious, acting on them is not easy. It requires bold investment decisions, efforts to build the skills of local teams, and the courage to operate in ways that are fundamentally different from what headquarters might regard as normal. When emerging-market consumers perceive a brand consistently and positively across the major touch points, including friends and family and the in-store experience, they are far more likely to choose that brand, profiting companies that spend smartly rather than heavily.

Other strategies that companies follow in emerging markets include:

- Launch mega-brands rather than standalone brands: Well-known brands reassure in the emerging markets. Multinational brands operating in emerging markets are learning quickly. Many have either expanded their footprints into adjoining categories or rebalanced focus in favor of the "master brand." For example, Nestlé's Maggi is a bouillon cube brand in developed markets, but in India, it is used to sell instant noodles, milk, sauces and soup.
- Adjust product to maximize value justification: Emerging market consumers are "nervously optimistic." International brands are more expensive compared to local competitors, new consumers are sensitive to "value for money" as opposed to low price. Marketers should concentrate as much on increasing perceptions of value as lowering out-of-pocket expense.
- Arbitrage on trends driven by stage of economic development: Other factors being equal, economies and consumer motivations evolve in rather predictable ways. As markets progress from emerging to developed, marketers can retain the initiative by launching products in niche categories destined to achieve broad scale.
- Compete across, not within, categories: Emerging market consumers are new consumers. Advertising should work hard to convey a compelling reason to switch from one category to another.
- Develop rational and contextual communications: Emerging market consumers are confused by excess of new brand alternatives and have not yet attained confidence in their material stability. Communications shift the balance from emotional to rational benefits and dramatize product value. The importance of developing market rationalism is apparent in many ways. Companies try to increase persuasion by in-store

activities in changing buying decisions near the point of purchase. Making available the information portals such as online opinion leaders aids in shaping consumer preference.

REFERENCES

Atsomon. Y. Kuentz. J.F. & Seong. J. (2012). Building brands in emerging markets. *McKinsey Quarterly*. Retrieved September 2 from, http://www.mckinsey.com/business-functions/marketing-and-sales/our-insights/building-brands-in-emerging-markets.

The Huffington Post (2014). Emerging Markets, Consumer Insight and Business Strategy. Retrieved September 2 from, http://www.huffingtonpost.com/tom-doctoroff/emerging-markets_b_4893113.html

Discussion Questions

1. Consumer behavior is becoming a recognized discipline—but it still needs to be understood as a process that is different for emerging markets and developed markets. What is your advice to the foreign retailers trying to venture in the country?
2. Which strategies do you think would play a crucial role in building brands in emerging markets?
3. What are the most important things to be learned from this case study in relation to understanding consumers and brand building in emerging markets?

REFERENCES

About Trent (2010). Retrieved October 29, 2010, from http://www.mywestside.com/aboutus.aspx

Ankur, B. & Aman, J. (2016). Apparel e-tailing in India. Retrieved July15, 2016, from www.technopak.com/Files/apparel-e-tailing-in-india.pdf

Bajpai, S. Jain, N. & Samtani. K. (2015). The Changing Connected Consumer in India. Retrieved August 1, 2016, from, www.bcgperspectives.com/content/articles/center-consumer-customer-insight-marketing-changing-connected-consumer-india/

Bhattacharya, P. (2009, Feburary 2). *India Quarterly: Indian Beauty Market Roundup.* Message posted from issue of *GCI Magazine*. Retrieved December 1, 2009, from, www.gcimagazine.com/marketstrends/regions/bric/38826982.html

Chattaraman, V. (2009). *The Indian Consumer*. Retrieved June 3, 2016 from, www.udel.edu/fiber/issue4/world/indianconsumer.html

Cosmoprof. (2015). India's Cosmetics Industry may Treble by 2020. Retrieved August 7, 2016 from, www.cosmoprof.it/2015/01/indias-cosmetics-industry-may-treble-by-2020/

Ernst & Young Inc. (2007), *The Great Indian Retail Story*. Retrieved October 4, 2007 from http://www.ey.com/global/download.nsf/ India/Retail_TheGreat_Indian_Retail_Story/$file/TheGreat_Indian_Retail_Story.pdf

Ernst & Young Inc. (2014). The Retailer. Retrieved August 4, 2016 from, www.ey.com/Publication/vwLUAssets/EY-the-retailer-july-september–2014/$FILE/EY-the-retailer-july-september-2014.pdf

Ernst & Young Inc. (2015). The Retailer. Retrieved August 4, 2016 from, www.ey.com/Publication/vwLUAssets/EY-the-retailer-july-september–2015/$FILE/EY-the-retailer-july-september-2015.pdf

Euromonitor International. (2016). Menswear in India, 2016. Retrieved July 15, 2016 from, www.euromonitor.com/menswear-in-india/report

Globus (2010). Retrieved October 20, 2010, from www.globus.in/v2/about_globus.asp

Images Yearbook 2009: The Business of Fashion (2009). Images multimedia pvt. Ltd., New Delhi, India (2009). Retrieved July 15, 2016 from, www.pwc.com/en_GX/gx/retail-consumer/pdf/india.pdf

Indian Chamber of Commerce (2015). Sector brief. Retrieved July 24, 2016 from, /www.indianchamber.org/sectors/retail/retail-notes-june-2015/

India Brand Equity Foundation (2016). Indian textile and apparel industry analysis. Retrieved July 24, 2016 from, www.ibef.org/industry/indian-textiles-and-apparel-industry-analysis-presentation

India Online (2016). E-commerce in Emerging Markets. Retrieved July 24, 2016 from, www.economist.com/news/leaders/21693925-battle-indias-e-commerce-market-about-much-more-retailing-india-online

Indian Retailer (2015). Mom-and-Pop Stores Fight Back. Retrieved July 25, 2016 from, http://retail.franchiseindia.com/article/whats-hot/trends/Mom-and-pop-stores-fight-back.a3513/

India Retailing (2014). Why Should a Retailer Move to Tier-II and Tier-III cities. Retrieved July 25, 2016 from, www.indiaretailing.com/2014/09/17/retail/why-should-a-retailer-move-to-tier-ii-iii-cities/

Jain, C. & Dutta, D. (2009). Explore Beyond the Obvious: India's Position in the Global Textile and Clothing Trade. Retrieved December 7, 2009 from, www.udel.edu/fiber/issue4/world/explore.html

Lifestyle Department Stores (2016). Retrieved July 19, 2016 from, www.landmarkgroup.com/retail/fashion/lifestyle/

Luxury Daily (2016). Retrieved July 17, 2016 from, www.luxurydaily.com/how-luxury-brands-should-target-indias-super-rich/

Madison, A. (2003). The World Economy: Historical Statistics, OECD, Paris.

Nielsen (2012). Emerging Consumer Demand: Rise of the Small Town Indian. Retrieved, Retrieved July 17, 2016 from, www.nielsen.com/content/dam/corporate/india/reports/2012/Emerging%20Consumer%20Demand%20%E2%80%93%20Rise%20of%20the%20Small%20Town%20Indian.pdf

On device research (2012). The Great Indian Consumer Market-A Close Up View From An Insider's Prespective. Retrieved July 17, 2016 from, https://ondeviceresearch.com/blog/the-great-indian-consumer-market-a-close-up-view-from-an-insiders-perspective

Retail (2009). Retrieved November 10, 2009 from, www.ibef.org/industry/retail.aspx

Sheth, K. & Vittal, I. (2007). *How Half the World Shops: Brazil, China, and India.* Retrieved July 4, 2016, from, www.mckinseyquarterly.com/Americas/How_half_the_world_shops_Apparel_in_Brazil_China_and_India_2075

Sridhar, L. Different Strokes, The Luxury Consumer in India Today is Difficult to Stereotype. Retrieved October 20, 2010 from, www.businessworld.in/bw/storyContent/2009_09_18_Different_Strokes.html

Textile Value Chain in India (2015). Changing Habits of Women's Wear in India. Retrieved July 16, 2016 from, www.textilevaluechain.com/index.php/article/industry-general/item/367-changing-habits-of-women-swear-in-india

The Economic Times (2012). Why Women Consumers Matter and What Companies are Doing About It. Retrieved July 20, 2016 from, http://articles.economictimes.

indiatimes.com/2012-03-27/news/31245046_1_indian-women-women-power-consumer-spending

Wessing, T. (2015). Foreign direct investment in the Indian retail sector. Retrieved July 20, 2016 from, www.lexology.com/library/detail.aspx?g=6654961d-a7e3-4cb8-839f-670bb32382fd

RUSSIA

Diana Bank Weinberg

Andrey Gabisov

Jaya Halepete

OBJECTIVES

After reading this chapter, you will

▸ Know the unique characteristics of Russian consumers

▸ Understand the Russian retail industry and its challenges

▸ Grasp the regulations for foreign direct investment in Russia

▸ Know the various entry formats chosen by foreign retailers

In 1991, Russia opened a new chapter in its history of more than a thousand years when the breakup of the 74-year-old USSR made it an independent republic. Russia was an isolated country by the end of the Cold War. Today, the Russian market continues to deal with: logistical issues, infrastructure problems (including delays at ports due to congestion), high custom fees and taxes, poor quality of products, red tape, and corruption. Nevertheless, economic reforms and an abundance of natural resources have helped Russia to return to its rightful place on the world stage (Table 6.1). Russia possesses one of the world's largest reserves of gas, oil, coal, and other minerals and energy resources (Worldatlas, 2016), and it ranks among the highest exporters of natural gas, oil, and steel. However, due to its over-reliance on commodity exports, Russia is vulnerable to changing commodity prices all over the world. The government is trying to develop diverse sectors of the economy, such as technology and retail, to reduce Russia's dependency on exports.

TABLE 6.1 Fast Facts about Russia (2015)

Capital	Moscow
Population	146,6004 million
Type of government	Federation
GDP (Purchasing Power Parity; in US$	$3.471 trillion ($14,000 per capita)
Age structure	0–14 yrs: 16.7 percent 15–64 yrs: 69.7 percent 65 yrs plus: 13.7 percent
Religion	Russian Orthodox: 15–20 percent Muslim: 10–15 percent Other Christian: 2 percent Unspecified or None: 63–73 percent
Ethnicity	Russian: 77.7 percent Tatar: 3.7 percent Ukrainian: 1.4 Bashkir: 1.1 percent Chuvash: 1 percent Other, unspecified and none: 14.1 percent

Source: CIA factbook.gov (2016); US Commercial Service Hong Kong, (2015)

Since 2008, a drop in the price of oil has hurt the Russian economy, but it still remains an attractive country for investment, also due to the devaluation of the ruble since Russia's annexation of Crimea in 2014, its ongoing conflict in eastern Ukraine and the imposition of financial sanctions by Western countries (Rogov, 2014). According to American consulting firm A.T. Kearney (Ben-Shabat et al., 2015), "Russia remains Europe's largest consumer market, with rising disposable incomes and an expanding middle class, and it offers massive growth opportunities for retailers with a long-term approach." The average per capita income is increasing, so consumers are spending more. Rising wages, increasing standards of living, and changing consumer habits, along with growth in the retail sector, are changing the face of Russian retail. The Russian market is highly fragmented. For example, the top five food retailers' sales account for only 7 percent of total sales, leaving room for large retail chains to enter the market, grow, and take the lead. It is not very expensive to acquire domestic companies, due to their low valuation.

The first quarter of 2010 saw a growth of about 57 percent in the Russian clothing market, spurred by an increase in customer demand, the entry of international retailers, such as Italian luxury fashion house Dolce & Gabbana and Japanese casualwear designer Uniqlo, and increase in sales of brands such as Zara and H&M. Many luxury retailers who exited the market during the recession of 2008 have been gradually returning. Hence, Russia as a retail market is regaining its popularity among international retailers due to its growth of 7.8 percent from 2006–2013. Nonetheless, the Russian retail industry is highly fragmented, with the top eight international players controlling under 20 percent of the market: X5 Retail Groups, Magnit OAO, Auchan Group, Metro AG,Dorinda Holding, Lenta OOO, Dixie Group OAO, and Sedmoi Kontinent chains. In 2012 Tander ZAO, X5 Retail Group and Dixi Group continued active organic growth by opening new stores. In the first six months of 2012, X5 Retail Group opened 171 new stores while closing only 12. Over the same period Tander ZAO opened 272 new stores under its Magnit brand. Intensified competition in major cities means it will need tremendous efforts for new stores to break even (Kolchenikova and Konstantinova, 2013).

THE RETAIL LANDSCAPE: WESTERN IS GOOD

Retail has been one of the fastest-growing markets in the Russian Federation. When the Soviet era ended, many Russians started small businesses in retail. Huge economic growth followed an economic crisis in 1998, in which the Russian economy was overwhelmed by massive debt, low energy prices, and a host of other political and economic issues. The Russian ruble dropped three times more than the United States dollar, wiping out many Russian companies, especially those with low levels of management and "Red Directors," CEOs with Soviet-only experience who failed to acknowledge the laws of the capitalist market, such as the need for marketing. Significant changes have occurred since 1998. The Soviet legacy has given way to new ideas and more professional management. Vladimir Putin ushered in accompanying economic and political changes when he became president in 2000. Under his government the system didn't become fairer and less corrupt, but it definitely became more economically and financially stable, which business requires. The retail industry has become more modern, and many foreign investors have entered the

▲ FIGURE 6.1 Saint Petersburg, Russia on December 25, 2016.

market, especially since 2012, when Russia joined the World Trade Organization (WTO).

In the mid-1990s, standards of living dropped significantly, and people had no money to buy basic consumer goods. There was no middle class, except for a small segment in Moscow, the capital and most populous city. A segment of extremely rich people became wealthy through shady and corrupt deals. This wealthy class had no idea which products were good or bad. After three quarters of a century of communist living, they were ready to consume everything from abroad and price was not a concern. Companies such as the premium multibrand apparel chain Bosco di Ciliegi and JamilCo, a retail chain that sells exclusive-right premium brands such as Burberry, Escada, and Sonia Rykiel, and middle-segment brands such as Timberland started their businesses during this period. They are industry leaders today.

Most future retailers and brands came from Russian distribution companies that were working with European brands. For example, Bosco Sport, which outfits the Russian Olympic team, is owned by Bosco di Ciliegi, which distributes many foreign premium brands. The Russian retailer Finn Flare was originally set up in Finland and has grown to more than 50 stores in Helsinki, Moscow, Saint Petersburg, and Astana. Its franchising network consists of about 130 stores across Russia and Kazakhstan. In 1969, Finn Flare hired a new export manager named Raimo Aaltonen, who would go on to develop the business to the highest standards and in 1991, he bought the business. During the same year, a young Russian entrepreneur named Ksenia Ryasova started her own business in Russia. She sold apparel from Vietnam, where she had lived for three years, and then started her own multibrand retail chain, "People in New." In 1996, she met Raimo Aaltonen and signed an exclusive distribution agreement for the Finn Flare brand in Russia. According to the agreement, she could produce her own apparel designs under the Finn Flare brand and mix them with the assortment that was coming from Finland. The "People in New" brand had to be terminated because of the overwhelming success of Finn Flare. The Russian Finn Flare distributor became a huge name in Russia, and in 2006, Ms. Ryasova bought Finn Flare and became its president.

The success of Finn Flare revealed Russian consumers' preference for Western goods and Western brands. In the 1990s, Russian manufacturers could not deliver either quality or stable production, but Russian distributing companies were growing rapidly. Unfortunately in 1998, the economic crisis killed many small and medium businesses. As many small companies went bankrupt, the time was ripe for introducing new formats and new business technologies.

▲ FIGURE 6.2 Russian President Vladimir Putin delivers a speech during the military parade March of the Victorious in Belgrade, Serbia. President Putin arrived in Belgrade to commemorate the city's liberation by the Red Army and Yugoslav Partisans in 1944, during World War II.

Retailers that survived the first wave of bankruptcies changed their marketing strategies. They began catering to middle- and low-income consumers. Imports of cheaper products from Asia picked up pace. Russian manufacturers had to rethink their production and were forced to create lower-priced products. Due to a lack of funds, many of the largest players could not invest in the retail sector.

By 2000, retailers began to enjoy economic growth. Retail chains developed. Strong retail chains that had established themselves in Moscow and St. Petersburg now looked to expand in other regions. Small stores began consolidating their businesses to compete with large retailers. Foreign investors entered the market, bringing new technology and increased competition. Retail chains became powerful and began dictating terms to producers and distributors. From 2005 to 2008, retail chains developed rapidly and their management became more professional. Large retailers enjoyed steady growth. The market became stable and transparent. The manufacturing industry was reborn. During this period, the level of competition was the highest among retailers.

Many retailers began expanding, and with money to spend, retailers began diversifying their businesses.

Since the end of 2008, competition among retailers has intensified. Political stability and economic growth in Russia prompted many foreign retailers to invest in the market. Some Russian retailers entered the middle-income segment. Due to the increasing number of retailers, the demand for real estate grew. Real estate in Moscow and St. Petersburg is very expensive, which hindered further expansion. During the world financial crisis of 2009, many retailers left the market. There was then availability of store space in malls, but it became hard to get financing and even harder to get consumers. Nevertheless, some mass-market foreign retailers (such as H&M) decided to enter the market. They had resources, cheap products, and little competition. Existing retail outlets and stores lacked cash to cover expenses. Small- and medium-sized businesses suffered from this more than large retail chains. They were not ready to face new competition. Large apparel companies such as those in other industries changed their business models to focus on low-income segments of the market. But apparel in Russia is still priced higher than in many other countries, which affects consumption.

Many industries in Russia are updates of Soviet state-owned enterprises, but retail is an exception. Entrepreneurs have introduced not only quality products from all over the world, but also all modern trading technologies, workplaces, and formats, thus creating a very different retail market.

CONSUMERS: DEPRIVED NO MORE

Russian consumers have shed their "sleeping bear" image, now spending more than other European consumers. Russian consumers are similar to consumers in the developed economies, but the level of importance given to various shopping attributes is different. Russian consumers pay more attention to communicating status and the need for uniqueness than consumers of developed nations (Karpova, et al., 2007). In the past, Russians were satisfied with cheap imitations. But now, the new consumer mantra is "Quality is worth the money." For a long time, consumers did not have many options when shopping for clothes due to a lack of established branded stores. These consumers were also not willing to overpay for apparel and were looking for better quality and a range of products. In 2007, foreign retailers entered the market to meet the demands of Russian consumers. Nonetheless, private-label store brands have had less success in Russia than in many other markets. 73 percent of the Gain

Report respondents still don't buy them (Kolchenkova and Konstantinova, 2013).

Consumers in large cities and regions beyond vary drastically. Retailers interested in expanding in different regions of Russia need to understand these variations and cater to distinct needs. For example, in St. Petersburg, women like Scandinavian style with less bijouterie and not very bright colors, whereas in Kazan, women like bright colors and sparkling jewelry.

Russian consumers spend twice as much on apparel as Europeans and Americans. About 28 percent of their income goes toward apparel purchases (Advertology, 2008). The majority of these purchases are made to update their wardrobes (Fashioner, 2009). Although it is difficult to generalize consumer behavior for all the cities in Russia, it is true for many regions with prominent retail chains. Fast fashion is very popular in major cities, but casual and sportswear is the most popular category in many regions. A market for evening-wear has developed only in Moscow and St. Petersburg.

Russian consumers mainly like to shop at large malls, followed by small stores and smaller malls, and an even smaller group buys from street vendors (Fashioner, 2009). As a rule, shopping malls located in city centers have one or more cinemas, restaurants, grocery retailers, durable goods retailers, souvenir stores, cosmetic retailers and beauty salons. Some property developers also allocate space for sports and fitness clubs under the roof of a shopping mall. In 2011, over 25 shopping centers were completed in Russia. Moscow and St. Petersburg still account for the highest number of malls in Russia. At the end of 2011, approximately 45 percent of all shopping centers in the country were in these two cities (Kolchenikova and Konstantinova, 2013).

The high cost of real estate and corruption make apparel in Russia very expensive. But premium segment consumers are willing to pay a lot more for apparel than their counterparts in other European countries. Paying more money for a product is in itself a status symbol (Levinskij, et al., 2010). Russians are brand conscious and willing to pay more for branded apparel than non-branded apparel and prefer foreign brands for durable goods. Many Russian consumers who were raised in the Soviet era desperately want to own Western brands, which were very scarce in their youth. This proclivity toward spending more to show status is one of the reasons why almost 71 percent of Russians do not have any savings at all (FDU, 2010).

In 1998, people spent more than half of their incomes on food, but that expenditure is now being replaced by spending on goods and services, recreation, and education, among others, mainly because of the increase in disposable income and the desire to emulate the Western lifestyle. Almost 15 percent of Russian shoppers like to experiment with new brands on a regular basis, and this number is even higher (22 percent) among 16- to 24-year-olds. Brand name is very important for Russian consumers, and they associate high quality with foreign apparel (Russia, 2004/2005).

MEN

In 2006, men's clothing and footwear represented only around 20 percent of the products available, and the lack of specialized stores for men came to the attention of leading retailers. For example, in 2006, the underwear retail chain Dikaya Orkhideya launched specialized stores selling men's underwear under the VI Legion brand. From 2009 to 2013, menswear from Europe to Russia increased from 502 million euros to 812 million euros, an increase of 62 percent during this period of time (Döpfer, 2014).

Who is the Russian male consumer? Russian men generally come to the store with an idea of what they want and what they need. They very rarely come to the store to buy something just for fun. Mostly, they don't get any pleasure from shopping. That's why they like quick and professional service. Fashion authority for them is a shop assistant, girlfriend, or wife. If teenagers check magazines for new trends, the older generation may not. Interestingly, men spend less money on apparel than women and also consume less. For example, in 2009 only 41.2 percent of men bought themselves something new (compared to 58.8 percent of all women).

The small male population accounts for a lower level of men's apparel consumption than women's. However, men's income is expected to increase as part of post-recession economic growth. In addition, a new generation is growing up. The 21- to 30-year-old group are children of modern culture with a keen attention to fashion. An impressive change in behavior patterns should result in more frequent consumption. It gives industry analysts reason to forecast that, notwithstanding the financial crisis, menswear and footwear retailers will grow faster than womenswear.

WOMEN

Andreyeva (2006), an associate professor who specializes in research on marketing of luxury goods and fashion marketing, describes Russian women this way: "The variety of fashionable images and modern fashionable women in Russia is amazing! All palette of style, all colors are present in the modern Russian fashion: from international trendsetters to unique Russian national authenticity.

Ability to change depending on a situation or context, as it seems to be is a unique feature of Russian women. It is not important whether there was this context at the time of Ivan the Terrible, Peter the Great, or Joseph Stalin. Russian women always possessed the unique ability to survive, love, and be fashionable."

Russians have a very specific nature. They differ from other Europeans. Twentieth-century English anthropologist Geoffrey Gorer (1962) has characterized Russian women with actions and feelings that are difficult to understand. Russians can combine humility and impudence, cruelty and goodness, heathenism and Christian Orthodox religion. Russians are known to run to extremes. A similar behavioral pattern still applies to apparel buying behavior. On the one hand, Russian women like to imitate Western ways, and their tastes are becoming more and more cosmopolitan. On the other hand, however, they display a distinctly Russian bent toward unpredictability. Russian women value the opinions of others very much, but they value the opinions of their men secondarily. They rate the opinions of other women and their girlfriends first. Russia is a huge country with many different nationalities and religions. It means that consumer behavior can vary considerably. But in most cases, these rules apply.

Most women can't afford to be only homemakers in Russia. They have to work and still fill traditional roles (Russian women in America, 2009). Women make up 46.9 percent of the employed population in Russia. Women are the majority in public health service (85 percent), education (81 percent), credit and finance (78 percent), and information and accounting services (75 percent), but only 22 percent of the labor force in the construction industry.

Russian women like to dress well and tend to invest heavily in their wardrobes, including shoes. Working women, who have husbands to support them, have more money to spend. A young woman between the ages of 20 and 25 spends two-thirds of the funds available to her on apparel and accessories. In the retail season in 2015, European merchandise of women's outdoor jackets and coats to Russia increased by 21 percent, while dresses increased by 17 percent, denim pants by 27 percent and trousers by 13 percent (Döpfer, 2014). Young women also make their boyfriends buy apparel for them. Married Russian women with children and single mothers have a negligible amount to spend. Women younger than 22 shop at street vendors and buy inexpensive apparel imported from China, South Korea, and Turkey. These younger women do not have any preference for brands.

Unfortunately, income never improves for many Russian women, who continue to shop at the street vendors and non-prestigious shopping centers

▲ FIGURE 6.3 Modern Russian woman dressed for a fashion show.

throughout their lives. Young single women earning well may shop for brands in the malls. Women over the age of 27 are considered "older." They tend to dress more conservatively. They wear knee-length skirts or longer, show less cleavage, and dress in suits. Although older women don't seem as provocative as the young women, even they wear outstanding clothes, transparent tops, and short dresses (Interesting facts, 2009).

Russian women like to buy jewelry, especially rings and necklaces. Brand reputation and craftsmanship are crucial (Style & Design, n.d.). The drab Soviet era is long gone, and today's Russian female consumers are fashionable, quality-conscious, and brand aware. Rather than buying simply because of the label or for the prestige of the brand, Russian consumers are increasingly looking for better designs, fabrics, and workmanship. Russian designer Valentin Yudashkin says, "In Russia, women always aspired to look and dress beautiful. Nowadays when everyone has more of an opportunity (to dress up), it is designers' duty to help women in that."

Although Russians have a deep-seated penchant for luxury clothes and jewelry, there is a fast-growing trend toward the casual (Russian passion for

▲ FIGURE 6.4 Chanel creative director Karl Lagerfeld appears at the fashion show of Chanel's Paris-Moscow ready-to-wear collection at the Maly Theater, 2009.

fashion, 2009). This trend, coupled with the "trading down" (buying less expensive clothing) and "back to basics" (buying more basic clothing such that more mix and match combinations are possible) approaches adopted by Russian buyers, may bolster clothing sales in Russia during bad economic times. Russian women, who comprise the major fashion customers, no longer slip on skyscraper-high heels to go shopping and are opting for a softer, less flashy look. As Russian consumers adopt a more casual lifestyle, business attire is giving way to comfortable clothes at the office. Many retailers believe that athletic clothing is poised to grow; there is a rising interest in sports and a greater awareness among Russian consumers of healthy lifestyles (Russian passion for fashion, 2009).

CHILDREN

Children constitute about 20 percent of Russia's 142 million people. With the middle class growing in Russia, the demand for better-quality and imported clothing for children is on the rise. Children's goods have been growing especially fast and Russia became the largest market in Europe for toys in 2011, overtaking Germany's market, formerly the biggest in Europe. In May 2012, the British toy store Hamleys opened a large 1,700 square meter store in central Moscow's Evropeisky shopping center (Aris, 2012). The demand for good-quality apparel exceeds supply. About 10 percent of higher-income Russian consumers shop for their children at malls and boutiques. They prefer to buy only imported clothing. About 30 percent of Russians cannot afford even inexpensive locally made products; they buy cheaper Chinese imports at open-air markets (Parshukova, 2004).

THE BEAUTY INDUSTRY IN RUSSIA

Russia is the fourth-fastest-growing beauty and toiletries market in the world (Blagov, 2007). More recently, a growing demand for high quality and individualized cosmetic products was created by both foreign and local manufacturers as the awareness of different skin and hair types has resulted in understanding the advantages of using a full range of products for each type. Previously considered only for beauty, cosmetics started to be viewed as a means to achieve general improvement in health. Beauty salons and spas are becoming more popular, although due to the recent economic downturn, there is a growing demand for professional products for home use. Additionally, with the local currency depreciating, prices on imported cosmetics and toiletries are increasing, thereby intensifying demand for mass market products with a combination of price and quality (US Commercial Service Hong Kong, 2015).

About 30 percent of Russians spend $90 per month on beauty products. The most profitable sector among all personal care lines is skincare. Maybelline, MaxFactor, and L'Oreal are the top brands in mass beauty products. But, for facial and body care, Kalina, a local brand, is the top seller. Russian consumers believe that a domestic product is best suited for Russian skin. This belief, however, does not apply to luxury brand cosmetics. Some of the niche luxury brands, such as Editions de Parfums and Frederic Malle, have been well received in Russia. International luxury brands have a sizable market.

More than seven decades of communism and its emphasis on function have left Russian women craving beautiful clothes and looks. Plastic surgery, skincare treatments, and other services that foreigners took for granted were only available for the Soviet elite. But there was a huge demand from the mass market after communism collapsed. The beauty industry has grown at the rate of 20 percent annually since 2000, with a slight slowdown around 2005. The Russian consumer is also showing greater interest in men's products along with natural products. Brands such as Givenchy for men are being heavily marketed to capture men's growing interest in beauty products. The beauty and personal care industry saw high current retail value growth in 2015. This was driven by increased unit prices as a result of ruble devaluation, despite companies' efforts to restrain hikes in unit prices by reducing pack sizes (Euromonitor International, 2015).

▶ *Beauty Industry and Women*

From 1997 to 1999, almost 40 percent of beauty products were sold through kiosks, open markets, or department stores. Today, specialty beauty stores, direct sales, and pharmacies are the most popular places for buying beauty products. Hypermarkets, the Internet, and drugstores are other popular shopping formats for beauty products. Consumer demand for higher-quality products along with a better shopping experience spurred the development of new formats. Russian women prefer shopping where they can get help from skilled staff and makeup experts. L'Etoile (one of the main distribution channels of cosmetics, enjoying 40 percent of the Russian market) and Ile de Beaute are the top two beauty retailers in Russia. Still, Russia is far from being a saturated market (Grishchenko, 2009).

Both mass-market (like Avon or Lumene) and niche brands (like MAC) are working on getting the attention of Russian consumers. Although the beauty segment is in its infancy, it is likely to become more popular towards the end of the decade. Intensive advertising helps consumers learn about a brand, which generates profits for it. Russian consumers who experience niche brands for the first time during foreign travel look for them when they get back home. The beauty industry should be a very attractive product segment for international retailers interested in entering the Russian market.

Retailers face certain challenges in this segment. This is the reason for the attractiveness of direct sellers such as Amway, Mary Kay, and Oriflame, among others. It is very difficult to find distributors who can deal with logistics issues such as lack of good roads and warehouses, the high price of fuel, and low level of infrastructure. Changes in import regulations (for example, uncertainty over a customs clearance regulation in 2010 when Russia, Belorussia, and Kazakhstan united in a Custom Union) can also create problems. So it is essential that foreign investors do their homework and plan their entry strategy carefully in order to succeed in the Russian market.

▶ *Beauty Industry and Men*

The men's cosmetic industry is becoming very important and is growing rapidly in Russia. The current growth projection is about 15 percent annually for the next ten years, which is anticipated by the results of 2005 that summed to $195.4 (Euromonitor International, 2016). Men between the ages of 30 and 50 show a high level of interest in beauty products. The most popular brands are Clarins, Lancôme, and Biotherm homme (Russian beauty products, 2010).

Skincare has become part of the daily routine of a large segment of Russian men. Initially women were the primary purchasers of cosmetics for their men, but now men buy beauty products for themselves. They visit stores to purchase cosmetics and are becoming active in learning about new products and trying them. They make purchases of cosmetics in specialized stores and beauty salons. Men use shower gels, deodorants, after-shave lotions, hand and foot creams, facial scrubs, and cleansing gels (Cosmetics in Russia, 2009). With the growing interest of Russian men, cosmetics are beginning to become a worthwhile market for foreign retailers.

LUXURY RETAIL IN RUSSIA

Moscow is considered one of Europe's most fashionable cities. Luxury fashion products are sold in many different formats including boutiques and are mainly dominated by foreign brands. Many international luxury brands, such as Louis Vuitton, Cartier, Prada, Chanel, Hermès, and Tiffany, have established themselves in this market. GUM, the ornate department store across Red Square from the Kremlin, saw Bulgari and Jimmy Choo boutiques open in

2015, while Hermès doubled its selling space, and BNS Group, which operates 180 fashion stores across Russia, opened four new high-end Michael Kors shops in Moscow last year (Khrennikov et al., 2016).

Despite this, demand for luxury products has dropped since 2009. One of the reasons for this is the drop in income forced by the global financial crisis. Stores have to offer a discount of 70 percent (which otherwise would sell even though they were priced higher in Russia than other countries) to match the price point of the same luxury brand products that are sold in Paris, Milan, and other European capitals. Russian consumers were not willing to pay high prices for a product that is available for less in neighboring countries. With discounts as high as these, it takes Russian storeowners five to seven years to break even (Luxury brands, 2010). In addition to this obstacle, the cost of operation in Russia is prohibitive because of high rents for retail properties

▲ FIGURE 6.5 Customer picks clothing at the boutique of fashion designer Sultanna Frantsuzova. These specialty stores sell exclusive high-margin products.

(Machnicka, 2008). Most luxury brand consumers in Russia prefer to shop in other European countries because of the price difference, although this has recently turned around, mainly because the ruble has devalued and created unprecedented bargains. Additionally, Chinese tourists have also helped in the increase of luxury sales in Russia. Chinese tourists account for 17 percent of buyers at St. Petersburg's luxury department store DLT and programs with Chinese tour operators hope to bring more Chinese shoppers (Khrennikov, 2016).

Luxury brand stores are mainly located in the malls of the regional capitals. The development of this segment depends completely on the Russian economy. An increase in demand for luxury products as a result of an improved economy can help the luxury market to grow. Foreign luxury retailers may need to watch and wait before making any further investments in Russian luxury retail.

APPAREL RETAIL FORMATS: A NEW WAVE

The development of retail trade in Russia led to the introduction of new formats. Today, about 94.3 percent of Russian trade turnover could be attributed to modern retail formats such as hypermarkets, supermarkets, and discounters. Open-air markets and older Soviet style stores including wet markets are declining in popularity and losing market share to modern retail formats (Kolchenikova and Konstantinova, 2013).

In the 1990s, private shops and stores served nearby residential areas. A small store served an entire street. But now everything is different. Trade centers occupy thousands of square feet. As in many developed countries, stores have become places not just for shopping, but also for leisure activities. Store size has increased not only because of the growing number of products, but also the growing number of services. A typical supermarket now includes a snack bar, laundry and many other services. Consumers can rest assured that all their needs will be met when they go to the store.

Today, there are many different store formats in Russia. They differ in size, pricing strategy, assortment offered, and services offered. Most of the retail formats present in other emerging markets are present in the Russian retail market. Apparel retail appears in many popular formats, such as small multiband outlets, stock centers, and supermarkets. Archaic Soviet-era formats with many counters and only one separate cash desk coexist with modern formats using modern technology and management strategies.

Russia's traditional retail formats (street vendors) still capture a major share of sales in different categories of products in most emerging markets. Modern formats are popular yet have a smaller share in overall sales in the country.

▶ *Street vendors*

Street vendors sell the most volume of all the apparel sold in Russia. Traditionally they occupy either big markets in the city (they usually are situated in suburban areas in highly developed cities like Moscow or St. Petersburg) or small markets near subway stations or railway stations. The shops may be covered by a roof, but most often they are tents or kiosks. Street vendors bring goods from China and usually try to avoid customs. Cheap rent and cheap logistics help them offer goods at very low prices. Usually illegal Chinese immigrants or immigrants from ex-Soviet republics (Armenia, Georgia, etc.) run these markets.

Moscow's Cherkizovsky was the biggest market in Europe until police shut it down in 2009. Over 45,000 immigrants from China worked there, along

▲ FIGURE 6.6 A woman sells vegetables at the street market in Ljubljana, Slovenia.

▲ FIGURE 6.7 State Department Store in Moscow.

with people from Russia, Korea, Vietnam, and the former Soviet republics. This market sold illegal goods and had a turnover of about $21 billion per year. Along with clothing, one could buy drugs and weapons. The police confiscated goods worth $2 billion. The government is now planning to close illegal street markets and convert them into organized markets (NST online, 2016). This will help increase apparel production in Russia and reduce competition from cheap imports from China.

▶ Department Stores

Department stores in Russia offer a wide range of goods including clothing, furniture, and food. Stores that carry multiple brands pay particular attention to the depth of assortment. The service level is very high, as are the prices. Both old and new retail chains operate in this format. Chains built before the founding of the Soviet Union are known for their beautiful interiors. Some of these stores are popular tourist sites, for example, Moscow's Gostiny Dvor (one of the most famous department stores in Russia; in the Soviet Union, it was called "TSUM"). Some department stores carry their own brands of clothing along with international brands. Offering a wide variety of merchandise makes the store more profitable. Stores created since 2000 have a clear positioning and marketing strategy. The Finnish department store chain Stockman is a good example of well-operating management. Stockman shops sell a wide variety of products. The assortment is broad, but not very deep. Prices are low to medium. Sometimes they sell products under their own brands just to increase the depth of assortment. These shops are decorated, with different sections of goods. They occupy a floor or two, and offer self-service.

GUM, which is another example, is one of the oldest and most beautiful stores in Russia. This department store is a major tourist attraction in Moscow. Since the seventeenth century traders have met at this site. At the end of the nineteenth century, Moscow merchants' guild decided to build a big store on it where every merchant could find a place and the customers would receive the best shopping experience. On December 2, 1893, Russian emperor Alexander III officially opened the new department store. It quickly became famous for its beauty and size. It became even more popular during the Soviet period, when it became a tourist attraction as a symbol of Soviet trade. In 1990, GUM, which was government property, was bought out by some businessmen. During the 1990s, it changed owners several times and, finally, in 2004 the Russian retailer Bosco di Ciliegi bought out a majority share. Before this deal, Bosco di Ciliegi was already renting a significant amount of square footage in the store. This deal helped them get control of the store and renovate it. Bosco di Ciliegi decided to make the store friendly for visitors. As the personnel became more professional, customer service improved. Today, GUM houses many high-end boutiques (Givenchy, Sonia Rykiel, Villeroy & Boch, Hugo Boss, Lacoste, Jimmy Choo, Jean Louis David, Dior Institut, just to name a few) along with independent brands. Bosco di Ciliegi has also opened several cafes and premium food stores in the building.

▶ Specialty Stores

These are one of the most popular apparel retail formats in Russia. These stores offer a limited range of products and focus on a target audience selected by strict and rigid marketing decisions. Most of these shops are small in size. They sell expensive products with high margins only for this target audience.

▶ Supermarkets, Hypermarkets, Superstores, and Wholesale Clubs

Russian supermarkets usually occupy between 5,400 and 22,000 square feet (500–2000 square meters) of area and are located in the city. Development of these formats is the main strategy for the biggest food retailers. Supermarkets usually offer a wide assortment with lower prices than other stores. The low prices are attributed to the fact that they have larger sales volume. Superstores are bigger—about 86,000 square feet (8,000 square meters)—and are located on the outskirts of the city. Retail chains Patterson (Russian retail chain owned by X5 Retail Group) and Perekrestok (retail chain owned by X5 Retail Group) (June 2010) use a supermarket format. X5 Retail Group likes to play with different formats. This company owns several of the biggest Russian retail brands in different segments. The company was created in 2006 after the merger of two big retailers—discounter Pyaterechka and middle-segment supermarket chain Perekrestok. After the merger, X5 Retail started a very aggressive expansion program. They buy more and more competitors like Patterson. But mostly the brands disappear after the merger and the assets are moved to one of the leading brands Pyaterochka or Perekrestok.

In big cities like Moscow or St. Petersburg it is hard to find space for big stores, so there are more hypermarkets. Prices in hypermarkets are much lower than in supermarkets, but the supermarket has a more convenient location. Superstores and hypermarkets usually build big retail chains, such as Krasnodar-based Magnit, the food retail chain with the most stores (3,464 stores as of June 2010), or O'key, a food retail chain from St. Petersburg, with 52 stores in Moscow and St. Petersburg. Another very popular format is the **wholesale club**, which offers a limited assortment of food, household products, clothes, and the like. To make purchases one has to be a member of the wholesale club, like Costco or Sam's Club in the United States.

▶Discount Stores

Discount stores are widely spread all over Russia. Most large food retail chains use this format to fight for market share. Discounters operate on the principle of self-service and sell mainly food products at very low prices. The range of goods is very low and usually doesn't include apparel. The biggest discounters are retail chains such as Pyaterochka, a discount food retail chain established in 1999 and owned by X5 Retail Group, with more than 1500 stores across Russia, and Dixie, a discount food retail chain with 552 stores across Russia.

▶Factory Stores

Factory stores are shops owned by producers and situated near the factory. Sometimes they sell the previous season's products or factory seconds.

► *Online Retailing*

People in big cities use not only traditional formats but also relatively new virtual stores (**online retailing**). Many of them are developing rapidly and will soon have visible market share. But Russia's undeveloped postal service has slowed the format's development considerably. In 2010, eBay entered the Russian market and immediately the postal service collapsed. Moscow's center for international post was overloaded with work. Postal services blamed customs and customs blamed the postal system. But in the end it was consumers who suffered.

By 2010, trade via the Internet was one of the fastest-growing formats. During 2011, growth of internet retailing in Russia remained high and exceeded growth rates of store-based retailing although it remains a very narrow market. Internet sales in Russia grew by 30 percent to reach $11 billion in 2011. More than 50 percent of consumers who buy goods online live in Moscow or St. Petersburg (Kolchenikova and Konstantinova, 2013).

Plenty of virtual apparel stores, such as boutique.ru, sell goods brought from either China or Europe, or goods they bought from retail chains at a discount. Some producers and retail chains have opened their own web stores. And some, such as Nike, offer exclusive online merchandise that cannot be found in traditional stores.

► *Catalog Retailing*

In the 1990s a very common way for Russians to purchase European goods was through **catalog retailing**. One of the most popular was a German catalog called "Otto," but there were plenty of others. In stores selling from catalogs the only problem was again the postal services. Big companies tried to avoid it by offering distribution to an office in the city, which took care of distribution. It helps the client to avoid all the bureaucracy and risks of Russian post by leaving it to the retailer. Buyers could place their orders either by mail or in the office of the company. The product could be delivered to the customer either at home or in the office with a warehouse.

► *Vending Machines*

Vending machines are not as developed in Russia as they are in the United States or Japan. But there are some very interesting examples of this format in Russia. Russia's biggest fruit importer, JFC, has its own brand of bananas, called Bonanza. To popularize its brand, the company put up vending machines that sell bananas (a common practice in Japan). The goal of this campaign was not so much to make a profit as to market their product. The vending machine was a medium for advertising.

STORE OWNERSHIP: PRIVATE OR PUBLIC?

The domestic retail chains in Russia have primarily been privately owned businesses. But since 2000, many retailers have gone public to help finance their retail activities. They need additional financing to grow their businesses to compete with foreign investors. Only a handful of retailers have been able to go public. The requirement of transparency of accounts and regulatory requirements deter most companies from attempting to go public.

FDI REGULATIONS: CORRUPTION IS THE DETERRENT

Russia offers a stable investment environment. The inflow of foreign direct investment in Russia has been increasing since 2000. The domestic market's increasing demands and consumers' increasing disposable income make Russia a premier emerging market for investment. The government is encouraging this investment by abolishing most of the constraints on foreign businesses and easing some of the regulations. Steps to encourage further investment include increased tax relief and decreased administrative barriers. The Russian government is also investing in infrastructure to promote foreign investment (Gerendasi, 2009).

There are no restrictions on the type of format in which a foreign retailer may enter the Russian retail industry. A foreign retailer can own land and open a store in Russia without any basic restrictions. The foreign retailer is expected to abide by anti-monopoly legislation and not engage in unfair competition or restrictive business practices. For example, a foreign retailer (as well as Russian) cannot cooperate with other retailers in order to fix the price of any product or force distributors to pay an entrance fee (payment for the right to work with the retailer) for their products (Nikiforov, 2005).

The government plans to implement several measures to decrease corruption and make the process of establishing new business much easier. These plans are designed to boost foreign retailers' interest by making it easy to enter the Russian market. As a case in point the Russian government plans to optimize its tax system and create preferential treatment for investors that will develop innovative technologies. These innovations are not limited to information technology (IT) and telecommunications but also extend to textile production.

INTERNATIONAL BRANDS: RISKY BUSINESS

The Russian market is very complicated when it comes to store management. The main question that all foreign retailers have to answer is: "Is it better to operate our own retail chain in Russia or to perform as wholesaler?" In apparel retail, not many companies operate their own chains. Zara and other Indetex brands, as well as H&M have independent store chains because they prefer to have complete control. Most companies perform as wholesalers or distributors. Nike and many other premium fashion brands follow this business model (finding a local Russian partner for a brand is much easier if the brand is popular in its parent country). They sign agreements with Russian companies and sell them fixed volumes of their goods. That way, the foreign chains minimize the risks but have stable distribution. The risk of an unreliable partner is much lower than the risk of operating independently. Franchise stores are another format that foreign retailers often choose. This format again reduces having to deal with various problems associated with doing independent business in Russia.

Business models in Russia are increasingly becoming oriented toward decreased costs. Owners have started thinking more about efficiency. But the market won't continue to grow without help from the government.

INFLUENCES ON APPAREL RETAILING: ENTER AT YOUR OWN EXPENSE

Many different factors influence the apparel retail industry in Russia. Most of these factors apply to retailing in general.

NEW MALLS

New malls are being constructed in Russia at a fast tempo. Russia was the leading European country by new malls commissioned in 2010. However, Russia's major cities still lack space for shopping areas, mostly because federal and regional legislation makes acquiring land extremely difficult. Russia is the biggest country in the world with a huge territory and abundance of people. The low level of retail development gives potential investors huge possibilities for new business development.

HIGH COST OF INVESTMENT

The cost of capital in Russia is high, and running a retail business is difficult under these circumstances. To survive in this kind of environment, retailers use semi-legal financial schemes by evading certain taxes (Russian Retail, 2005). But this factor can be compensated for by rapid growth of business. The growth of the Russian economy is highly dependent on oil and gas prices. Russian growth will thus be unpredictable in the next few years as these prices continue to fluctuate constantly.

BUREAUCRACY

There is a complex bureaucracy in Russia. This results in a lot of red tape for importing goods and buying real estate in the country. Import regulations and customs lack transparency. Another problem is undeveloped legislation. Some laws are very complicated and extremely hard to follow. The regulations in Russia differ by region. This conflicts with retailers' interest in cost effectiveness by using a centralized supply chain. Investors should consider employing local talent in the companies because they may better understand the legal requirements.

IMPORTS INCREASE COST OF PRODUCTS

The majority of the clothing sold in Russia is imported and is very expensive owing to the high cost of importing. Logistics expense increases the manufacturer's price by 12 percent, and the customs clearance step increases this price by a whopping 40 percent (if the customs clearance is done officially, which is very rare). Store markup is 300 to 500 percent to cover all the overhead expenses, such as rent, personnel, electricity, credit payouts, taxes, and transactional costs connected with communicating with the government.

POOR INFRASTRUCTURE

Lack of proper infrastructure in the country causes transportation problems. The roads are in poor condition, and traffic is heavy. A lack of electricity and poor communication lines also create major problems for retailers.

GETTING TO KNOW DOMESTIC COMPETITORS: PRICE MATTERS

Foreign investors interested in the Russian market should look at some of these highly successful domestic retail chains.

- ▶ **Sela wear and accessories:** Sela Corporation was founded in Russia in 1991. It is a vertically integrated company operating more than 443 stores across the country. It is also present in other countries, including Ukraine, China, Estonia, and Israel. Sela sells mass-market apparel for kids, teens, women, and men. It operates in a small store format with a limited assortment. The clothing is made in China. The capability to produce inexpensive clothes under qualified management helped this company achieve great success in Russia. It has a sourcing office in China that looks for factories across the People's Republic of China (PRC) to carry out its production. The company now also has some of its production in Russia. Sela is one of the leading apparel retail chains in Russia that continues to grow in its regular store format along with franchise operations.

- **OGGI (OODJI):** OGGI has been in existence since 1998, with its first store opening in 1999 in St. Petersburg. This retail chain has 252 stores in Russia and also has a presence in some other nations. It is a mass-market apparel retail chain selling apparel and accessories for women. They plan to expand worldwide and rebranded themselves as OODJI in 2010. The name change was because it was easier to pronounce OODJI in various languages, and the company believed that the new name had a better appeal.

- **Gloria Jeans and Gee Jay:** This company has existed since 1988 and now has about 250 stores in Russia. It is a vertically integrated company selling mass-market apparel for teenagers, kids, and young adults. Gloria Jeans is the biggest apparel producer in Russia.

- **Incity:** This company was created as a mass-market brand for urban women in the age group of 18 to 35. They carry classic lines, casual lines, and jeans. The company was founded in 2005. In 2010 they had 228 stores all across Russia. Their pricing strategy, which includes putting low-priced products on sale and other promotional techniques, makes their products low cost.

- **Savage:** Since its founding in 2000, Savage has provided mass-market apparel for urban men and women in the age range of 25 to 35 years. They have about 160 stores in Russia and are also present in Ukraine and Kazakhstan. They are expanding using the franchising model.

HOW MATURE IS THE RETAIL INDUSTRY? LONG ROAD HOME

The Russian market is far from mature. In 2010, stores satisfied the needs of about 60 percent of the population, a figure that reveals room for more retailers in the country. A large retail network in Russia has about 15 stores on average, compared to 1,000 stores in the United States. The Russian market is by no means saturated and as a fast growth emerging market, it still has much room to expand, especially as Russians are eager shoppers.

Foreign retailers are introducing more sophisticated formats. The low valuation of domestic chains makes it easy for foreign retailers to acquire them. In 2009 and 2010, the French food retail chain Carrefour and Walmart reconsidered the market for potential acquisitions (Walmart later exited the market). Domestic retailers in Russia use mergers and acquisitions as the main instrument for expansion. A good example of domestic acquisition is Eldorado, one of Russia's leading electronic retail chains. Established in 2004, Eldorado was originally a regional retail operator with its first outlets in Samara and Kazan. It moved into the Moscow retail market by acquiring three shops of the small electronic retailer Mikrodin in 1998, and nine Electrical World shops (another small electronic retailer) in 2002, making Eldorado one of the biggest players in the capital. Similarly, in 2003 the food retail chain Kopeika rolled out about $30 million to acquire Prodmag, a Moscow-based network of discount shops. In 2010, Russia's most active retailer in mergers and acquisitions was the X5 Retail Group, which has consolidated many competitive retail chains. It now owns Kopeika, which will be terminated.

Since 2009, rents and the cost of construction materials have dropped significantly, opening up a window of opportunity for foreign retailers. The growing GDP of the country, a growing middle class with higher disposable income and a desire to spend money, and lack of good-quality products make Russia a very alluring market for foreign investors.

BUYING FOR APPAREL RETAIL STORES: IMPORTING IS IN

After the financial crisis of 1998, the price of imports in Russia skyrocketed by almost 300 percent. This increase created a niche for domestic Russian manufacturers and producers of raw materials, thereby increasing domestic production. The stabilization of the Russian currency has returned prices to pre-crisis levels, so products can be imported into Russia again. The domestic industry faces several issues, such as shortage of raw material, obsolete production equipment, and lack of funds. Because of these problems, domestic producers cannot compete with imported products in either price or quality. Therefore, products such as fashion items, knits, and synthetic fabrics are largely imported from various countries into Russia.

The low volume of textile production in Russia is another challenge for domestic clothing manufacturers. Almost all textiles come from abroad. Most apparel is imported from China (35 percent), Turkey (12 percent), Germany (8 percent), and Italy (6 percent) (Advertology, 2008). Customs clearance creates additional costs, and in the end production in Russia becomes very expensive. In 2009 Russian clothing producers introduced initiatives to help their industry. They asked the government to create Special Economic Zones for producers, which would lower taxes for Russian apparel producers. They also wanted the government to allow them to import textiles without customs payments.

Buyers for small retail chains and outlet stores (excluding premium brand stores) buy apparel from outlet representatives. They buy goods either in stores that offer them discounts, or in discount outlets. Most of last season's apparel is bought in Milan. Buyers visit Milan once a season and buy large quantities of clothing on sale. Then all the goods are shipped to Russia by air. After customs clearance in St. Petersburg or Moscow, the goods arrive at the store. Some products get to Russia illegally and many are fake. They are brought mostly from Italy and Turkey.

Large retail chains import apparel into Russia from Italy, Turkey, China, and Germany. Russia covers more area than any other country and straddles the Ural mountain range that divides Europe and Asia. Most goods come to western Russia by ship from Guangzhou, China. Large amounts of apparel are brought to eastern Russia via the Trans-Siberian Railway or trucks from China.

RETAIL CAREERS: FOREIGNERS NOT WELCOME

Retail is one of the fastest-growing and dynamic segments in the Russian economy. It offers a rare opportunity to quickly build a successful, high-paying career. Many retailers pay for higher education because they want their employees to be highly qualified. Retailing is one of the most competitive job markets, and top companies understand that people are key assets.

Store personnel or sales associate is one of the positions most in demand in the Russian retail industry. There is also a very high demand for middle management and senior managers because of the rapid growth and expansion of retail chains. Only educated professionals can manage complex store formats such as department stores. Unfortunately, such personnel are still lacking, even in big cities like Moscow and St. Petersburg. People do not have the required educational backgrounds. Even if they have experience, it is not enough for working in a modern retail chain. Managers in accounting, logistics, and finance are always welcome and can easily find work as long as they have a good education and work experience.

Traditionally, students start their careers working part-time in a store. Most merchandisers and promoters are students. These are good part-time jobs because they give students a foothold in a big company. Sales assistants are also in demand. After graduation, most students go directly to offices and do not work in stores. Starting out as low-level assistants, they can advance over time to become heads of divisions. These positions are not restricted to business graduates. After a couple of years as a merchandiser, an employee can join a corporate education program to gain the knowledge that is needed to obtain a management-level job. Food retailers have the hardest competition and the highest-growing rate in the industry. They invest in their employees, as they need to have good people working for them.

To build a successful career in retailing requires a good educational background. Professional education for the retail industry is not very well developed in Russia. Several good business schools and universities prepare students as marketers and specialists in finance, accounting, and logistics. In addition, some institutes teach courses that prepare students to be assortment managers. But in general the education level is low and qualified students are lacking. Most companies are looking for employees with an education in economics and knowledge of foreign languages. Some websites where one can look to find jobs in the Russian retail industry are www.job.ru, www.hh.ru, and www.rabota.mail.ru.

Development of the retail industry has forced many retail chains to rethink their management strategies. Big chains need professionals in top-management positions in order to secure stable growth and business development. The lack of professionals in Russia has led to a demand for foreigners as managers. Unfortunately the Russian government is not very welcoming of foreign workers. The paperwork to obtain a work permit and visa can take anywhere from 12 to 24 months to process. The process is complicated not only for the employee but for the employer as well, who has to deal with employee registration and tax calculations. These obstacles are one of the main reasons that foreign talent steers clear of Russia. The 2010 law allows foreigners (especially those highly qualified) to stay longer in the country and obtain all permissions much quicker (Freshfields Bruckhaus Deringer LLP, 2015). A work permit would take only a month. Unfortunately, it would be available only for highly skilled professionals who must prove their exceptional skills. But the new regulations would be the first step toward leniency. There are still many things that need to be improved before the world's top managers will consider Russia a good place to work. The main problem is still the quality of life, which is not very high in Russia. Corruption, the absence of infrastructure for foreigners, and the lack of English speakers make Russia unattractive to foreign employees. Both government and citizens understand the need to make Russia more comfortable and safe for foreigners. The country is changing and Russians are keen to shed their country's unfriendly image.

THE FUTURE OF APPAREL RETAIL: OPPORTUNITY KNOCKS AGAIN

Apparel retail in Russia is a very complicated business. One faces many obstacles in this market. The biggest problem is finding a place for the store. When you find a location, there are the hurdles of high rent, bureaucratic red tape, and corruption. Even in big cities like Moscow, Yekaterinburg, St. Petersburg, and Kazan, where there are rather large numbers of trade outlets, rent is high. According to *Forbes* magazine (Russia), retailers spend up to 30 percent of their proceeds on rent (Levinskij & Zhegulev, 2010), which is twice the rent in other European cities. The number of trade outlets is still lower than in Europe or the United States. For example, Moscow, Russia's most developed city, has fewer trade outlets for every 1,000 citizens than Madrid, Stockholm, or even Prague (Levinskij & Zhegulev, 2010). But despite the pitfalls, many foreign retailers operate successfully in Russia. For example, the French retail chain Auchan is one of the most successful food retail chains in Russia. They had second place by income per square foot in 2009, and by 2013, they were one of the top three retailers by total income, alongside Russian retail monsters X5 Retail Group and Magnit (Trade House Land, 2013). Key elements of their success are good store locations and low expenses. Their success strategy seems simple, but it is in fact a hard-won achievement because food retail is one of the most technological and complicated businesses.

The cost of credit in Russia is very high. Foreign companies have an advantage over Russian retailers because they can find investments outside of Russia much more easily than Russian companies. Credit rates in Europe and the United States are significantly lower than in Russia. This difference can give foreign companies a huge competitive advantage especially now that the market has shrunk.

The market situation is very advantageous for foreign retailers. Many local retailers have gone bankrupt since the 2008 economic downturn, so there are more opportunities to acquire existing retail chains and obtain good retail properties, which are a scarce commodity in Russia. In addition, the market began to grow and for early 2017, it is expected to grow again by one percent (Andrianova, 2016) 2010 was expected to regain the pre-crisis sales levels.

However, there are some difficulties. A foreign retailer needs to be aware of the high transactional cost connected with communicating with the government. Starting at the Russian border, retailers have to find their way through the complicated Russian law. Russian officials are not keen to help the businesses. After customs, the next issue may arise with tax officials. It is not always possible to negotiate officially. Even the courts don't help much. In the end, a retailer faces a dilemma: either close the business or find ways around the regulations. Even big multinationals like IKEA face tax problems. All these costs increase the risk that net income will be very low, about 10 percent. These hindrances affect competition in the market and the way foreign retailers enter the Russian market. The government is taking steps to fight corruption and force banks to lower credit rates. If these measures are implemented, they will have positive effects on the apparel retail industry and make the Russian retail market a lot more attractive to international investors.

In sum, some of the challenges that a foreign retailer needs to keep in mind before considering investing in Russia are:

- Lack of space with adequate infrastructure, parking facilities, and so on
- High rent for properties and competition for prime real estate
- Different types of customers in big cities as compared to outer regions
- Complicated regulations and high cost of imports
- Prevalent corruption
- Lack of trained and experienced retail professionals

SUMMARY

After 1991, when the USSR dissolved, a new retail landscape started to emerge in Russia. As commodity prices hit all-time highs during the decades that followed and the economy became more stable, Russia emerged as Europe's largest consumer market with rising disposable incomes and an expanding middle class. Even though the market is highly fragmented, many foreign retailers have entered this thriving market, which saw it turn in 2008, but recently somewhat recovered. Many brands such as premium Dolce & Gabbana, Escada or Burberry, and lower-cost Uniqlo, Zara and H&M took advantage of the opening of the Russian market to enter with full force, especially after 2012, when Russia joined the World Trade Organization.

By 2000, retailers began to enjoy economic growth. Retail chains developed. Strong retail chains that had established themselves in Moscow and St. Petersburg now looked to expand in other regions. Small stores began consolidating their businesses to compete with large retailers. The top eight international players controlling around 20 percent of the market are X5 Retail Groups, Magnit OAO, Auchan Group, Metro AG,Dorinda Holding, Lenta OOO, Dixie Group OAO, and Sedmoi Kontinent chains. Online retail also saw continued growth since 2010.

Foreign investors entered the market, bringing new technology and increased competition. Retail chains became powerful and began dictating terms to producers and distributors. From 2005 to 2008, retail chains developed rapidly and their management became more professional. Premium multibrand apparel chains Bosco di Ciliegi and JamilCo in the big cities of Moscow and St. Petersburg are examples of this. Due to this consolidation, real estate prices have increased and become quite expensive, although this did not hinder the entrance of mass-market foreign retailers (such as H&M), as the middle class was also becoming larger and demanding cheaper European products at affordable prices.

Because of the development of their retail economy throughout, Russian consumers are spending more than other European consumers, whose shopping attributes are different: Russians want status products and give attention to good quality brands. The Russian beauty and toiletries markets are the fourth-fastest-growing in the world with growth rates of 20 percent a year since 2000. Russian consumers mainly like to shop at large malls (primarily in Moscow (the new mall GUM across Red Square is a shining example) and St. Petersburg, followed by small stores and smaller malls, and an even smaller group buys from street vendors. From 2009 to 2013, menswear from Europe to Russia increased 62 percent. Russian women like to dress well and tend to invest heavily in their wardrobes, including shoes, jewelry and accessories. A young woman between the ages of 20 and 25 spends two-thirds of her income on apparel and accessories. Similarly, Russians buy mainly imported products for their children at malls and boutiques.

CRITICAL THINKING QUESTIONS

1. What are some of the economic issues involved in entering the Russian retail market?
2. What are some of the legal and investment issues a foreign retailer needs to know when entering the Russian market?
3. How can international companies wanting to enter the Russian market take into account the differences between cities and rural areas?
4. What are some of the mistakes that foreign retailers have made in entering the Russian market?
5. Russian women and men are demanding consumers. What are some of the factors and characteristics to take into consideration when marketing to them?
6. What marketing strategies can a local Russian retailer use to market to Russians?

Case Study

BUSINESS IN RUSSIA: RETAIL'S ROCKY ROAD

Pundits leapt on French retailer Carrefour's decision to pull out of Russia last autumn as more evidence of "foreigners fleeing Russia." The company had opened its doors in the midst of the international financial storm that made many Russian consumers stay indoors until the weather improved. But lost in the flood of bad news was the fact that Carrefour's rival, fellow French supermarket chain Auchan, was not only staying but continued to expand.

Carrefour was not alone in its retreat. In 2007, Germany's Edeka Zentrale AG closed its Marktkauf hypermarket, whereas Turkish company Ramenka spent most of the last couple of years gradually closing its chain of Ramstore hypermarkets and supermarkets. However, other international players are thriving: cornflakes, after all, do not enjoy the same geopolitical significance as oil and gas.

Auchan has been the most active of the burgeoning number of foreign companies hoping to cash in on Russia's 142-million-strong consumer market. It nipped in to buy Ramenka's hypermarkets and continues to expand its operations in Russia (just as it has next door in China).

Rapidly earning a strong reputation in emerging markets, the privately held retailer from Lille entered Russia early and is now one of the most popular anchors among property developers, according to Jacob Grapengiesser from East Capital, a fund manager concentrating on Eastern Europe and a significant holder of shares in Magnit, the country's largest grocery retailer.

Auchan has 91 hypermarkets and 176 convenience stores with over 41 thousand employees (Auchanholding, 2015). Jean-Pierre Germain, CEO of Auchan Russia, said the company is willing to "adapt to different markets in different regions of Russia." As an illustration, a rollout of Raduga stores—a new, low-cost outlet—has begun in smaller cities with populations of fewer than half a million people. By 2015, the company had a total of 91 hypermarkets in Russia.

According to Natasha Zagvozdina from investment bank Renaissance Capital, the French company is joined in the list of the country's top five grocery retailers by Germany's Metro, which has been expanding aggressively across the region, alongside three Russian operators; foreign retailers are now the third- and fourth-largest retailers in the Russian market.

It's also the size and early development of Russia that makes the prize so tempting; Grapengiesser predicts that "[modern grocery chains] will continue to grow for many years." In fact, despite continuing to capture business from outdoor markets and other independent operators, grocery chains still enjoy less than a 40 percent share of food sales across Russia, according to Zagvozdina. "The consolidation opportunity in Russia is absolutely huge," she states, a view backed by the claim of Lev Khasis (CEO of the leading grocery retailer X5) that over the next decade his company hopes to double revenue every three years.

Magnit's deputy CEO Oleg Goncharnov told Russia Now: "Today the Russian retail sector has a turnover of $200 billion a year. We are the second-largest player, but we only have a 3 percent market share. There is an enormous potential and Russia is one of the most dynamically developing retail markets in the world."

Not only did Magnit leave its expansion plans for 2009 unchanged, it even saw revenues increase that year by a third, easily beating 2008 (a record year for the company), which continued to grow until 2014, when net income grew by 42 percent (Hille, 2014), despite Russia's overall economic decline of just under nine percent. But there is a lot of work still to do. The size of Russia, its poor transport infrastructure, and an absence of experienced third-party logistics operators make supply and distribution key. Those activist investors believed to have pressured Carrefour. Try convincing them to live with five years of losses while distribution networks are built.

Auchan is not the only retailer with ambitious plans after seeing its position strengthened in the last year or two then. Magnit, for instance, with the aid of a successful second public offering at the end of October (which raised $365 million) plans to plow $1 billion into opening up to 580 new stores in 2010 (to add to the 3,228 it already operates, the vast majority smaller stores outside the major cities), as well as strengthening its logistics infrastructure. Russia's food retail business was already the fastest growing in Europe, and as of 2016, the economy is expected to recuperate and grow.

Source: "Business in Russia: Retail's Rocky Road," Rossiyskaya Gazeta (Russia). Retrieved on December 15, 2010 from http://www.telegraph.co.uk/sponsored/russianow/business/7256781/Business-in-Russia-Retails-rocky-road.html

Discussion Questions
1. Auchan has 91 hypermarkets and 176 convenience stores with over 41,000 employees. Jean-Pierre Germain, CEO of Auchan Russia,

said the company is willing to "adapt to different markets in different regions of Russia." What are your thoughts on Auchan's adaptation decision?

2. What are some of the risks involved with mergers and acquisitions in a developing economy?

REFERENCES

Andreyeva, A. (2006). Designer Brand in Fashion Business; Cases of Armani Group and Gucci Group. Saint-Petersburg State University Publishing, p. 256.

Andrianova, A. (2016). Russian Economy Edges Near End of Recession as Contraction Eases. Bloomberg. Retrieved on September 15, 2016 from www.bloomberg.com/ news/articles/2016-07-28/russian-economy-edges-near-end-of-recession-as-contraction-eases

Anonymous. Average spending on menswear. *RBC*. Retrieved on August 31, 2009, from http://marketing.rbc.ru/news_research/31/08/2009/ 562949970677727. shtml?&investigations=1

Anonymous. Biggest Russian Retail Chains Rating. *Opt Union*. Retrieved on April 9, 2007, from www.opt-union.ru/publications.php?id=46

Anonymous. Children's Apparel Retailers want to Compete with Street Vendors. *3A-marketing*. Retrieved on December 3, 2007, from www.3a-marketing.ru/ news/1196667990

Anonymous. Clothes by Need. *Fashioner*. Retrieved on November 13, 2009 from www. fashioner.ru/index.php?path=node/3/news/read/1292

Anomymous. Cosmetics in Russia. *Cosmetics in Russia*. . Retrieved on May 23, 2010, from www.cosmeticsinrussia.com/showart.phtm?reg=full&type=f&num= 2039

Anonymous. Food Retail Chains in Russia, 2008 (demo version). RBC, 2008, p. 29.

Anonymous. In Jeans. *Sostav*. Retrieved on March 6, 2008 from www.sostav.ru/ news/2008/03/06/issl2/

Anonymous. Russian Apparel Market Growth. *Advertology*. Retrieved on July 13, 2008 from http://advertology.ru/article63623.htm

Anonymous. What for Do the Russians Spare. FDU: Personal Finance. Retrieved on March 3, 2010 from http://www.fdu.ru/investment/news0006401B20/default. asp

Aris, B. (2012). Retail Wave hits Russia. beyondbrics. Retrieved on June 1, 2016, from http://blogs.ft.com/beyond-brics/2012/04/03/retail-wave-hits-russia/

AuchanHolding (2015). A Worldwide Presence. Retrieved on June 2, 2016 from www.groupe-auchan.com/en/who-is-auchan/international-presence/

Belyanina, Jana. (2009, October 13). "Europe and China Attack Russian Apparel Market." *Geopolitica*. Retrieved on October 13, 2009 from http://geopolitica.ru/ Articles/773/.

Ben-Shabat, H., Moriarty, M., Kassack, J., Torres, J. (2015). Global Retail Expansion. An Unstoppable Force. The 2015 Global Retail Development Index. Retrieved on

May 29, 2016 from www.atkearney.com/consumer-products-retail/global-retail-development-index/current-research-detail

Blagov, S. (2007, May 14–20). To Russia, with Love. ICIS Chemical Business Americas, p. 24.

Döpfer, R. (2014). Clothing Market Report Russia in Spring 2014. European Fashion and Textile Export Council. Retrieved June 1, 2016, from www.cpm-moscow. com/download/exhibitor/ClothingMarketReport_2014.pdf

Euromonitor International (2016). Beauty and Personal Care in Russia: Country report. Retrieved May 25, 2016 from www.euromonitor.com/beauty-and-personal-care-in-russia/report

Federal Service of Government Statistics (2009). Retrieved on May 21, 2009, from www.gks.ru/bgd/regl/b09_13/Main.htm

Freshfields Bruckhaus Derlinger LLP (2015). Important Changes in Russian Immigration Law. May. Retrieved on September 12, 2016, from: www.lexology. com/%28F%28YwBl6Hv_dR6jzVB68XIJkrQhh64p-txs3fa-WAIZEDPENU8DO3W 2iZWg21X6Itvaqm85xVOdXIUPUClP0DJg-xQm5cTkFp1GNfvq4s_ DJ9p793qFEebj15PfVBV0TOvcUTyM13kX1RqeBiYr9xhIPGo5yo42-- G_M2Lb6njO1FTccWM1FML54QwF1f2MX0EQNG pbGHedznEWLTkKOuqji6Io-Do1%29%29/library/document.ashx?g=f8f06d08- bb9c–48a2–910f–7c490c70dab0&b=Lp3fmEyNKU3PFlfrbdpwnpHRsyBoiOjHT5 Py1INBqTo%3D&bt=2015–03–24T22%3A24%3A43.6807458%2B00%3A00&nored irect=1

Gerendasi, P. (2009). Doing Business in Russia. Retrieved on May 21, 2010, from www.pwc. com/ru/en/doing-business-in-russia/assets/doing-business-in-russia-2009.pdf

Gorer, G. (1962). *The People of Great Russia: A Psychological Study*. W.W. Norton and Company

Grishchenko, G. (2009, September). Facing Challenges, Russian Beauty Industry Maintains Potential. Retrieved on January 15, 2010, from www.gcimagazine. com/marketstrends/regions/bric/ 57017582.html

Golubev, Pavel. Baltic Status, March 2009. Interesting Facts about Russian Women and Womens' Rights in Russia. (2009, August 14). Retrieved on May 17, 2010 from www.waytorussia.net/WhatIsRussia/Women/Facts.html

Hille, K. (2014). Magnit keeps Crown as Russia's Leading Grocer. *Financial Times*. Retrieved on June 3, 2016, from https://next.ft.com/content/5a3f788c-8d85- 11e3-9dbb-00144feab7de

Karpova, E., Nelson-Hodges, N. & Tullar, W. (2007). Making Sense of the Market: An Exploration of Apparel Consumption Practices of the Russian Consumer. *Journal of Fashion Marketing and Management, 11*(1), 106–121.

Kolchenikova, O. and Konstantinova, I. (2013). Russian Federation, Retail Foods, Retail Sector Continues to Expand. *Gain Report*. Number RSATO 1312. USDA Foreign Agricultural Service.

Khrennikov, I, Lemeshko, A. & Gretler, C. (2016). When the Going Gets Tough, Russia's Rich go Shopping. *Bloombergpursuits*. Retrieved on June 2, 2016 from www. bloomberg.com/news/articles/2016-02-04/what-recession-rich-russians-snap-up-luxury-goods-with-gusto

Loshakova, Darya. (2009). Market of Cheap Apparel will Grow. *Sostav*, No. 2 (670). Retrieved on February 27, 2009, from www.sostav.ru/articles/2009/ 02/27/ko3/

Levinskij, A., Zhegulev, I. & Red, P. (2010). *Forbes Russia*, January; pp. 92–98.

Luxury Brands no Longer in Demand in Russia (2010, March 16). Retrieved on May 21, 2010, from http://english.pravda.ru/business/companies/112598-0/

Machnicka, M. (2008). Russian Clothing and Footwear Market: Much Room for Foreign Retailers. Retrieved on January 15, 2010 from www.pmrpublications. com/press_room/en_Russian-clothing-and-footwear-market_-much-room-for-foreign-retailers.shtml

Ministry of Economic Development of Russia (2009). About Social-Economic Development of Russia in 2009. Retrieved on February 3, 2010 from www.economy.gov.ru/minec/activity/sections/macro/monitoring/ doc20100203_01

NST online (2016). Moscow Bulldozes 100 "Illegal" Shops. New Straits Times Online. Retrieved on September 16, 2012 from www.nst.com.my/news/2016/02/126618/ moscow-bulldozes-100-illegal-shops

Nikiforov, I. (2005). The Commercial Laws of the Russian Federation. Part 4. Foreign Direct Investment. Retrieved on May 21, 2010 from www.epam.ru/index. php?id=22&id2=400&l=eng

Parshukova, M. (2004). The Market for Children's Apparel in Russia. *Apparel and Textiles*. Retrieved on May 21, 2010 from www.musavirlikler.gov.tr/upload/RF/ The%20Market%20for%20Children.doc

Rogov, K. (2014). What Will Be The Consequences of the Russian Currency Crisis? European Council on Foreign Relations. Retrieved May 30, 2016 from www.ecfr. eu/article/commentary_what_will_be_the_consequences_of_the_russian_ currency_crisis385

Russian Beauty Products (2010). Retrieved on May 21, 2010, from www.beautytipshub. com/russian-beauty/russian-beauty-products.html

Russian Retail Industry: Structure and growth forecasts (2005). Retrieved on January 15, 2010 from www.russiajournal.com/node/19099

Russian Passion for Fashion (2009, March). Retrieved on May 25, 2010, from www. hktdc.com/info/mi/a/tq/en/1X000AWA/1/HKTDC-Trade-Quarterly/Russian-passion-for-fashion.htm

Russian Women in America (2009, June 14). Retrieved on May 24, 2010, from www. russianwomendating.us/2009/06/russian-women-in-america.html

Shienok, D. (2010) Middle Class is out of Clothes. *Retailer.* Retrieved on February 27, 2010, from www.retailer.ru/item/id/16146/

Style & Design: Global Luxury Survey (n.d). Retrieved on May 30, 2010, from http://205.188.238.181/time/specials/2007/article/ 0,28804,1659346_1659333_1659199,00.html

Trade House Land (2013). Food Retail Chains on Russia. Retrieved on September 16, 2016, from https://proagria.fi/sites/default/files/attachment/ash.pdf

US Commercial Service Hong Kong (2015). Cosmetics & Toiletries Markets Overview, compiled by US Commercial Service Hong Kong. Retrieved on June 1, 2016, from http://trade.gov/industry/materials/ITA.FSC.Cosmoprof.2015_final2.pdf

Worldatlas (2016). The World'S Largest Oil Reserves by Country. *Worldatlas.* Retrieved on May 29, 2016, from www.worldatlas.com/articles/the-world-s-largest-oil-reserves-by-country.html

TURKEY

7

Elida Camille Behar
Shubhapriya Bennur
Serkan Yalcin

OBJECTIVES

After reading this chapter, you will

- ▶ Understand the characteristics of apparel retailing in Turkey
- ▶ Comprehend traditional and contemporary retail establishments in the Turkish apparel industry
- ▶ Know international apparel retailers in Turkey and foreign investment policy in Turkey
- ▶ Understand factors affecting retailing in the Turkish apparel industry
- ▶ Grasp characteristics of apparel consumers in Turkey
- ▶ Know career retailing in the Turkish apparel industry

In 1923 the Turkish Republic was established upon the remnants of the Ottoman Empire, with a visionary named Kemal Ataturk at its helm. After the end of the stagnant Ottoman Empire, Ataturk helped Turkey to recover many aspects of Turkish life, including the alphabet, government structure, and dress. He and his successors, known as Kemalists, helped to lay the foundation for Turkey's present economy.

Turkey had an average annual growth rate in GDP of 3.93 percent from 1999–2015, according to TradingEconomics.com (May 2016). Its GDP ranked #18 out of 200+ countries according to The World Factbook (2015).

TABLE 7.1 Fast Facts about Turkey

Capital	Ankara
Population	79.4 million
Type of government	Parliamentary Republic
GDP: purchasing power parity: in U.S. $	$1.576 trillion (2015 est.)
Age structure	0–14 yrs: 25.4 percent 15–64 yrs: 67.6 percent 65 yrs plus: 6.0 percent
Median age	Total: 30.1 years Male: 29.7 years Female: 30.6 years
Religion	Muslim: 99.8 percent (mostly Sunni) Other: 0.2 percent (mostly Christians and Jews)
Ethnicity	Turkish: 70–75 percent Kurdish: 18 percent Minorities: 7–12 percent

Source: CIAfactbook.gov

Euromonitor recently reported that Turkey's real GDP will grow by 3.3 percent in 2016 (May 2016). Twenty-first century Turkey is the fourth largest labor force in relation to EU countries according to TurkStat (May 2014). Turkey has a large population of qualified, cost-effective, and motivated people; this population also means a large consumer base, especially in terms of increasing purchasing power. Foreign companies often find the Turkish labor force to be educated, skilled, motivated, and effective. The Turkish population has seen increased employment, higher wages, many young people (50 percent are under the age of 30), and a mainly urban population. Many foreign companies consider these characteristics of the Turkish population as being favorable to doing business in Turkey.

As the Ottomans knew as they built their empire 700 years ago, Turkey's strategic location in the world makes it a hub country suitable for regional

headquarters. Turkey is located between Europe, Central Asia, and the Middle East. Turkey has close ties with the European Union. The Ankara Agreement was signed on September 12, 1963 to establish closer ties between the European Economic Community and the Turkish people. Turkey has been in the European Customs Union since 1996 and a European accession country since October 2005. The Customs Union increased trade liberalization between Turkey and the European Union. Such liberalization opens more doors to European retailers in the Turkish market, especially when they want to bring their products with them instead of producing them in Turkey. A liberal investment climate in Turkey has made it attractive to international retailers, which has resulted in large foreign direct investment by multinationals. The World Bank states that it takes 7.5 days to start a business in Turkey and it is ranked 55 out of 189 countries in the Ease of Doing Business Rank (May 2016).

Foreign companies benefit from many features of the Turkish economy. In particular, Turkey's young population and strategic location are big draws for foreign companies that choose the country as a site for both production and sales. Foreign companies prefer to operate in Turkey to get the benefit of its large consumer base. In addition, many multinational companies choose Turkey as their regional headquarters to manage their operations in the Middle East, Africa, the Balkans, and the independent states of the former Soviet Union. For example, BASF has been conducting business in Turkey for 135 years. Since the founding of the Turkish Republic, BASF has been a contributor to their economy. By 2005, BASF had combined its two separate headquarters into one operation in Istanbul: Business Center Turkey, Middle East and North Africa (BCT). Approximately 900 people work in this center, which manages 34 nearby countries. BASF Turkey has six production facilities in the country. Its product categories are: chemical, functional materials and solutions, performance products, and agricultural solutions (www.basf.com). Turkey's geographic location has evidently made it a very attractive market for many international businesses.

Attractive as Turkey's location is to foreign investors, they must keep in mind the country's mixed national and business culture. Understanding consumer behavior and business practices requires an understanding of Turkey's unique blend of European and Asian cultures and business practices. Islamic values mean a great deal to many people as well as to some companies. Such values affect the apparel purchases of a considerable number of women. However, such values are not as important to the Turkish government as they are in some Arabic countries. Successful foreign investors understand Turkey's unique characteristics.

THE RETAIL LANDSCAPE: A PROMISING MARKET

The retail sector in Turkey saw an 8.6 percent increase in 2015 over the prior year, totaling $438 billion. Since 2010, retail has grown by 36.3 percent. Forecasters expect the retail sector to grow to a sales volume of $473 billion by the year 2020. Of particular note is the explosion of internet retailing in Turkey. This grew by 31.8 percent in 2015 to $9.2 billion from the previous year. Since 2010, the internet retail channel has increased by 325 percent. The trust of the Turkish consumer in paying online, the spread of multi-channel retail, and the acceptance of mobile e-tailing have all contributed to this growth.

According to Euromonitor, the shopping mall has had the most significant effect on the increase in retail in 2015 (January 2016). Euromonitor also mentioned that informal retailing has now entered a period of decline in Turkey, while at the same time domestic and international retailers have been opening stores on popular, Fifth Avenue-like streets. Strong employment and the move to the cities will keep consumers on this shopping pathway.

Less than half of the retailing is organized, the rest of it is done through informal formats. Shopping malls are still being built in Turkey, particularly in Istanbul. Mall construction will continue to increase the percentage of the organized retail format along with an increase in people employed in the retail sector. According to Hulusi Belguthe, the president of the Shopping Malls and Investors Association (AYD), "the amount of shopping malls in Turkey has reached 354 and there are around 22–23 cities left which do not have a shopping mall" (www.realestatenews.com, Dec 2015). A.T. Kearney has reported that there are 150 shopping malls in Istanbul (2016). Although it is declining, a segment of the Turkish population does not like shopping at the organized shopping channels, perceiving that the products they sell are more expensive than at informal retail setups. Informal retailing is most popular in rural parts of the country where incomes are more limited. People still feel the need for small grocery stores, once and still the most popular retail outlet (for many people) for groceries due to convenience and habit (Euromonitor, 2016). Taken together, these factors reveal a dynamic and growing economy attractive not only to new domestic entrepreneurs but also to foreign investors.

Since the 1980s, international activity in the Turkish retail industry has been on the rise. Some companies, such as Procter & Gamble, have been present in Turkey for more than a decade with Istanbul serving as their headquarters for operations in Turkey, the Caucasus, the Central Asian Republics, and Israel. Benetton, Turkey's first international ready-to-wear company, has been operating in the country since 1985 and has used Turkey as a springboard for doing business in Turkmenistan, Georgia, Uzbekistan, Tajikistan, Kyrgyzstan, and the Middle East. Benetton Turkey employs more than 3,000 people in production, retail, and management. Until 2012, Boyner Holding and Benetton Giyim were 50/50 licensing partners. Both companies had mutual strategies to restructure and change growth plans. Benetton retains its vital business in Turkey with 119 store locations in the country.

Foreign retailers began entering the Turkish market through joint ventures or licensing agreements. The largest cities offered considerable opportunities to foreign investors to enter the retail market. In Turkey, the textile industry is one of the largest and earliest-established industries. The apparel industry was established during the 1950s and initially served only the domestic market. It did not grow much until the 1970s. With new export-oriented economic policies in 1980 and related investments, the textile and apparel industry began to develop and has since increased in international competitiveness (State Planning Organization, 2004). Among the strengths of the Turkish textile and apparel industry are domestic cotton production, proximity to the European Union market, skillful labor, investment in infrastructure and telecommunication systems, and a large domestic market. In addition, with the increased education of the Turkish consumer, they are now aware of sustainability and eco-friendly textiles. As a result, more organic cotton is being produced in Turkey, which has benefitted the consumer, particularly in childrenswear—Turkish parents feel that is a better, safer, alternative for their child.

As reported by Euromonitor, apparel and footwear showed a 9.2 percent current value growth from 2014 to 2015 (see Table 7.2 for the category breakdown).

POPULATION AND CONSUMERS

According to the 2015 Revision of World Population Prospects by the United Nations, Turkey is among the Top 20 Countries (#18 rank) accounting for 75 percent of the world's population. Urban population is increasing across the globe. It is forecasted by the UN that city populations will increase by 380 million people within the next five years (2015).

TABLE 7.2 Percentage of current value growth from 2014–2015	
Childrenswear	14.0 percent
Footwear	8.8 percent
Menswear	8.0 percent
Womenswear	8.5 percent
Accessories	8.2 percent
Sportswear	9.8 percent
Apparel and Footwear	9.2 percent

Source: *Euromonitor* Category Briefing February 2016

Turkey already has a vast majority of its people living in urban environments (92.1 percent TurkStat). Istanbul (formerly the ancient city of Constantinople) is the most populated city with 18.6 percent or 14.7 million people, followed by Ankara with 6.7 percent or 5.3 million people, then Izmir with 4.2 million (5.3 percent), Bursa having 2.8 million (3.6 percent), and Antalya with 2.3 million people (2.9 percent). Looking at these population stats from a broad perspective, it shows that the top five cities house 37 percent of the Turkish population. These city dwellers are no strangers to the many benefits of urban living, such as employment opportunities, higher salaries, and access to the best retail shopping experiences.

CONSUMERS: A MIX OF OLD AND NEW TRADITIONS

Ataturk's 1925 Hat Law and the 1934 Clothing Law tried to change the way people dressed to give them a Westernized look. These laws restricted the wearing of religious clothes outside prayer places and banned laypeople from wearing them, especially a kind of hat (known as the fez or traditional turban) and coat favored by men. Kemal Ataturk wanted the Turkish people to wear collared shirts, fedora hats, and oxford shoes. Today, these laws are still in existence and are part of the Turkish Penal Code.

These two laws led the way toward Western modes of dress. Since that time, blogs, magazines, movies, TV, celebrities, and all social media have influenced Turkish consumers' preference for apparel. In addition,

▲ FIGURE 7.1 Shops in the Grand Bazaar, Istanbul. The bazaar contains 4,000 shops and dates back to the fifteenth century.

▲ FIGURE 7.2 Cheerful Turkish friends looking at a jewelry store window.

166.5 million Turkish airline passengers (TurkStat) bring back the latest in European fashions.

In Turkey, regional differences also create distinct consumer preferences. People dress more conservatively in small rural areas and more fashionably in big cities which are also tourist destinations. Ads for fast fashion retailers show Turkish youths wearing trendy apparel. When surprised parents tell their children that such clothes are not appropriate, the youth respond, "We are in Istanbul," indicating that they prefer the fashions of metropolitan cities.

The media's effect on clothing is enormous in Turkey. More and more liberal lifestyles are emphasized in movies, TV/cable series, commercials, magazines, and all social media. Turkey's government is secular, yet, it has recently become more conservative due to regional volatility. Although Muslims are in the majority, religion does not have any impact on the government or the media, unlike many other Islamic countries surrounding Turkey.

Turkey is a developing country with a per capita GDP of $10,515 compared to $5,443 in Iran, $12,736 in the Russian Federation, $24,407 in

▲ FIGURE 7.3 Inside Trump Towers Shopping Mall in Istanbul.

Saudi Arabia, $42,726 in France, and $54,630 in the US (The World Bank, 2014).

Although high-end luxury apparel retailers are present, especially in malls and streets in wealthy neighborhoods, the number of consumers for expensive luxury is not as high as in developed countries. The majority of Turks fall into the low-to-middle income range and are best served by their domestic retailers, such as LC Waikiki, Mavi, Colin's, YKM, and Boyner. These domestic retailers offer relatively inexpensive, quality products. Womenswear produces the highest level of apparel sales, so international retailers need to understand them well.

WOMEN

Females make up 50.8 percent of the Turkish population with womenswear constituting 42 percent of all apparel sales, making this the largest segment in apparel retail sales. Generally speaking, womenswear around the globe makes up the majority of apparel purchases due to the variety of product categories for women, such as dresses, jeans, leggings, tops (knit and woven), shorts, skirts (short and long lengths), blazers, sweaters, to name a few. As is typical of all female consumers, those who live in large cities will buy more fashion-forward items than those who live in small/rural environments who will dress more conservatively or lag behind in fashion.

In recent years, obesity has become an issue for Turkish women and the Turkish population in general. Euromonitor has reported that 38 percent of the Turkish population is now overweight (2016). Eating habits have been gradually changing with the adoption of fast food as an easy option. More women are now educated and have entered the Turkish workforce making time available for purchasing and preparing fresh food a rarity. This change in diet and weight has led to an increase in plus-size fashions for women.

Due to the increase of women in the workforce and global influence, the business attire worn by Turkish women has been changing. The formal look of a business suit is diminishing and being replaced by the ubiquitous legging and denim-style legging worn by Western women for almost a decade. Euromonitor reported that this product category increased by 12 percent in current value growth in 2015.

Because Turkish consumers are mostly Muslim, many Turkish women prefer to wear clothes (at least outside their homes) that cover their bodies. Muslim women are not allowed to show their body parts (except face, hands, and feet) to men other than their husbands and immediate male family members. Families sometimes force their daughters to cover their bodies, but there are no such restrictions among Turkish female consumers who do not practice Islam. However, women who do practice Islam sometimes do not cover their bodies due to their job requirements or depending on where they live. Unlike some Arabic countries, Turkey does not have laws that require all women to cover themselves when they go out.

It is very hard to calculate the number or ratio of female consumers living by Islamic principles. Muslim women in small cities and neighboring villages generally follow Islamic covering style. Even in big cities, the number of such female consumers is not low. In fact, in May 2016, the first Istanbul Modest Fashion Week was held at Haydarpasa Station in Istanbul. The aim of this event was to promote Turkish fashion, particularly fashion for the modest consumer. This new event was sponsored by Modanisa.com, an online multi-brand retailer, in conjunction with the Islamic Fashion and Design Council (2016). At the start of 2016, Dolce & Gabbana began producing a collection for its Muslim customers, consisting of hijabs and abayas. Although the D&G collection is at the high end of the spectrum, it caused a sensation because it was catering to a specific target market in the Middle East. Dominique Soguel of the Associated Press stated, "In Turkey, an estimated two-thirds of women wear a headscarf, according to industry experts." (2016). Steff Yotka of Vogue reported, "According to a report by Thomas Reuters, Muslim shoppers spent $266 billion on clothing and footwear in 2013 and are expected to spend $484 billion by 2019." (2016). This market is finally being recognized by the international design community with specific fashions for the modest consumer.

Among other female segments, especially the millennial demographic, there is more fashion or brand consciousness, and they welcome products from international retailers selling clothing, handbags, accessories, fragrances, and cosmetics. Handbags are especially desired by Turkish women. Among young Turkish female consumers, brand consciousness is high. Turkish women have recently embraced colorful nail polish and headscarves. Both product categories have become trend driven. Euromonitor reported that in fashion apparel accessories, scarves had the largest percentage value growth in the 2014–2015 period with an 8.6 percent current value growth (2016). As mentioned earlier, the recent rise in conservatism in Turkey is influencing Turkish women to wear headscarves on a daily basis. It should be noted that Turkish veiling fashion emerged as early as the 1980s followed by veiling fashion shows in the 1990s using famous Turkish models. This trend resulted in the launch of veiling fashion magazines, such as *Ala*, *Aysha* and *Enda*. There is

▲ FIGURE 7.4 Cigdem Akin—Runway—Mercedes-Benz Fashion Week
Istanbul—October 2016.

much written about the rise of veiling fashion in the 1980s as a Turkish female
rebellion against the conservative dress requirements for Muslim women by
purposely wearing very colorful headscarves to thumb their nose at the
practice. Nonetheless, the headscarf in its array of colors is quite a beautiful
fashion statement.

MEN

Sales of menswear constitute the second largest segment (25 percent) with
respect to total apparel sales. As in the women's apparel segment, the young
male millennial has a high regard for well-known international brands. Euromonitor reported a number of new trends for the fashion conscious Turkish
male (2016). New among the trends are colorful pants and shorts, in colors
such as red, yellow, green, and blue, sleeveless coats, and an increase in casual
business attire for the urban male—not very different from the global male
consumer. Skinny jeans are very popular with males and females alike. The
Turkish male also favors masculine deodorants and shaving products due to
aggressive advertising campaigns on the part of the brands. AXE known for its

deodorants and fragrances ran a sexy YouTube video in 2013 targeting this market segment (https://youtu.be/ThUawhqtDBg).

Travel experts are known to report that it is still customary to wear shorts to the knee or longer when touring Turkey because clothing customs are still dictated by strong Islamic traditions. They also report that Turkish men rarely wear tank tops. More formal clothes and accessories such as jackets, suits, high-quality shirts, pants, shoes, and watches are among some favorite products worn by Turkish male consumers, in the villages and small cities. Middle-aged and older male consumers usually wear casual pants, not denim, and shirts. In many eastern Turkish villages, both men and women tend to wear baggy pants (*salvar* in Turkish), which are comfortable for doing farm work.

THE BEAUTY INDUSTRY IN TURKEY

An improving standard of living and an increasing young employed population, along with growing interest in looking young and attractive, has led to a greater demand for beauty and personal care products in Turkey. Euromonitor has reported that for the past two years, this industry has been dominated by the large global players such as Avon, L'Oréal, Nivea, Procter & Gamble, and Unilever (2016). These multinationals have large budgets which support the necessary research and development, advertising and promotional activity to be successful in this business segment. Not to say that small and medium-sized enterprises (SMEs) are left out. Cosmetics Business reported that there are 3,250 cosmetics and personal care product manufacturers in Turkey with a total of 14,000 employees; most of these SMEs are located in Istanbul (2015).

As the Turkish consumer becomes more educated, they have become more aware of the benefits of products that use natural ingredients. These products have great appeal for Turkish women. It has been the Turkish heritage to use a wide range of natural products, such as black soap, olive or grape-seed oil in hair care, rose water, yogurt treatments, and henna scalp treatments. This desire for natural products has led to an increased demand or micro-trend for halal beauty products. Halal means permitted or lawful according to Islamic law. The halal beauty and personal care products sector is growing. The products do not contain any animal ingredients and may also be made under Islamic supervision; although what actually constitutes a halal product is not yet clearly defined. A few of the early entrants are Amara Cosmetics, SamPure Minerals, Shiseido (brand name Za), Sahfee Halalcare, and Mihri Istanbul.

One of the key trends reported by Euromonitor is the "selfie" which monopolized all social media; this trend is driving the creation of new make-up products (2016). The selfie-obsessed Turkish female consumer now desires products which will give a camera-ready appearance. So, products which will enhance the complexion with a radiant glow, translucent look, or contrasting color are becoming popular.

The hair care category has the largest share of Turkish beauty and personal care USD 670.4 million, followed by skin care USD 567.8 million, and color cosmetics USD 429.7 million. As reported by Euromonitor, within hair care, conditioners showed the strongest growth; specifically, conditioners which address problems such as dull hair, over-treated hair, or hair loss.

Men's grooming reached USD 350 million in 2015. More and more Turks are living in cities and have professional jobs. These metro males are willing to spend their money on grooming products which will improve their looks. Men's skin care had the highest percentage increase in current value growth, increasing by 20 percent in 2015; the largest category within men's grooming are men's razors and blades at 45 percent of the overall grooming category (Euromonitor). Previously, men living in rural environments did not need to shave often. With the increase in professional jobs located in cities, Turkish men will continue to shave more frequently.

CHILDREN

Turkey's total fertility is 31 percent higher than Europe, or 2.1 Turkish children versus 1.6 European children for every woman (UN World Fertility Patterns 2015). In 2015, there were 20.2 million Turkish children between the ages of 0 to 14 years old. In recent years, as early as 2013, the Turkish government has been giving monetary incentives to couples for having at least three children, in order to boost the young population.

With both parents working, there has been a trend toward higher quality products. In addition, in the past, parents have tended to hand down clothes from one child to the next, now parents prefer to buy new clothes for the additional children in the family. These factors lead to higher sales in childrenswear. Euromonitor reported that childrenswear had a current value growth of 14 percent in 2015, reaching USD3.1 billion.

Some of the recent trends for childrenswear have been colorful clothing items, cartoon/licensed character products, fashions from grown-up trends, and more items for the daughter. Parents enjoy shopping for their children while they are shopping for themselves, so they prefer the large formal retail stores. LC Waikiki is the market leader for childrenswear with 29 percent market share. Koton has had strong growth in childrenswear by offering more product choices and aggressive advertising on TV, outdoor and online. YKM and Boyner are the leaders in private label product offering in the kids' market. Gap Kids, H&M, Jacadi, and Zara Kids are among the international retailers present in Turkey.

LUXURY RETAIL IN TURKEY

Turkey's luxury goods sales grew by 5 percent in the period 2014/2015 as compared to global luxury goods sales growth of 4 percent or USD 317 billion (Euromonitor April 2016). Turkey has an extremely wealthy middle and upper-middle class. It is also among the top 20 countries in the world based on income of individuals in USD. Consumers in Turkey are also known to spend freely when the economy allows for it. They also save and so have money to spend on luxury products. Uniqueness is a very important attribute for a luxury consumer in Turkey and limited edition products sell very well in this market. Turkey has some new malls that have opened in the last five to six years, for example, Kanyon mall, which houses many luxury brands such as Lacoste among others.

Counterfeit luxury brand products are the biggest issue for luxury retailers in Turkey. The copies are impeccable and look very much like the original. Because the leather industry is very well developed in Turkey, counterfeit goods are easy to produce and sell in the market. The stores that sell these products get away with bribing the officials who might otherwise stop them from selling the fakes (Amed, 2008).

APPAREL RETAIL FORMATS: FROM BAZAAR TO ISTINYE PARK

Among the key organizations in the apparel sector are the Turkish Clothing Manufacturers Association, the Turkish Fashion and Apparel Federation, to which many local apparel associations belong, and the Istanbul Textile and Apparel Exporters Association. The format of Turkish apparel retail industry has four major retail establishments: malls or shopping centers; apparel shops (outlets generally on busy streets); apparel in supermarkets, hypermarkets, or megamarkets; and local bazaars organized weekly.

INTERNET SHOPPING

Fifty-six percent of Turkish consumers buy online because it is cheaper; another 36 percent buy online because of the convenience. In addition, Turkish

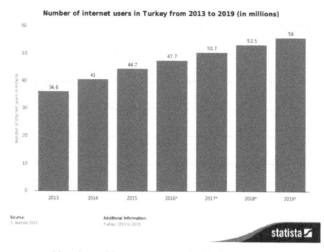

▲ FIGURE 7.5 Number of Internet users in Turkey.

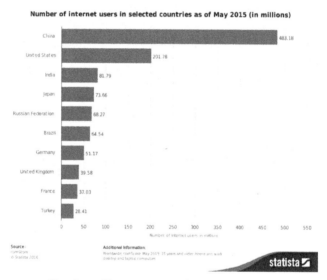

▲ FIGURE 7.6 Number of Internet users in select countries.

consumers (56 percent) value the product comments, reviews and feedback that they read online via social media (PWC April 2016).

TRADITIONAL RETAIL FORMATS

Turkey has put its own spin on the same traditional formats that exist in many other countries.

▶ Apparel Shops (Outlets)

Compared to the American apparel retail market, Turkey has substantially more sales through apparel stores located on busy streets and in local bazaars. Apparel stores on streets are not generally as sophisticated as their counterparts in shopping centers. However, it is possible to find high quality and unique apparel in such stores. Istanbul's Bagdat Street and Nisantasi (a small neighborhood popular for apparel shopping) include high quality and luxury outlets.

▶ Local Bazaars

Apparel retailing in Turkey also includes retailers in **local bazaars**, in which fruit, vegetables, grocery items, shoes, and textiles are sold. Such bazaars, established along various streets, are very informal and not common in developed countries. Sellers get permission from local authorities to set up sales stands. Payments in such bazaars are generally in the form of cash with no receipts given to the buyer. Sellers are individuals rather than companies. Sellers get products from various producers or they themselves produce or grow products (as in a farmer's market). The Turkish Council of Shopping Centers and Retailers estimates that around 4,000 local bazaars are organized weekly (2009). However, the apparel sold in these bazaars is not of high quality. A beloved organized local bazaar was Sali Pazari, which was held every Tuesday and Friday in the Kadikoy neighborhood of Istanbul. It ceased to exist in 2008 due to modernization efforts. There is now a more organized market instead. This bazaar was a good representation of local bazaars in Turkey. The clothes sold in this market were considered to be the cheapest in town. Shoppers could find not only apparel but also furniture, jewelry, and antiques. Many neighborhoods have their own weekly bazaars (generally on different days in different neighborhoods) where people go on foot with their own small shopping carts and have the opportunity to buy many different things. Grocery items are fresh and of much better quality than those sold in stores.

MODERN RETAIL FORMATS

These are formats that are usually seen in all developed nations.

▶ Supermarkets, Hypermarkets, Megamarkets

Until the late 1980s, shops—whether grocery, jewelry, apparel, or other kinds of retail—were generally located on the first or ground floor of buildings where

▲ FIGURE 7.7 Cloth and lace on sale at Istanbul's Grand Bazaar, one of the largest covered markets in the world.

people lived. It was normal for a person, especially a mother, to call for grocery items (bread, cheese, newspaper, etc.) from her balcony to be delivered in a basket hanging from a rope on the balcony down to the grocery store. Grocery shopping does not get more timely or convenient. The number of such small retail stores is on the decline, and many people miss them. These small stores are being replaced by big stores (called supermarkets, hypermarkets, or mega-markets). These stores aren't convenient in terms of location but make up for it in low prices and convenience as many products can be found in such big markets. As car ownership increases in Turkey, more and more people tend to choose to travel to these big stores.

Since the early 1990s, such big stores have trended more and more toward selling their own brands (also called store brand or designer brand) in many product categories, including apparel. Migros pioneered selling own-brand products. Other stores and chains such as Metro (Germany), Gima (Turkey), Tansas (Turkey), Kipa (Turkey), Ismar (Turkey), Continent (Turkey), and Carrefour (France) also sell many own-brand products. Migros Ticaret, one of the largest retailers owned by Turkey's Andolu Endustri Holding, carries its food retailing across three brands. Migros covers super and hypermarket sales, while discount stores operate under the Tansas umbrella with Macro Center being responsible for more up-market gourmet options. Migros Ticaret, originated as a joint venture between Swiss-based Migros Co-operatives and the Istanbul Municipality—exemplifying the success of foreign firms in Turkish food retailing (Market Insights, 2014).

▸ Malls/Shopping Centers

Together with increases in industrialization and modernization, more and more malls or shopping centers have opened, especially in big cities. Istanbul, the trade capital of Turkey, hosts the highest number (61 in 2010) of shopping centers. In addition, the recent trends have seen the spread of shopping centers to secondary cities. For example, in 2013 new centers were seen in Gaziantep, Sanliurfa, Kahramanmaras and Samsun. The second trend is the opening of exclusive outlets in the more developed market of Istanbul. For example, the Zorlu Centre, opened in 2013, houses a variety of luxury outlets, initiating a new wave of exclusive, high-end retail malls (Oxford Business Group, 2014).

The rapid growth of the shopping mall sector in Turkey without detailed regulation has led to a new law (Draft Law) in January 2015 on the Regulation of Retail Trade focusing on opening, activities and audit of retail businesses, mainly shopping malls, department stores and chain stores. The draft high-lights are below (CMS Law Now, 2015):

▸ *Working Hours*: The working hours of certain or all retail businesses may be determined by the relevant governor, pursuant to obtaining the opinions of the relevant municipality, chamber of commerce and other craftspeople's associations.

▸ *Common Areas*: Every shopping mall must have common areas such as emergency medical response units, places of worship and children's play areas. For existing shopping malls, these common areas must become operational within one year from the date the Draft Law enters into effect.

▸ *Areas for Social and Cultural Activities*: An area equal to 5 per thousand of the shopping space must be reserved for social and cultural activities.

▸ *Allocation of Space for Craftspeople*: At least 5 percent of the total shopping mall area must be leased to craftspeople. Especially to those engaging in traditional crafts having a cultural or artistic value which is under risk of extinction.

- Chain and department stores must allocate at least 1 percent of shelf space for the sale of local goods produced in the region in which the store is located.
- *Regulation of Outlet Stores*: The outlet stores must display the sign on the facade of the store. However, in order for shopping malls to be able to display such sign, at least 70 percent of stores within the shopping mall must be outlet stores.

The Mall of Istanbul (MOI) is one of the biggest malls in Turkey developed by Torunlar GYO. It opened to visitors on May 23, 2014, with its 350 stores, gourmet center, MOIPark (the first specially designed theme park), traditional street arts and performance arts center. MOI hosts both national and international leading brands with a total of 350 stores. Some of the brands to been seen here are Migros, Koctas, Media Markt, Teknosa, Zara, Mudo, and YKM. Victoria's Secret has a full concept store while Debenhams opened its second store with a new concept. Furthermore, Decathlon of France and Miss Selfridge of the UK are only some of the global brands that have opened locations for the first time in malls owned by Torunlar. In 2007, the upscale Istinye Park opened in Istanbul. It includes 300 stores and the first IMAX theater. In 2013, the Zorlu Center opened in Istanbul. It features a luxurious shopping center, a center for performance arts, a five-star hotel, offices, and residences. It houses 180 different stores. Apple introduced the iconic cube store concept in its first Turkish store. Beymen has opened its largest department store here. Brooks Brothers, Industrie Denim, Cos, Lanvin, Pomellato, Stella McCartney, and Superdry are other brands who opened their first Turkish stores here.

▶ Department Stores

Major department stores in Turkey are as follows: Begendik, Beymen, Boyner, Mudo, Vakko, and YKM (Yeni Karamursel Magazasi) (www.mymerhaba.com). Begendik is located in Ankara and sells everything a consumer could need from textiles to cosmetics and kitchenware; everything except alcoholic drinks. The prices are mostly for the middle class. Begendik operates 46 supermarkets and 13 hypermarkets throughout Turkey. Due to fierce competition in the retail market many international chains have recently pulled out of Turkey. This, in turn, has helped domestic players such as Begendik, who bought 12 stores from German food retailer Metro AG in 2014.

Beymen provides its customers with stylish but wearable clothing, shoes, and accessories for everyone in the family under their own exceptionally high quality, locally manufactured brand name. It also carries a selection of world-renowned brands such as Donna Karan, Dice Kayek, and Sonia Rykiel, among others. Beymen also has a sleek yet comfortable range of home decor items. Beyond the quality of their goods, Beymen is known for providing extraordinary service. Beymen has also a brand of both casual and elegant clothing for children and the younger sportier crowd called "BM Club."

Boyner Holding, one of the leading holdings and the owner of Beymen, opened Boyner (formerly Carsi), which stands by its motto, "Buy quality for less," and produces goods under the name Altimod as a sister to the Altinyildiz brand, a high quality name in Turkey. Boyner has since become a well-known department store with branches in almost all shopping malls. In addition to clothing, it sells sports gear, kitchenware, home decor, glassware, fashionable bags and shoes, as well as internationally known brands of cosmetics. Mudo is one of Turkey's best fashion companies. Mudo goods are stylish, and include a range of both professional and casual men and women's clothing, as well as children's fashion and a selection of attractive rustic home decor.

Vakko: "Fashion is Vakko" has long been the motto of this ultra-chic Turkish style house. It started in 1934 when Mr. Vitali Hakko started small millinery called Şen Şapka (Merry Hat). As the business expanded the name was changed to Vakko, and the company began to produce haute couture scarves made of Turkish silk, cotton, and wool. When the first Vakko store opened at Beyoğlu, Istanbul in 1964, it was the biggest store that had ever been built there and made Vakko the biggest brand-name phenomenon on the Turkish clothing scene. Vakko has continued to develop its wares by creating a line of home decor, a clothing line for men, perfumes V de Vakko (for men), Katia (for women) and Piu Piu (for children). The Vakko Company also opened Vakkorama stores that cater to younger tastes and is home to Power FM, a radio station that focuses on international pop music. One of the traditional gifts that Turks give to one another is a box of chocolates or stylishly wrapped candies. If you want to impress a Turk, choose from Vakko's wide assortment of chocolates, which always have that perfect finishing touch, which is Vakko's trademark.

YKM is one of the oldest department stores in Ankara. Its principal aim is to meet the needs of the entire family. With its own credit card, YKM allows its customers to make interest-free installment payments.

▶ *Specialty Stores*

There are several small specialty stores selling specific items such as scarves, sports apparel, leather apparel, and so on. One famous specialty store in Turkey is Derimod, which has produced leather apparel since the 1970s.

STORE OWNERSHIP: FAMILIES RUN THE SHOW

Over 50,000 companies operate in the Turkish textile and apparel industry. More than 90 percent of these companies are family owned, and more than 80 percent of these are small and medium-sized enterprises employing fewer than 250 employees (Eraslan, Bakan, and Kuyucu, 2008). Children take over these businesses when their parents retire. This family dominance is prevalent even in very large firms in Turkey. Koc Holding, a Fortune 500 company, was established and managed by textile magnate Vehbi Koc, it was then managed between 1984 and 2003 by his son Rahmi Koc; his grandson Mustafa Koc is the current honorary chairman of the board of Koc holdings. Vehbi Koc (1901–1996) was a brilliant entrepreneur. Through his partnership with Ford, General Electric, and Mobil prior to the 1950s, and his other business ventures afterwards, his company quickly developed into one of the largest groups in Turkey.

LC Waikiki started in France in 1985, continuing after 1997 as a Turkish brand under the umbrella of LC Waikiki Mağazacılık Hizmetleri Ticaret A.Ş. LC Waikiki has 651 stores in 31 countries (2016). LC Waikiki, which was selected as Turkey's "Favorite Company in the Ready-to-Wear Industry of 2013" was actually established in 1988 by the Dizdar family from Safranbolu, and the Küçük and Kısacık families from Malatya. The Dizdar, Küçük, Kısacık and Amouyal families currently hold most of the shares of LC Waikiki Retail Company.

FDI REGULATIONS: WIDE OPEN

In 1954, the Turkish Government passed the Foreign Capital Incentives Law, which outlined restrictions on and conditions for foreign investments in Turkey. A new foreign direct investment law enacted in 2003 canceled this law and its restrictions, and made Turkey one of the most liberal OECD countries with respect to foreign direct investment. Turkey's regulatory environment is extremely business friendly. The key features of this law are (Investment in Turkey, 2016):

▶ Foreign investors are free to make foreign direct investments and are to be treated the same as domestic investors. Thus, foreign companies will not be restricted in terms of ownership, income or management rights. This freedom levels the playing field for foreign companies in competition with domestic companies, and ensures their full ownership. In addition, foreign investors no longer face pre-entry or pre-establishment screening requirements, nor do they need to notify the Undersecretariat of the Treasury of Turkey. They just need to follow the same regular company establishment procedures as domestic Turkish firms.

- ► Foreign direct investments cannot be expropriated or nationalized. (Nationalization is where the host country governments take over companies.) As this law prevents nationalization, expropriation is not an issue in Turkey.

- ► The new law removed any financial restrictions related to foreign investment. Foreign investors can freely transfer abroad: profits, dividends, proceeds from the sale or liquidation of all or any part of an investment, amounts arising from license, management and similar agreements, and reimbursements and interest payments arising from foreign loans through banks or special financial institutions. Foreign companies may freely acquire real estate (in lieu of rent).

- ► For the settlement of disputes arising from investment agreements subject to private law and investment disputes arising from public service concessions contracts and conditions concluded with foreign investors, foreign investors can apply either to the authorized local courts or to national or international arbitration or other means of dispute settlement, provided that the conditions in the related regulations are fulfilled and the parties agree thereon. In any dispute or law suit, foreign investors have the right of dispute settlement in local courts or international arbitration agencies.

The bottom line of this law is that foreign companies are treated equally and are subject to the same regulations as domestic Turkish firms. Turkey also has double taxation prevention treaties with 82 countries. A double taxation treaty means that a foreign company will not be taxed twice on the same income by both its home government (country A) and host country government (country B). If there is no such treaty between two countries, then country A would tax the company's income generated in the foreign market as the company belongs to or is registered in the home country; the host country B would also tax this company for generating profit in country B. So, this company would have to pay income tax (on the same income, the one generated in the foreign country) twice, which would make international operations less profitable and less attractive. To prevent this double taxation and ease the tax burden, countries sign double taxation prevention treaties. Foreign investors are encouraged to read the *Investors' Guide for Turkey* published by the Republic of Turkey Prime Ministry Investment Support and Promotion Agency of the Republic of Turkey (ISPAT).

INTERNATIONAL BRANDS: STRATEGIC LOCATION IS THE KEY

There is no restriction on entry for multi- or single-brand international retailers. International apparel retailers target menswear, womenswear, and childrenswear, but their presence in the womenswear segment is the most visible, in both the malls and on the high street. The womenswear segment accounts for 35 percent of all apparel sales in Turkey. Many international apparel retailers (such as Bottega Veneta, Gant, Ermenegildo Zegna, Nine West, Paul & Shark, Marks & Spencer) serve middle and upper class customers. In addition to multinationals in the clothing industry, multinationals in the beauty, personal care, and cosmetic industries also operate in Turkey. Many large cosmetics and personal care companies (such as Procter & Gamble, Henkel, Colgate Palmolive, and Unilever) have production and marketing centers in Turkey and operate through either licensing or joint ventures. Taking advantage of Turkey's strategic location, Unilever exports goods produced in Turkey to more than 30 countries while their Istanbul HQ manages its operations in 35 countries in Central Asia, the Middle East and North Africa. In the Turkish market, domestic companies, such as Evyap (seller of soaps, hand gel, and shower gel under many different brand names, such as Duru, Fax, Activex, and Ava), offer stiff competition.

Turkish consumers are generally brand-conscious consumers in many product categories, such as clothing, cars, fragrance, and shoes. In the 1980s, when foreign trade policies changed and import substitution policies were abandoned, many foreign brands entered the Turkish market. Turkish consumers were much more obsessed with foreign brands in the 1980s and early 1990s than they are now. For example, in the 1980s and early 1990s, many young men and women had to have a pair of Levi's. Although many foreign brands are still in demand and are regarded as superior, the emergence of many domestic producers and nationalistic advertisements has increased the popularity of domestic brands. Fragrance is perhaps the exception, because famous brands are always in high demand despite much higher prices in Turkey than in Europe or the United States, owing to import costs and the fact that average personal income is two to four times higher in the West.

ENTRY FORMATS BEING CHOSEN BY INTERNATIONAL BRANDS

International retailers choose different entry formats to enter different countries based on their expansion plans and the regulations for foreign direct investment in the country. Common formats in Turkey are export, subcontracting, joint venture, licensing, and distribution.

▸ Export

An international retailer may choose the export mode to enter the Turkish market. The choice of export results from the decision of the exporter not to engage in direct investment, such as local production, in Turkey. Although Turkey offers many advantages for companies regarding local production, such as availability of resources, labor, and favorable foreign investment laws, some companies may have better production choices (locations) and prefer exporting over local production. The main advantage for such companies in adopting the export mode would be to avoid high investment costs that are associated with local production. If such retailers have efficient production bases, they produce in these locations and export to their sales markets from their production location. However, export may not be the best way to enter Turkey because export is generally associated with low profits. Also, export does not allow foreign companies to become aware of further opportunities in Turkey because their involvement level is low. At the end of the day, export choice is related to the retailers' strategic orientation and commitment level towards Turkey. Unilever and Colgate/ Palmolive both produce in and export to Turkey, whereas Procter & Gamble, L'Oreal, Wella, and J&J mostly export to Turkey.

▸ From Subcontracting to Joint Venture

Some Turkish apparel producers have long served international apparel companies as subcontractors. Others have operated through licensing. However, to increase their effectiveness, international apparel retailers have preferred the joint venture format to benefit from their Turkish partner's knowledge of the domestic market. For example, in 2005, Benetton signed a licensing agreement with the Boyner Group to initiate its Turkish operation. Boyner Group manages all commercial activities of the United Colors of Benetton, Sisley, Playlife, and Killer Loop brands in Turkey (Benetton, 2005).

▶ Licensing

Other international brands have not committed as much as Benetton, preferring the franchising entry format. For example, Fiba Holdings purchased franchising rights from Marks & Spencer and GAP and thus has the right to open and manage Marks & Spencer and GAP stores in Turkey.

▶ Distributor

Some international retailers have entered the Turkish market through distributorship agreements. For example, Jones Apparel Group (the designer and marketer of Jones New York, Nine West, Anne Klein, Gloria Vanderbilt, Kasper, Bandolino, Easy Spirit, and Evan-Picone, among others) entered Turkey via a distributorship agreement with Park Bravo. The Canadian premier lingerie retailer La Senza also chose Park Bravo when it entered the Turkish market in 2005.

INFLUENCES ON APPAREL RETAILING

According to Ali Babacan (Deputy Prime Minister of Turkey for Economic and Financial Affairs) Turkey is expected to average an annual GDP growth of 5.2 percent; over the next 10 years it will be the fastest growing country in Europe. Even as many parts of Europe experienced high unemployment, Turkey was able to create 4.9 million additional jobs since 2009 mainly because of its growth as a tourist destination. Turkey is the sixth largest country in the world for incoming tourists. This growth signifies existing opportunities for retail development across the country (Turkish Retail News Portal, 2014).

FASHION-CONSCIOUS CONSUMERS WITH MONEY

According to a report by London-based BMI Research published in October 2015, total household spending in Turkey is expected to grow by about 4.8 percent during 2016–2019; this indicates a strong growth of opportunities for retailers in the country. Young, fashion-oriented Turkish consumers spend remarkable amounts of money on designer goods and clothes. Together with increases in GDP, more and more consumers will be able to afford such products. Not only are rapid economic expansion and higher standards of living enabling Turkish consumers to purchase higher-value products, but a consumer survey conducted by IBS also indicates that Turkish consumers are becoming more brand-oriented and seek to purchase international brands.

ESTABLISHED DOMESTIC RETAIL SECTOR

Turkey's retail sector offers vast opportunities because the country is relatively underdeveloped, has a large population, and has new plans for shopping schemes. However incumbent domestic companies have already adopted modern retailing logic, and this means that foreign brands may struggle to establish themselves. Foreign retailers will no doubt face intense competition from such domestic retailers, as Turkish companies establish their own brands rather than serve as subcontractors. BMI research forecasts that 4.4 million more people will move to cities in Turkey by 2019. Urbanization and increasing levels of income will rapidly change the retail landscape in the country. The number of women in the workforce is rapidly increasing in Turkey—it is now about 34 percent—and women prefer to shop in one place due to lack of time. Retailing thus calls for "one-stop shopping" for consumers (Business, 2015).

The apparel retail sector has grown in line with the rapid growth of the general retail sector in Turkey. Two major factors are affecting this growth: increasing investment by foreign retailers, and an increase in the number of malls, shopping centers, and other retail outlets driven by the fact that Turkish textile producers switched to apparel retailing during the financial crisis of 2008. This forced companies to merge or switch to retailing due to decreasing profit margins in apparel production.

BRAND-BASED COMPETITION

Brand awareness has grown to the point that price competition and the sale of basic textile goods will not contribute much to the sector's development. In response to the demand for brands, the Turkish apparel industry has launched a nationalist branding campaign. "Turquality" was introduced in January 2004 by the Under Secretariat of Foreign Trade, the Turkish Exporter's Association, and the Istanbul Association of Textile and Apparel Exporters. "Turquality" unites the words "Turk" and "quality" in an effort to highlight the quality of Turkish products and services and upgrade the international perception of these products. The project also aims to provide a stimulus for the textile industry to upgrade its technology and reposition itself in the international market as producers of higher-end, quality apparel. The "Turquality" project now provides Turkish companies with financial support, professional consultancy and helps in the branding process of Turkish companies in the global market place in accordance with the 2023 vision for Turkey (Branding to the Top, 2014).

Brand-based competition is most intense in the sports and denim sectors. In sports apparel, Adidas, Nike, Kinetix, and Puma are among the leading retailers, whereas Levi's, Lee, Mavi Jeans, Rodi, and Leke lead in denim. Effective marketing campaigns, advertising, and orientation toward a target market are among some key success factors in apparel retailing. However, the availability of a vast number of brands in the sector prevents brand loyalty because consumers often switch brands. The chairman of Benetton underlined the importance of the Turkish population for its youth, increasing income, and fashion wisdom. Statistics show that 16 percent of the Turkish population is aged between 15 and 25. This age segment has a 26 percent share of total apparel purchases in Turkey; it is also more responsive to fashion trends.

GETTING TO KNOW DOMESTIC COMPETITORS: RISING FROM THE CRISIS

The Turkish textile sector heavily felt the effects of the global financial crisis of 2008–2009. Many factories and subcontractors closed their doors or went bankrupt. Textile firms generally chose one of the three options: engage in a merger, switch to apparel retailing, or invest in other sectors. Many chose to become apparel retailers by creating their own brands. In addition, foreign retailers coming to the market have helped to substantially increase the level of competition.

Some examples of textile firms that switched to apparel retail include (Eraslan, et al., 2008):

- ▶ Fabric producer Ozon Group, under the brand name Defacto
- ▶ Thirty-six-year-old leather producer Desa
- ▶ Fabric producer Tohum Holding, with 30 stores
- ▶ Textile producer Tedi, by opening 57 stores in one year
- ▶ Oz-El Groups, the world's third largest textile accessories producer, operating under the A'Plus brand

In addition, other textile manufacturers have collaborated on forays into retail. Seventy-eight textile producers worked together to create MOL, retail outlets that sell quality products at prices so cheap they beat East Asian imports.

Such collaboration is not widespread. As many as 15,000 different brands in the apparel sector indicates a preference for individualism among apparel producers. These apparel producers and retailers are engaged in intense competition. The Italian integration model of manufacturing, branding and marketing, which some Turkish economists have proposed to increase the competitiveness of both the textile and apparel sector, argues that small companies should merge to create big and powerful companies and that major specialized production facilities should replace many small production facilities, which are inefficient in their use of assets. Another essential component is to produce an entire collection and sell it as a brand (Foreign Market Consulting Report, 2014).

There is also the Asian effect. Turkey, like China, is a giant in the export of textile and apparel products. They are direct competitors. Products imported from various Asian countries, especially those from China, have had some market share in the Turkish clothing and footwear markets. The quality of such products is not high, but because of competitive prices they have found many Turkish buyers. This competition is perhaps more intense in the European Union (EU) market because Turkey is a key apparel exporter to the EU. Turkey has a customs union agreement with the EU, indicating that Turkey will abide by EU customs rules. Although this agreement has opened some doors to Turkish textile and apparel producers benefiting from common customs, it also brought some disadvantages. For example, the EU removed customs barriers (especially quotas) with China in 2005, leading to a considerable increase in levels of Chinese exports. These increases also affected Turkey, which had to adopt this customs removal as well. When the domestic market became vulnerable to a flood of Chinese products, Turkey applied the protection rule of the customs union agreement. To restrict the market penetration of Chinese manufacturers, the Turkish Government required them to apply for certification. Thus, Turkey was able to minimize the effect of Chinese textile and apparel exports. Whereas some Turkish textile and apparel companies preferred the cheap Chinese products, others raised concerns about their sustainability and their quality.

The textile and apparel sector focused on production and export for decades before reorienting itself towards organized, brand-based retail chains in the apparel sector. Domestic chains such as Collezione, LC Waikiki, Ipekyol, Vakko, and Sarar together with international chains such as Benetton, Bata, LaCoste, Nine West, Zara, Mango, H&M, Topshop, Adidas, and Nike are well established based on brand or experience in the Turkish market. Leading Turkish brands can be seen across the world, from Las Vegas and Dubai to Berlin, Tokyo and Moscow. For example, LC Waikiki, which is Turkey's biggest fast-fashion brand, has about 407 stores across the country and a further 106 across the globe. Sarar, a Turkish brand has about 15 stores across the US and aims to add 100 stores within the next 10 years. Sarar and brands such as Mudo and İpekyol are making inroads into the Middle East. Besides, Turkey's young, stylish, urban population along with growing number of working women are demanding higher-quality, stylish yet affordable designs to suit their busy lives. Several fashion bloggers promote foreign brands such as Michael Kors, Chanel, Primark, Mango, and Zara, showing fashion fans how to mix and match with local brands (Holland, G, 2015). For international retailers willing to enter the Turkish market, these four formats are recommended:

1. If their brand is well known, international retailers can capitalize on this through sole ownership. Prada, which opened two stores in fashionable Istanbul neighborhoods in 2009, is a good example.
2. If a brand does not provide very high leverage in competition, a joint venture with a well positioned Turkish firm would be a good option for entry. Even well-known brands choose this option because the apparel sector is very sensitive to the cultural and religious differences between Turkey and Western countries.
3. Purchase an established brand in the Turkish market.
4. Enter the market and then try to gradually increase brand awareness. This may take time, and there are many established brands in the market. This may prove difficult for unknown brands.

BUYING FOR APPAREL RETAIL STORES: LOOK NO FURTHER, IT'S ALL AT HOME

The Turkish apparel industry makes sourcing easy for retailers in many ways: richness in materials (Turkey is the world's sixth-largest cotton producer and also an important producer of man-made fibers); proximity to major markets (especially the EU); the ability to respond quickly to orders; qualified labor; the presence of apparel-related industries; the capacity to create fashionable, well-designed, and innovative products; participation in a customs union agreement with the EU; and free trade agreements with many countries (State Planning Organization, 2004).

There are more than 50,000 companies in the Turkish textile and apparel industry. About 95 percent of these companies are family owned, 85 percent of these companies are small and medium-sized enterprises, and 25 percent engage in exports. Technology-oriented production is realized only by big firms. In the Turkish textile and apparel sector, there are two kinds of manufacturing companies: those who set standards in the sector by producing high-quality thread, yarn, and fabrics, and those producing ready-made, no-brand clothing using domestic and imported fabrics. These second category producers sell their no-brand apparel to retailers through intermediaries. No-brand apparel makes up a large portion of domestic apparel production and export. However, Turkey is keener on building brands as their goal for 2023. In addition, there are wholesalers and retailers that are not producers.

Foreign apparel is marketed in Turkey through foreign sourcing firms and distributors, which organize sales and marketing programs according to consumer base or demand characteristics. Many international apparel and textile firms have procurement and contact offices and retail outlets in Istanbul, which they use as the procurement center for their European and Asian outlets. In addition to Istanbul, cities such as Izmir, Bursa, Ankara, Denizli, Gaziantep, Kayseri, Tekirdag, and Adana are major apparel sourcing sites.

International retailers either export their apparel products to Turkey or use domestic subcontractors or companies if they are in a joint venture or licensing agreement. For example, Benetton has many subcontractors in both Italy and Turkey. Levi Strauss has production facilities in Turkey and Levi's Turkey also exports to many countries in the Middle East, the Caucasus, and Central Asia. Turkey has emerged as one of the major suppliers for international textile and fashion brands mainly due to its dynamic and flexible production capacity and cost-efficient logistics by fulfilling a near-sourcing solution for Finnish textiles and apparel companies. In 2014, Turkey was ranked as the world's seventh biggest apparel exporter (USD 18.7 billion) with global market share of 3.4 percent. Turkey is also the third biggest apparel supplier to the EU market after China and Bangladesh. Turkey is a major sourcing hub for many international buying offices, trading houses, and international retailers including Adidas, Gap, Hugo Boss, Inditex Group, Arcadia Group, Kappahl, Marks & Spencer, H&M, Debenhams, Varner, Next Sourcing and French Connection.

RETAIL CAREERS: NEED MORE TALENT

The growth of the Turkish retail sector demands qualified labor. Unfortunately, the supply of qualified sales representatives for the increasing number of shopping centers and stores is falling far behind demand. Retailing in Turkey is not seen as a career but just temporary work. Educational programs in retailing are very limited. Anadolu University and Kocaeli University offer retailing certificates and college degrees, and some vocational high schools offer courses in retailing. Some companies (such as Mudo, Teknosa, and Hatemoglu) train their employees themselves and are thus able to decrease labor turnover in their retail outlets to a certain extent. However, managers and college professors agree that there is a huge demand for qualified employees in the retail sector in Turkey (Konuk, 2008).

The Ministry of Labor and Social Security is the government agency dealing with the work permits that foreigners need to work in Turkey. The agency organizes work permits under three categories: work permit for a definite period; work permit for an indefinite period; and independent work permit.

DEFINITE PERIOD

Unless there are other provisions in the bilateral or multilateral agreements to which Turkey is a party, permission to work is valid for a maximum of one year. After one year, the permit may be extended up to three years, on condition of working for the same company and in the same job. At the end of that three-year period, the work permit may be extended for a maximum of three years to work in the same profession with any employer. The work permit may also be granted to the spouse of any foreigner who has come to Turkey to work, as well as the children under the foreigner's care, under the condition that they have legally resided with the foreigner without interruption for at least five years.

INDEFINITE PERIOD

Unless there are other provisions in the bilateral or multilateral contracts to which Turkey is a party, foreigners who have resided in Turkey legally and continuously for at least eight years, or who have legally worked in Turkey for a total of eight years, may be granted a work permit without terms.

INDEPENDENT WORK PERMIT

The Ministry of Labor and Social Security may grant an independent work permit to foreigners who want to work independently on the condition that they have resided in Turkey legally and uninterruptedly for at least five years and that their work will have a positive effect on national employment and economic development (Ministry of Labor and Social Security, 2015).

Some useful web resources on Turkish retail jobs are: www.elemanara. com (Turkish), www.cvtr.net (Turkish), www.eleman.net (Turkish), and

TABLE 7.3 Selected Clothing, Footwear, and Accessories Retailers in Turkey in 2015

Chain	Owner/Franchisee	Store Count 2015
LC Waikiki	LC Waikiki Magazacilik Hizmetleri Tic AS	407
Mavi	Mavi Giyim San ve Tic AS	339
Zara Group (all brands)	Inditex	1931
Lacoste	Eren Holding AS	120
Mango	Mango Turkiye Tekstil ve Ticaret Ltd Sti	120
Benetton	Benetton Giyim San ve Tic AS	119
Vakko	Vakko Tekstil ve Ticaret AS	87
H&M	H&M Hennes & Mauritz AB	46
Marks & Spencer	Marks & Spencer/Fiba Holding	46
GAP	GAP Inc/Fiba Holding	30
C&A	C&A	26
Apple	Apple	3
Michael Kors	Michael Kors	3

Sources: C&A Istanbul—Fashion Turkey. (n.d.). Retrieved May 24, 2016, from http://www.fashionturkey.co.uk/C&A-istanbul

[1] 2014 Store Count

www.kariyer.net (Turkish). Some industry websites are www.perakende.org, www.ampd.org. (Turkish), www.perakendehaber.org, and www.perakende.tv.

THE FUTURE OF APPAREL RETAIL: AN OPPORTUNITY CALLING

Being a very large sector, the textile and apparel sector plays an important role in the Turkish economy and generates huge employment. The Turkish retail sector is continuing to grow despite tough trading conditions. General retailers hold the largest share of retail sales in 2014, and will continue to dominate the market in 2019.

Online retail channels are seeing the fastest growth, followed by department stores. The electrical and electronics category is expected to grow the fastest, followed by apparel, accessories, luggage, and leather goods over the next five years (ASD reports, 2015).

Four distinct trends emerge from the examination of publications, speeches, and sector reports related to the Turkish apparel sector:

1. More and more investments by foreign apparel retailers
2. Establishment of new shopping centers, not only in big cities but also in others
3. Tendency on the part of domestic textile firms to become apparel retailers
4. Growing brand awareness and creation of brands and quality products as Turkey 2023 initiative (for example, the "Turquality" campaign)

As the Turkish economy becomes more stable and the government enacts favorable foreign investment laws, foreign investors become more willing to operate in the Turkish market. So, competition from foreign investors is expected to increase in the apparel retailing sector. An increasing number of stores or retail outlets by the incumbent apparel firms and the establishment of new shopping centers are indications of retail growth in general and apparel retailing growth in particular. The conversion of domestic textile companies into apparel retailers will no doubt intensify the competition in international apparel retailing, especially as more and more Turkish apparel brands make their debuts in international markets in the spotlight of the "Turquality" campaign.

Growth in apparel retail requires success in creating a brand. Turkish apparel firms have not been as successful in this area as their foreign counterparts. The transfer of foreign knowledge through experience would be valuable to them. Malgorzata Machnicka, retail analyst at PMR, indicates that large European retailers have difficulty surviving in Turkey. The joint venture is a preferred means of entry into the Turkish market. Joint ventures offer an excellent opportunity for shared knowledge (Machnicka, 2009). Joint venture agreements with Turkish companies that have proved a profitable model for international companies include British DIY company Kingfisher's 50 percent joint venture with Turkish Koc Group's to form KocTas, which resulted in the

▲ FIGURE 7.8 Bridal Wear Seller on Mahmutpasa Shopping street, Istanbul, Turkey. The narrow climbing street Mahmutpasha is the place where those of a conservative nature come to buy a coat or a headscarf, or to kit their boys out in the costume they wear on circumcision day at weekends. Located in the area between Grand Bazaar and Eminonu, it is a symbol of cheap shopping in Istanbul.

creation of a market leader. Overall the growing economy, affluent consumer trends and increase in spending levels have created opportunities for international businesses in Turkey. The key to market success lies in responding to cultural behavioral patterns and sensitivities.

International brands or retailers began to enter the Turkish market during the 1980s, mostly through licensing agreements or joint ventures. In the apparel sector, these included such stores as Benetton in 1986, Mothercare in 1988, Levi's in 1989, and LC Waikiki in 1991 (Ar & Saydan, 2004).

SUMMARY

Twenty-first century Turkey is the fourth largest labor force in relation to EU countries, having a large population (79.4m) of qualified, cost-effective, and motivated people; this population also means a large consumer base, especially in terms of increasing purchasing power. Foreign companies often find the Turkish labor force to be educated, skilled, motivated, and effective. Turkey's young population and strategic location are big draws for foreign companies that choose the country as a site for both production and sales.

Attractive as Turkey's location is to foreign investors, they must keep in mind the country's mixed national and business culture. Understanding consumer behavior and business practices requires an understanding of Turkey's unique blend of European and Asian cultures and business practices. Islamic values mean a great deal to many people as well as to some companies. Such values affect the apparel purchases of a considerable number of women. However, such values are not as important to the Turkish government as they are in other Arabic countries. Nevertheless recent political events are beginning to affect this former status quo.

The retail sector in Turkey has held strong in 2015 with an 8.6 percent increase from the prior year for a total of $438 billion. Retail forecasts remain optimistic through 2020. As with other emerging markets, internet retailing has been explosive. In addition, informal retail formats are on the decline, giving way to the shopping malls. Turkey now has more than 350 shopping malls; Istanbul alone is home to 150!

The textile and apparel industries have long been established in Turkey. Among the strengths of the Turkish textile and apparel industry are domestic cotton production, proximity to the EU market, skillful labor, investment in infrastructure and telecommunication systems, and a large domestic market.

Turkey has a vast majority of its population living in urban environments, 92.1 percent according to TurkStat. These consumers are increasingly educated due to formal schooling and the Internet. Clothing laws have been part of Turkish law since the early twentieth century and have changed the way people dress, encouraging a more Westernized look. Blogs, magazines, movies, TV, celebrities, and all social media have influenced Turkish consumers' preference for apparel. In addition, with easy travel to Western Europe, Turkish tourists constantly bring back the latest fashions from European capitals. Urbanization and increasing incomes are rapidly changing the retail landscape in the country. The increasing number of women in the workforce in Turkey has changed the preference of shopping among women. They have more disposable income and prefer to shop at one place due to lack of time. Retailing thus calls for opportunity in one-stop shopping for consumers. Turkey is the fastest-growing market for luxury goods in the world. In 2014, luxury sales in Turkey jumped by 37 percent to an estimated $3 billion. By 2018, the market is expected to reach $5.4 billion. A key component of Turkey's luxury market is not only its rising economy but also its position as a tourist destination. These well-heeled travelers account for 20 percent of Turkey's total luxury market, with a majority of them arriving from the Middle East, Russia and Central Asia (McKinsey & Company Report, 2014)

As more middle-class consumers and newly wealthy, entrepreneurial elite emerge across the country, a greater share of spending is happening outside of Istanbul. For example in Ankara, Izmir, Bursa, Konya, Antalya, Mersin and Kayseri, four-fifths of the households have annual incomes greater than $75,000 and better purchasing power. There is much growth ahead in the use of digital and mobile shopping, Young aspirational and new entrant consumers are going online to shop and search for discounts.

Key marketing strategies for brands entering and expanding within Turkey start with securing the right retail space. Finding the right location not just in Istanbul, but ultimately in cities beyond the capital, like Ankara and Antalya, is vital. Next is to ensure affordability and create brand awareness. Turkish consumers are still somewhat price sensitive. This is evidenced, for instance, by the department store Beymen, which organizes "Butterfly Days" on the last day of each month, offering selected items at half price and arranging special promotions for their loyalty card holders. Finally, it is important to attract and capitalize on digital consumers by engaging with them on their multichannel journey.

CRITICAL THINKING QUESTIONS

1. The Turkish Republic was founded in 1923. Shortly thereafter, Ataturk's 1925 Hat Law and the 1934 Clothing Law were established to give the Turkish people a Westernized look. Both these laws are still in existence. Would it be possible to pass such laws today in Turkey? Why or why not?

2. Modest fashion is finally being recognized by the international design community. In 2016, Modest Fashion Week was started in Istanbul and Dolce & Gabbana produced a collection for Muslim consumers. If you were a Turkish retail company, how would you market this trend as fashion to increase sales volume?

3. The halal beauty and personal care products sector is growing in Turkey. There are many successful vegan beauty brands such as Pacifica, skyn ICELAND, and Color Proof hair care. Would you introduce a vegan

beauty brand in Turkey? If so, how would you enter this market from both a retail format and Foreign Direct Investment (FDI) perspective?

4. As nations develop and grow their middle class, obesity becomes a concern. Thirty-eight percent of Turkish people are currently overweight. Obesity has become a growing tendency in many developing markets. Is fashion now being influenced by obesity?

5. As a foreign retailer planning to expand your apparel business within Turkey how would you capitalize on the burgeoning luxury consumers?

Case Study

LC WAIKIKI: THE MOST LOVABLE BRAND

LC Waikiki, the leader in the Turkish clothing industry, is a good example of the establishment and growth of a Turkish apparel firm. LC Waikiki was originally a French apparel firm established in 1985 by George Amoual, the French designer and his partner. In 1988, LC Waikiki was searching for a subcontractor to meet its increasing demand. LC Waikiki signed a subcontractor contract with Taha Textile, and later became Taha Group, a branch of Tema Holding, the current owner of LC Waikiki. Taha Group was then the subcontractor of many big companies. Taha Group established Tema Textile to operate in the retail sector and introduced LC Waikiki products to Turkish consumers in 1991 (LC Waikiki, 2009).

LC Waikiki entered the Turkish ready-made clothing market with a line of childrenswear and later added adult clothing to its range of products. Within a short time, LC Waikiki expanded its product line to include collections designed for infants, children, youth, and adults. Tema Textile purchased the LC Waikiki brand in 1997. The number of retail outlets increased from 21 in the early days to 250 in 2009. Today LC Waikiki trades in 684 stores in 32 countries. After the purchase, the company introduced many other sub-brands. By combining superior product quality and reasonable pricing policies with wise investments, LC Waikiki has quickly become a leader in the apparel market in Turkey. It continues to reinforce its position through ongoing investments, the provision of uniform service and product quality throughout the country, and the importance it attaches to its customers. In 2009, the company set its sights on being among third biggest brands in Europe by 2020 (LC Waikiki, 2009).

LC Waikiki has had the growth problem, or rather the growth vision. The following actions have been taken. First, the company focused on further developing its identity by opening contemporary stores that have a Western look just like typical stores seen in the U.S. malls. Then, the company established Zirve Architect, an affiliate, to develop store concepts for Tema Group and Taha Clothing. They also opened procurement offices in China, Bangladesh, and Egypt. Other collections and brands (such as Southblue and XSIDE) were also introduced. Southblue targeted adult male and female consumers desiring elegant clothes, whereas XSIDE targeted younger consumers desiring casual apparel. However, Tema Group did not limit itself to production and sales of only its own brands. Rather, Tema Group also tried to increase its growth and competitiveness through production for the world's leading brands such as Marks & Spencer, Top Shop, Decathlon, and Tommy Hilfiger among others (LC Waikiki, 2009).

Today, Tema Group produces apparel sold in LC Waikiki stores through both domestic and global supply chain systems. The performance of the company is very significant. The company achieved sales growth rates of 45 percent and 46 percent in 2007 and 2008, respectively. With its 250 stores in 51 cities of Turkey, it serves millions of consumers. In 2003, the company ranked 185 on the Capital 500 list, a Turkish company ranking similar to the Fortune 500. The company has increased five points in 2016 and is now ranked 26 on the Capital 500 list. It has become the third largest company in the Turkish retail industry and the third highest employer. According to "100 Women-Friendly Companies Research" conducted by Capital Magazine in 2015, LC Waikiki ranked 2 in terms of the number of female employees and 1 in terms of female managers. According to the research results of *Perapost Magazine* based on 2014 sales, LC Waikiki was ranked 1 in the readymade garment category and 3 on the general list among the first 100 retail companies (LC Waikiki, 2016).

The case of LC Waikiki (Tema Group, Taha Holding) exemplifies a successful business strategy through brand development and global supply chain establishment. The company was initially a subcontractor of LC Waikiki and later purchased the brand. It may use a similar strategy to further grow in international markets because it currently produces for other brands. Such a carefully planned growth strategy may also suit other companies.

Discussion Questions

1. Tema Holding produced for LC Waikiki long before purchasing it. Is long experience in an industry and especially in the apparel industry a must for success? Would new apparel companies or brands have little chance of success?
2. Is acquisition a good way to grow in the Turkish apparel industry? What factors should be considered before acquisition decisions?
3. LC Waikiki initially sold children's clothing and then expanded to other segments as well. How can an apparel firm assess whether its brand will be successful in other segments?

REFERENCES

Amed, I. (2008, October 16). Turkey: Counterfeit Culture. Retrieved October 14, 2010 from www.businessoffashion.com/2008/10/turkey-counterfeit-culture.html

Ar, A. A., & Saydan, R. (2004). Marka olusturulmasinda konumlandirma strateji ve Mavi Jeans ornegi, *Mevzuat Dergisi*, 7(81), Retrieved December 6, 2009, from www.mevzuatdergisi.com/2004/09a/02.htm.

Articlebase (2009). The history of Mavi Jeans brand. *Articlebase.com*, Retrieved December 9, 2009, from http://www.articlesbase.com/clothing-articles/the-history-of-mavi-jeans-brand–1556413.html

ASD reports. (2015). Retrieved June 30, 2016 from https://www.asdreports.com/market-research-report–217152/future-retailing-turkey

BASF Turkey. (n.d.). Retrieved May 30, 2016 from www.basf.com/tr/en/company/about-us/basf-tuerk.html

Benetton (2005). Press Release. *Benetton*, Retrieved December 23, 2009 from http://press.benettongroup.com/ben_en/releases/2005–04–21

Branding to the Top (2014). Retrieved June 30, 2016 from www.turkeydiscovert hepotential.com/en/news/get/the-turkish-perspective–2014–25-branding-to-the-top.

Business (2015). Retrieved June 30, 2016 from www.dailysabah.com/money/2015/10/16/turkish-retail-sector-grows-despite-tough-conditions

C&A Istanbul—Fashion Turkey. (n.d.). Retrieved May 24, 2016 from www.fashionturkey.co.uk/C&A-istanbul

CIA, The World Factbook (2009a). Maps, Political World, *CIA*, Retrieved October 19, 2009 from www.cia.gov/library/publications/the-world-factbook/docs/refmaps.html

CIA, The World Factbook (2009b). County Information. *CIA*, Retrieved December 17, 2009, from www.cia.gov/library/publications/the-world-factbook/index.html

Clover, J. (2106). Apple Planning to Open Third Retail Store in Turkey in 2016—Mac Rumors. Retrieved January 28, 2016 from www.macrumors.com/2016/01/28/apple-third-turkey-store-coming–2016/

CMS Law Now (2015). New Regulation for Shopping Malls in Turkey. Retrieved June 8, 2016 from www.cms-lawnow.com/ealerts/2015/01/new-regulation-for-shopping-malls-in-turkey?cc_lang=en

Demography and Labor Force—Invest in Turkey. (n.d.). [Turkish government]. Retrieved May 30, 2016, from www.invest.gov.tr/enUS/investmentguide/investorsguide/Pages/DemographyAndLaborForces.aspx

Eraslan, H., Bakan, I., & Kuyucu, A. (2008). Turk tekstil ve hair giyim sektorunun uluslararasi rekabetcilik duzeyinin analizi. *Istanbul Ticaret Universitesi Sosyal Bilimler Dergisi, 7*(13), 265–300.

Euromonitor (2009). Clothing and footwear in Turkey: Market Report, *Euromonito*r, October 2009. Retrieved October 25, 2009 from www.euromonitor.com/ Clothing_And_Footwear_in_Turkey

Euromonitor Passport. (2016). Euromonitor International—Turkey: Country Profile (Turkey: Country Profile). Retrieved May 15, 2016 from http://libproxy.fitsuny. edu:2141/portal/analysis/tab

Foreign Market Consulting Report (2014). Retrieved May 15, 2016 from www. slideshare.net/FMConsulting/fmc140709de-textile-industry

Gap—Fashion Turkey. (n.d.). Retrieved May 24, 2016, from www.fashionturkey.co.uk/gap

Genc, K. (2013, November 11). Turkey's Glorious Hat Revolution—Los Angeles Review of Books. Retrieved May 30, 2016 from https://lareviewofbooks.org/article/ turkeys-glorious-hat-revolution/

Ghanem, K. (2016, January 5). What is Halal Makeup? | Style.com/Arabia. Style.com/ Arabia. Retrieved from http://arabia.style.com/beauty/beauty-counter/what-is-halal-makeup-explained/

H&M Annual Report 2015. (2016). (Annual Report) (p. 110). Sweden. Retrieved from http://about.hm.com/content/dam/hm/about/documents/en/Annual%20 Report/Annual%20Report%202015_en.pdf

Haber Turk (2006). Kizlar Gece Dekolteli Gunduz Dusuk Belli: Genclik Arastirmasi, *Haber Turk*, Retrieved December 23, 2009, from www.haberturk.com/haber.asp ?id=3867&cat=200&dt=2006/10/24

History of Turkish Clothing. (n.d.). Retrieved from www.turkishculture.org/fabrics-and-patterns/clothing–593.htm

Holland. G (2015). The Best Turkish Fashion Brands. Retrieved May 30, 2016 from www.globalblue.com/destinations/turkey/istanbul/best-turkish-fashion-brands

How Many Shopping Malls Are There in Turkey? (2015, December 2). Real Estate News. Retrieved from http://realestatenews.com.tr/how-many-shopping-malls-are-there-in-turkey/

HTP Arastirma ve Danismanlik and Retailing Institute (2003). Turkiye Hazir Giyim Tuketim Endeksi. Retrieved November 4, 2009 from www.ampd.org/ images/.../02_TurkiyeHazirGiyimTuketimEndeksi.ppt

Inditex Annual Report 2014. (2015) (p. 318). Retrieved from www.inditex.com/ documents/10279/18789/Inditex_Annual_Report_2014_web.pdf/a8323597–3932–4357–9f36–6458f55ac099

Invest in Turkey (2009a). 10 Reasons to Invest in Turkey. *Republic of Turkey Prime Ministry, Investment Support and Promotion Agency.* Retrieved January 4, 2008, from www.invest.gov.tr/en-US/investmentguide/Pages/10Reasons.aspx

Invest in Turkey (2009b). Cisco, Success Stories, *Republic of Turkey Prime Ministry, Investment Support and Promotion Agency.* Retrieved January 15, 2008, from www.invest.gov.tr/SuccessStories.aspx?ID=15

Invest in Turkey (2009b). Nortel, Success Stories, *Republic of Turkey Prime Ministry, Investment Support and Promotion Agency.* Retrieved November 15, 2008, from www.invest.gov.tr/SuccessStories.aspx?ID=8

Investment in Turkey (2016). *The Republic of Turkey Prime Ministry Investment Support and Promotion Agency (ISPAT).* Retrived June 8 2016 from www.invest.gov.tr

Kearney, A. T. (2016). The 2016 Global Retail Development Index™: *Global Retail Expansion at a Crossroads* (Global Retail) (p. 31). Retrieved from www.atkearney.com/documents/10192/8226719/Global+Retail+Expansion+at+a+Crossroads%E2%80%932016+GRDI.pdf/dc845ffc-fe28–4623-bdd4-b36f3a443787

Kocak, A. (2006). Turkey in Transition. Expectations in the Textile and Apparel Industry for the Next Two Decades, *The Woolmark Company,* Retrieved November 8, 2009 from www.remarkablesolutions.com/Turkey_in_Transition.pdf

Konuk, C. (2008). Buyuyen perakende sektorunun insan kaynaklari ihtiyaci da artiyor. *Perakende.org,* Retrieved December 18, 2009, from http://perakende.org/haber.php?hid=1200989474

Lambert, J. (2006). One Step Closer to a Pan-European Shopping Center Standard: Illustrating the New Framework with Examples, *Research Review, 13*(2), 35–40.

LC Waikiki (2009). Corporate History. LC Waikiki, Retrieved November 15, 2009, from www.lcwaikiki.com

Machnicka, M. (2009). Turkey Attracting Foreign Retailers. Report: Retail in Turkey 2009. Market Analysis and Development Forecasts 2009–2010. *PMR Publications.* Retrieved November 12, 2009, from www.ceeretail.com/wp_705/Turkey_attracting_foreign_retailers___April_2009.shtml

Market Insight (2014). Turkey's Top 5 Supermarkets Profiled. Retrieved June 5, 2016 from www.transport-exhibitions.com/Market-Insights/Cold-Chain/Turkey-Biggest-Supermarkets-Guide

Mavi Jeans (2009). Retrieved November 15, 2009 from www.mavi.com

Michael Kors Stores in Turkey | Michael Kors. (n.d.). Retrieved May 24, 2016 from www.michaelkors.com/stores/turkey

McKinsey & Company Report. (2014). Size Isn't Everything: Turkey's Fast-Growing Luxury Market. Retrieved June 15, 2016 from www.mckinseyonmarketingandsales.com/size-isnt-everything-turkeys-fast-growing-luxury-market

Ministry of Labor and Social Security (2009). Types of Permissions, *Republic of Turkey, Ministry of Labor and Social Security Department of Work Permits for Foreigners,* Retrieved December 23, 2009, from www.yabancicalismaizni.gov.tr/eng/index.html

Oxford Business Group (2014). Turkey's New Retail Law Driving Formalisation in the Sector, While Local Retailers Expand Internationally. Retrieved June 8, 2016 from www.oxfordbusinessgroup.com/overview/growth-market-sector-being-formalised-through-new-retail-law-local-retailers-seek-new-opportunities

PWC and AMPD (2007). Turk Perakende Sektorunun Degisimi ve Ekonomi Uzerindeki Etkileri, *PriceWaterHouseCoopers and Turkish Council of Shopping Centers and Retailers.* Retrieved November 4, 2009, from www.pwc.com/tr/tr/publications/retail-sector.jhtml

PMR Publications (2009). Turkey Attracting Foreign Retailers (April, 2009). Retrieved November 10, 2009, from www.pmrpublications.com

Savasci, I. (2003). The New Trends in Retailing: The Development of Private Labels and Applications in Turkey. *Yonetim ve Ekonomi. 10*(1), 85–102.

State Planning Organization (2004). Sector Profiles of Turkey: A General Outlook, *General Directorate for Economic Sectors and Coordination, Turkish Prime Ministry,* Retrieved November 14, 2009 from http://ekutup.dpt.gov.tr/imalatsa/2004.pdf

Store locator—M&S Türkiye. (n.d.). Retrieved May 24, 2016 from http://global.marksandspencer.com/tr/en/store-locator/

Superbrands—Vakko. (2015). Retrieved May 27, 2016 from http://superbrandsturkey.com/markalar/Vakko/en-vakko.html

Suzer, H. (2005). The Most Powerful Foreigners, *Capital* (March 1, 2005), Retrieved November 17, 2009 from www.capital.com.tr/haber.aspx?HBR_KOD=2117

The Undersecretariat of Treasury (2009). Retrieved November 17, 2009 from www.treasury.gov.tr/irj/go/km/docs/documents/Treasury%20Web/Legislation/Foreign%20Direct%20Investment%20Legislation/FDI%20Law.pdf

Turkish Council of Shopping Centers and Retailers (2009). *Sektorel Bilgiler.* Retrieved November 15, 2009, from www.ampd.org/sektorel_bilgiler/liste.aspx?SectionId=5

Turkish Retail News Portal (2014). Retrieved June 15, 2016 from www.turkishretail.com/world-retail/opportunity-knocks-for-retail-development-in-turkey–1340189827h.html

WowTURKEY (2009). Retrieved November 15, 2009 from www.wowturkey.com

Yilmaz, N. (2007). Istanbul Becomes Management club. *Turkish Daily News.* Retrieved December 17, 2007 from www.turkishdailynews.com.tr/article.php?e newsid=91518

THAILAND

8

Takeshi KN
Monthinee Tricharoenrat
Shubhapriya Bennur
John Walsh

OBJECTIVES

After reading this chapter, you will

▶ Understand why Thailand is an important emerging market

▶ Grasp various aspects of retailing in the country

▶ Recognize the unique characteristics of a Thai consumer

▶ Know about foreign direct investment regulations for
investing in Thailand

Thailand is a middle-income country located in the mainland of Southeast
Asia. In 2015 it had a per capita income of around $15,319 (PPP) according
to the International Monetary Fund. It is the second-largest economy in Southeast Asia (Thai economic performance in Q1 and Outlook for 2013). According
to the Asian development outlook 2016 issued by the Asia Development Bank,
the percentage of GDP growth, inflation and current account balance of
Thailand for 2016–2017 in comparison to Southeast Asian countries will be
3–3.5 percent, 0.6–2.0 percent and 7.5–4.0 percent, respectively. It is about twice
the size of Wyoming. The current population of Thailand is about 68 million and
it is ranked 20 in the list of countries by population. Its capital, Bangkok, has a
population of around 8.5 million urban residents and about 50 percent of the
population is urban. It has the reputation for being the hottest capital city in the

world, with an average maximum daily temperature of around 90°F. Standards of living are much lower outside Bangkok, and there are sharp divisions between the cities and the countryside. Beside Bangkok city, the largest cities in Thailand by population are Nonthaburi (population 270,609), Nakhon Ratchasima (population 174,332), and Chiang Mai (population 174,235) and over the past decade, modern retailing, driven by international investment, has spread to these cities whereas before it had been limited to the capital city. Although not listed as one of the biggest cities in Thailand, Pattaya, Phuket and Ko Samui are smaller towns/islands that are tourist destinations and make a significant contribution to Thailand's retail environment. They offer a concept of tourism shopping to spa resorts. Thailand has its own royal family and has been a constitutional monarchy since the 1932 Revolution, which overthrew the absolute monarchy system. It is a parliamentary democracy with a prime minister (see Table 8.1). His Majesty the King is the head of state.

TABLE 8.1 Fast Facts about Thailand	
Capital	Bangkok
Population	68 million
Type of government	Constitutional monarchy
GDP: purchasing power parity: in US$	$1.108 trillion
Age structure	0–14 yrs: 17.41 percent 15–64 yrs: 72.73 percent 65 yrs plus: 9.86 percent
Religion	Buddhist: 93.6 percent Muslim: 4.9 percent Christian: 1.2 percent Other: 0.2 percent
Ethnicity	Thai: 95.5 percent Burmese: 2 percent Other: 1.3 percent Unspecified: 0.09 percent

Source: CIA factbook.gov

Thailand has become an important emerging market, especially since the beginning of the twenty-first century. With a cost structure that is reasonable, a stable economy, skilled workforce, a good regulatory system, and desirable incentives for investments, Thailand has become an attractive country for foreign investors (Thailand's investment, 2008). The country's government is trying to work toward improving the conditions further to simplify and attract foreign investment. It has identified fashion as a centerpiece of its campaign to move the economy away from low-cost manufacturing to more creative activities because fashion is a large part of Thai consumption and exercises a powerful hold on the imagination. According to WTTC Travel & Tourism Economica Impact 2015, the country has generated more than Thai Baht 1,309.1bn in vistor exports, with 87.6 percent of this leisure travel spending (inbound and domestic) and 12.4 percent for business travel. Thailand also expects to attract around 25 million interational tourists. The country also represents a complex marketplace in which Western and local goods compete against increasingly influential Korean and Japanese products. Due to the large size of the market, apparel producers need to look at local factors or neighboring countries when designing the merchandise for both Thai consumers and the foreigners who live and work in Thailand, as well as to the international tourists

THE RETAIL LANDSCAPE: MODERN FORMATS GAINING POPULARITY

In 1966, Feneny, Vongpatansin and Soonsatham mentioned the "cho-huay" known as "mom-and pop" grocery shops, a tradiational retail format in Thailand, that allows the Thai family to run their business on the ground floor while they lived on the second or upper floor. In the concept of "cho-huay", there was no such thing as fixed and listed prices. The buyers and sellers made their purchases by bargaining, the productions were displayed inside cupboards, or on shelves and the concept "do-it-yourself" did not exist prior to 1955. The first major step in the modernization of Thai retailing emerged in Bangkok; the Central Department store, the country's first modern retail center, had opened its doors for business (Watcharavesringkan, Karpova, Hidges and Copeland 2012). Although many new department stores were established locally like Tai Fah, no retailers from outside of Thailand could operate until 1999 after the Alien Business Law was repealed. The two large retailers in Thailand now are Tesco Lotus with over 1,800 stores located nationwide with various formats (Extra, Hypermarket, Department Store, Tald, Express) and Big C with 122 stores again with various formats (Hypermarket, Extra, Jumpo). Thanks to the convenient transportation system like BTS and MRT and rapidly growing infrastructure in Bangkok, consumers can access the stores more easily than before; some stores are located far from the city center such as IKEA, which is located in the Bangna area. Thai consumers have a strong buying behavior in relation to leisure time. Although Thai consumers are happy to travel some distance to stores around the city for both leisure, entertainment, culinary and shopping, increasingly they also prefer to shop from a single location, especially those who are living in the smaller cities and even within Bangkok. Retailers are responding to this by ensuring a wide range of goods and services are available in every space. Although there have been many changes in retailing in this country, collectively the department stores, hyper/super markets, traditional market (ta-lad), wholesale and weekend fair/market (i.e: Chatuchak), family-businesses, small household businesses and those trading on (wet-markets) street (both food and apparel) as well as e-retailing have created one of the most diverse and vibrant environments in Thailand.

Apparel retail is an important part of this process. As a central part of the manufacturing industry that has helped pull Thailand out of poverty, textiles and apparel occupy a significant part of modern Thai history and continue to be a major strength of the economy. Apparel is a notable part of Thailand's crucially important export effort (it is one of the most open countries in the world in terms of international trade and, therefore, very vulnerable to changes in the international business environment). The value of garment exports was about USD 7.8 billion at the end of 2014. Exports of apparel are increasing as the quality of fashion items increases, partly thanks to government-sponsored initiatives, while costs remain comparatively constant. Although there have often been internal political issues this has had little effect on to the garment manuafcturing and export sector according to Sukji Kongpiyacharn, president of the Thai garment manufacturers association.

With increasing competition from all fields, and from China in particular, Thai manufacturers are striving to add value to their products in all categories, by improving technology and design and increasing the unique qualities of "Thainess" to make distinctive and often exotic items. These factors are clearly evident in the domestic retailing sector, where foreign and homemade items compete directly against each other in all but the most high-end sectors (where foreign brands dominate) and the low-end sectors, which are dominated by locally made products or imports from neighboring countries (Jitpleecheep, 2009a). Due to the establishment of new factories

▲ FIGURE 8.1 A storefront display indicating "Thainess". Thainess is introduced in a store or a product to make it appear more exotic and, therefore, appealing to a customer.

and facilties in off-shore branches, with cheaper labour costs, Thailand has seen a fall in orders from the US, EU and Japan of 6.7 percent and 1.1 percent in knitted clothes and woven clothes, repectively (April, 2015). The production of fabric also slumped by 12.2 percent due to competition from the ASEAN market, espcially Myanmar and Cambodia. However, trade in textile fiber, bedding and towels and lace fabric increased by 5.6, 1.1 percent and 15.4 percent, respectively, resulting from a greater volume of domestic consumption (Industrial economic status report, May 2015).

CONSUMERS: MOVING TOWARD MODERNISM

As a developing, middle-income country that was economically depressed at the end of World War II, Thailand has changed rapidly over the past few decades. Whereas there has been an emergence of a new middle class with often considerable spending power and aspirations in terms of consumer goods, they preserve a number of cultural practices and superstitions concerning the type and variety of apparel that should be worn. Clothing has traditionally been subject to sumptuary laws in most of mainland Southeast Asia; this practice continued until the twentieth century, in which several of the despotic paternalists who led the government between the 1930s and 1960s sought to ensure that urban residents dressed in ways that were recognizably "modern" and based on Western modes. Historically, Thais have worn Indian cotton or Thai silk *phanung* or sarong-type clothes and very little else. In rural Thailand, many people, especially the poor, continue with this style; this further restricts the penetration of modern retailing methods in the Kingdom.

Two other factors of Thai apparel that are unusual from a Western perspective are also worth mentioning. The first is that there are approximately 700,000 or more ethnic minority people resident in Thailand, most of whom are hill tribespeople living in different parts of the north of the country (in addition to unknown numbers of unregistered or undocumented ethnic minority people). In many cases, cultural traits, which may have been

▲ FIGURE 8.2 Traditional Thai Dance Girls at the Elephant Round-up Festival in the city of Surin in Northeastern Thailand.

intensified by the desire to pander to the interests of tourists, extend to the clothing that the women of these ethnic minority people wear on a daily basis. Because these clothes are made within the community and are homemade where possible, the people wearing these clothes are outside the market system when it comes to most forms of apparel.

Second, all male Buddhist Thais are expected to be ordained and live as a monk at some period of their lives. Buddhist monks wear distinctive saffron-colored robes, and presenting new robes to monks on special occasions, as well as to boys and men about to be ordained, is a regular feature of apparel buying. These robes are now available in supermarket chains, and there is no need for specialist buying.

The Buddhist religion (which is professed by more than 94 percent of the population according to most estimates) includes a superstitious component that often manifests in the use of apparel to protect the body, the family, and important physical items. This superstitious component is most commonly seen in the amulet industry. Amulets are worn on chains around the neck,

▲ FIGURE 8.3 This amulet depicts a superstitious component of Buddhist religion. Amulets are blessed by the monks and considered to have supernatural powers to protect the wearer.

either under the clothes or on the outside in more flamboyant cases. Amulets are usually made by or at least in conjunction with particular Buddhist monasteries; they are blessed by the monks and many believe they have supernatural powers. In other cases, this superstition is manifested by sacred or magical tattoos worn on the body or on white cloth worn as a singlet. Cosmetic tattooing has also become popular among younger people, and in some cases the traditional, sacred images are incorporated into new designs.

Separate and specific marketing efforts toward men, women, and children are predominantly the preserve of the urban middle and upper classes. Outside of these classes, apparel purchasing is based primarily on need and convenience; that is, the need based on a hot and wet climate and the nature of work and daily life. In the case of footwear, for example, the flip-flop or thong-type sandal is generally the only type of footwear required because it is the most practical in wet conditions (they dry much more quickly than other shoes) and it is hardy enough to survive being drenched in mud or water. The following sections, therefore, relate primarily to the privileged and urban classes.

WOMEN

Apparel retailing is dominated, by the size, shape, and coloring of Thai women, which differs from those of Western women. Western visitors to Thailand can shop only at big outlets of franchised/distributed foreign brands, because clothes sold in other places do not fit them well. Even those sized XL or above are too small for the majority of European or American women. However, the development of social media, has seen a change in both training and design education. Customers in Thailand can now easily find any designs, styles, color and size ranging from the luxury and high-end brands to clothes from onstreet markets. However, in the many luxury and high-end stores in Bangkok, the senior buyer tends to order styles for their wealthy local customers, so visitors may struggle to find clothes that will fit them. Although the shopping and tourism concept is now developing in Thailand, the luxury or high end sector is not yet focused on Western visitors, except for traditional Thai textile and home furnishings. However, customers from Asian countries could easily find all they need in both fashionable and traditional style, shape and color, as the cultural and buying patterns are quite similar, to Chinese, Southeast Asian and also to East Asian customers. Local designers and distributors are beginning to produce items that suit visitors from Western countries. This requires attention to detail with respect to size and shape for clothing, as well as coloring not only for clothing and textiles, but also for cosmetics and health products. The high-end cosmetics and beauty products that are widely available tend to be those with a reputation for high-technology (for example, Clarins, Body Shop, and L'Occitane) or those that are aimed specifically at East Asian women (for example, Oriental Princess and Anna Sui). The same is, broadly speaking, true of clothing, in that the most prestigious brands are available along with those that are more tailored to the Thai consumer. Some hybrid brands cling on at the margins; for example, H&M, Uniqlo, and Zara are brands that are gaining some traction for their value-cost equation, while catering to the larger Thai consumer bases. Nowadays, customers from ASEAN countries can easily buy a ticket and spend the weekend in Thailand for both shopping and entertainment, due to visa exemptions within the ASEAN and low-cost airlines like Air Asia, Tiger Air, Jesstar and Nok Air.

MEN

There tends to be a lack of role models for men who are fashion conscious and acceptable to a modern audience. The traditional image of a Thai man consists of deference, diligence, and obedience, which is disliked by the young, with its more attractive obverse of the *nak leng* ("tough man"), a sharp-dressed (usually in neo-colonial style), hard-living individual whose wealth and success is demonstrated by the ostentatious display of material goods (for example, gold jewelry, prestigious foreign car, muscular servants, and numerous *mia noi* or "little wives," whose presence is widely tolerated in a supposedly monogamous culture). This is a normal image and is anti-modern, which has had a knock-on effect on modern marketing techniques. Whereas media personalities are permitted to display a more modern image, such an image is nearly always combined with an eventual display of obedience, combined with a return to traditional values (including, of course, appearance). All of this sets a limit to the extent to which Thai men will accept or be interested in having goods and services marketed to them, apart from the forms that are essentially traditional or conservative in nature. This is truer of older men than younger men, who are generally more comfortable and familiar with the internationalized Thai society and economy. There are also a larger number of younger male role models who appear in the media in a variety of different fashions. In addition, Thailand's tolerance for the "lady boys" (or *katoey*), means that some such flamboyant individuals have been able to push the envelope for what is considered acceptable in terms of apparel and fashion. Retail tastes have become internationalized; teenagers and younger men have shown more openness to clothes and items that would be considered unacceptable to older consumers. Most of the young consumers feel comfortable wearing modern outfits for daily working and business. Similar to other Asian countries, national dress is still worn for more formal occasions such as weddings or engagements. Women wear one of eight national dresses (e.g. Ruean Ton, Chit Lada, Amarin, Borom Phiman, Chakkri, Chakkraphat, Dusit, Siwalai), while men wear a jacket known as a suea phraratchathan.

CHILDREN

Children outside of the urban, middle classes have few opportunities to choose apparel because of lack of resources (and, owing to the climate and conditions, lack of need for a choice). Children within those classes are commonly enrolled in so many extra-curricular activities that they do not have the time to work to buy their own apparel. Inevitably, therefore, marketing to children involves extensive use of the "nag factor" and peer pressure.

In the case of younger children, advertising presents images of happy and contented Asian children—that is, they portray traditional Asian values of family orientation and obedience. Older children and teenagers generally find themselves looking at the vaguely rebellious Western style that is known, somewhat inaccurately, as hip-hop or, more recently, Korean or Japanese pop or R&B styles. Moreover, the variety shows originally produced from the West such as "The Kid Voice", "Thailand's Got Talent" or the "X Factor", in additon to the local productions and Asian shows as "Daddy, Where are we going?", "Supper man return", etc are acting as the main points of reference not only for the children but also for younger parents.

THE BEAUTY INDUSTRY, SKIN CARE AND SPA PRODUCTS IN THAILAND

HIGH QUALITY LOCAL BRANDS VS INTERNATIONAL BRANDS

Thailand has many beauty salons, hairdressers, spas, and clinics that are primarily aimed at women. Even when service retail outlets are explicitly unisex in nature, customers as well as staff are overwhelmingly female. Although massage and the pursuit good health are acceptable to all ages, only younger women are considered suitable to use beauty products related to those activities. Older women do use massage services but mostly on a medically therapeutic basis. The massage stores located on the streets have masseurs that have been trained professionally in the massage school, and some masseurs are trained in traditional setings such as the temple or study-centers, where they can develop their

▲ FIGURE 8.4 A girl wearing typical Thai dress.

skills but pay no tuition. Few older women use spas for cosmetic purposes rather than for health; however, as the extent of middle class in Thailand spreads and the number of older female role models increases, marketing to the older and less economically privileged has also increased. Beauty products, for example, are broadly defined to include natural remedies and dietary supplements, and are now available through the multiple convenience stores that are so prevalent throughout the Kingdom. In this way, the range of items that was previously reserved for younger, richer women is now increasingly being diffused to the mass market. Traditional, herbal and oriental medicine is still practiced in Thai skin care and spa production and this has fed into the increasing demand for organic products. . Customers both local and tourist do prefer these to the new technology lab skin care brands and can choose between many international brands, but there is high demand for local herbal brands, especially spa productions (compressed herb, foot massage, oil, lotion, diffusers) using exotic ingredients such as lemon grass, orchid, ginger, jasmine, etc. Interestingly, local brands are trusted by local customers and tourists alike (Nguyen et al, 2015). Brands such as Panpura, Harnn, Thann, BsaB, Satira and others are now dominating the market and expanding their business in Asian countries. Although all the listed brands are targeted at different customer bases, they are professionally marketed not only in quality but also regarding improvement in store design, visual merchandising, packaging and design, promotion and service, so they are considered to be more mainstream. The market for men's skincare is also consid-red to have potential due to the influence of K-pop and drama, and because of the climate and pollution issues in Thailand.

Women's beauty products are extensive and increasing in scope, not just in terms of the range and nature of products and services provided but also in the age range of women who like to use them. In urban settings, the target market for beauty products for women is increasing in age. In terms of range of goods, women are offered the opportunities not just to appear younger and to conform more closely to specific ideals of beauty as exhibited by professional models and celebrities but also to change their bodies so as to become more Westernized in nature. In Thai society, the most beautiful people are often considered to be those with mixed Thai-Western parents, and the beauty industry promotes the idea that appearance can be enhanced by whitening the skin, increasing bust size, and having cosmetic surgery to change the shape of the nose and eyes in particular. Thailand is considered a center for this kind of cosmetic surgery because of its expertise in the particular physiognomy of Asian people and also the economy of scale available through providing gender reassignment surgery to local people and international visitors. In this industry, modern high-technology products can merge with longstanding traditional remedies to provide the supposed advantages that are possible.

Thai people have an interest in appearing both beautiful and fashionable if they can afford it. This interest is evident in the extensive network of beauty parlors, spas, massage centers, cosmetic beauty clinics, and, increasingly, weight loss clinics that are common throughout urban Thailand. This has been intensified in the twenty-first century by a new emphasis on healthy eating and living, which has led to the distribution of a variety of products that promote one or more of the qualities of aesthetic beauty and good health. A number of these products are sourced from China or at least from ethnic Chinese communities because of the respect paid to traditional Asian medicines and methods. It is quite common, for example, to find Chinese shampoos that promise to reverse hair loss in men. Korean ginseng, meanwhile, is also growing in prevalence because of the belief in its health-promoting activities and because of the trendiness of Korean products and ideas.

Men are more likely to have beauty products directly marketed to them because of their health-promoting aspects rather than their ability to enhance aesthetic appeal. Beauty products are usually promoted directly through point-of-sale activities in hairdressers' salons and similar locations. A variety of men's interest magazines now offer new ideas for male grooming. The majority of these magazines use licensed content from Western countries where they originated, often with local additions and the use of local talent as models and role models. These magazines are more open to promoting beauty products than are mass media such as television, where male beauty products are still viewed by a large part of the audience as either an excessive embrace of non-Thai globalization or as being effeminate.

LUXURY RETAIL IN THAILAND

Although luxury retail opportunities are possible in Thailand, they are still only a feature in a few urban areas because of the unequal distribution of income in the country and in terms of access because most people cannot afford to buy those kinds of products. In spatial terms, luxury is available in a small number of central Bangkok shopping malls and department stores such as Emquartier, Emporium or the long-established Gaysorn. New projects are under construction around Bangkok, such as the Siam Icon near the Chao Phraya river, the Muse near Victory Monument and others, high-end hotels, mostly in the capital, but in a small number of locations in other parts of the

Kingdom as well, for example in the international airport and various malls such as the Galleria, King Power Phuket, King Power Sivaree, etc. This includes products such as luxury cars (there are special distributors for brands such as Lamborghini and Ferrari), speedboats, jewelry, and the usual range of consumer goods. Given the relatively low cost of labor, especially in the service sector, providers of goods and services may come to the customer rather than vice versa. Service standards also tend to be high because of the competition with Singapore and Hong Kong as a destination for international shoppers. Due to IPSOS Singapore PtD Ltd (2013), in Asia, the top five countries whose visitors spend the most in Thailand are India, Hong Kong, Singapore, Australia and Russia. Also, in 2012, 15 million tourists from the Asian Pacific have visited Thailand. Clearly there is potential to open-up Thailand as a luxury retail sector for Asian customers. In order to do that sucessfully, Thailand should plan to have a strong connection between the goverment and retailers to provide the best fit to meet the needs of national and international consumers.

Historically, the ability to shop for luxury goods in Thailand was highly correlated with the ability to travel overseas. These days, despite the many ways in which such travel has been simplified through the removal of visa requirements for most citizens of the Association of Southeast Asian Nations (ASEAN) and the rapidly increasing provision of budget air travel, the assumption that ability to shop for luxury goods is related to ability to travel overseas still remains. Those who enjoy luxury items are those, by and large, who can go overseas to shop for them. Preferred destinations in this context are Europe and North America. Because Thailand has never been formally colonized in the modern age, there is not one particular overseas country to which people immediately look for comparison and fashionable trends, although Europe is generally preferred to the United States because of previous historical connections. However, given what has been said about the nature of Thai consumers, other Asian countries are the critical locations for shopping trips. In particular, Hong Kong and Singapore are primary shopping destinations, due to their proximity and range of available brands and outlets, combined with suitable service, food, and accommodation.

In the first decade of the twenty-first century, the development of retail opportunities in central Bangkok has ensured that, in practical terms, travel overseas for shopping is not required anymore because the same products are available in Thailand, and tourists can travel to Bangkok to shop. In 2005, the Thai government introduced the Thailand Elite Card for foreign visitors to Thailand. Members pay up to $50,000 (1.5 million baht) to receive free first-class

▲ FIGURE 8.5 Apparel sold in these street stalls is similar to those sold in local stores.

travel from Thai Airways, special VIP services, and an enhanced visa. The program has struggled due to lack of interest and various complaints. The lack of joined-up government thinking among the relevant agencies and ministries has meant that projected benefits of membership, such as privileges in buying and owning land, have failed to be realized, and the project was considered to be a failure (Saengsawang, 2009). In 2010, lengthy pro-democracy demonstrations closed down much of the central luxury shopping region of Bangkok and, after the military launched a series of violent attacks that left more than 90 dead and thousands injured, one of the large shopping centers burned to the ground.

APPAREL RETAIL FORMATS: NEW IS IN, BUT OLD IS NOT OUT

Retailing in Thailand has changed significantly since the 1960s. From a situation of temporary markets selling low-cost goods, the country now offers a large number of high-end retail-based shopping malls offering fashion items from all around the world. However, this development is very limited spatially and in terms of population. The bulk of economic development takes place in the capital city Bangkok, which dominates the economic, political, cultural, and institutional spheres in Thailand. Although retail development has been spreading to other towns and cities since the turn of the century, these sites are also subject to strong segmentation within the population as most people, especially in rural areas, continue to rely on such traditional formats as temporary markets and street vendors for apparel purchases.

The most common traditional retail formats in Thailand are temporary markets, mom-and-pop stores (family owned shops), and street vendors. Historically, Thai shops were part of businesses operated by small-scale entrepreneurs, often ethnic Chinese in origin who would frequently open a venture known as a Chinese family business (CFB), which was characterized by family ownership and control, hierarchical management, unwillingness to expand beyond the limits of what one person could manage, and opportunistic diversification in new ventures that could be spun off to be managed by other family members. Even today, a large number of Thai firms are family owned rather than publicly owned through stocks and shares (and there are also combination ownership structures) even among the very largest firms.

Shops were usually opened in the rows of shop-houses, which are so characteristic of Southeast Asia, and for marketing relied primarily on word-of-mouth, passing foot traffic, and personal networks of connections. When larger stores did emerge, they usually acted as wholesalers as well as retailers, redistributing goods sourced from overseas or from domestic manufacturers to the neighborhood retailers in addition to direct sales. Overall, the retail and wholesale industry was fragmented, with no national or multinational chains in operation. This situation changed as a result of the presence of American and allied troops using Thailand as a base for fighting in Vietnam, Cambodia, and Laos. The troops provided a stimulus to the creation of a more modern retailing system in which larger, partly foreign-owned stores could provide economies of scope and scale to provide items for consumption primarily by foreigners and high-society Thai people with international tastes.

A feature of most shopping centers, especially those not located in central Bangkok, is that they are usually surrounded by street vending space.

Vendors might draw lots on a daily basis to determine their particular location or else a more permanent system might be in place as vendors pay the center's owners a fee for opening their stalls outside. Shoppers can adjust their shopping preferences based on cost and other personal preferences. Shopping inside offers higher prices in an air-conditioned environment, with generally higher levels of quality and range of sizes; shopping outside is less comfortable and may require haggling. Street vendors have developed a reputation for tough bargaining and, in a low-trust society like Thailand's, shoppers are concerned that they will lose face if they pay more for an item than their friends and family members believe they should have done.

Items provided by street vendors need not be inferior to those available within the shopping center and not just because it is possible for some entrepreneurs to source the same items from the same factories where they are manufactured. Within the overall population of street vendors, there exists a subset of trained and enterprising entrepreneurs who have been adding value to their stalls by such measures as personal brand creation, batch manufacturing of personally designed items, international sourcing, and franchising of stalls. These entrepreneurs are in contrast to the majority of vendors who operate stalls largely undifferentiated from each other, with items sourced by wholesalers or family members and relying on calling out to passing individuals as the principal means of marketing. These stalls are staffed by individual owners, family members, or hired staff who are mostly paid low wages (possibly below statutory minimum wage levels) but offered some measure of commission. Street vendors may occupy a permanent position in one market area or may rotate their business around a variety of different temporary or seasonal markets.

In Bangkok, wholesale markets and nearby factories represent important sources for products. Outside Bangkok and especially in rural areas, traveling merchants will supply and resupply a number of different stalls with the same range of goods, leading to repetition of product offerings and few opportunities for vendors to add value to their businesses.

MODERN FORMATS

The traditional retailing continued until the inauguration of the 1999 Foreign Business Act, after which major changes became evident. This act enabled foreign investors, for the first time, to create majority-owned retail outlets that were less than $3.3 million (100 million baht) in extent, and that did not deal in food and beverages or any agricultural products. Large-scale retailers felt obliged to use nominees (that is, Thai individuals or organizations guaranteed to act as sleeping partners) to circumvent the regulations. Using this approach, large companies such as the UK's Tesco Lotus and France's Carrefour established ownership of their chains by buying out local partners and then embarking on a period of rapid expansion that gave rise to local protests and environmental concerns (Kanchoochat, 2008), including demonstrations and boycotts. Tesco Lotus now employs 36,000 people in Thailand and has 8,400 franchisees in the country in a variety of formats, from hypermarkets to express services.

▶ Hypermarkets

These formats devote ample space to various categories of apparel products, mostly in the low-cost sectors in which the chain specializes.

▶ Specialty Stores

New ventures such as the Tesco Plus Shopping Mall at Srinakharin district in Bangkok offers specialty stores with more up-market brand names, including Body Glove (USA), Bossini (Hong Kong), and City Chain (Thai-Chinese). New entrants have also emerged in the large retail malls, including PC Land Co, which is planning to open a $50 million (1.5 billion baht) project at Bang Bua Thong district in Bangkok called The Square. In Chiang Mai, the Thai-owned Renova Group will open Vian Panna on a piece of land measuring seven rai (one rai is 1,600 square meters or 17,200 square feet).

Retail sales increased by 4 to 5 percent in 2009, despite the economic crisis and ongoing political instability throughout the year, largely because of the opening of new stores that were supported by previous government development in Bangkok of the public transport system (including light rail and underground train services) and the metropolitan infrastructure. The government's version of economic stimulus programs created around the world is called Thai Khem Kaeng ("strong Thailand") and, although funds were disbursed throughout 2009 at a snail's pace, it is hoped that this spending will help sustain retail sales through 2010. Clearly, retail sales are supported more in the higher-end sectors rather than the lower end, where most suffering is felt and the great majority of jobs lost.

▶ Department Stores

Within retail malls, apparel is available both within department stores (for which rent is payable and service costs are shared to various extents) and in specialty stores outside of the department store but within the mall. Most of the international brands found in the high-end stores retain their international ownership but may have an extensive presence at the board and management level; it is a generally held belief that Thai senior management is essential in business success, not just because of their local business knowledge but also because of their access to requisite connections in the public and private sectors.

STORE OWNERSHIP: REGULATED BY LAW

Thai investors ostensibly hold ownership of retail space, but it is clear that foreign investors ultimately hold control. Future government activity may force international investors to reveal their real level of ownership of retail companies and comply with the law, but given the fragility of investor confidence in the Kingdom and the fact it has persisted since at least the military coup of 2006, it is more likely that sleeping dogs will be allowed to lie.

▲ FIGURE 8.6 The Emquartier District building is one of the leading high end and luxury department stores in Bangkok adjoining the Bangkok Emporium.

Ownership of retail outlets is regulated by various laws, which are in turn based upon the developmental principles of the Thai state. These principles promote export-oriented economic growth with low labor cost competitiveness and are based on the desire to ensure that no land falls into foreign ownership. The need to strike a balance between these two impulses has been met in part by the 1999 Foreign Business Act and possible much-discussed but not yet seen future legislation, which may be countered by the investment incentives to foreign investors provided by the Board of Investment (BOI). In other words, more restrictions from one arm of government are usually balanced by concessions from another arm of government.

Thailand is very vulnerable to external economic shocks (such as recessions elsewhere in the world or sudden changes in commodity prices) because of its reliance on exporting, particularly low-value-added agricultural products, as well as the importance of the tourism industry and the large proportion of GDP devoted to purchasing oil and gas from overseas. As a result of these various factors, the foreign business lobby has historically had an important role in influencing the legal framework and environment. The most important member of the lobby has been Japan, most of whose investment has been in manufacturing (and distribution of some of the automotive products made or assembled in Thailand) and whose requests have by and large been granted. More vociferous foreign investors, including Americans and Europeans, who have had more interest in retailing, have had less success in achieving their goals because of resistance to the concept of cultural hegemony in much of the state government and the desire to protect local jobs and lifestyles. There is also the need to protect vested Thai interests in the retail industry. Consequently, until 2008, all or nearly all of the retail outlets in Thailand were officially locally owned. It is not known, although there is much anecdotal evidence, to what extent retail outlets were in fact controlled by foreign investors who had placed official ownership in a local partner, perhaps a Thai spouse.

FDI REGULATIONS: A NOT-SO-OPEN MARKET

The industry was governed by regulations introduced in 1972, which permitted ownership of up to 49 percent of a business, by foreign interests—land was and is not available for sale to a foreigner at all. Foreign investors have, therefore, always been required to take a Thai partner or partners to go into business. The regulations also provided for various other ways in which business could be organized, including local partnerships and cooperatives.

In considering Thai law, it may be helpful to understand that Thai law generally provides for freedom in positive rather than restrictive ways: In most Western cultures, an individual is free to do anything unless restricted by a specific law; in Thai culture, people, organizations, and institutions can perform any act only if there is a valid law that specifically gives them the right to do so, for example, in opening new types of business operations currently unregulated. Consequently, adoption of innovations and exploitation of new forms of retailing are hindered by the need to create and implement the necessary law to permit these acts to take place legally. Lawmaking can be a lengthy business.

As Thailand enters into more types of economic integration, in the form of free trade agreements and other treaties, the ability of foreign investors to own and operate retail outlets or retail distribution businesses in the country will certainly increase. In some cases, increased opportunities are push-led (that is, the dynamic comes from an agreement making opportunities available and investors then taking advantage of them) and some are pull-led (that is, investors petition government to make opportunities available to them and, presumably, others). Foreign investors have become accustomed to working through semi-legal ownership structures when existing legislation prevents them from exercising the level of control they desire. Whereas liberalization of ownership progresses at a slow pace, it is unlikely that the restrictions on ownership of land in Thailand by foreigners will be lifted in the foreseeable future.

A barrier to entry that is maintained by the private rather than the public sector is the patronage system that, in Thailand, restricts access to resources and public goods to a limited group of well-connected people. Although it is possible to break into the required networks through the use of capital, it nevertheless makes it difficult for new arrivals to compete on a level playing field. In sectors such as property development and tourist resort management, access to patronage is manifested through extortion by organized criminal gangs. In apparel, new entrants have to operate with a restricted number of partners and at disadvantageous terms. For example, the supermarkets and hypermarkets of Thailand generally operate in the same way that those in many other Asian countries do by making shelf space and position available to intermediaries prepared to pay. The same is said to be true of attracting media attention to PR activities or just considering products and events. Product placement is also a significant part of Thai media, particularly on television.

INTERNATIONAL BRANDS

The 1999 Act enabled an increase in the extent of ownership and control of shops in various categories, which encouraged an increase in international investment, from Britain, France, and the Netherlands in particular. Multiple retail chains and shopping malls operated by the British-Thai Tesco Lotus Group, the French Carrefour chain, and the Dutch-Thai Makro warehouses opened in Thailand. Smaller shops are almost entirely Thai owned, and franchising is often managed through contract with a local partner, such as Thai company CP (Charoen Pokphand) does for the 7-11 chain in Thailand (4,030 stores) and its Lotus franchises in China (79 supercenters) under the Chia Tai Group brand (Charoen Pokphand Group, 2010). Department stores routinely are operated and owned by Thai management companies, with the exception of Japanese investment in some department stores, which has witnessed only mixed levels of success.

INTERNATIONAL BRAND MARKET ENTRY STRATEGY

International brands entering Thailand generally do so through joining existing distribution chains leading to the large shopping centers and their networks. There are some alternatives to this, as for example the alternative distribution network created to support the successful Amway Multi-Level Marketing venture, in which members sell to their families and friends and recruit new people to join as members from whose sales they are able to claim a fee. However, particularly as a result of legal changes initiated by the Asian meltdown of 1997, powerful incentives have been put in place to encourage new entrants to join existing channels.

Having been one of the most open economies for inward investment for some decades, as well as having joined the World Trade Organization (WTO) in 1995, Thailand has few formal barriers to investment in the country. However, those few barriers can be significant in effect. For example, it is illegal for foreign individuals or corporations to own land in Thailand, with a few minor exceptions. Unable to buy land, foreign corporations must operate at a level of uncertainty that is uncomfortable for them. To reduce that uncertainty, investors will generally try to circumvent the regulations through a joint venture agreement with a local partner in which the international investor is the principal active partner. Such joint ventures give undue power to the local partner. By contrast, using what is called a "nominee" (i.e., the person whose name appears on forms as the official owner but who may not actually be the real owner) the local partner flirts with illegality because an accusation can be made at any time, including an admission made by the nominee. The same problems affect any foreign national who marries a Thai person and then tries to buy a house. However, despite numerous representations at all levels of government, the Thai state has resolutely refused to concede any meaningful changes to the law.

A second informal barrier to entry is the occasional use of outbreaks of nationalism and xenophobia in the popular media, which may then be used to color public and political discourse. Generally, xenophobia is aimed at neighbors for political reasons—for example, at the end of the first decade of the new century, both Cambodia and Singapore were vilified for supposed transgressions. People at even the highest levels of government are known to repeat long-standing accusations about the perfidies of foreigners of all nations, which has the effect of keeping these ideas in the minds of the public. On the other hand, many Thai people continue to have the belief that overseas items are inherently superior to their locally produced counterparts.

CULTURAL INFLUENCES ON TEXTILE AND APPAREL RETAILING

Clothing plays a role in informal ritual moments in Thailand. For example, it is a practice among young people to use their first-ever month's salary to buy new clothes for their parents to show gratitude for raising them. It is also a practice to "clothe" images of Buddha and statues by adding some golden decorations or adornments, depending on the size of the image concerned. On numerous occasions, on a regular or seasonal basis, religious, cultural, or superstitious influences are influential in determining what people wear, as well as various aspects of behavior and language. These are one of the many factors that structure the wardrobe of Thai people and limit it in marketing terms, especially for foreign brands or innovative products.

In addition to cultural influences, physical and climatic influences also affect apparel retailing. Despite some changes brought about by urbanization and changing dietary and lifestyle patterns leading to emergent obesity (Escobar, 2009), Thai people are generally shorter and slighter than Westerners. This difference is especially noticeable among women, who find Western clothes as carried by, for example, Marks and Spencer to be unsuitable, as well as expensive in comparison with the quality. Marks and Spencer and others in both South Korea and Japan face a similar problem. Indeed, it is fashion from these two countries that is condidered more fashionable in Thailand, particularly among young people and women. Since around 2005, Korean and Japanese media products have increasingly influenced the cultural scene of the Kingdom, as manifested by the popularity of Korean and Japanese food, soap operas, pop music, and fashion. Hairdressers specialising in Korean and Japanese styles have begun to open, and the Japanese Daijiro Enami has been named an ambassador for Thai tourism (South China Morning Post, 2015).

INFLUENCES ON APPAREL RETAILING

Thailand uses a similar retailing environment to other East Asian countries: That is, shops tend to be staffed by many assistants who approach and attend customers as soon as they come near their products. Consumers expect high level of service and may express dissatisfaction if the attendant is insufficiently knowledgeable, impolite, or does not show interest in the customer. Thai consumers are often characterized by faddishness and by a desire for personal aesthetic appeal that is also reflected in the large number of beauty salons, hair salons, spas, and massage outlets that may be found and is typical of many East Asian societies. In some cases, faddishness becomes controversial when it leads people, generally but not exclusively young women, into spending money on cosmetic surgery on the one hand and, on the other, the use of decorated teeth braces and spectacles that have no medical purpose or value. Some other features of apparel retailing are discussed in the following sections.

CUSTOMER SERVICE EXPECTATIONS

Customers expect not only retail assistance but also additional services at low cost. For example, trousers for both men and women are usually produced in a range of waist sizes but at the same length. It is understood that, after the purchase has been made, shop assistants will hem the pants within 45 minutes to an hour (outside of peak shopping hours) and for a low cost—less than US$1 per item—or sometimes this service is free of charge. If this service is not available, many tailors operate street businesses or small shops in which adjustments of various types can be made. Individuals will often use a regular tailor who is known to them and who can be trusted to make the adjustments correctly (perhaps after two or three attempts). This work supplements the principal work of tailors or, for some, it may represent their main line of business. Shoe and boot repairs, for example, as well as watch repairs, may be conducted both inside and outside shops. Especially for the latter, using the

▲ FIGURE 8.7 Thai glamour magazines at a newspaper and magazine shop in Bangkok.

service tends to be a case of caveat emptor, and it is considered important to know who the service provider is.

COLOR-CODING OF CLOTHING

In Thai tradition, colors have been assigned to each day in a week according to astrological rules. Yellow is for Monday. Pink is for Tuesday. Green is for Wednesday. Orange is for Thursday. Light blue is for Friday. Purple is for Saturday and red is for Sunday. Moreover, it can be seen that Thai people wear Yellow shirts showing respect to His Majesty the king because he was born on Monday. Light blue is worn to show the respect to HM the queen as she was born on Friday. Thai society has, especially since the political events of 2006, become increasingly color coded in terms of clothing. It is customary to wear different colored clothes to mark certain ritual or celebratory occasions. For example, attending a funeral requires black clothes while attending a wedding, New Year or other celebration require bright colors to represent joy and happiness. For Chinese descendants, red is always worn on propitious occasions. Additionally, certain days of the week were marked down for special remembrance of His Majesty (HM) the King, when people wear yellow, and HM the Queen, whose color is blue as mentioned above. For some years, this was a sporadic custom, but it intensified in 2006, when street protests led by the fascist "People's alliance for democracy" (PAD) movement made a big play of wearing yellow on most days, with the implication that anyone who did not was in some way disloyal to the throne, which is very nearly the most damaging thing that can be said against any Thai person. Street protests were followed by a military coup and, despite the martial law and cancellation of the Constitution that followed, pro-democracy demonstrations began to emerge. The protestors chose to wear red as their own color. Political disputes, which continued into 2010, remain characterized by the use of rival colors, which has had a considerable impact on the clothes that people wear and buy. Generally, most people now avoid wearing a color that would mark them as politically active for fear of negative consequences—for example, people were encouraged to avoid wearing the traditional red for the 2010 Chinese New Year and wear pink instead (Wancharoen, 2010).

GOVERNMENT INFLUENCES

The Thai establishment has been enforcing nationalism upon the country for a number of decades and because of this, the clothes that people wear have become politicized. In the years leading up to World War II, Western attire was promoted as a form of modernization of the country and, although this is no longer necessary as policy, uniforms of various kinds are still widely used throughout the country. Civil servants and government officials wear uniforms on a daily basis or for special occasions, while high school and university students are expected to wear a standardized uniform when at the institution. Sometimes Thai traditional clothes or fabrics have been worn at the end of weekday (although private universities have a little more latitude, if they choose to take it). Corporate uniforms are also prevalent throughout the banking sector, particularly those at the front desk who work closely with customers as this conveys an image of each company. On the one hand, this is because some people do not have much money and cannot afford many suitable changes of clothing, especially in workplaces where the clothes might be damaged or dirtied. One consequence of this situation is that most working people have a more limited range of clothes than do people in comparable positions in many Western countries. On the other hand, this is the way to make everyone in society equal to each other since they do not have to compare prices and brands of clothes worn. Furthermore, the hot climate means that

▲ FIGURE 8.8 Protesters wearing red clothing. Street protestors wear a particular color to show affiliation with a particular political party. This influences the choice of color among clothing worn by regular people.

fewer types of clothes are necessary; even in winter, people rarely wear more than an extra sweater or a light jacket. Shawls have become fashionable among office workers in air-conditioned spaces but, in general, most people content themselves with T-shirts and shorts in their nonworking hours.

THE FOREIGN RETAIL BILL

The Foreign Retail Bill divides new stores into four categories based on size—120 to 299 square meters, or 1,292 to 3,218 square feet; 300 to 999 square meters, or 3,229 to 10,753 square feet; 1,000 to 2,999 square meters, or 10,764 to 32,281 square feet; and 3,000+ square meters, or 32,292+ square feet—and establishes location and opening hours' guidelines for each (Theparat & Phusadee, 2009). It also specifies the nature of committees sold to determine whether individual projects can be given permission to proceed. Given the nature of Thai committees, this step will certainly lead to a lengthening of the process by which permission may be received. Representatives of local retailers and wholesalers are concerned that the proportion of the total retail market controlled by large retail chains has been estimated at up to 60 percent of the 1.4 trillion baht ($47.7 billion) annual market.

INFRASTRUCTURE DEMANDS

There appears to be a trend for consumers to try to find all their shopping needs within one center, which affects the marketing of goods within such a center. In the past, shopping tended to be a family-oriented or at least social experience in Thailand, much more than in most Western countries, and routinely includes at least one meal. Transportation, in Bangkok in particular, is such that the majority of people will travel by car; consequently, there is a need for extensive (and comparatively cheap) parking. The air conditioning in shopping malls is also a big draw, and a number of people will visit malls simply or at least partly as a means of staying cool while passing the time. Currently, there is a new trend of lifestyle shopping. Community malls with individual themes and decoration are everywhere in Bangkok and its urban areas. This allows the Thai people to feel superior if they know about new and incredible places. So, photos from these place will be posted via online social network such as Facebook. Another trend in Thailand is the flea market where everyone can sell anything, particularly clothes, accessories and food. However, it is not only the normal flea market but it is like an event with some activities like live music. Unlike India, for example, where guards ensure that "undesirable" persons are not permitted to enter shopping malls, the power of peer pressure and social exclusion tends to ensure that malls are filled with people who are of the class or status at which the goods are marketed.

INTERNET RETAILING

Internet retailing in Thailand has gradually grown in recent years. This is due to government regulation to support education via online and cable networks. However, a phoneline is required for an internet connection so access is limited. Internet access in middle class urban areas is widely used. There are several internet cafés in almost every area in cities particularly near educational institutions since their main customers are students and teenagers. Unfortunately, they often use the internet for online gaming rather than for educational puroposes.

Nowadays, small villages also have access to the internet. It is always available at the temple as this is the place where people tend to gather. Due to the rapid growth of online shopping, there are some customers who buy more online rather than in traditional shops. However, Thai people are not yet used to buying things online; they choose to pay by transfering money in traditional way and letting the seller know by telling them via an online chatting program. Although, more people are using credit cards, they still do not trust online card payments as Thailand is a low-trust society. In general, the widespread use of credit cards is comparatively recent; although penetration of the market is quite strong, use of individual cards is comparatively slight.

GETTING TO KNOW DOMESTIC COMPETITORS: THE RACE TO ACQUIRE PRIME RETAIL LOCATIONS

Big C which was founded and operated by Central Group (later acquired by Carrefour Thailand) is one of the great players in Thailand hypermarkets. At present, BJC supercenter has the biggest share of Big C which it bought from the Casino group. Apart from Big C, Tesco Lotus is a big player in this market. There are two major influential players in the department store market: the Central Pattana Group and the Mall group. Both own stores ranging from local to high-end. Owing to Thailand's restrictions on land ownership and control of retail businesses, local property developers remain very influential. They are generally responsible (in whole or in part) for developing the large shopping centers that are now opening beyond the major cities of the country for modern retail methods, as well as operating many of the more important centers in Bangkok itself. Foreign brand managers customarily look for some sort of partnership with a local developer both to gain access to location-specific knowledge but also for legal requirements and the need to navigate complex zoning and administrative requirements. It is only when the foreign investor has gained extensive experience of the Thai market that it is able to move ahead independently. This has been the case for Tesco Lotus and also for the Minor Group, whose American founder Bill Heinecke has lived in Thailand for many years and which provides cluster marketing for a range of food and beverage brands (e.g. Sizzler [US-Australian] and American brands Swensen's, Dairy Queen, and the Pizza Company).

As mentioned above, the principal department stores in Thailand mostly from Central Retail group and the Mall group, with smaller numbers of Japanese stores like Tokyu and Isetan. The Central Retail group, has both Central Embassy as the high-end store which connects with Central Chidlom, the main brand of the group. However, Robinson, focusing on middle income customers and above is also operated by Central. Central group was founded in 1947; its first department store in Thailand was opened by the expansion of an existing general merchandise operation in 1957 around Yaowarat area (China town). It then opened the one-stop department store, Central Chidlom, in 1973, this sold apparel, furnishings, and various other categories of consumer goods.

There are more than 100 shopping centers in Bangkok, including the figurehead Siam Paragon Center at peak-retail center Siam Square and the enormous Seacon Square in Srinakarin, which was the fifth-largest shopping center in the world at the time of its opening. The brand new Em District is on Sukhumvit road at Prompong area. Moreover, Central Embassy selling only premium and high-end brands including exclusive restaurants is situated in the Rajprasong area which is the popular shopping center in Bangkok. Well-known international brands are represented in nearly all shopping centers in one form or another, although there is some division into higher- and lower-end markets. For example, the recently opened Union Mall center on the eternally busy Ladprao Road is positioned as a lower-end mall for local residents (Bangkok residents customarily drive everywhere) and people using the attached subway. Most outlets are aimed at lower-middle-class customers on the ground floor, with low-cost originals and accessories for young shoppers on the upper floors and an extensive food court area and supermarket in the basement, which has a few bulk staple goods available. High-end goods are not available in this center, but most malls will segment customers according to location within the mall overall.

In terms of business strategy, there is little to differentiate among rival department stores and retail chains from the perspective of consumers. Key competitive advantages lie in the ability to acquire land in attractive areas and the right to develop it, especially when the land is set to increase in value in line with anticipated improvements in physical infrastructure (e.g., new public transport facilities are built). Critical competencies involve the ability to move in the right circles, to have deep pockets for future investments, and the willingness to subcontract other functions to specialists. This tends to make the large retail spaces rather homogenous places to go shopping.

Other than retail stores and malls, there are alternative selling formats that are creating competition in the retail market. Bangkok has some very important, large, wholesale and retail market complexes such as Pratunam, Bobae, and Chatuchak. Each of these consists of numerous outlets offering smaller or larger ranges of products, be they permanent or temporary in nature, and inside or outside. A wide range of customers may be found, and some specialization of retail space is evident to deal with the different segments of the market. Customers range from teenagers shopping for accessories and fashion items to export agents.

At the brand level, the market divides into three distinct strategic groups of products competing against each other:

- At the top level are products sold in department stores and specialty shops within shopping centers, which are often foreign branded goods marketed through reputation and placed within the retail space, supplemented by point-of-sale activities. Loyalty schemes are popular, with multistore cards made available for use in a broad range of outlets and points schemes linked to cash discounts and other benefits. These loyalty schemes are in addition to store-based credit or debit cards. Additionally, both Western and Asian festivals are used as the basis for sales and other promotions. Christmas is followed by Chinese New Year and then Valentine's Day. Some sales are themed, and sales staff is expected to participate by wearing appropriate costumes. In other cases, the sale is simply an excuse for additional discounts.

- The second level of products is contained within shopping centers or retail districts but is separate from the high-level brands. This level includes individual shops on different levels from the department store within the shopping center or removed from it; because Thai consumers are, by and large, not willing to walk very far, the spatial location of an outlet within a larger mall indicates the quality and price of the products likely to be sold there. In some cases, the more (relatively) remote locations shade into illegality as pirated goods are made available. Periodic sweeps of shopping centers aimed at confiscating pirated goods and arresting those involved in their distribution and sale are often made public beforehand so that little difference is made in the long term after the immediate sweep. Goods at this level are generally marketed through availability and perhaps individual sales abilities. It is common for all products in a similar category to be sold in a specific area, which has the effect of reducing price as a means of determining sales: Just as in a traditional wet market selling fresh meat, fish, and vegetables, market vendors must live and work cheek by jowl with each other on a long-term basis, and the antipathy that might be caused by aggressive price reductions is deterred for that reason.

▶ The third level of goods is sold outside or in low-quality shop-houses, as they are perceived (although the location within a city or town of the shop-house might lend it additional cachet). Haggling over the price is common, and customers will need to have a good idea already of what is fashionable in order to find something that they like because vendors will try to sell all of their stock as if it were of equal trendiness.

HOW MATURE IS THE RETAIL INDUSTRY?

There is considerable scope for apparel retailing to grow in Thailand. Although Bangkok appears to have reached a saturation phase for new retail developments, further schemes continue to be built. Shopping centers have been opened in the coastal resort Pattaya and in the northern capital of Chiang Mai (e.g., Central Airport Plaza) and are planned or opening in Khon Kaen (Central Plaza) and elsewhere. Shopping centers tend to have clusters selling the same group of brands: Central malls offer the Tops supermarket, B2S (stationery and books), Office Depot, Power Buy (consumer electronics), and Robinson department store. Similarly, the Minor International Group clusters leading restaurant outlets (Sizzler, Burger King, Swensen's, Dairy Queen, and others), which may then be attached to a shopping complex managed by a retail chain. So the shopping experience is becoming homogenized across the country.

BUYING AND SOURCING FOR APPAREL RETAIL STORES

In most retail chains, professionalization of local staff has meant that Thai employees have been inducted into internationalized best practices. In the

Body Shop chain, for example, newly hired employees are expected to work at every level of retail activity before being permitted to enter into management training. Staff training is generally considered to be an important component of assimilating new employees into corporate culture. In few areas of retail management is this more true than in buying, which in Thailand has traditionally been an activity founded on the creation and re-creation of existing network connections. The attempt to professionalize the buying function is assisted by the presence of extensive manufacturing capacity throughout the Kingdom, both Thai and internationally owned. It might also be pointed out that the continuing weakness of the labor movement in the country enables the buyers, like all managers, to minimize any mistakes by requiring workers to rework any items at what is effectively their own expense. In recent times, the professionalization of Thai retail staff has been so successful that some are now being recruited internationally (Sruthijith & Chakravarty, 2010).

At the individual entrepreneurial level, buying can be quite sophisticated, although for the majority of street vendors or small shops, the buying function extends no further than a convenient nearby wholesale market—indeed, in many provincial markets, stall owners are tied to wholesalers who oblige them to stock whatever goods they might make available. However, on a more sophisticated level, there is a subset of street vendors and small shop owners in Bangkok who, as white-collar victims of the 1997 financial crisis, decided to remain in the city and put to use their business skills rather than return to rural, agricultural underemployment. Accordingly, they have established in some cases international supply chains, importing in one case clothes from Korea (in crates marked for charitable causes) and, in others, establishing their own brands that could be serviced through contract manufacturing in the Rayong region of southern Thailand, which enabled small-scale batch production in a variety of different configurations. In the event that goods are not sold on a timely basis, they may be passed on first to secondary-value locations (marked up because further from the center of fashion) and then to non-urban locations.

In Bangkok in particular, rental costs for retail spaces are very expensive, and entrepreneurs cannot afford to keep unsold products on the premises. Vendors revealed that, in the case of fashion-conscious Bangkok-based university female students (hence, mostly middle- or upper-class individuals), items are bought and worn no more than two or three times before being discarded. As a result, if products are not sold more or less immediately, it is unlikely that they will be sold in the location concerned and so they are at once pushed on to the next place in the selling chain.

As in many other developing countries, local authorities have for some years maintained a fairly lax attitude toward intellectual property rights (IPR). This attitude stems from a lack of capacity to police the issue properly, a lack of political will to do so, and the strong incentives that exist for entrepreneurs to reduce costs and risks in producing new items through copying existing intellectual property. IPR piracy manifests itself in Thailand in several ways: direct replication of existing products with inferior materials for sale as fakes through outdoor markets; passing off inferior products for protected branded items (which can be dangerous for customers when it involves medication or some kinds of cosmetics); copying of protected designs or elements of trade dress (e.g., patented or copyrighted elements) and using them in products under other brands; or obtaining samples from factories contracted to produce branded goods under license and using these for sale or as production prototypes. Some of these manifestations are clearly examples of theft and may be punished by the courts, when the police are able and willing to identify miscreants. In other cases, however, a general tolerance toward copying the work of others throughout society can be witnessed at all levels. That high-quality products are so far beyond the reach of most people tends to promote the idea that it is perfectly rational to use fake goods, even when most, if not all, people know they are fake.

The degree of IPR piracy has reduced the willingness of international investors to invest in Thailand and has reduced the reputation of certain branded products (as consumers do not realize that they are fakes), while allowing some entrepreneurs to benefit from the work of others. However, following the example of South Korea, the Thai Government has been inspired to take action against pirated goods in the main markets and malls of Bangkok and, to some extent, in the other urban centers. Thai manufacturers themselves have gained sufficient experience to be able to eschew piracy and can instead develop their own brands, with the assistance of CAD technology and flexible manufacturing systems. As more free trade agreements are signed and membership of the World Trade Organization intensifies, internationally accepted norms concerning IPR are becoming more embedded in Thai society. Most developed Western countries had similarly lax attitudes toward IPR during their own periods of development and have only recently changed their tune now that they have the power to protect their own products.

RETAIL CAREERS

Thailand was a poor country at the conclusion of World War II but has since become a middle-income country. It has managed this transformation by export-oriented manufacturing with competitiveness based on low labor costs. As wages have slowly risen over the years, combined with the emergence of China and Vietnam as alternative targets for investment in manufacturing, Thailand's factory-based economy has become less and less sustainable. In response, the government made plans to identify suitable alternative sunrise industries and industrial clusters in which it could invest and develop. It identified the fashion industry as a suitable future industrial cluster, owing to the size of the domestic market and sources of supply, existing manufacturing capacity, and the possibility of training skilled designers. The 2006 military coup significantly decelerated these plans because emphasis was placed on social conservatism and promoting the role of the military in the country. However, led to a considerable extent by the private sector, the fashion industry is being developed at every stage of the value chain. This has meant that career opportunities are emerging in the retailing of apparel in Thailand.

There still remain certain skill deficiencies that are not being met by local staff. For example, the head of one very prominent international cosmetic chain complained that he had to go to Hong Kong to find competent visual merchandising staff. The government responded by promoting a series of industrial clusters in which it was hoped a long-term competitive advantage could be established and sustained. Clearly, providing the conditions for new jobs was an important part of that process, and the flagship Bangkok Fashion City event showcased the talents of young designers, as well as numerous models and, less visibly, support staff, technicians, manufacturing agents, and the like. Inevitably, policies such as this are difficult to evaluate accurately and do not produce results in predictable time frames.

Further, the legacy of the 3Ls (low-skilled, low-wages, and long-hours) labor market strategy makes new jobs in retailing less attractive. Thai workers have one of the longest work weeks in the world, but their productivity at work remains disappointingly low and careers in retailing have tended to follow this pattern. Although many Thai executives have benefited from international education and exposure to international best practices, by and large innovations have yet to spread to the retail or personal service sectors of the economy.

A non-Thai person wanting to work in Thailand must be in possession of a valid work permit. These are available in various categories and, for professional or management positions for people from Western countries in particular, the process of obtaining a permit has become much less onerous than it was even a few years ago. The employer is responsible for collecting the paperwork required and the representative, together with the prospective employee, is required to visit a specific office, depending on where the head office of the business concerned is located. This office is not the same as the immigration office because the functions belong to different ministries. For management positions, the employer will routinely meet all fees, which are comparatively minor in any case. For brief assignments in Thailand not involving payment by an organization incorporated in the country, a work permit is not generally required, and visas are also not usually required for most residents of developed countries; however, it is always wise to check requirements beforehand because these might change.

The number of college-level courses available has increased notably, and more are expected to open (*The Nation*, 2006). Educational institutions now offering courses in fashion design or related subjects but these are very limited for fashion merchandising or retailing. There are about 20 institues which promote apparel & textiles both in teaching, facilities and employment, including

▲ FIGURE 8.9 Bangkok fashion week.

local schools as Chulalongkorn University (ranked 253 in World QS, 2015), Kasetsart University, Srinakharinwirot University, and Silpakon University (for design), Thammasat University (for textile and design), Bangkok University (design), and international schools such as CIDI Chanapatna International Design Institute (design) and Raffles International College (design and management). Interestingly, most of the design and management programs are offered in and around Bangkok. Clothing and textile design studies has strong support from both the Thai Goverment and external agencies such as department stores and malls. Courses such as merchandising, marketing, and retail management or fashion communication are lacking, although there are some courses (research for graduate level only) in intensive management schools like Sasin (a business school of Chulalongkorn University) or Mahidol University (QS ranking 295, 2015) but these are not really focused on development and support for the industry. In 2012, the Luxellence center was set up under the direction of CP Group (CP group limited company) for courses in luxury corporate programs with IFA Paris, and consulting and research in lifestyle and luxury focused on the Bangkok market.

The government has made efforts to promote the role of entrepreneurs in the economy, together with all kinds of small and medium-sized enterprises (SMEs). It has established the SME Bank, the Department of Industrial Promotion, and the Office of SME Promotion. Managers can obtain some training from governmental agencies and support for production and, in particular, exporting. Of course, these schemes suffer from the usual problems of lack of supply and the difficulties entrepreneurs face in finding time for the right kind of training.

THE FUTURE OF APPAREL RETAIL

The future of retailing as a whole is at something of a crossroads in Thailand as a result of the conservative, nationalist approach first taken by the junta from 2006 to 2008 and then its successor, the military-installed Abhisit regime. This government is at best ambivalent toward the business sector in general and international investment in particular. Retailing has been a very visible part of its policy approach because the extension of modern retailing through Thailand has been very closely associated with the spread of international investment and capitalism in the country.

Initially, international investors started retail investment as part of joint ventures with locally owned companies, but the government slackened the requirement to do so in the early years of the twenty-first century. After this, international companies began buying out their local partners and assuming more control over operations and growth. The most rapid and extensive growth has been undertaken by supermarket-based chains like Tesco Lotus (nearly 400 stores of different sizes nationwide), Carrefour (39 branches nationwide), Tops (114 branches nationwide), and Big C (67 branches nationwide) (MacKinnon 2008; Carrefour 2009; Tops Supermarket, 2008; Big C Supercenter 2010). These chains are also important centers for apparel marketing, both as centers for sale themselves and as part of shopping complexes, which have external space open for street vending (Maneepong & Walsh, 2009).

As of the end of 2010, the administration was still delaying implementation of the Foreign Retail and Wholesale Bill, which is intended to regulate further the ways in which international investment projects might be approved (or not) and where such projects could be located. Zoning regulations in Thailand have for many years been widely considered to be subject to compromise through corruption, and those charged with protecting local interests have vociferously complained that irregularities have taken place between international investors and colluding politicians. Whether or not these irregularities actually took place was secondary to local advocates' ability to gather local support among communities and individuals who felt threatened by the spread of retail chains. The announcement of any new branch of Tesco Lotus was for a while met by a campaign of opposition by local people and pressure on local planning authorities.

To summarize the previous points, when investing in Thailand, it is important to remember that:

▶ Thailand is undergoing a retail revolution not just in terms of the types of products available but the types of retail opportunities provided and the extent of locations at which consumers can access items.
▶ Thai consumers require adaptations to many products in terms of size, shape, color, and with respect to some cultural factors.
▶ Despite evolving regulations concerning foreign investment, it is almost certain that investors will require a local partner to assist with ownership of land, navigation of regulations, and providing location-specific information.
▶ The marketplace is becoming a battleground in which emergent local brands are competing with Western brands on the one hand and increasingly popular Korean and East Asian styles on the other hand.

▶ Another aspect of Thailand that foreign investors need to know about is the labor laws in the country. Although the principles of freedom of association and collective bargaining are recognized in Thailand, in practice the nature of labor law means that labor unions have relatively little power and few rights compared to Western countries. Although this attitude seems unlikely to change much in the 2010s, the pressure applied by newly signed free trade agreements may have an impact.

SUMMARY

Thailand is a middle income country located in Southeast Asia and Bangkok is the capital city with 8.5 million urban residents. Since the beginning of the twenty-first century, Thailand has become one of the important emerging markets due to its stable economy, skillful workers, a good regulatory system and some incentives in investment. So, these are the reasons why Thailand is so popular among foreign investors. The country's government also works hard to improve conditions and regulation to attract more foreigners.

Apparel retail market is very important to Thailand's economy. In the past, Thailand was one of the biggest producers. There are many factories located throughout Thailand. However, the competition is more intense as other countries in ASEAN have opened up for investors and are providing lower production costs. So, Thai producers have to adapt themselves by use Thainess in their style and this turns out good. Moreover, there are many Thai-owned brands that adapt to the society like add more sizes to fit western travelers. The men's apparel market has also expanded due the effect of western, Japanese and Korean media. For children's apparel, the media has a great deal of influence in their fashion. For example, parents buy outfits depicting the characters in the popular Korean variety show "The return of the Superman."

The beauty industry in Thailand is also very popular, particularly Thai spa products. Skincare products and the cosmetic surgery market are expanding more than ever before. There are wide ranges of products suitable for all skin types and age ranges.

Luxury goods, hotels and condominiums have some potential in Thailand's market in urban areas. However, the competition in Asian countries is intense and Hong Kong and Singapore are top destinations for shoppers. In this case, the government should promote Thailand tourism along with the shopping experience.

In Thailand, there is a type of grocery shop called "Cho-Huay" which is a traditional format run by the owner. This type of shop is always small and located at the first floor of owners' houses. Street vendors are almost everywhere.

In 1957, the first modernized "Central department store" was opened. Nowadays, there are a lot of chain stores, both Thai and foreign operated such as Tesco Lotus, Big C, Central, Robinson, the Mall in addition to many more independent stores nationwide. Furthermore, there are two retail companies which play an important role in the market: "The Mall group" and "Central group". There are more than 100 shopping centers in Bangkok and several in stores in urban cities. These prove that the market is still growing.

Thai regulation limits investment in Thailand to those of Thai nationality. In the case of industry, foreigners can own up to 49 percent of shares. However, foreigners will let their spouses or Thai nominees hold their shares for them.

However, international retailers often operate via contract with local partners e.g. Tesco-Lotus and 7-Eleven. Yet, department stores in Thailand are generally owned and operated by Thai management companies.

Thailand has some formal barriers to entry. First, it is illegal for foreigners to own land in Thailand. Second, there are occasional outbreaks of nationalism and xenophobia in the media.

For Thai people, culture plays an important role in their daily life and also in apparel retailing. As can be seen, Japanese and Korean culture have a lot of influence as lots of TV dramas are aired on Thai free TV.

Inside the retail store, the environment is like that of other East Asian countries. Each shop has staff who approach and try to sell products to customers. Apart from this, customers expect an extra service with low cost, e.g. garments adjusted for free.

Color-coding is used to represent some special events or groups while governors still need to wear a uniform.

Thai people who are fashion-conscious will buy clothes and use them less than three times before being discarded. So, the seller should sell the items that are on-trend at that time in a good location even though the cost of rental is very high.

The main problem for retail careers in Thailand is the fact that the workforce lacks the skills to support the whole process of the company. However, many Thai institutions have opened fashion, textile and apparel courses to support skilled staff into the market. The Thai government is supporting entrepreneurs in this field.

CRITICAL THINKING QUESTIONS

1. Why is Thailand an important emerging market?
2. What area of industry in Thailand is focused on improving the efficiency of the economy?
3. What is the difference between "Cho-Huay" (Traditional Thai retail) and general retail?
4. Could you explain the behavior of a Thai consumer when visiting a retail store?
5. How does Thailand overcome China and other competitors in the world market of producers?
6. What is apparel retail in Thailand like, in general? Explain the differences between the women's, men's, and children's market.
7. Explain an industry regulation in Thailand.
8. What are important things to know before investing in Thailand?
9. What would be an appropriate strategy for a multinational company that would like to open a new market in Thailand?
10. How do culture and society influence the Thai textile and apparel market?
11. How would you source for an apparel store in Thailand?
12. What are some potential problems in the Thai retail career market?

Case Study

GAP IN THAILAND

A number of foreign ventures in Thailand have ended in failure or at least only partial success for a variety of reasons. Burger King, for example, drastically reduced its scope after the enormous increase in popularity of the goddess Kuan Yin. The attendant voluntary abstinence from beef led a spokesperson to observe that "Thailand is a chicken country." The Sogo department store ran into trouble due to financial problems in its home country of Japan. Others have been victims of the financial crises in 1997 and 2008, or have held off investing because of political instability, pandemics or natural disasters. Achieving success has required not just vision and understanding of the marketplace but, in many cases, the patience to wait until sufficient consumers exist who might be attracted to the products and who will be willing to resist counterfeited goods. An example of such a firm is Gap, which did not open its first dedicated shop in Thailand until 2010 (through Minor International PLC), partly because of the presence of so many fake goods and the lack of maturity in the market. However, having determined that 2010 is the correct moment to enter the market, at present, there are seven Gap stores in Bangkok and also in Chiang-Mai. This late-market entry means that the company has more choice in terms of appropriately qualified and skilled senior and middle-ranking staff, while also being able to take advantage of best practice from rival brands. It also means that Thai consumers have had a chance to become accustomed to Western styles, colors, and prices, and so should be more willing to accept the products. The downside, of course, is that rivals have had time to build customer loyalty and familiarity. However, because Thai consumers are characterized by desire for the new, brand loyalty is not generally seen as a powerful barrier to entry in consumer goods markets.

Source: Jitpleecheep, Pitsinee, "MINT Expects Food Response to Gap in Thailand," *Bangkok Post* (March 6, 2010). Retrieved on December 15, 2010 from http://www. bangkokpost.com/business/marketing/33991/mint-expects-good-response-to-gap-in-thailand.

Discussion Questions
1. In a country in which intellectual property rights are only loosely respected, to what extent is it worthwhile for an international investor to try to suppress pirated versions of its products?

2. How can brand loyalty be developed in consumers who, through rapid globalization, seem to have become addicted to whatever is new?
3. In the case of opening the Gap store, what market segments is this strategy appropriate and whereabouts in Thailand should Gap focus?

REFERENCES

NESDB Economic report, Thai economic perfromance in Q1 and Outlook for 2013 and 2016. Macroeconomic strategy and planning office, Press release, May 16, 2016.

http://data.un.org/CountryProfile.aspx?crName=THAILAND

Travel and tourism economic impact 2015 world, The authority on world travel and tourism council, London, 2015

REFERENCES

Asia Development Bank (ADB) (2008). Key Indicators for Asia and the Pacific 2008 (Manila: ADB, 2008). Retrieved March 10, 2010 from www.adb.org/Documents/Books/Key_Indicators/2008/pdf/Key-Indicators–2008.pdf

Big C Stores (2010). Big C Supercenter. Retrieved March 10, 2010 from www.bigc.co.th/en/stores/

Carrefour, Thailand—Opening of the 37th Carrefour Hypermarket (2009). Retrieved March 1, 2010, from www.carrefour.com/cdc/group/current-news/thailand-opening-of-the–37th-carrefour-hypermarket.html

Charoen Pokphand Group (2010). *Marketing and Distribution Business.* Retrieved March 1, 2010, from www.cpthailand.com/Default.aspx?tabid=242

Dressed for Success (2006). *The Nation.* Retrieved March 10, 2010, from www.nationmultimedia.com/smartlife/20060327/

Escobar, P. (2009). Superfat Hits Asia, *Asia Times Online.* Retrieved March 1, 2010 from www.atimes.com/atimes/Southeast_Asia/KG02Ae01.html

Feeny, A., Vongpatanasin, T. & Soonsatham, A. (1996). Retailing in Thailand. *International Journal of Retail and Distribution Management, 24*, 38–44.

Honomichil, J. (2013) Global Top 25 Report. IPSOS Singapore.

Jitleecheep, P. (2009). Improvement in Store. *Bangkok Post Economic Review, Year-End 2009* (2009a), p. 16.

Kanchoochat, V. (2008). Services, Servility, and Survival: The Accommodation of Big Retail, in P. Phongpaichit & C. Baker, eds., *Thai Capital after the 1997 Crisis,* Chiang Mai: Silkworm Books, 85–104.

Maneepong, C. & Walsh, J. (2009). A New Generation of Bangkok Street Vendors: New Businesses, Old Policies. *Paper presented at the 8th International Symposium of the International Urban Planning and Environment Association (IUPEA),* March 23–26, 2009, at the University of Kaiserslautern, Germany.

Nguyen DK.; Kunchornsup W., Suriwong S., Wachirawarakarn S., Innanchai S. (2015). The Effect of Styling in Visual Merchandising as a Design Element: Case Study on Thai Spa and Skincare, unpublished, CIDI Chanapatana International Design Institute Resource.

Saengsawang, W. (2009). Special Report: Thailand Elite Card on Bumpy Road," *National News Bureau of Thailand Public Relations Department* (December 22, 2009). Retrieved from http://thainews.prd.go.th/en/news.php?id=255212220007

Songkran Fun Gets Under Way in Earnest (2007, April 14). *The Nation* Retrieved March 10, 2010, from www.nationmultimedia.com/search/read.php?newsid=30031869

Sruthijith K. K. & Chakravarty, C. (2010). Reliance Retail Hiring Professionals from Thailand. *The Economic Times of India.* Retrieved February 10, 2010, from http://economictimes.indiatimes.com/news/news-by-industry/services/retailing/Reliance-Retail-hiring-professionals-from-Thailand/articleshow/5474885.cms

Sukasame, N. (2008). The Essence of Online Retailing: A Case Study of Thailand. *Journal of International Business and Economics, 8*(2), 117–21.

Summary of Industry Economic Status. The Office of Industrial Economic_Industrial Economic Status Report, May 2015. Thailand.

Thailand's Investment Market Retains its Attractiveness (2008). *The Nation.* Retrieved March 15, 2010 from www.nationmultimedia.com/2008/05/09/business/business_30072622.php

Tesco Lotus (2010). Retrieved October 25, 2010, from www.tescolotus.com/left.php?lang=en&menu=corporate_th&data=profile

Tops Supermarket (2008). Company Profile. Retrieved January 15, 2010 from www.tops.co.th/companyprofile/index.html

Wancharoen, S. (2010). New Year Revelers Will Be Pretty in Pink. *Bangkok Post.* Retrieved February 15, 2010 from www.bangkokpost.com/news/local/32614/new-year-revellers-will-be-pretty-in-pink

Watcharavesringkan, K., Karpova, E., Nelson Hodges, N. & Copeland, R. (2010) The Competitive Position of Thailand's Apparel Industry. *Journal of Fashion Marketing and Management: An International Journal, 14*(4), 576–597.

MEXICO

9

Diana Bank Weinberg

Mohammad Ayub Khan

Jaya Halepete

OBJECTIVES

After reading this chapter, you will

► Understand the evolution of the Mexican retail market from the 1980s onwards

► Grasp the role of foreign direct investment policies in the Mexican retail market

► Determine the effects of the Mexican consumer's preferences on buying decisions

► Understand cultural factors influencing the retail market in Mexico

Mexico's location at the crossroads of North and Latin America, and the Pacific and Atlantic Oceans is a compelling factor for many international investors. They see Mexico as a logical place to invest to spring into the North and South American markets. Its two coastlines provide easy access to ports for international businesses. Mexico is a regional power in economic development and international business, and the only Latin American member of the Organization for Economic Cooperation and Development (OECD), which it joined in 1994.

As the "rich men's club," the OECD has been very careful whom it accepts. As Mexico started with entry negotiations, it had to open its economy and

TABLE 9.1 Fast Facts about Mexico	
Capital	Mexico City
Population	121,736,809 million
Type of government	Federal Republic
GDP at Purchasing Power Parity (USD)	$2.22 trillion
Age structure	0–14 years: 27.59 percent
	15–24 years: 17.9 percent
	25–54 years: 40.55 percent
	55–64 years: 7.19 percent
	65 years and over: 6.77 percent
Religion	Roman Catholic: 82.7 percent
	Protestant: 6.3 percent
	Pentecostal: 1.6 percent
	Jehovah's Witnesses: 1.4 percent
	Other: 5.0 percent
	Unspecified: 2.7 percent
	None: 4.7 percent
Ethnicity	Mestizo (Amerindian–Spanish):
	62 percent
	Predominantly Amerindian:
	21 percent
	Amerindian: 7 percent
	Other (mostly European): 10 percent

Source: CIA Factbook.gov (2015); INEGI (2015).

submit to deep economic changes, which it did. Because Mexico has always managed to recover well from its economic woes and is considered an upper-middle-income country, economic ups and downs have reinforced government intentions to develop new policies, restructure the economic system, and participate in international business. In the 1970s, during what was termed the "Mexican Miracle" by historians, Mexico advanced relatively quickly in terms of economic development. However, in the 1980s, the lack of economic competitiveness threw Mexico into a deep financial crisis, and the economy stagnated to the point that the country defaulted on its payments. In 1986, Mexico joined the World Trade Organization's (WTO) precursor, the General Agreement on Tariffs and Trade (GATT), which resulted in the reduction of taxes imposed on imports and exports. Furthermore, Mexico started to liberalize foreign trade by reducing tariffs on most imported goods accompanied by industry deregulations, such as opening many sectors, including the retail sector, to foreign ownership (Marinov, 2006). Since then, and due to OECD and WTO membership, the country has made steady progress, except for the 1994 devaluation of the peso due to bad internal macroeconomic decisions and the global financial crisis in 2008.

Mexico's economy has a couple of perennial weak spots. It is highly dependent on the U.S. economy, which receives over 80 percent of Mexico's exports. The country also contends with environmental challenges, including massive earthquakes such as the 1985 event that destroyed Mexico City and left many thousands homeless, and hurricanes mainly in the Gulf of Mexico and the Caribbean. In spite of all this, Mexico remains one of Latin America's leading emerging economies.

Mexico's is the fifteenth-largest economy in the world, according to GDP. The creation of the North American Free Trade Agreement (NAFTA), a 1994 trade agreement between Mexico, Canada, and the United States, has significantly and positively influenced Mexico's image for investors, both foreign and domestic. Mexico's trade figures with the United States and Canada—including textile and apparel products—have tripled since NAFTA was established (Villareal & Fergusson, 2015).

Mexico has one of the highest percentages of young consumers in the world (see Table 9.1). Of its estimated 122 million people, 59 million are 30 years old or younger (INEGI, 2016). That is close to 50 percent of the total population. The percentage of potential consumers between the ages of 20 and 44 is substantially high in Mexico (41 percent). This portion of the population is crucial for retail markets, including apparel products. Other tendencies, such as increasing urbanization in Mexico (over 29 cities have reached the half-million inhabitant mark), are positive indicators for national and international retail businesses. Furthermore, government institutions are introducing checks and balances to eradicate malpractices related to industrial policies and standards. By improving quality, price, and service, Mexico continues to improve its business practices in a highly competitive world.

THE RETAIL LANDSCAPE: AN EMERGING MARKET ALL THE WAY

Mexico's retail market dates back to the 1930s and 1940s in Mexico City. By the early 1960s, retail stores started expanding into other cities; they found potential markets in Monterrey and Guadalajara, the biggest urban areas after Mexico City. Though the retail business saw periodic ups and downs throughout the last century, with uncooperative government business policies, an unstable political environment, and increasing poverty and financial crises, the retail business continued to evolve and gained momentum in the late 1980s and early 1990s. There was a slight break in the momentum in 1994–1995 because of the sharp peso devaluation. Since 2008, Mexico has been the second-largest retail market in Latin America after Brazil, with a value of US$310 billion (Economist Intelligence Unit, 2009), and more recently, second in e-commerce, accounting for 12.3 percent of all e-commerce in Latin America (Smith, 2016). In 2015, retailing in Mexico recorded current value growth of five percent, reflecting the recovery of the industry after 2014, which saw consumer confidence fall as a result of comprehensive new tax laws which negatively affected disposable income (Euromonitor International, 2016). Another positive sign is that Mexican per capita consumer spending is forecasted to increase by 30 percent by 2017 (PwC, 2014). Moreover, retail is one of the biggest sectors in the Mexican economy, accounting for seven percent of GDP and employing 10 percent of the labor force, therefore it holds enormous potential to help drive Mexico's continued economic growth (Bolio et al., 2014).

Traditionally, retail businesses have concentrated their business efforts in urban areas with a large population of economically powerful consumers. They provide one job in five outside agriculture (Tilly & Alvarez Galván, 2006). About 44 percent of the Mexican population lives in one of 25 big cities, and retail businesses have focused on these cities. Of the dominant apparel products (womenswear, menswear, and childrenswear), the womenswear segment was the industry's most lucrative in 2011, with total revenue of $2.415.5 billion, equivalent to 45.1 percent of the industry's overall value (PwC, 2014).

Research analysts expect the Mexican apparel retail industry, which did not show attractive growth indicators from 2004 to 2009 (Economist Intelligence Unit, 2009), to have relatively slow retail sales growth until 2016 and competition among an increasing number of new retailers (Gap, H&M, American Eagle Outfitters and Forever 21, among other) to intensify. The country's retail sales are expected to grow from US$217.35 billion in 2013 to US$264.61 billion by 2017, a rise of 17.8 percent in five years (PwC, 2014).

Large retail outlets have existed in Mexico since the 1940s, but the growth of super- and hypermarkets accelerated only after 1994, with NAFTA. For instance, the number of supermarkets in Mexico nearly doubled from 544 in 1990 to 1,026 in 2000 (Reardon & Berdegué, 2002). Furthermore, in 2001–2002, the share of the top five supermarket chains was 80 percent of the food sales, and the share of foreign multinational chains in supermarket sales was over 70 percent (Reardon and Berdegué, 2002). Despite this dominance by large retailers, in areas with low population densities or low income, consumers prefer to buy produce, dairy products, and meat from traditional retailers (Euromonitor, 2005). As such, Mexico is a hybrid country, where new, world-class retail development shares the street with an estimated 2.3 million mom-and-pop stores and traditional markets; all these venues serve a highly diversified and continuously growing base of consumers (PwC, 2014), whose attitudes and buying behavior could prove to be an impediment for further concentration of retail trade.

CONSUMERS: FROM "MALINCHISTA" TO MAINSTREAM CONSUMER

Mexican consumers are culturally similar across the country, as they derive from a common ancestry, mainly a mixture of Mexican Indian and Spanish descent (Marinov, 2006). Mexican consumers shop once or twice a week for themselves but several times a week for their children. Most consumers are price sensitive, but those with purchasing power tend to buy products with popular brand names. Socio-demographic factors also define the purchasing behavior of Mexican consumers. Around 20 percent of the population belongs to the high-middle and upper class (INEGI, 2010), so the preferences of these consumers will differ from those with lower annual earnings. Older consumers traditionally shop in small local shops. Younger consumers, especially those employed who do not have time to shop on a daily basis, shop once a week in large outlets (Marinov, 2006). Also, working women and women with children, who are in charge of everyday household purchases, are the targets of super- and hypermarket commercials and promotions.

Coming from a traditional collectivist society, consumers in Mexico tend to be group-oriented (Hofstede, 2015) and are attentive to the wishes and feelings of others (Albert, 1996). In addition, Mexican consumers are status-oriented and exhibit their social standing through their possessions. For a Mexican, "*él que dirán*" (what will people say) is a very important consideration when shopping. In addition, Mexicans are known as "*malinchistas*." The word is derived from the name of a woman nicknamed "La Malinche." She was kidnapped by Spaniards and used as a translator after she had learned Spanish. For many Mexicans, she helped Spain in its Mexican conquest, and was hence considered a traitor to her people. Today someone who chooses a foreign product over a Mexican product is called a "*malinchista*," which shows that Mexicans have a preference for foreign products as they consider them to be of better quality. For foreign retailers, this "*malinchismo*" part of the Mexican culture can be used in their sales and retail endeavors.

Mexican consumers like to buy high-fashion apparel. Lack of fashionable merchandise in the market has led consumers to buy fakes of American brands. "Mexican manufacturers can't bring the same design, color, fashion, durability, and excitement of the U.S. brands, so unless they work to change this, consumers will continue to buy U.S. brands in the illegal markets," said Miguel Angel Andreu of the industry think tank Instituto Textil Nacional (Freeman, 2010). According to apparel chamber Canaive, which represents 8,600 manufacturers, Mexicans spend about $21 billion a year on clothing, of which 60 percent is believed to involve stolen, smuggled or counterfeit garments acquired in street markets (PwC, 2014).

Although the buying habits of the upper and middle classes may not be the same as those in poorer classes, mainly due to income differences, factors such as group influence, affiliation, interpersonal relationships, social distinction, brand reputation, and individual aspiration also influence their buying decisions. Therefore, international retail businesses trying to penetrate the Mexican market should focus on marketing strategies that reflect emotional appeal, brand quality, and reference group.

Characteristics that distinguish Mexican consumers from others include:

- ▶ Mexicans like to buy products imported from other countries like the United States, Europe and Canada, and many Mexicans go to U.S.–Mexican border supermarkets for shopping.
- ▶ They are highly quality-conscious, but will sacrifice quality for a lower price.
- ▶ Store name and location are highly important to Mexican consumers.
- ▶ Consumers in Mexico like personal attention from providers and distributors of products or services. Customer service is very important.

- Whereas low-income consumers purchase generic products because of their lower price, higher-income groups buy branded products for their perceived quality.
- They perceive that foreign products in Mexico are better in quality than Mexican products, are competitively priced, and are available in multiple variations, in addition to giving the potential buyer a feeling of belonging to a higher society. For instance, the brand Gap is highly valued by the higher classes as a status symbol to show everyone that they have enough money to go to the United States and shop.
- The middle-aged, urban, educated upper-class prefer to buy foreign products and world-recognized brands.
- Mexican consumers are looking for the hottest fashions, the biggest brands and the best quality they can find.
- Mexico is considered to be a collectivist society, and Mexicans tend to be group-oriented and concerned about feelings of other people.
- Affluent Mexican consumers tend to purchase brands that convey status and power, and even poor Mexican consumers display a tendency toward conspicuous consumption (Vaezi, 2005).

WOMEN

Mexican women tend to be the primary shoppers and, therefore, the main decision makers. In Mexican society, men have tended to be the breadwinners, and women are those who control household finances, raise the children, and take care of their husbands. Because women tend to be more sensitive to their surroundings, the buying behavior of their peers affects their shopping habits (Galindo, n.d.).

Status is important for Mexican women, and their homes, cars, and other material possessions reflect who they are, or who they aspire to be. They spend a large part of their income (or their husband's) in providing clues to their social class. Mexican women take particular pride in a clean and orderly home. Similarly, they tend to be very conscious of their looks. On Saturday mornings, many Mexican women can be found at the hairdresser's, chatting with their friends and reading the latest gossip columns, on which they will freely comment to the woman sitting under the next hair dryer.

Therefore, regardless of the social class to which they belong, women are the main providers of a nice, clean home (although they themselves will not do the cleaning) and are impeccably dressed. Their shopping habits largely depend on those of the social class to which they belong.

MEN

Some studies (Rausch, 2002) have shown, against reasonable expectations, that Mexican men tend to be more brand conscious than women, especially those under the age of 22. This is especially true for certain beauty products, as well as branded clothing and home goods. Nevertheless, these purchases will be mainly made by the woman of the house, which could be a wife, mother, or even grandmother, because many Mexicans continue to live with extended family. Because men of working age provide the family income, they want to be taken care of and appreciated. This includes having a nice, clean, and orderly home, food on the table, and the respect and gratitude of their children.

Therefore, although males seem to have a strong preference for brands that confer status, they leave those decisions to the women in their households. Cars or home electronics, for instance, are considered bastions of men's knowledge for which they will shop personally.

THE BEAUTY INDUSTRY IN MEXICO

Mexico's cosmetics and toiletries market is ranked 11th in the world and second to Brazil in Latin America. The high-end cosmetics market is estimated to be between $330 and $400 million. The top brands in Mexico are Lancôme, Estee Lauder, and Chanel. Although television is the primary influence for choice of beauty products, particular influences vary by region. For example, Mexicans near the U.S. border use more hair colors, and color cosmetics are most popular in Guadalajara, the second largest city in Mexico. Hair products are the most consumed cosmetic products in Mexico. Almost 98 percent of women wash their hair daily. As they tend to have long hair (a sign of femininity and Latin beauty), they require lots of hair products. Mexican women generally do not use conditioner due to a myth that it weakens hair (Joynes-Burgess, 2008).

The changing role of Mexican women, with 33 percent at work as executives, is increasing the demand for anti-aging products. A new market for natural products is also growing in Mexico. Makeup brands with minerals are expanding in the country. Sales of beauty products in the country rose by 3.4 to 3.8 percent in the first half of 2015, as Mexico is expected to be among the top 10 growth markets for luxury goods, with sales rising 34 percent by 2019 (Stillman, 2015).

Mexican men were not interested in beauty products until the media brought news of beauty product trends in Europe and the United States after Mexico started opening its economy in 1986. Until 2005, hardly any

▲ FIGURE 9.1 Actress Paulina Gaytan attends the Esquire Mexico Magazine 2nd Anniversary Masquerade Party. Mexican consumers are influenced by international fashion and like to buy high-end apparel.

information was available about facial and body treatments. Brands such as Carlo Corinto Skin Essentials (France) have now started producing their products for the male Mexican market. Mexico has over 30 million men between the ages of 20 and 75, with 40 percent spending an average of $50 a month on personal care products, making it a very attractive market for beauty retailers (Canseco, 2007). Between 2008 and 2013, sales of male grooming products increased by 36 percent (CentralAmericaData.com, 2014).

LUXURY RETAIL IN MEXICO

In the upper echelons of Mexican society, "cosmetics trends come from Europe and the United States," says Silvia Tapia, who heads the fragrance department at El Palacio de Hierro's swank Santa Fe store. As the economy improves, even with their limited purchasing power, Mexican consumers look for luxury items (Magana, 2007). As their spending power increases, they are becoming more interested in luxury brands such as Louis Vuitton, Zegna, and Hermès, among others. They look for exclusive brands that make them feel special. Mexico has boutiques as well as shopping malls such as Perisur mall in Mexico City that sell luxury products. In 2008, Saks Fifth Avenue opened its first store in Centro Santa Fe in Mexico City, attracted by the large metropolitan area of 22 million people and about 2 million households with incomes of US$100,000 or more (PwC, 2014). The luxury market may be worthwhile to consider for foreign retailers interested in the Mexican market.

APPAREL RETAIL FORMATS: HISTORY IN THE MAKING

The retail market in Mexico is divided into different segments: grocery retailing (hypermarket, supermarket, discounters, small grocery retailer, food/drink/tobacco specialists, open-air markets or *tianguis*); non-grocery store-based retailing; and non-store retailing (health and beauty specialists, clothing and footwear specialists, electronics, and appliance specialists). Although large modern outlets account for around 40 percent of formal retail sales, around 60 percent of the population is likely to make frequent small purchases at street stalls or independent outlets (The Economist Intelligence Unit, 2009).

TRADITIONAL FORMATS

Traditional formats are made up of street vendors, who sell at stoplights and door-to-door, and open-air markets, where sellers congregate.

▲ FIGURE 9.2 Model in a white summer dress.

▶ Street Vendors

Mexico's street markets are estimated to be worth about 2 billion pesos ($163 million). There are about 200,000 street vendors across the country, and they are an important part of the informal economy. Street vendors in Mexico belong to a union that protects them against agencies that try to shut them down. They often sell fake brand-name products, do not provide any guarantee, do not pay taxes, and offer much lower prices than modern retail formats. Subway stations and street locations are common places where one can find these street vendors. These vendors pay union fees and also pay rent. Street vendors contribute to the nation's economy by means of self-employment and generating wealth, so the government is not inclined to take strong steps to remove them from the market, although it has tried to include them in the formal economy, mainly unsuccessfully (Laya, 2014).

▲ FIGURE 9.3 Flea market in Mexico City. Street vendors are members of unions and form a large percentage of retail income in Mexico.

According to a report of the U.S. Department of Commerce, a substantial percentage of U.S.-made apparel products of all prices and quality levels are illegally imported to Mexico and sold in informal, open-air markets, sometimes *tianguis* or "markets on wheels." They may be located in a city center, near subway stations, in front of formal stores, inside the malls, at beaches, or anywhere with pedestrian traffic. They are family owned and sell cheap products, including vegetables, clothes, food, toys, and furniture, among other things (Zimmerman, 1997).

FLEA MARKETS OR *PULGAS*

Flea markets or *pulgas* are temporary markets that sell knockoffs of American brands to Mexican consumers in search of fashionable products. They also sell handmade local products. Almost 60 percent of all the apparel sold in Mexico is from counterfeit trade that takes place in these markets. These markets are set up on certain days of the week.

MODERN FORMATS

Mexico has formats that are similar to the modern formats in other countries, such as warehouse clubs, hypermarkets, savings clubs, supermarkets, and department stores. The Internet has the lowest penetration in Mexico of all OECD countries (OECD, 2010), so Internet shopping has not been a form of shopping widely adopted. Nonetheless, direct or home shopping does exist (Tupperware, Mary Kay or Natura are good examples) and is counted as part of the informal economy.

▶ Department Stores

These include high fashion stores such as Casa Palacio, Sanborns, Sears, Liverpool, Palacio de Hierro, and Suburbia, all of whom have a presence in the Centro Santa Fe, probably the most posh of all malls in Mexico. As such, these are not found on a stand-alone format, but as part of indoor or outdoor malls. The store format and product range are similar to those in American department stores (such as Macys).

▶ Specialty Stores

These are high-end, niche-market stores that sell apparel products at high prices in exclusive retail stores and boutiques featuring the likes of Armani, Saks Fifth Avenue, Calvin Klein, Hugo Boss, Versace, Zara, Dolce & Gabbana, and Gianfranco Ferre. For the most part, these are part of indoor or outdoor malls.

▲ FIGURE 9.4 Mexican market. These types of flea markets may be located in any area and sell inexpensive and a wide range of products. Some also sell knock-offs of American brands.

▲ FIGURE 9.5 Saks Fifth Avenue, Santa Fe Mall, Mexico City. Saks Incorporated has expanded its international presence by opening its first Saks Fifth Avenue store in Mexico today. The tri-level, 150,000 square foot store is located in the Santa Fe Shopping Center, an upscale development in Mexico City.

▶*Hypermarkets and Warehouse Clubs*

Large American chains, such as Walmart, Costco, and Sam's Club, have all expanded aggressively into Mexico and have penetrated the Mexican shopper's pockets, mainly via store credit cards. In addition, Mexican stores such as Chedraui, Casa Ley, Comercial Mexicana and Soriana (with its wholesale club, Clubes City Club) are no less important in the Mexican market.

STORE OWNERSHIP: MULTIPLE FORMATS

Mexico's retail industry has many different ownership formats. Many retail giants, such as Gigante, own many stores in different formats (warehouse clubs, savings clubs, and so on). There are some joint ventures between American and Mexican retailers, such as Radio Shack, that have performed very well, and some alliances, such as the one between Grupo Cifra and

Walmart, which brought Sam's Club to Mexico. By 1997, Walmart had acquired Grupo Cifra to become Walmart de México y Centroamérica. Franchise stores have been a very popular format in Mexico since the early 1980s. Gap Inc. is present in Mexico as a franchise store, while Willliams-Sonoma Inc. announced a strategic franchise partnership with Liverpool for 2015 (Businesswire, 2014).

FDI REGULATIONS: MEXICO OPENS UP

Foreign investments started flowing into Mexico in the early 1980s as a result of unilateral moves to liberalize the country's economy. Mexican entry into the General Agreement on Tariffs and Trade (GATT) in 1986, followed by the establishment of NAFTA in 1994, accelerated the process of creating an open economy, which increased foreign direct investment (FDI) into the country. This influx stimulated the national government to design new laws to provide legal certainties for foreign investment in Mexico, to guide investments into productive activities, and to promote competitiveness. Political events further enhanced the credibility of the country as a solid investment hub when the first free presidential elections were held in 2000.

Since 1994, Mexico has signed free trade agreements with the European Union, the European Free Trade Association (EFTA) countries, Honduras, El Salvador, Guatemala, Costa Rica, Colombia, Chile, Bolivia, Nicaragua, Israel, and Japan. It has also signed agreements of economic cooperation with Argentina, Brazil, Peru, Paraguay, and Cuba. Additionally, Mexico has signed 27 agreements for the promotion and reciprocal investment protection, which protect foreign capital flows by law inside the country. Several double taxation treaties have been signed so that companies in certain countries are protected against being taxed in both home and host countries; are not tempted to evade taxes; reduce taxes on dividends; and decrease taxes due to income consolidation. Currently, Mexico is negotiating the Trans-Pacific Partnership (TPP) with American and Asian countries.

According to Mexican laws, foreigners may:

- ▶ Hold equity in Mexican corporations or partnerships
- ▶ Acquire fixed assets, such as factories, via FDI
- ▶ Enter new fields of economic activity or manufacture new lines of products, such as biofuels
- ▶ Open and operate establishments (branch offices, agencies, stores)

- Expand or relocate existing establishments via joint ventures for industries considered strategic by the Mexican government (petroleum being the most sensitive of all)

After Mexico's entry into the OECD in 1986, the country had to change its investment laws so that in certain sectors, such as the retail industry, foreign investors could now own 100 percent of the companies of this sector. For example, Walmart entered the Mexican market in 1981 through a joint venture with Grupo Cifra, the largest retail group in Mexico. In a 50 percent equal equity stake, both companies established Sam's Club in Mexico. By 2000, Walmart had acquired a 100 percent stake in Grupo Cifra. Table 9.2 shows the changes in amounts of FDI in the Mexican retail sector from the early 1980s on.

The NAFTA negotiations brought about a substantial lowering of trade tariffs (from an average of 27 to 10 percent). NAFTA members follow domestic regulations in each other's countries. Imports of U.S. apparel products in particular increased significantly with NAFTA, a welcome development for the well-off Mexican consumer. The acceptance of American-made products, an increasing ease in establishing direct operations in Mexico, and cheap labor costs motivated many U.S. apparel companies to move production into Mexico as Mexico was starting to open its economy in the early 1980s (Wade, 1997).

TABLE 9.2 Foreign retailers' entry modes and formats in Mexico

Name	Date and Mode of Entry	Type of Store
Walmart (USA)	• 1981: Buys 49 percent of Operadora Futurama in Northern Mexico • 1991–1993: 50/50 JV with Cifra for different formats, including SAMS Club de México and Wal-Mart Supercenter • 1997: Acquisition of majority ownership stake in Cifra; all stores change name to Wal-Mart de México.	All big formats and specialized stores (clothes; consumer goods) and restaurants

Name	Date and Mode of Entry	Type of Store
	• 2005: Largest private employer in Mexico with 702 stores in 64 cities in Mexico	
Carrefour (France)	• 1994: JV with Gigante to develop hypermarket chain • 1998: Acquisition of Gigante stake in JV • 2005: Announces the end of its activities in Mexico	Hypermarkets
Auchan (France)	• 1995: 50/50 JV with Comercial Mexicana to open hypermarkets • 1997: End of JV with Comercial Mexicana • 2002: Sells its five hypermarkets to Comercial Mexicana	Hypermarkets
Safeway (USA)	• 1981: Enters a 49 percent JV in Casa Ley	Supermarkets
HEB (USA)	• 1997: Opens five stores in northern Mexico • 1991: JV of price club with Comercial Mexicana	Supermarkets
Costco (USA)	• 1995: Costco buys the Price Club share one year after the merger between Costco and Price Club	Discount Club
Pricesmart (USA)	• 2002: JV to open membership club discount stores	Discount Club
Fleming (USA)	• 1992: JV with Gigante to open supermarkets • 1998: sells stake in JV	Supermarkets

Kmart (USA)	• 1993: JV with Puerto de Liverpool • 1997: Kmart and Liverpool sell their four stores to Comercial Mexicana	Supermarkets
Falabella (Chile)	• 2008: Looked into acquiring Comercial Mexicana • 2012: Announces its interest in entering the Mexican market • 2013: Tried unsuccessfully to acquire/fuse with Sanborns • 2016: JV with Soriana to open Sodimac (home improvement) and CMR (financial services), 600 million USD investment in five years	Supermarkets

Source: Durand, C. (2007), Externalities from Foreign Direct Investment in the Mexican Retailing Sector, *31*(3) *Cambridge Journal of Economics*, 393–411; México se convierte en el séptimo Mercado latinoamericano en que participará Falabella, *America Economía*, 18/04/2016. Retrieved from www.americaeconomia.com/negocios-industrias/mexico-se-convierte-en-el-septimo-mercado-latinoamericano-en-que-participara-fal; Bourlier, A. (2016), Falabella Partners with Soriana for Mexico Expansion, *Euromonitor International*, 18 April 2016, http://blog.euromonitor.com/2016/04/falabella-soriana-mexico-partnership.html

INTERNATIONAL BRANDS: TRANSFORMATION TO MIDDLE CLASS

Globalization and the emergence of newly industrialized economies such as Mexico have made the mobility of brands internationally a common phenomenon. Mexico's northern neighbor is a huge market where most international brands can be found. Brands such as Zara, Kenneth Cole, Dockers, and Julio, among many others, are popular in Mexico. Mexican demand for imported brand names is increasingly high, especially among the well-off and consumers who perceive that owning an imported brand puts them in a high class. Because the apparel retail market is fragmented and growing, the likelihood of new competitors entering the market is substantial. International brand owners see the Mexican market as an attractive supplement to their national markets. Benetton Group, the Italian clothing company, has signed an agreement with Sears Mexico to expand the United Colors of Benetton brand in Mexico. Under the terms of the deal, the Italian clothing manufacturer will open 250 points of sale by 2010, of which 200 will be located in Sears stores across the country (Zargani, 2008). A Mexican consulting group, Grupo AXO, is advising Tommy Hilfiger, Guess, DKNY, Coach, and Thomas Pink on the best strategies to enter the Mexican market (Clark, 2008). Slim's Grupo Sanborns will acquire the license of Saks Fifth Avenue in Santa Fe Mall, one of the most luxurious malls in Mexico City (Jones, 2006).

Mexican consumers continue to show an interest in foreign products, ranging from electronics, upscale consumer goods, and novelty items. Furthermore, Mexican consumers view U.S.-made apparel products as being of high quality, in addition to projecting a good fashion image (Frastaci, 1999). As they tend to have a high brand loyalty, Mexicans are ready to pay for product features (mainly ease of use) that come with owning foreign-owned brands. Women in particular are more loyal to a particular designer than a retailer.

Product attributes including brand name, price, design, and service are important criteria of a purchase decision in Mexico. Although Mexicans have a preference for U.S.-made products (which they consider of good quality and innovative), Mexican products are also in great demand because they are cheaper and attractive to price-sensitive consumers.

FACTORS INFLUENCING APPAREL RETAILING

Retailers interested in investing in Mexico's retail market will feel the impact of these factors on their businesses: free trade agreements, cost of doing business, history, culture, social classes, brand names and brand loyalty, and market segmentation.

FREE TRADE AGREEMENTS

Among the most important factors influencing apparel retailing in Mexico are the myriad free trade agreements Mexico has negotiated with the United States, Canada, Japan, and the European Union, among others. NAFTA's provision of unilateral access to Mexican and U. S. textile markets has increased the potential and profitability of the textile sector. Mexican exports increased, which led to the growth of the industry and an increase in investment, both foreign and domestic, in the sector. The textile sector saw a downturn after China's entry to the WTO in 2001, an event that brought a flood of cheap textile products into Mexico. And trade pacts with Caribbean, African, and Andean countries have increased the competitive environment in Mexico. The recession that hit in 2008 also hampered the steady growth of textiles in the country, although these have recuperated more recently.

BUSINESS COST

Mexico traditionally held competitive advantages in its abundance of raw materials, low taxes, and cheap labor. But in recent years, due to increasing Chinese competition, Mexico has lost some of its competitive advantages. Production costs have risen because of modernization of infrastructure and industrial reforms, and the costs of labor, energy, and water have gone up enough to have substantial impact on the apparel retail market. The industry is furthermore challenged by smuggling, theft, and other illegal activities; poor faculty in developing new products; low-quality products; and decreasing quality of service (Ochoa, 2005).

HISTORY AND CULTURAL ASPECTS

Mexico shares a number of cultural and historic milestones with many Hispanic countries of Central and South America: European colonization, wars of independence, struggles for democracy, rigid class structures, and a wide rich/poor divide. But there is a marked distinction between Mexico and other Hispanic countries when it comes to buying behavior. Research shows that Mexicans appear to have a strong affinity with typical American values, such as a strong inclination for consumerism. Mexico forms an emotional as well as physical bridge between the United States and the rest of the continent. The unique relationship with the United States partly explains Mexican consumerism. At the same time, most Mexicans feel a degree of antipathy for their northern neighbor. They feel that Americans do not understand them and reject the idea that they share similar values. For most Mexicans, the loss of almost half their country to the United States in 1848 is still fresh. They deplore the populist view that regards them as aliens in the southwestern U.S. states in which they live and work in large numbers, while rich Americans party in Mexico's resorts, which only a few privileged local people can afford to visit. The population of Mexicans living and working in the United States is growing, and the flow of human and cultural traffic across the border continues (there are 11 million illegal immigrants in the US, most of them are Mexican). Sixty-seven percent of approximately 42 million U.S. Hispanics are Mexicans. Twenty-eight million Mexicans or people of Mexican descent (roughly one third of Mexico's total population) now live in the United States.

SOCIAL CLASSES

Mexicans are a proud people, passionate about their own identity, and yet envious of the wealth they perceive comes with living in the United States. They aspire to American wealth and power, but do not necessarily envy the United States. When Latin American consumers are asked about generosity and wealth in a social context, they talk about sharing knowledge and giving time and advice as well as money.

Mexican consumers almost exaggerate the use of brands to display status. The Mexican drive to display success can take the most unexpected forms. For example, working-class households keep oversized American refrigerators in the living room rather than the kitchen because they represent financial success. Working class and elite are affected alike by the drive to display status. Fake and counterfeit products span the drink, fashion, and accessory categories. If you order a bottle of premium spirit at a reputable bar, it is customary for the seal to be broken at your table to ensure it is not just a genuine bottle filled with imitation liquor.

ROLE OF BRAND NAMES

Upper- and upper-middle-class Mexicans tend to demonstrate status and economic power by ownership of branded products, especially foreign ones. These Mexicans can pay a high price for a premium branded product. Brand names such as BMW, Chivas Regal, Rolex, and Gucci are popular among this group. Hence, the tendency among high-end, educated consumers is toward buying products based on fashion, function, and service.

BRAND LOYALTY AND MARKET SEGMENTATION

The relationship between brand loyalty and market segmentation based on age is obvious in Mexico. Teens and young adults tend to buy the same products or brands as their peers. Additionally, this market segment responds to marketing efforts more than other segments, and they will change brands and products. In contrast, mature customers over 40 years old are more loyal to brands and less likely to change brands. However, the availability of choices has moderated such behavior, leading customers to compare purchase options and shop across sectors. A traditional department-store shopper of the past now shops in different formats, looking for choices, convenience, and availability. Consumers also shop frequently and visit retail stores in the hope of finding new products or brands that offer good design, leading fashion, and a competitive price.

GETTING TO KNOW DOMESTIC COMPETITORS: DIFFERENT PLACES FOR DIFFERENT PEOPLE

The biggest competition for a foreign retailer interested in investing in Mexico comes from Walmart, Soriana, Comercial Mexicana, Chedraui, and S-mart. These five companies are corporate entities that own stores in various formats such as supermarket, hypermarket, warehouse clubs, and so on. As the foreign company of the group, Walmart faces price wars against a purchasing co-operative formed by the four domestic companies, which gives them greater bargaining power.

WALMART

Walmart operates around 2,300 units (Viswanatha, 2015) and was the lead retailer in Mexico in 2015 (Euromonitor International, 2016), thanks to its strong presence in the country through seven retail formats: Bodega Aurerra (discount stores that carry food and clothing), Sam's Club (for bulk purchases, same as in the United States), Walmart Supercenter (grocery and general merchandise), Superama (general stores located in residential areas), Suburbia (aimed toward middle-income families), Vips (restaurants serving international cuisine), and Banco Walmart (banking). Another chain called El Palacio de Hierro, a luxury department store, is expanding quickly and may offer competition for luxury retailers interested in entering the market.

COMERCIAL MEXICANA

Established in 1930, Comercial Mexicana acquired retailers such as Sumesa Kmart and Auchan, among others, to establish stores in many different formats in Mexico. They have 214 retail stores in various formats. It is known in the market as a "very Mexican store" because it carries many typically Mexican products such as candy with hot spices, hot salsa, and so on that have been displaced by imports in other chains. It is also known for its low pricing to cater to various socioeconomic segments of the market. It sells food, perishable products, and clothing.

SORIANA

One of the oldest retail businesses in Mexico, Soriana began developing in the 1930s. In 1998, the company became more customer-service oriented. It is a public limited company that has recently expanded into almost every state of Mexico with 471 stores. Soriana is the second-largest retailer in Mexico. This retail chain focuses on local markets to bring the right regional product to the right location. The store sells food, toys, clothes, health and beauty products, and basic services for home. They also offer the lowest price for 100 goods every day. In early 2016, the Chilean retailer SACI Falabella and Soriana announced a joint venture, facilitating Falabella's entrance into Mexico via the expansion of its CMR financial services (including retail credit cards) and the development of Falabella's home improvement specialist chain, Sodimac. The venture calls for the investment of approximately $600 million over the next five years split between the two companies and to open 20 Sodimac outlets in Mexico (Euromonitor International, 2016).

CHEDRAUI

Chedraui is the fourth-largest Mexican retailer. It is a convenience store that sells groceries, apparel, and other nonperishable items. It was founded in 1927. In 2005, it bought 29 supermarkets from the French chain store Carrefour. Carrefour left the Mexican market as their stores were underperforming due to intense competition from Walmart.

▲ FIGURE 9.6 Mexico becomes Falabella's seventh market in Latin America, where the company also sponsors fashion shows.

S-MART

S-Mart is a Mexican grocery store chain that competes with Walmart and Soriana. S-Mart is an associate of Topco, which is a cooperative owned by other retailers' cooperatives and independent grocery stores and chains. It provides services such as procurement, quality assurance, and packaging for retailers. The store sells frozen and fresh food, health and beauty products, and so on. There are 46 branches of S-Mart in the northern region of the country.

GIGANTE

Gigante opened its first store in Mexico City in 1962. The company went public in 1991. They bought an existing Mexican supermarket, Blanco, and converted it into warehouse formats called Bodega Gigante. They brought the American companies Radio Shack and Office Depot into Mexico through joint ventures. The company then expanded internationally by opening a store in California. It also has a savings club format in a joint venture with American company Price Smart. The company does not compete with Walmart in the lowest price field, but it does have promotional deals on an everyday basis.

EL PALACIO DE HIERRO

El Palacio de Hierro (The Iron Palace) is a chain of prestigious high-end department stores in Mexico. It is a part of the Mexican conglomerate Grupo Bal. It offers both national and international brands at competitive prices. The store sells high-end clothing, beauty products, furniture, electronics, entertainment products (such as video games), and so on. This group has 22 stores in Mexico.

HOW MATURE IS THE RETAIL INDUSTRY? NOT QUITE THERE

Mexico has over 121 million consumers. Consumer expenditures are increasing with greater opportunities for employment and an increase in the per capita gross domestic product (Marinov, 2006). According to the Asociación Nacional de Tiendas de Autoservicio y Departamentales, A.C. (National Association of Retail and Department Stores, ANTAD), there are approximately 46,666 retail stores in Mexico, including grocery, apparel, pharmacy, toy, and pet stores (ANTAD, 2016). After they have covered major cities, large- and medium-sized retailers fan out from metropolitan areas to smaller cities with small stores in the country as a market penetration strategy (Euromonitor, 2008).

The market for apparel products seems to have matured in large cities due to urbanization and the emergence of new regional markets. Real estate newcomers to the market, such as the American Kimco Realty Corporation, have increased choices for consumers and brought better-quality products to market because they have expanded the physical space used for retail stores and allowed for increased infrastructure (Journal of Property Management, 2008). Mexican apparel retail businesses are in search of new market options because the local market is saturated with large-format foreign competitors (Díaz, 2009). A highly fragmented Mexican market has room for many small players, making it a very attractive one for international expansion.

BUYING FOR APPAREL RETAIL STORES: SHOP TILL YOU DROP

In the international textile industry, Mexico ranks fourth—behind the United States, China, and Hong Kong—in terms of market share (Portos, 2008). In the 1990s, production shifted from Asia to the Americas, and North American supply shifted from assembly to full production (which includes manufacturing fabric, cutting, and sewing the product). This dynamic lowered the share that Hong Kong, Taiwan, South Korea, and China held in the U.S. market. In Mexico, the production chain from fiber to textile to clothing is a leading production activity.

The textile and apparel industry is a top manufacturing sector in Mexico, second only to manufacturing since the 1990s (Rodriguez, 2006). Local industry supplies knit and woven woolen fabrics, but woven cotton and man-made fiber need to be imported. Most woven cloth for shirts, blouses, dresses, and summer skirts are imported without duty or restriction (according to NAFTA rules), and come primarily from the United States, which supplies over 75 percent of them. The remainder comes from Korea, Taiwan, and China, even though they have tariffs of over 500 percent.

How does a foreign apparel-product manufacturer establish a relationship with retailers in Mexico? A broad range of activities are required:

- ▸ Understand the Mexican market and consumer.
- ▸ Commit to local partners over the long term.
- ▸ Offer innovative products.
- ▸ Reflect up-to-date fashion with your products.
- ▸ Keep prices affordable.
- ▸ Provide personalized service.

Foreign manufacturers should provide value-added products, which should include better-quality products as well as innovation in fashion. Additionally, Mexican retailers demand high margins, on-time deliveries, and point-of-sale help. The Mexican market is competitive and sophisticated and demands a good amount of service. Other strategies involve offering flexible payment arrangements and wholesale prices or discounts because tariffs on imported goods are high, which makes them very expensive for local customers. For instance, Chinese textiles enter Mexico with a 500 percent tariff.

Foreign manufacturers who are interested in the Mexican market must be aware that women make up more than half of the population and represent the most important customer segment of the Mexican market. Women do (or guide) most of the shopping, for themselves as well as for their families.

As for distribution strategy, most international companies hire local distributors, but some open direct sales offices and subsidiaries in Mexico. Around 400 franchisers operate in Mexico, 40 percent of which are of foreign origin; growth in sector was nine percent in 2013 and around 12 percent in 2014 (U.S. Commercial Service, 2014). It can take time to identify a suitable geographic location, understand the local distribution network, establish a network, and build the necessary infrastructure. Furthermore, it is critical to conduct market research in order to understand the nature and degree of competition among the existing retailers, including the unofficial or informal retail market in Mexico, which trades products at throw-away prices.

RETAIL CAREERS: IN LINE WITH ECONOMIC GROWTH

Because the retail market in general and apparel retailing, in particular, are growing sectors in Mexico, opportunities for employment in the sector are growing. The apparel industry is attractive to entrepreneurs because ownership does not demand much seed capital, technology, or sophisticated skill. Small investors either in groups or individually can enter the market and position themselves with new brands.

In general, salary structure varies among states or regions in Mexico. Salaries are relatively high in Mexico City, DF (Federal District), Nuevo Leon, Guadalajara, and Quintana Roo. Foreign companies in Mexico offer better compensation programs than their local counterparts as well as company's size, which can be a decisive factor in defining a salary structure for its employees. For example, a big company in Mexico City with 100 to 500 employees may pay its CEO a base salary of $10,000 per month, whereas in Monterrey, the capital city of Nuevo Leon, the base salary may be $20,000 per month. But in the city of Hermosillo (a relatively less-developed region of the country), the base salary may be only $5,000 per month. Other factors that influence pay include the university from which the employee graduated, whether they have a foreign degree, and their level of education. Connections and references can also play an important role in salary negotiations in Mexico.

Students coming from abroad to study in Mexican universities can find internship opportunities in local companies in different sectors, including retail, as most universities run internship programs in collaboration with neighboring businesses. For example, the Monterrey campus of Tecnológico de Monterrey (ITESM) in Nuevo Leon runs an internship program in which students who spend a semester or two in a company receive academic credit. Such programs are available for both undergraduates and graduate-level students.

International Business Strategies is a website that provides interesting and updated reports on the retail industry in different countries, including Mexico (http://www.international businessstrategies.com/market-research-reports). Fibre2fashion.com is another website that provides countrywide information on different industrial sectors, including job opportunities (http://jobs.fibre2fashion.com/). The website http://www.jobofmine.com/job/search/country/Mexico/ also provides job information.

THE FUTURE OF APPAREL RETAIL: MORE ROOM TO GROW

The contribution of the textile and apparel industry to the national economy is significant. Mexico is a world-class producer and exporter of textile and apparel products. In this sector, Mexico has several competitive advantages, such as the infrastructure for textiles, that have been around in the country since the early twentieth century and that have the ability to supply the American as well as the domestic market, and have a wealth of export experience (Portos, 2008). Despite Mexico's competitive edge in this sector, it remains vulnerable to certain economic situations. According to a 2008 survey (Rodriguez and Ulises 2008), in economic and financial crises, consumers tend to spend less money on apparel products and even less on more expensive imported brands. Nonetheless, the young Mexican population ensures a steadily growing customer base for retailers (Latin America Monitor, 2005) and presages a potentially large market as the Mexican economy continues to grow (Frastaci, 1999).

▲ FIGURE 9.7 A model walks the runway during the Liverpool Fashion Fest Autumn/Winter 2016 at Televisa San Angel in Mexico City.

Since the early 1990s, Mexico has made itself an attractive destination for foreign direct investment, became an open market, and carried out extensive privatization in different industries. Some useful things a foreign investor should know about Mexico include the following.

- Although informal-retail formats take away some market share, modern-format stores can compete with them by providing variety, convenience, good pricing, quality, and personal service.
- Mexicans visit malls for entertainment as well as for shopping. Successful malls include entertainment venues, such as movie theaters or ice-skating rinks.
- Convenience matters to Mexican consumers. Ample parking space is a big draw to the mall.
- About 45 percent of Mexicans have a monthly income of less than $500, making this a worthwhile segment on which to focus.

SUMMARY

Until the mid-1980s, the retail market in Mexico had been fragmented and closed off, as Mexico was highly protectionist. After the 1982 financial crisis, the government decided to start opening the country to the world and the retail market underwent many fast changes.

Already an important player in Latin America due to the "Mexican Miracle" in the 1970s, Mexico joined the General Agreement on Tariffs and Trade (the precursor to the World Trade Organization), signed the North American Free Trade Agreement with Canada and the US in 1994, and also joined the Organization for Economic Cooperation and Development that same year. With these acts, Mexico liberalized foreign trade by reducing tariffs on most imported goods accompanied by industry deregulations, such as opening many sectors, including the retail sector, to foreign ownership. The first one to enter the market was Walmart, in a joint venture with Cifra in 1991. It has become the biggest and most profitable Walmart in the world with over 250 Walmart supercenters and an additional 2,600 retail stores under the brands Superama, Suburbia, Zona Suburbia, Sam's Club, Bodega Aurrerá, Mi Bodega Aurrera, Bodega Aurrera Express, and Farmacia de Walmart. Of special interest is the luxury retail in Mexico with the presence of luxury stores, such as El Palacio de Hierro or Liverpool, where famous international luxury brands (Chanel, Louis Vuitton, Saks Fifth Avenue) are being sold.

Being a middle-income economy, Mexico has one of the highest percentages of young and eager consumers in the world with 59 million people aged 20 to 44. Additionally, urbanization has allowed the retail sector to become more consolidated and be one of the most vibrant Latin American markets (second only to Brazil) with Monterrey, Mexico City, and Guadalajara being the main purchasing urban centers. The recent growth of five percent a year and e-commerce accounting for over 12 percent of all e-commerce in Latin America. Additionally, employing 10 percent of the labor force and accounting for seven percent of GDP, the retail sector is poised to drive Mexico's continued economic growth. Today, the country's retail sales amount to over $220 billion and it is expected to reach over $265 billion by 2017, a rise of closer to 18 percent in the last five years.

As women's beauty industries are the most lucrative sector and it is Mexican women who do most of the shopping anyway, many new retailers have targeted this market, spilling-over to menswear and childrenswear. Some of the biggest and newest players are GAP, H&M, American Eagle Outfitters and Forever 21. Despite this, Mexico continues to be a hybrid country, where new, world-class retail development shares the street with an estimated 2.3 million mom-and-pop stores and traditional markets. This fact could prove to be an impediment for further concentration of retail trade, as would stolen, smuggled or counterfeit garments acquired in these street markets.

The retail sector in Mexico is one of the most vibrant and will continue to be so, as the Mexican middle-class and eager consumers continue demanding international brands. Retailers will be more than happy to oblige.

CRITICAL THINKING QUESTIONS

1. Globalization has taken a hold of our economies. How do you see its role in the Mexican retail sector?
2. How can Mexico take further advantage of its membership in the WTO and NAFTA to continue growing its retail sector?
3. How has the internationalization of the Mexican retail sector affected the national producers?
4. Should retailers expand their presence to other Latin American markets? Why or why not?
5. How can Mexico fight stolen, smuggled or counterfeit garments acquired in street markets?
6. What is your opinion on the sustainability efforts of Walmart in Mexico?

Case Study

GRUPO SANBORNS: ON THE ACQUISITION TRAIL

Grupo Sanborns is the retail sector of the holding company Grupo Carso, one of Mexico's largest conglomerates, with stakes in many different industries, ranging from retail to technology. Its initial acquisitions included Mexican companies such as Sanborns, Fábricas de Papel Loreto y Peña Pobre, Empresas Frisco, Industrias Nacobre, and Porcelanite. Its owner, Carlos Slim Helú, is considered the wealthiest man on earth. In 1997, Grupo Carso acquired 70 percent of the American retailer Sears Roebuck Inc., with 66 stores in Mexico. This first entry into the retail sector proved profitable and augured well. By 2004, the group owned almost 85 percent of the company. In 2010, Sears represented 48.5 percent of the consolidated sales of the Grupo Sanborns. Although most of Sears' providers are Mexican, quality goods from Asia and other countries can also be found in the store (Grupo Carso, 2010). In 2008 the Italian retailer Benetton went into partnership with Sears. Carlos Slim Domit, son of Carlos Slim Helú and chairman of Sears Roebuck Inc. in Mexico, said that: "Benetton is a highly prestigious international brand, and this partnership will allow us to continue offering fashion and high-quality products to our clients" (Zargani, 2008).

In 1994, Grupo Carso acquired Dorian's, a Mexican retail company founded in 1959 in Tijuana and serving the north of Mexico. Dorian's has around 71 selling points in most northern states and targets different Mexican markets. It has around 394 thousand square feet in sales areas. With this inroad the conglomerate increased its competitive advantage in the Mexican market and consolidated its position as one of the most important and successful Mexican conglomerates. In 2010, Dorian's constituted three percent of the total sales of Grupo Sanborns (Grupo Carso, 2010).

By 2003, after eight years of operating in the Mexican market with great success, Grupo Carso acquired JC Penney's six stores in Mexico, thus expanding the retail company's coverage into a wide range of national, private, and exclusive brands with style, quality, and competitive pricing. By merging JC Penney with Dorian's, it has further consolidated its position in the Mexican retail market.

Discussion Questions

1. Would you say that Grupo Carso implemented the right acquisition and consolidation strategy?

2. Carlos Slim Domit, son of Carlos Slim Helú and chairman of Sears Roebuck Inc. in Mexico, said that: "Benetton is a highly prestigious international brand, and this partnership will allow us to continue offering fashion and high-quality products to our clients." In the United States, Benetton and Sears don't necessarily cater to the same customers. Why do you think this partnership works in Mexico?
3. The Mexican retail market seems to be saturated by companies both foreign and domestic. And yet, more and more international retailers keep entering the Mexican market. How do you think Grupo Sanborns can continue to compete in an increasingly globalized industry?

REFERENCES

Anderson, J. (2010). Effects of increased trade and investment on human development in the US and Mexican border communities. *The Journal of Developing Areas, 43* (2), 341–362.

ANTAD (2015). Retrieved on May 24, 2016 from www.antad.net/.

Apparel Retail Industry Profile: Mexico (2008). *Datamonitor*, pp. 1–24.

Bailey, W. & Gutierrez de Pineres, S. A. (1997). Country of Origin Attitudes in Mexico: The *Malinchismo* Effect. *Journal of International Consumer Marketing, 9* (3), 25–41.

Baker, S. (2007). Global market review of discount apparel retailing: Forecasts to 2012: 2007 edition: The Global Market for Discount Apparel. *Just Style: Global Market Review of Discount Apparel Retailing*, pp. 5–36.

Bissell, B. (2003). Practical advice for investing in tourism and lodging projects in Mexico. *Journal of Retail & Leisure Property, 3*(1) 93–103.

Bolio, E., Remes, J., Lajous, T., Manyika, J., Ramirez, E. & Rosse, M. (2014). Bridging the Gap: Modern and Traditional Retail in Mexico. McKinsey on Marketing & Sales. McKinsey&Company. Retrieved on May 24, 2016 from www.mckinseyonmarketingandsales.com/bridging-the-gap-modern-and-traditional-retail-in-mexico.

Businesswire (2014). Williams-Sonoma, Inc. Announces Strategic Franchise Partnership and Expansion to Mexico. Retrieved on May 24, 2016 from www.businesswire.com/news/home/20141001005323/en/Williams-Sonoma-Announces-Strategic-Franchise-Partnership-Expansion-Mexico.

Canseco, O. C. (2007). Latin Male Cosmetics Sales Grow. Retrieved March 1, 2010 from www.latinbusinesschronicle.com/app/article.aspx?id=1186.

CentralAmericaData.com (2014). Trends in beauty market in Mexico. Retrieved on May 25, 2016 from www.centralamericadata.com/en/article/home/Trends_in_Beauty_Market_in_Mexico.

Clark, E. (2008), Mexico-based Firm Looks to Steer Retailers South for Growth, *Women's Wear Daily, 195* (41), p. 28.

Daniels, W. (1997). Guess Again: Not All Apparel Jobs Flee US. *The Christian Science Monitor, 12*, 8.

Di Gregorio, D., Thomas, D. & de Castilla, F. (2008). Competition between Emerging Markets and Multinational Firms: Wal-Mart and Mexican Retailers. *International Journal of Management, 25*(3), 532–545.

Díaz, U. (2009). Visten con éxito su negocio. *Negocios y emprendimiento*. Retrieved on February 2, 2010 from www.negociosyemprendimiento.org/2009/03/los-casos-de-diez-emprendedores-que.html.

Durand, C. (2007). Externalities from Foreign Direct Investment in the Mexican Retailing Sector. *Cambridge Journal of Economics, 31*, 393–411.

Euromonitor International (2016). Retailing in Mexico. Retrieved on May 24, 2016, from www.euromonitor.com/retailing-in-mexico/report.

Frastaci, M. (1999). Approaching Mexican retailers. *Apparel Industry, 60*(5), 26–31.

Freeman, I. C. (2010). Mexico: Apparel investment needed to counter contraband. *Just Style News*. Retrieved October 18, 2010 from www.just-style.com/news/apparel-investment-needed-to-counter-contraband_id108921.aspx.

Galindo, A. (n.d.). Psicología del consumidor mexicano. IDM Group. Retrieved on March 2, 2010 from www.greenbook.org/company/Investigacion-de-Mercado-Grupo-IDM.

Gereffi, G. (1997). Global Shifts, Regional Response: Can North America meet the Full Package Challenge? *Bobbin, Vol. 31*(3), 16–31.

Gereffi, G. (2009). Development Models and Industrial Upgrading in China and Mexico. *European Sociological Review, 25*(1), 37–51.

Gregorio, D. D., Thomas, D. E. & Castilla, F. G. (2008). Competitive dynamics between emerging market firms and dominant multinational rivals: Wal-Mart and the Mexican retail industry. *International Journal of Management, 25*(3), 532–547.

Grupo Carso (2010). Retrieved March 9, 2010 from wwwgcarso.com.mx.

Growing Opportunity (2007). *Chain Store Age, 83*(3), 1–2.

Hofstede, G. (2015). The Hofstede Center. Retrieved May 22, 2015 from https://geert-hofstede.com/mexico.html.

INEGI (2016). Edad mediana, población, comparación internacional. Retrieved May 18, 2016 from www.inegi.gov.

Institute of Real Estate Management (2008). Shopping Centers Head Down to Mexico (2008) *Journal of Property Management, 73*(4), 6.

Jones, F. (2006). Upscale Retail. *Latin Trade*, p. 13.

Joynes-Burgess, K. (2008). Mexico: Courage in challenging times. Retrieved March 1, 2010 from www.katejb.com/work/CourageinChallengingTimes.pdf.

La industria textil y del vestido en México (2014). *Instituto Nacional de Estadística y Geografía*. Retrieved on May 10, 2016 from www3.inegi.org.mx/sistemas/biblioteca/ficha.aspx?upc=702825068448.

Laya, P (2014). In Mexico, street vendors trump retailers in tough times. *Bloomberg*. Retrieved on May 20, 2016 from www.bloomberg.com/news/articles/2014-08-19/in-mexico-street-vendors-trump-retailers-in-tough-times.

Major Mexican Soft Goods Retailers (2007) Retrieved February 10, 2010 from www.trendexmexico.com/retinfo/msgret.html.

Magana, M. (2007). The road to Eldorado. *Landor.* Retrieved March 4, 2010 from www.landor.com/index.cfm?do=thinking.article&storyid=558&.

Marinov, M. (2006). *Marketing in the Emerging Markets of Latin America.* UK: Palgrave Macmillan.

Mexico Company: JCPenney Pulls Out (2003) *EIU ViewsWire.*

Mexico: Just the Facts (2006). *Journal of Commerce,* p. 1.

Mexico Monitor (2010). Retrieved March 5, 2010 from www.latinamericamonitor. com

Mexico Retail Report (2008). Bharat Book Bureau. Retrieved February 10, 2010 from www.bharatbook.com/Market-Research-Reports/Mexico-Retail-Report.html

Min-Young, L., Youn-Kyung, K., Lou, P., Dee, K. & Forney, J. (2008). Factors affecting Mexican college students' purchase intention toward a US apparel brand. *Journal of Fashion Marketing and Management, 12*(3), 294–307.

Ochoa, S. M. (2005). Corrupción y contrabando en el sector textil en México. *Cámara de Diputados Reporte Temático N. 5.*

Olaf, C. (2002). Salary Survey: Part II. *Business México, 12*(3), 19–20.

Olvera, S. & Violeta, M. (2009). "Pega el dólar caro a idas de 'shopping'." Retrieved on March 5, 2010 from http://norte-monterrey.vlex.com.mx/vid/pega-dolar-caro-idas-shopping–77635433.

Portos, I. (2008). La industria textil en México y Brasil: Dos vías nacionales de desarrollo. *Universidad Nacional Autónoma de México.*

PriceWaterhouseCoopers (PwC), S.C. (2014). Retail Sector. Retrieved May 22, 2016, from https://www.pwc.com/mx/es/international-business-center/archivo/2014–04-retail.pdf

Ramirez, Z. (2005). Adquiere Slim tiendas de JCPenney en México. Retrieved on March 9, 2010 from http://archivo.eluniversal.com.mx/finanzas/36634.html.

Rausch, L. (2002). Cross-cultural Analysis of Brand Consciousness. Retrieved on April 5, 2010 from www.uwlax.edu/urc/JUR-online/PDF/2002/L_Rausch.pdf.

Reardon, T. and Berdegué, J.A. (2002). The Rapid Rise of Supermarkets in Latin America: Challenges and Opportunities for Development. *Development Policy Review,* 20(*4*) 371–388.

Smith, C. (2016), The Latin-American e-commerce report: The Region's Top Markets, Biggest Growth Opportunities, and Foreign Retailers Making Inroads. *Business Insider International.* Retrieved on May 22, 2016 from www.businessinsider.de/the-latin-america-e-commerce-report-the-regions-top-markets-biggest-growth-opportunities-and-foreign-retailers-making-inroads–2016–3?r=US&IR=T.

Stillman, A. (2015). Mexico's Beauty Market Lures World's Biggest Brands. *Financial Times* Retrieved on May 23, 2016 from www.ft.com/cms/s/0/d20b4faa–57d5–11e5-a28b–50226830d644.html#axzz49ZxXh5Zo.

Tilly, C. & José L. A. G. (2006). Lousy Jobs, Invisible Unions: The Mexican Retail Sector in the Age of Globalization. *International Labor and Working-Class History, 70,* 61–85.

U.S. Commercial Service (2014). Doing Business in Mexico; 2014 Country Commercial Guide for U.S. Companies.

Vaezi, S. (2005). Marketing to Mexican Consumers. *Journal of Brand Strategy*, No. 190, 43–45.

Villareal, M. A and Fergusson, I. F. (2015). The North American Free Trade Agreement. *Congressional Research Service.*

Viswanatha, A. and Barrett, D. (2015). Wal-Mart Bribery Probe Finds Few Signs of Major Misconduct in Mexico. *The Wall Street Journal.* Retrieved May 18, 2016 from www.wsj.com/articles/wal-mart-bribery-probe-finds-little-misconduct-in-mexico–1445215737.

Zargani, L. (2008). Benetton Inks Deal with Sears Mexico. *Women's Wear Daily, 195*(113), 1–7.

Zimmerman, S. (1997). Shopping in Mexico: The *Tianguis.* Retrieved March 3, 2010 from www.mexconnect.com/articles/152-shopping-in-mexico-the-tianguis.

QATAR

Shubhapriya Bennur
Md. Rashaduzzaman
Samirah Alotaibi
Yiyue Fan

THE RETAIL LANDSCAPE: AN EMERGING MARKET

The State of Qatar is situated on a peninsula projecting into the Arabian Gulf, bordering Saudi Arabia to the south. Prior to the discovery of oil, the Qatari economy was largely based on pearl fishing. Within its 11,586 km², Qatar holds the world's third-largest gas reserves and the largest single non-associated gas field. Today, through the careful exploitation of these massive hydrocarbon resources, Qatar ranks as one of the richest nations in the world, achieving GDP (purchasing power parity) of US $334.5 billion in 2016. The Qatari government enacts equitable economic and social policies that are pro-business, encourages foreign investment and the growth of the private sector (About Qatar, 2016). Qatar's economic diversification strategy continues to create foreign investment opportunities across its burgeoning retail market, despite sustained low oil prices. According to Alpen Capital, the Qatari retail market is expected to grow at a compound annual growth rate (CAGR) of 9.8 percent reaching $284.5 billion in 2018, the fastest in the GCC region. The government has ambitious plans to develop its retail landscape to meet the rising demand of the growing population's high level of personal consumption. Key projects already underway include the Mall of Qatar, Doha Festival City and Place Vendome (Qatar's burgeoning retail market, 2016).

The continued low oil price means the Qatari Government is seeing its state revenues decline. As such, the country is actively seeking foreign and private sector investment. The development of the retail sector will help to shore up its economy and presents excellent opportunities for foreign investors. In 2015, the country was ranked as the fourth most attractive retail market according to the Global Retail Development Index (GRDI), placing it first in the Middle East.

TABLE 10.1 Fast Facts about Qatar

Capital	Doha
Population	2.258 million
Type of government	Absolute Monarchy
GDP: purchasing power parity: in U.S. $	$334.5 billion (2016)
Age structure	0–14 yrs: 12.57 percent
	15–24 yrs: 12.62 percent
	25–54 yrs:70.45 percent
	55–64 yrs: 3.41 percent
	65 yrs and over: 0.94 percent
Median age	Total median age :33 years
	Male: 24.1 years
	Female: 28.1 years
Religion	Muslim: 77.5 percent
	Christians: 8.5 percent
	Hindu and other: 14 percent
Ethnicity	Arab: 40 percent
	Indian: 18 percent
	Pakistani: 18 percent
	Iranian:10 percent
	Other 14 percent

Source: CIA factbook.gov

QATAR'S BURGEONING RETAIL MARKET

Qatar is a small country with very large natural resource reserves, mostly natural gas, and so solid GDP growth is to be expected. The economy is seeing the benefits of the government's long-term economic plan to diversify, with over 60 percent of its GDP now derived from non-hydrocarbon industries (Wealth and Finance, 2016). Qatar is emerging as the most attractive market for retailers in the Middle East, according to a new index produced by AT Kearney.

The GRDI placed a total of six Middle East countries in the top 30 most attractive markets for development opportunities in retail. Following a year that saw oil prices drop, AT Kearney said the region has remained an attractive destination for retailers: "Despite the record drop in oil prices, retail sales growth is expected to continue. Indeed, the retail space pipeline remains strong, with several major projects underway in Qatar, the UAE, and Oman. Kuwait has felt the impact disproportionately, due to its high reliance on oil and relative lack of diversification."

Alpen Capital said in its "GCC retail industry report" "While retails sales growth across all the GCC countries is expected to remain positive between 2013 and 2018, the outlook for Qatar is the most optimistic during the period."

The study added: "The Middle East continues to welcome international brands such as Macy's (in the UAE) and Harvey Nichols (in Qatar), and expansion from existing retailers."

The ultra-luxury brands, such as Chanel, Prada and Gucci, also are interested in opening second stores in Doha (Arabian Business, 2015). The region has one of the most attractive corporate tax regimes, which works as an "attraction" to retailers. Over the years, the region has emerged as an international tourist hub, enjoying popularity among leisure travelers, international shoppers and pilgrims. The Gulf is also gearing up to host events such as the World Expo 2020 and FIFA 2022, leading to a growing influx of tourists and creating immense opportunities for existing and new retailers in the region (Gulf Times, 2015).

Until recently, international brands were limited by insufficient retail supply. This is changing as Doha exprcts to welcome 1 million square meters of retail space in the next two to three years. Ambitious retail development projects in 2015 and 2016 include Doha Festival City, the Mall of Qatar, and the Gulf Mall, which will significantly enhance the retail landscape. Like its neighbor Saudi Arabia, Qatar also opened one of the world's few women's-only malls, the Souli Mall. For now, brand penetration in Qatar remains behind regional leaders such as the UAE. In the grocery sector, supermarkets and hypermarkets are expected to expand; for example, Carrefour plans to be an anchor tenant in the Mall of Qatar. Qataris' affinity for luxury goods has also triggered entry plans by high-end retailers such as Harvey Nichols, which will open its first store in 2017 in Doha Festival City. Other market entrants include Karl Lagerfeld and Juicy Couture (AT Kearney, 2015). The massive infrastructure investments and the sharp increase in the country's population were behind the high expectation that the non-oil sector will register over 10 percent growth by the end of 2014 and the size of Qatar's retail market will touch 32 BN QR (8.9 billion USD) mark. As a result of growing demand and higher purchasing power, the sector is expected to grow by more than 7 percent annually during 2014 and 2017 (Qatar Country Report, 2015).

MARKET PROFILE AND RETAIL SECTOR

▸Recent Developments

Qatar's real GDP growth expanded by 4 percent year-on-year (YOY) in Q4 2015 on the strength of its non-oil sector. The country's growth is projected to expand by 3.4 percent in 2016 due to massive infrastructure investment and further economic diversification (Qatar Market Profile, 2016).

In preparation for the 2022 FIFA World Cup, along with the Qatari bid to host the 2024 Olympics, large-scale infrastructure projects are underway, including the construction of stadiums, rail systems and highways. The government plans to spend up to US$ 205 billion on infrastructure during 2013–2018.

China's FDI stock in the country has surged in recent years, leaping from US$77 million in 2011 to US$354 million in 2014.

CURRENT ECONOMIC SITUATION

▸Policy of Trade

Qatar is a member of the World Trade Organization (WTO) and maintains a liberal trade regime. Non-Qataris are barred from engaging in distribution activities in Qatar. Importers, who must be Qatari nationals, must register in the Importers Register and be approved by the Qatar Chamber of Commerce and Industry (QCCI). Qatar maintains a strong tie with other members of the Gulf Cooperation Council (GCC), which consists of Saudi Arabia, Kuwait, Oman, the UAE, Bahrain and Qatar. In 1999, the GCC agreed to form a customs union, which took effect from 2003 to zero-rate goods traded within

TABLE 10.2 Major Economic Indicators

	2014	2015	2016*
Population (million)	2.2	2.4*	2.6
GDP (US$ billion)	210.1	185.4*	170.9
GDP Per Capita (US$)	93,990	76,576*	66,265
Real GDP Growth (percent)	+4.0	+3.3*	+3.4
Inflation (percent)	+3.3	+1.7	+2.4
Exports of Goods (US$ million)	126,702	77,294	64,490
Export (percent change)	−5.0	−39.0	−16.6
Imports of Goods (US$ million)	31,145	28,496	33,763
Import (percent change)	−1.0	−8.5	+18.5
Exchange Rate (Riyal: USD)	3.64	3.64	3.64

Source: IMF, EIU, Qatar Ministry of Development Planning and Statistics

* IMF, EIU estimates

the GCC (Qatar market profile, 2016). The standard rate of external tariff is 5 percent (*ad valorem*) in accordance with the GCC customs union. Currently, Qatar's government is encouraging foreign investment by streamlining licensing and financial sector regulations, with the corporate tax rate set at 10 percent. More recently, Qatar has started work on the country's new special economic zones, which will be divided into three projects: the Ras Bufontos, the Umm Al Houl and the Al Karaana, which will all focus on different sectors. These three zones are expected to be completed in phases between 2017 and 2022 and will offer favorable tax and duty incentives.

▶ *Free trade agreements*

Qatar is a member of the Greater Arab Free Trade Area Agreement (GAFTA) that came into force in 1998. Under the GAFTA, Qatar enjoys free trade with Algeria, Bahrain, Egypt, Iraq, Kuwait, Lebanon, Libya, Morocco, Oman, Palestine, Saudi Arabia, Sudan, Syria, Tunisia, the UAE and Yemen (Qatar market profile, 2016). As part of the GCC, Qatar also holds free trade agreements (FTAs) with Singapore, New Zealand and the European Free Trade Association (EFTA).

Qatar is about to enter a period of strong growth in retail supply with a number of new retail malls nearing completion. Despite the large number of retail malls under construction, no new malls have opened since the Gulf Mall in early 2015. Based on DTZ's assessment, the overall supply of purpose-built, retail mall accommodation in Qatar is 643,000 sq m, contained in 14 purpose-built malls. The two largest shopping centers, Villaggio Mall and City Centre Mall, account for 39 percent of the current supply. DTZ estimates that in excess of 1.3 million square meters of retail space is currently in various stages of construction and is scheduled to open by 2019. This represents a 220 percent increase on current supply; if completed as planned, this will have a major impact on the dynamics of the retail market in Qatar (Qatar market report, 2016).

The showroom retail market is estimated to comprise more than 800,000 sq m of leasable space in Salwa Road and Barwa Commercial Avenue. Elsewhere, on The Pearl Qatar, Medina Central opened in 2015, and following a period of tenant fit-outs, the majority of retail units have now opened for business. Porto Arabia has also seen an increase in activity with a number of new arrivals on the retail promenade in recent months.

Qatar is ranked fourth among the top five in the world and the top in the GCC countries in the Global Retail Development Index (GRDI), a report

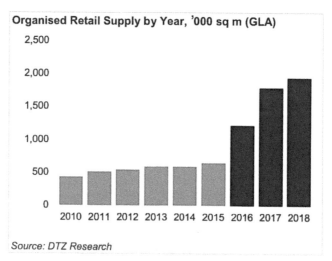

Source: DTZ Research

▲ FIGURE 10.1 Organized retail supply by year

released by AT Kearney. Overall, Qatar saw total retail sales as high as $12.4bn with a 9.7 percent annual growth over the past four years. Bolstering Qatar's global position is its projected growth in retail space, which will reach 1 million square meters in the next three years (Gulf Times, 2016). The proliferation of malls in the country, paired with the Doha Shopping Festival, will also enhance the retail landscape. It is likely a variety of retail outlets will make their way to the country, ranging from hypermarkets to luxury goods.

The GRDI includes an analysis of the 15 leading luxury brands and their presence in the GRDI's top 30 countries. The analysis shows that emerging markets fall into three tiers of luxury development, with different implications for brands looking to enter or expand in these markets. Qatar currently hosts 13 of the top 15 brands, indicating a strong local demand for luxury brands and an opportunity for luxury retailers to further penetrate the market.

APPAREL RETAIL FORMATS

As Qatar prepares to host the 2022 FIFA World Cup, investors are already moving to build more new shopping malls to support it (Foreman, 2014; Upadhyay, 2016). The major department stores and specialty stores are the major distribution channels for clothing in Qatar. However, online retailing is now the fastest-growing sales channel.

MALLS

A mall is defined as "an enclosure having different formats of in-store retailers all under one roof" (Dani, 2014). As one of the most attractive destinations for luxury shopping in the Middle East, Qatar has many shopping malls includes: the Gate Mall, the Villagio Mall, the Mall of Qatar, and Doha Festival City.

Geographically, people who belong to the Arab states of the Persian Gulf, generally, enjoy a high standard of living. As the result, this area attracts many high-profile luxury brands (Marciniak & Mohsen, 2015). The retailers are trying to provide a unique experience for their customers. For instance, the Mall of Qatar offers shoppers an exciting collection of world-class luxury brands including Dior, Chanel, FENDI, etc. and high street fashion such as H&M. Moreover, it offers over 100 foods and beverage outlets and fine dining options, kid's play room, a 19-screen movie theater, and even a five star luxury hotel (www.mallofqatar.com.qa/en/shop.aspx).

Some of the shopping malls in Qatar are currently in the early stages of development (Foreman, 2014). Doha Festival City, which is designed to be

▲ FIGURE 10.2 Villaggio Mall is a shopping mall located in the Aspire Zone in the west end of Doha, the capital city of Qatar.

Qatar's largest retail and entertainment destination, will offer more than 500 brands; some of these will be entering the Qatar market for the first time (Doha festival city, 2015).

DEPARTMENT STORES

According to Michael Levy and Barton A. Weitz (2012) "department stores are retailers that carry a broad variety and deep assortment, offer customer services, and organize their stores into distinct departments for displaying merchandise (p. 41)." Qatar contains a variety of department store chains including Salam, Harvey Nichols, LuLu Centre, Galeries Lafayette, and Fifty One East (Marciniak & Mohsen, 2015).

Levy and Weitz (2012) determined that department chains in Qatar can be categorized into three tiers. The first tier contains high-fashion chains with exclusive designer merchandise. For instance, Salam is a unique boutique department store concept whose primary goal is to bring world-class luxury brands to the Middle East. Nowadays, Salam offers more than 350 of the world's top brands in a variety of areas including fashion and accessories, beauty, jewelry, watches, and home decor collections in Doha, Dubai, Abu Dhabi, Al Ain, and Muscat (Middle East's Home-Grown Fashion Destination 'Salam Stores' Hosts Paris Hilton in Dubai, 2009).

The second tier of department stores provides less customer service and offers more moderately priced merchandise. For instance, Debenhams, which is the leading UK department store, provides exclusive and affordable fashion collections from leading designers.

Quality Centre is an example of the third tier of department store in Qatar, targeting "more price-conscious consumers" (Levy & Weitz, 2012). According to its official website, it is located in the Airport road in Doha. Quality Centre offers a variety of product chains such as electronic, home appliances, footwear, home furnishing, luggage, and clothing.

SPECIALTY STORES

"Specialty stores concentrate on a limited number of complementary merchandise categories and provide a high level of service" (Marciniak & Mohsen, 2015). Shopping in Qatar is easy, fun, and great value. There are many global specialty retailers in Qatar's clothing market, for instance American Eagle Outfitters, Armani Exchange, Gap, Lacoste, Zara, etc.

Since Qatar is an Islamic country, people dress in a very traditional manner, so some of the global specialty retailers need to change their strategies to be able to get better fit with their Middle East expansion plans. The Middle East market will not accept a brand with an overtly sexual image. Abercrombie & Fitch changed its advertisements to "a more sophisticated, fully clothed look" (Bain, 2016). It plans to open stores in Qatar in 2017.

BRANDED STORES

Branded stores are "exclusive showrooms either owned or franchised by a manufacturer" with certified product quality (Dani, 2014). Since the Gulf Region is a geographical area, people still like to dress in a very traditional manner, for instance, women in the Arab Gulf states wear a loose overgarment over their street clothing known as the abaya. Some key brands and labels are targeting Muslim consumers. Debaj is one of Qatar's leading luxury abaya brands, which combines traditional abaya silhouettes with glamorous, modern cuts and patterns (Dani, 2014). Fufi Stylist Abayas brings together design elements from Libya, Italy and Qatar. There are other brands which focus on modest dressing such as Jo La Mode, Almotahajiba, and Fanilla Couture (Dani, 2014).

SUPERMARKETS

Supermarkets are the "extremely large self-service retail outlets" which provides a one-stop shop catering to varied customers needs (Dani, 2014). A growing number of supermarkets is driving Qatar's retail expansion. The average growth is expected to be around 12.1 percent annually until 2018 (Walker, 2015). Moreover, during the preparation for the 2022 FIFA World Cup, which will be hosted in Qatar, the ongoing population boom, international demographic, and its infrastructure development are some of the factors which will increase supermarket sales in the coming years (Foreman, 2014; Walker, 2015).

Examples of supermarket chains in Qatar are MONOPRIX, AL MEERA, Grand Mart and Safari Shopping Complex. The ZAWYA news service recently reported that the leading supermarket chain Grand Mart has partnered with Doha Sooq, the award-winning e-commerce portal hosted by Doha Bank, to launch the first online supermarket in Qatar. Groceries and a wide range of consumer products will be offered on the website for their customers across the country (Doha Sooq partners with Grand Mart, 2016).

HYPERMARKETS

A hypermarket is the combination of a supermarket and a department store, usually 100,000 to 300,000 square feet. It provides a large variety of low-priced

▲ FIGURE 10.3 Bridal shop window display at Villaggio Mall.

products (Dani, 2014; Levy & Weitz, 2012). At the moment, the brand penetration in Qatar is among the strongest in Middle Eastern countries; as a result, hypermarkets are expected to expand (Atkearney, 2015).

There are some major hypermarkets in Qatar such as Safari, Masskar, and Lulu. According to Wikipedia.org, Lulu is a hypermarket chain built by Lulu Group International which is based in Abu Dhabi. It has grown into a chain with several outlets across many countries including the UAE, Qatar, Kuwait, Saudi Arabia, and Oman and is the biggest hypermarket brand in the Middle East. There are six stores in Qatar so far, and Lulu Hypermarkets have become the preferred shopping destinations for Qataris.

More hypermarkets in Qatar will be developed in the next few years. Hill International, a US company, will be providing project management services on the Boulevard Mall scheme in Doha including a hypermarket, a cinema, and a family entertainment center which will open during 2017 (Foreman, 2014). At the same time, the hypermarket in Doha Marina

▲ FIGURE 10.4 Doha Qatar Market place.

Mall will be built in City Lusail. It has a USD 411 million budget (Foreman, 2014).

OVERVIEW OF QATAR'S MODEST FASHION RETAIL MARKET

There is substantial demand for modest fashion in Qatar. Due to the emergence and success of home-grown brands, such as Debaj and Fufi Stylist Abayas, there is push at national level to develop the country's fashion industry.

As a subset of the retail sector, the country's retail clothing market was estimated at $1.3 billion in 2013, according to BMI and national estimates. Assuming growth in line with the broader retail market, the market could be estimated at $1.6 billion in 2015 (Global Islamic Gateway, 2016). According to Dinar Standard analysis, Qatar's 1.7 million Muslims spent an estimated $1.1. billion on clothing and footwear in 2015.

LUXURY BRANDS

Despite a small population of 2.2 million, Qatar has the third-highest GDP per capita in the world—close to $82,000 in 2015, according to the IMF. Given the country's high disposable income, both Qatari nationals and expats have a high propensity for acquiring luxury goods. American Express Middle East estimates show that Qatari nationals are the GCC region's biggest buyers of high-end merchandise, spending up to $5,000 a month on luxury goods.

Qatar is one of the most attractive destinations for luxury shopping in the Middle East with five major shopping malls: the Landmark Mall, the Mall, the Villagio Mall, Royal Plaza Qatar and the Salam Mall. These have attracted several leading international clothing brands including Dolce & Gabbana, Karen Millen, Prada and Mango. Doha also has the women's-only Souli Mall (Global Islamic Gateway, 2016).

KEY BRANDS AND RETAILERS

Debaj is one of Qatar's leading luxury abaya brands. Fufi Stylist Abayas also infuses luxury and sophistication into traditional garments. Darz Design, founded in 2010, focuses primarily on manufacturing abayas incorporating Middle Eastern designs. Although not focused on modest fashion, Fanilla Couture's scarves and other pieces appeal to a large section of Qatar's Muslim consumers. Given Qatar's focus on modest dressing, there are numerous

▲ FIGURE 10.5 Foreign retailers such as Banana Republic and Zara at Qatar mall.

outlets dedicated to modest fashion. Jo La Mode is a leading upscale boutique with multi-brand modest fashion offerings. Other retailers include Almotahajiba, an upscale, luxury fashion brand for abayas, jalabiyas, and sheilas, and Hanayen, a Dubai-based retailer with stores in Qatar, known for its abayas and sheilas. Qatari fashion bloggers also have an important role in the country's blossoming fashion industry. Noor Al-Thani and Layla Asgar Al Siyabi are two bloggers with a huge number of followers.

DRIVING FORCES BEHIND QATAR'S RETAIL GROWTH

Qatar's retail sector is expected to be the fastest-growing in the region over the coming years. The most important driving forces behind Qatar's retail expansion are the opening of modern malls, supermarkets and hypermarkets, rapid population growth, purchasing power, favorable government policies, and retail space expansion.

GOVERNMENT POLICY

Favorable government policies and investments provide critical support to retail growth. Qatar National Vision 2030 and the Qatar National Development Strategy 2011–2016 both stress diversifying the economy away from oil and gas. Retail and other services are a critical part of this strategy (Oxford Business Group, 2016).

INVESTMENT IN INFRASTRUCTURE

The government has invested significantly in infrastructure such as roads, airports, seaports, power and other utilities that have helped drive growth in retail. Major events like the 2022 FIFA World Cup have also provided momentum. The surge in construction activity is also creating a host of new opportunities for retail companies.

CONSUMER DEMOGRAPHICS

Rapid population growth, driven largely by a burgeoning expatriate community, has continued to expand the consumer base. Qatar's population reached 2.22 million in 2015, growing by 9.5 percent from the previous year, according to the Ministry of Development Planning and Statistics (MDPS). Qatari nationals accounted for roughly 12 percent of this figure or an estimated 273,000 in 2014, according to the Qatar National Bank (QNB). The population is young: those between the ages of 20 and 39 account for more than 57 percent of the total, and are predominantly male, according to QNB.

INCOME AND SPENDING PATTERNS

The middle- and high-income expatriates and Qatari nationals are the retail sector's main target market. While income distribution figures show that much of the country's wealth is concentrated within a minority of the population, the average monthly salary for Qatari men and women is still quite high at QR29,000 ($7,949) and QR21,000 ($5,756), respectively, according to the MDPS. Thus, strong purchasing power per capita drives the growth of the retail sector.

EXPANDING RETAIL SPACE

The retail landscape will change dramatically over the next three years as a number of retail mega-projects come online. DTZ data suggests that the total GLA in Qatar's organized retail sector will almost triple from 590,000 sq meters to more than 1.7m sq meters by 2016. The GCC Retail Industry Report predicts an annual average rise of 7.9 percent in the space dedicated to "modern retail sales" in Qatar, from 445,600 square meters in 2013 to 651,200 square meters by 2018. In 2014, the un-organized retail sector secured 70 percent of total retail spaces. On completion of all ongoing downtown enhancement projects and the 14 malls under construction, the mall percentage share will change to 65 percent from the current 18 percent. This means that by the end of 2018, the major retail activities would be managed from the malls.

MIDDLE-MARKET EXPANSION

Mid-market retailers are also expanding in Qatar. One supermarket chain, Al Meera, opened 10 new stores in 2015 in areas like Al Thumama, Al Wajba and Jeryan Njeima. As of April 2016, it had 47 stores in total, with plans to increase this number to 55 by the end of 2017. The Spar Group is set to open its first supermarket in 2016 and plans to launch a further four stores by the end of 2017.

TABLE 10.3 Available retail construction space and mall distribution		

Proposed New Retail Malls

Project	Location	Estimated Completion Date
Mirqab Mall	Al Mirqab Street	2016
Al Hazm Mall	Markhiya	2016
Doha Mall	Abu Hamour	2016
Katara Mall	Al Qassar	2016
Tawar Mall	Duhail	2016
Mall of Qatar	Al Rayyan	2016
Katara Mall	Katara	2016
Doha Festival City	Umm Salal	2017
Northgate	North Doha	2017
Place Vendome	Lusail	2017
Marina Mall	Lusail	2018

Source: *DTZ Research*

FOREIGN DIRECT INVESTMENT (FDI) IN QATAR

Qatar is currently undergoing massive transformation under the rubric of the 2030 National Vision, which aims to modernize infrastructure, establish an advanced, knowledge-based, and diversified economy, which is no longer reliant on the hydrocarbon sector. As Qatar plans to spend USD 200 billion in the lead up to the 2022 FIFA World Cup and in implementation of the 2030 National Vision, there are enormous opportunities for foreign investment in various sectors including infrastructure, distribution (retail), health care, education, tourism and financial services, among others (Investment Climate Statement—Qatar, 2015).

For the second year in a row, Qatar lost several places in the 2016 Doing Business report issued by the World Bank, ranking 65th out of 189 countries. In 2012, FDI flows to Qatar reached over USD 30 billion, according to the latest

TABLE 10.4 Foreign Direct Investment

Foreign Direct Investment	2013	2014	2015
FDI Inward Flow (million USD)	−840	1,040	1,071
FDI Stock (million USD)	31,058.0	32,098.3	33,169.2
Number of Greenfield Investments***	78.0	53.0	35.0
FDI Inwards (in percent of GFCF****)	−1.4	1.4	1.2
FDI Stock (in percent of GDP)	15.4	15.3	17.9

Source: UNCTAD—2016

Note: * The UNCTAD Inward FDI Performance Index is Based on a Ratio of the Country's Share in Global FDI Inflows and its Share in Global GDP. ** The UNCTAD Inward FDI Potential Index is Based on 12 Economic and Structural Variables Such as GDP, Foreign Trade, FDI, Infrastructures, Energy Use, R&D, Education, Country Risk. *** Green Field Investments Are a Form of Foreign Direct Investment Where a Parent Company Starts a New Venture in a Foreign Country By Constructing New Operational Facilities From the Ground Up. **** Gross Fixed Capital Formation (GFCF) Measures the Value of Additions to Fixed Assets Purchased By Business, Government and Households Less Disposals of Fixed Assets Sold Off or Scrapped.

official data on foreign investment. According to estimates, FDI are expected to have since declined. Qatar is currently seeking to attract FDI in several sectors, including tourism, to continue its policy of economic diversification. Thanks to its large foreign exchange reserves, the country is also a key investor abroad (Santander Trade Portal, 2016).

The corporate tax rate is currently 10 percent.

FOREIGN DIRECT INVESTMENT—NET INFLOWS

Foreign Direct Investment (FDI) in Qatar increased by 116 QAR million in the first quarter of 2016. Foreign Direct Investment in Qatar averaged 519.33 QAR million from 2011 until 2016, reaching an all-time high of 3777 QAR million in the third quarter of 2012 and a record low of −1744 QAR million in the fourth quarter of 2012. Foreign Direct Investment in Qatar is reported by the Qatar Central Bank (Trading Economics, 2016).

TABLE 10.5 Country Comparison for Corporate Taxation

	Qatar	Middle East & North Africa	United States	Germany
Number of payments of taxes per year	4.0	19.0	10.6	9.0
Time taken for administrative formalities (Hours)	41.0	221.0	175.0	218.0
Total share of taxes (percent of Profit)	11.3	32.1	43.9	48.8

Source: Doing Business—2016

LAWS/REGULATIONS OF FOREIGN DIRECT INVESTMENT IN QATAR (SIMMONS & SIMMONS, 2015)

► Foreign investors may only invest in Qatar in accordance with the provisions of the Foreign Capital Investment in Economic Activities Law (No. (13) of 2000), as amended.

► Foreign investors may invest in all parts of the national economy (other than exceptions) with a Qatari partner who must normally own at least 51 percent of the enterprise.

► The Ministry of Economy and Commerce may permit foreign investors to own more than 49 and up to 100 percent of a company in specified sectors called the "Priority Sectors", namely business consulting; technical services; information technology; cultural, sports and leisure services; **distribution services**; agriculture; manufacturing; health; tourism; development and exploitation of natural resources; energy and mining.

► Foreign capital is guaranteed against expropriation (although the state may acquire assets for public benefit on a non-discriminatory basis, provided full compensation for the value of the asset is paid).

► Foreign capital (meaning shareholding by non-Gulf Cooperation Council ("GCC") entities or individuals) in public shareholding companies listed on the Qatar Exchange is limited to 49 percent in aggregate, unless the articles of association of such company provide for a higher percentage.

- A foreign company which has a contract with the Government of Qatar or a quasi-Government entity may be able to register a branch office (as opposed to incorporating a Qatar company) if it has entered into a contract in respect of a "government qualified project".
- The incorporation and organization of companies is governed by the Commercial Companies Law (No. (11) of 2015) (the "Commercial Companies Law") which came into effect in August 2015. The Commercial Companies Law regulates the types of company which may be established Qatar.
- Gulf Cooperation Council (GCC) nationals under certain circumstances are treated the same as Qatari nationals. The Ministry of Economy and Commerce has put in place internal regulations by virtue of which GCC nationals can fully own a Qatari company, under certain exempted activities.
- There is a separate and distinct regime for establishing companies in the Qatar Financial Centre which allows 100 percent foreign ownership. That regime is explained in outline in Section 9.

NEW QFC LAW

Qatar Financial Centre (QFC) will pass a new law in 2016, simplifying procedures for foreign investors and giving them more access to the local market, CEO Yousuf Mohamed al-Jaida has said. The revised QFC law will attract more Foreign Direct Investment (FDIs) to Qatar and allow international investors access to the local market (Gulf-Times, 2015).

PUBLIC-PRIVATE PARTNERSHIPS

Qatar's plan to pass a law to introduce the use of public-private partnerships (PPPs) is a positive move which will likely attract further foreign investment (Links Group, 2016). PPPs can be described as joint working arrangements between the public and private sector. Specifically, the Qatari Government intends to use PPPs as a form of procurement model for certain sectors including education, health and sport.

▲ FIGURE 10.6 Arab male consumers walking at Aspire Zone mall in Doha, Qatar.

CULTURE AND CONSUMERS

Due to the rapid rise in middle class incomes in Qatar in the past few decades, more people have been able to afford goods and services that were once the reserve of the wealthy. The result of this is that there is increased consumerism in the whole country and that consumer behavior is changing and becoming more intense across most demographics in the country ("Consumer Lifestyles in Qatar", 2016). There is, therefore, a record increase in the consumption of goods, especially those from foreign retailers, that are deemed to be indicators of a high-class lifestyle since many citizens of the country have a desire to be perceived as rich (Bhuian et al., 2013). There have been several studies that have sought an explanation for the new trends in consumerism in the country, and some psychological theories have been put forth as possible explanations for human behavior that transcends cultures and boundaries. These theories have a common underlying ideology: that consumer behavior is determined by an innate desire for social status or conformity.

One major indicator of consumer behavior is consumer confidence. This is quantified by the spending of the population under study. Consumer confidence has been at an all-time high in the past few years since most of the middle-income households in the country have had some considerable income at their disposal ("Consumer Lifestyles in Qatar", 2016). As more households are increasingly able to afford imported goods, the market for such goods has grown at an almost exponential rate and there has been a rush by international retailers to fill the resultant demand gap in the country (Dahl, 2013). Consumer confidence has been sustained all over the country despite recent economic issues such as the steep drop in global oil prices that has had a significant impact on the economy of Qatar.

There is also a very high demand for luxury goods in Qatar. This has been attributed by consumer psychologists to a desire for high social status, which is common in most middle class families and households across the world, including in Qatar. Such luxury goods include high-end cars, brand name clothing, and cutting-edge consumer electronics. There is also a significant increase in the consumption of processed foods from western countries, which a significant number of people in Qatar perceive to be of higher quality that the local delicacies. The psychological explanation for this trend is that people want to be perceived by their neighbors and friends as being rich, and the western indicators of wealth have permeated the Qatar culture; they are a major influence of how the Qatar consumers behave (Williams, 2014).

Aside from actual stores, many of the products from international companies are dispensed through online shops. The use of online retailers is still in the early stages in Qatar, but it is rapidly catching on among most consumers. Some of the global online retailers such as Amazon and Alibaba have already made their debut in the Qatar market either directly or through third-party partners and they are making considerable profits with a rapidly increasing market share. The online retailers in Qatar receive a lot of exposure through advertising on social media platforms and other popular websites. However, the popularity of online retailers is projected to catch on among younger consumers, but not so much among the older ones.

The culture of Qatar has a great impact on the consumer behavior of the different demographics in the country. Being an Islamic country, there are certain cultural expectations for men and women; these expectations have an impact on the products that people consume on the basis of their gender. A study showed that men in Qatar are more likely to purchase clothing such as suits from western retailers, while women were more likely to adhere to traditional Islamic dress codes. This indicates that the culture of the country has an impact on the retail products that are successful in the Qatar market. Products such as women's clothing from western retailers, which are considered indecent in the Qatar culture, are not likely to catch on among the consumers. The same applies to products such as alcoholic beverages, whose consumption is restricted in Islamic culture.

Some studies have found that affluent Qataris tend to overspend in a manner that is unnecessary and alarming. Social and cultural drivers have been identified as the causal agent of the irrational consumption behavior among a significant portion of the population of the country. They include unplanned shopping, which is a common characteristic of the middle class in the country, most of whom don't have to worry about sticking to a strict budget (Doha News Team, 2012). The availability of easy to use payment options such as credit cards has also made it possible for people to carry out complex transactions without fully appreciating the financial implications of such transactions.

Another factor that is been credited for the worrying consumer behavior of Qataris is the fact that there are so many malls in the cities and suburbs, which are frequented by many young people on a daily basis. Malls are viewed by young people as places for social interaction, and regular visits to these malls increases the likelihood of unplanned purchases (Doha News Team, 2012). The competitive nature of consumers has also been identified as a common cause of unplanned buying across all demographics in the country. Many people buy luxury or expensive items because their peers or family members have similar items, and they don't want to be left behind (Williams, 2014). Studies have also found that there is a lack of distinction between a necessity and a luxurious product in the minds of most consumers in Qatar (Doha News Team, 2012). Consumers are more likely to make purchased based on emotional reactions rather than rational thought.

For the retailers who seek to enter the Qatar market, there are lots of opportunities to explore. However, these retailers need to carry out a thorough cultural study of the country in order to understand how social dynamics and traditions influence the reception of certain goods and products within the country (Doha News Team, 2012). For their part, the consumers in Qatar have the ability to modify their behavior so as to gain the highest possible benefits from their shopping experiences.

SUMMARY

Qatar's rapidly growing population, coupled with its strong purchasing power per capita are strong fundamentals driving the growth of the retail sector. The country's affinity for luxury goods has already triggered entry plans by high-end retailers, and it is expected that more brands will follow suit given an additional 1 million square meters of retail space that is scheduled to become available in Doha in the coming years. Foreign investors definitely stand to gain from Qatar's burgeoning retail market. Growth-enhancing policies coupled with sound macroeconomic policies foster a healthy rate of return for investment and hence attract FDI. To maximize the benefit of FDI, Qatar should establish investment agencies, improve the local regulatory environment, develop the local financial market, and enhance transparency in macro-economic policies. A sound and transparent legal system governing financial transactions should also be put in place.

CRITICAL THINKING QUESTIONS

1. Why do you think Qatar is an important emerging market?
2. What opportunities do foreign retailers have in the Qatar market? What strategies do you suggest for foreign retailers entering the Qatar market?
3. Explain industry regulations in Qatar.
4. How do consumers in Qatar influence the luxury market of Qatar?

Case Study

LUXURY AND SOPHISTICATION: OVERVIEW OF QATAR'S MODEST FASHION MARKET

Before entering the Qatar market, companies must familiarize themselves with the market scenario. According to AT Kearney Qatar's retail sector is estimated to be about $13 billion in 2016. Qatar's 1.7 million Muslims spent an estimated $1.1. billion on clothing and footwear in 2015, according to DinarStandard analysis. Given the country's high disposable income, both Qatari nationals and expats have a high propensity for acquiring luxury goods. According to Euromonitor, the 15–34 year old age group has a strong preference for international brands. Qatar is one of the most attractive destinations for luxury shopping in the Middle East with five major shopping malls: The Landmark Mall, The Mall, The Villagio Mall, Royal Plaza Qatar and Salam Mall. These have attracted several leading international clothing brands including Dolce & Gabbana, Karen Millen, Prada and Mango. Doha also has the women's-only Souli Mall.

With population growth and an increasing number of expats, Qatar is no longer a market to ignore. The 2022 FIFA World Cup is also leading to infrastructure projects that will benefit the economy in the long term, such as the airport expansion and the construction of Doha Metro. Until recently, international brands were limited by insufficient retail supply. This is changing as Doha welcomes 1 million square meters of retail space in the next two to three years. Qataris' affinity for luxury goods has also triggered entry plans by high-end retailers such as Harvey Nichols, which will open its first store in 2017 in Doha Festival City.

Demand for fashion: There is substantial demand for modest fashion in Qatar, and there is a push to develop the country's homegrown fashion industry, in particular, modest fashion. Sheikha Moza bint Nasser al-Missned, the mother of current emir Sheikh Tamim, has played a key role in promoting the growth of Qatar's indigenous fashion industry, seeking to turn Qatar into a key manufacturing hub for premium clothing. Efforts to develop homegrown designers and brands are beginning to pay off for modest fashion, with brands such as Debaj and Fufi Stylist Abayas emerging since 2012.

Key Brands and Labels: Some of the key players of luxury brands in Qatar include "Debaj", Founded in 2012, Debaj combines traditional abaya silhouettes with glamorous, modern cuts and patterns. It has frequently partnered and participated in Qatar's major fashion gatherings, including the Heya Arabian Fashion Exhibition and the Luxury Network.

Fufi Stylist Abayas, founded by Libyan-born Fatma Ghanem in 2012, infuses luxury and sophistication into traditional garments. Fufi's collections bring together design elements from Italy, Libya and Qatar.

Darz Design, founded in 2010, also focuses primarily on manufacturing abayas incorporating Middle Eastern designs.

Although not focused on modest fashion, *Fanilla Couture's* scarves and other pieces appeal to a large section of Qatar's Muslim consumers. Founded by designer Razan Suliman, the brand carries a broad stylistic clothing range for men and women.

Retailers: Given Qatar's focus on modest dressing, there are numerous outlets dedicated to modest fashion.

Jo La Mode is a leading upscale boutique with multi-brand modest fashion offerings. It is owned by Jawaher Al Kuwari, Head of Advisory at Design Creationz, the organizing company of Heya Arabian Fashion Exhibition.

Other retailers include *Almotahajiba*, an upscale, luxury fashion brand for abayas, jalabiyas, and sheilas, and *Hanayen*, a Dubai-based retailer with stores in Qatar, known for its abayas and sheilas.

Qatari fashion bloggers also play an important role in the country's blossoming fashion industry. Bloggers such as Noor Al-Thani and Layla Asgar Al Siyabi have a huge number of followers.

Challenges and market assessment: There are several key considerations to addressing the modest fashion opportunity in Qatar.

Understand how the customer differs in Qatar and what exactly they prefer. Speaking from the perspective of a foreign modest fashion label selling into Qatar, Selma Bamadhaj, a co-founder of Singapore's Lully Selb, said, "Qatari women are all about class, luxury and sophistication. In terms of designs and styles, silhouettes are still pretty much abaya, kaftan, or kimono-inspired." With high purchasing power, Qatari women are highly selective when it comes to selecting materials and designs, yet they are less price-sensitive. Bamadhaj added "We gathered that the [Qatari] consumers have high spending power and if you have the right product, good quality, [there are] no questions asked on the price. When we got some orders, the customers did not even negotiate or ask for discounts."

Study the existing landscape: Growing support for emerging local fashion entrepreneurs is beneficial to boost the growth of Qatar's modest fashion industry. However, small-scale foreign labels might find it difficult to compete with homegrown brands due to a lack of understanding of Qataris' discerning tastes, the high cost of setting up a business in the country and a nascent e-commerce ecosystem. Entering Qatar's modest fashion industry must be predicated upon a solid customer research and distribution strategy.

REFERENCES

Afia Fitriati (2016). Luxury and Sophistication: Overview of Qatar's Modest Fashion Market. Retrieved from www.salaamgateway.com/en/fashion-art-design/story/luxury_and_sophistication_overview_of_qatars_modest_fashion_market-salaam14062016073242/

Qatar named Middle East's most attractive retail market, ahead of UAE (2015). www.arabianbusiness.com/qatar-named-mideast-s-most-attractive-retail-market-ahead-of-uae-594945.html

Discussion Questions

1. Who are the major players in Qatar's fashion market?
2. If you are looking to launch a fashion brand in Qatar—how attractive is the market?
3. What are the major challenges and opportunities for new fashion labels that want to enter the market?

REFERENCES

About Qatar (2016). Retrieved from http://udcqatar.com/English/Pages/AboutQatar.aspx

Arabian Business (2015). Retrieved from www.arabianbusiness.com/qatar-named-mideast-s-most-attractive-retail-market-ahead-of-uae–594945.html?tab=Article#.V_x7_uUrLIU

Bain, M. (May 10, 2016). After ditching sexy ads, Abercrombie & Fitch is looking to the Middle East. Quartz. Retrieved from http://qz.com/680213/after-ditching-sexy-ads-abercrombie-fitch-is-looking-to-the-middle-east/

Bhuian, S., Share, K., Muzaffar, A., Ahmed, H., Ghaida, R., & Dorgham, R. (2013). Consumer Online Shopping Attitude-Intention and their Determinants in Qatar. *International Journal of Electronic Finance, 7*(2), 146. http://dx.doi.org/10.1504/ijef.2013.057279

Consumer Lifestyles in Qatar. (2016). *Euromonitor.com.* Retrieved from www.euromonitor.com/consumer-lifestyles-in-qatar/report

Dahl, D. (2013). Social Influence and Consumer Behavior. *Journal of Consumer Research, 40*(2), iii–v. http://dx.doi.org/10.1086/670170

Dani, S. (2014). Middle East Retail: Fostering Growth Despite Challenges. *International Journal of Management and Social Sciences Research*, 3(4), 41–47. Retrieved from http://irjcjournals.org/ijmssr/Apr2014/9.pdf

Doha News Team. (2012). *Study addresses why Qataris overspend, how to tackle irrational consumer behavior. Doha News.* Retrieved from http://dohanews.co/study-addresses-why-qataris-overspend-how-to-tackle/

Doha Sooq partners with Grand Mart to launch Qatar's first online supermarket. Zawya. Retrieved from www.zawya.com/story/Doha_Sooq_partners_with_Grand_Mart_to_launch_Qatars_first_online_supermarket-ZAWYA20160508060159/

Doha festival city to launch the first ever Harvey Nichols luxury department store in Qatar. *World Market Intelligence News.* Retrieved from http://libproxy.csun.edu/login?url=http://search.proquest.com.libproxy.csun.edu/docview/1664624120?accountid=7285

Fitriati, A. (June 14, 2016). Luxury and sophistication: Overview of Qatar's modest fashion market. *Global Islamic Economy Gateway.* Retrieved from www.salaamgateway.com/en/fashion-art-design/story/luxury_and_sophistication_overview_of_qatars_modest_fashion_market-salaam14062016073242/

Foreman, C. (2014). Mall development begins in Doha. *MEED: Middle East Economic Digest,* 58(26), 14. Retrieved from http://web.b.ebscohost.com.libproxy.csun.edu/ehost/detail/detail?sid=e0076009–9a2a–4573-a082-e66cda3dae6f

%40sessionmgr106&vid=2&hid=107&bdata=JnNpdGU9ZWhvc3QtbGl2ZQ %3d%3d#AN=97001193&db=buh

Global Islamic Gateway (2016). Retrieved from www.salaamgateway.com/en/fashion-art-design/story/luxury_and_sophistication_overview_of_qatars_modest_ fashion_market-salaam14062016073242/12. Strong baseline indicators support growth in Qatar's retail market

Global retail expansion: An unstoppable force. (2015). *AT Kearney.* Retrieved from www.atkearney.com/consumer-products-retail/global-retail-development-index/2015

Gulf Times (2016). Retrieved from www.gulf-times.com/story/441667/Retail-market-Qatar-ranks-top-in-GCC

Gulf Times (2015). Retrieved from www.gulf-times.com/story/425898/Qatar-retail-market-growth-to-top-Gulf

Gulf-Times (2015). Retrieved from www.gulf-times.com/story/462477/New-QFC-law-to-attract-more-foreign-direct-investm

Investment Climate Statement—Qatar (2015), Retrieved from www.state.gov/e/eb/rls/ othr/ics/ 2015/241709.htm

Kearney AT (2015). Retrieved from www.atkearney.de/consumer-products-retail/ featured-article/-/asset_publisher/S5UkO0zy0vnu/content/global-retail-expansion

Levy, M., & Weitz, B. A. (2012). *Retailing Management.* New York: McGraw-Hill/Irwin.

Links Group (2016). Retrieved from www.linksgroup.com/2016/05/qatars-plan-to-introduce-public-private- partnerships-ppps-law.

Marciniak, R., & Mohsen, M. (2014). Homogeneity in Luxury Fashion Consumption: An Exploration of Arab Women. *The Business & Management Review*, 5(1), 32–41. Retrieved from http://libproxy.csun.edu/login?url=http://search.proquest.com. libproxy.csun.edu/docview/1558853907?accountid=7285

Middle East's home-grown fashion destination 'Salam stores' hosts Paris Hilton in Dubai. (July 9, 2009). *PR Newswire Europe Including UK Disclose.* Retrieved from http://search.proquest.com.libproxy.csun.edu/docview/365982717?accountid= 7285&rfr_id=info%3Axri%2Fsid%3Aprimo#

Oxford Business Group (2016). Retrieved from www.oxfordbusinessgroup.com/ overview/peak-view-large-increase-supplypipeline-high-spending-and-sophisticated-retail-market

Qatar's burgeoning retail market (2016). Retrieved from www.linksgroup. com/2016/07/qatars-burgeoning-retail-market

Qatar Country Report (2015). Retrieved from www.multiplesgroup.com/wp-content/ uploads/2015/02/Qatar-Country-Report–2015.pdf

Qatar Market Profile (2016). Retrieved from http://emerging-markets-research.hktdc.
com/business-news/article/Middle-East/Qatar- Market-Profile/mp/
en/1/1X4U1FO3/1X06O28M.htm

Qatar Market Report (2016). Retrieved from http://dtzqatar.com/press_releases/
q1–2016-qatar-market-report-retail-market-overview

Santander Trade Portal (2016). Retrieved from https://en.portal.santandertrade.com/
establish-overseas/qatar/investing–3

Simmons & Simmons (2015). Doing Business in Qatar—10 key points. Retrieved from
www.google.com/search?q=Doing+Business+in+Qatar+%E2%80%93+10+key+
points%2C+Simmons+%26+Simmons&ie=utf–8&oe=utf–8

Shimek, E. D. (2012). The Abaya: Fashion, Religion, and Identity in a Globalized World.
Lawrence University Honors Projects. Paper 12. Retrieved from http://lux.
lawrence.edu/luhp/12

Trading Economics (2016). Retrieved from www.tradingeconomics.com/qatar/
foreign-direct-investment

The Global Economy (2016). Retrieved from www.theglobaleconomy.com/Qatar/
Foreign_Direct_Investment/

The Mall of Qatar. Retrieved from www.mallofqatar.com.qa/en/shop.aspx

Upadhyay, R. (2016, August 11). Qatar sees construction boom ahead of 2022 World Cup.
Women's Wear Daily, 14. Retrieved from http://wwd.com/business-news/real-
estate/qatar-construction–2022-fifa-world-cup–10500112/

Walker, L. (2015, February 5). Growing number of supermarkets driving Qatar's retail
growth. *Doha News.* Retrieved from http://dohanews.co/growing-number-
supermarkets-driving-qatars-retail-growth/

Wealth and Finance (2016). Retrieved from www.wealthandfinance-intl.com/qatar--a-
haven-for-emerging-markets-investors

Williams, P. (2014). Emotions and Consumer Behavior. *Journal of Consumer Research,*
40(5), viii–xi. http://dx.doi.org/10.1086/674429

World Factbook. (n.d.). Retrieved from www.cia.gov/library/publications/resources/
the-world-factbook/geos/qa.html

FUTURE OF EMERGING MARKETS

11

Jaya Halepete
Shubhapriya Bennur

OBJECTIVES

After reading this chapter, you will

- ▶ Understand the cycle of emerging markets
- ▶ Be able to compare various emerging markets
- ▶ Understand the pros and cons of investing in various emerging markets

Emerging markets remain attractive for an average of five to ten years, after which they become saturated or the level of competition increases tremendously. During this period, foreign retailers enter the market, and the government of the country works at making the market investment friendly. Some investors succeed and some fail based on the mode of entry, time of entry, and level of understanding of the market.

Of all the emerging markets discussed in the preceding chapters, some countries are closer to being saturated, such as China and Thailand, than others such as India. Increasing competition and growing real estate prices make the market less attractive to foreign investors. Being close to maturity does not necessarily mean that there is no opportunity in the market, but it means that one has to be well prepared when entering that market. Retailers face major investing challenges in countries such as Russia; other countries such as Turkey have friendly investment environments and encourage foreign direct investment. Although there is always a chance of success for innovative

TABLE 11.1 Investing in Brazil

Pros	Cons
• World's fifth-largest country	• Bureaucracy
• Fashion oriented	• Corruption levels still high
• Flourishing middle class	• High taxes
• Public policies focusing on low income families' revenue improvement	• Complex tax system
	• High taxes for imported goods
	• Informal and gray markets
• Relatively young population	• Infrastructure bottleneck: airports, roads, ports, etc.
• Democratic system	
• Economic stability	• Competition, both domestic and foreign, is fierce in some industries (banks, retail, etc.)
• Institutional stability	
• No major geopolitical issues	
• Steady economic growth	• Extremely high interest rates
• Positive attitude toward imported goods	• Still a very unequal country, measured by HDI (human development index)
• Regional (Latin America) leadership	

concepts, most retailers selling a basic mix of merchandise will need to look for newer countries to invest in. The following sections look at the pros and cons of investing in each country discussed in this book (Tables 11.1–11.9).

COMPARISON OF EMERGING MARKETS

The emerging markets included in this book share some factors that make them attractive to foreign investors. Most of them have a large population with increasing income levels. The consumers of these countries also have a favorable outlook toward foreign brands and retailers. The countries are working to make it easy for foreign investors to invest in the country by relaxing foreign direct investment policies.

Some common drawbacks of investing in the emerging markets are lack of proper infrastructure and prevalence of corruption. These are common problems in a lot of emerging markets due to lack of availability of funds to

TABLE 11.2 Investing in Qatar

Pros	Cons
• The sixth-largest market for the European Union • Increasing incomes of population • The lowest tax rate in the region • Still low competition in some markets • Positive consumer attitude toward foreign products • Healthy economic growth • Availability of labor force especially from foreign countries • Increasing levels of productivity	• Gender roles are relatively distinct. Men engage in the public sphere more frequently than do women • Qatari businessmen prefer to do business with people they are familiar with, and who they feel they can trust. • The business culture of Qatar is typically Arabic, in that a lot of emphasis is placed on personal relationships between associates.

TABLE 11.3 Investing in China

Pros	Cons
• Second-largest economy in the world • Trend of increasing consumer spending • Growing affluent middle class • High level of interest of consumers in foreign brands • Hub for sourcing apparel • Open market for foreign investors	• Consumption power varies tremendously among cities, making it a very diverse market • Intense competition • Need to customize products for Chinese market • Market saturation in premier cities

keep up with infrastructure-related issues. Because retail is not very well developed in most of these nations, there are problems with the supply chain not being streamlined like in the United States or some European countries (such as the United Kingdom and France, for example).

TABLE 11.4 Investing in India

Pros	Cons
• Second-largest population in the world and growing • Increasing disposable income among a very large middle class • Market dominated by unorganized traditional retailers • Government relaxing regulations for foreign direct investment	• High level of corruption and bureaucracy • Lack of qualified retail talent • Infrastructure problems • Complex market with tremendous cultural differences among the local population • Very few cities with upper-class population for luxury retailers • High cost of real estate • High importing duties

TABLE 11.5 Investing in Russia

Pros	Cons
• Huge market (10th country by population in the world) • Huge premium segment potential • Considerable high amount of free-market niches • Positive attitude toward foreign products • Economic growth	• High level of corruption and bureaucracy • Obsolete legislation • Lack of qualified domestic managers for senior and top positions • Probable problems with logistics

Emerging countries such as China and India have a lot of diversity in their population. Due to the complex nature of consumer makeup, it is difficult to customize products to satisfy the needs of all the consumers. These emerging markets are varied with very low levels of brand loyalty. Many companies are tweaking their products to suit local tastes, such as Unilever making foamier

TABLE 11.6 Investing in Turkey

Pros	Cons
• Large population (80 million)	• Slight political instability
• Favorable investment laws	• High local competition
• Brand-focused consumers	• Differences among Turkish
• Large segment of young and	consumers in various
brand-conscious consumers	segments
• Positive attitude toward foreign	• Regional differences
products	
• Economic growth and increasing	
purchasing income	
• Key location as potential regional	
headquarters	
• Qualified and relatively cheap labor	
• Raw material availability and quality	

soaps and shampoos for these markets as compared to their Western counterparts (Easier said than done, 2010). Foreign investors need to spend extra time to understand these diverse groups of consumers and research their needs to be successful in these markets.

FUTURE EMERGING MARKETS

Over the past three years, Brazil, Russia, India, and China have outperformed many developed European markets as well as the U.S. market. Investors in these markets have profited from being the first movers (Turner, 2010). In the 1990s only Asia was considered to be the most attractive market in which to invest due to a large population and a growing middle class in countries like China and India. But many oil-rich Middle Eastern countries with urban populations and lack of organized retail markets will soon become attractive investment markets. Latin America has also been quick to recover from the latest economic downturn, making it attractive to foreign retailers.

A.T. Kearney has conducted research to find the most attractive emerging markets, taking into consideration market attractiveness, country risk, market saturation, and time pressure. Based on this research, some countries such as

TABLE 11.7 Investing in Thailand

Pros	Cons
• Government trying to attract foreign investors	• Culturally different consumers
• Opening up of the market for foreign direct investment	• Lack of skilled retail professionals
• Large market size	• Corruption
• Room for growth	• Products require adaptation in terms of shape, color, and size
• Good regulatory system	• Need to have a local partner to assist with ownership of land, navigate through regulations
	• Intense competition

TABLE 11.8 Investing in Mexico

Pros	Cons
• Large, free-market economy (123 million people; 14th-largest economy in the world)	• High level of corruption, cronyism, and bureaucracy, which favor large established Mexican monopolies
• Wealthy minority who demand high-quality brands	• Growing violence and insecurity due to the war on drugs
• Growing middle class who are changing buying and consumption patterns due to increasing purchasing power	• Brain drain of college-educated managers due to low salaries and lack of incentives
• "Malinchista" attitude toward foreign products	• Probable problems with logistics in the south of the country due to a lack of infrastructure
• Proximity to the U.S. market (largest border between a developed and a developing nation)	
• Country with the most free trade agreements in the world, including the wealthiest economies	

TABLE 11.9 Investing in South Korea

Pros	Cons
• Large, free-market economy is the fourth largest economy in Asia and the 11th largest in the world. (50 million people)	• Foreign investors and expat employees wanting to do business in South Korea are expected to adjust and conform
• Incredible economic growth and global integration to become a high-tech industrialized economy	• Although gender relations are becoming more equitable, men still dominate the Korean workplace
• Highly motivated and educated populace is largely responsible for spurring the country's high technology boom and changing buying and consumption patterns	• Personal relationships, hierarchy and saving face are all major factors in the Korean work environment

Kuwait, Saudi Arabia, the United Arab Emirates, and Chile, have been included in the top ten most attractive emerging markets. The research also includes countries such as Tunisia, Albania, Egypt, Vietnam, and Morocco to watch out for in the future. These countries will be the next set of emerging countries to study to understand the market for investment.

Countries such as Qatar, Albania, Macedonia, the Dominican Republic, Bosnia, and Herzegovina will soon be considered as the most important emerging markets based on their current retail performance. The global recession has brought out these smaller markets that have been insulated from foreign competition for a long time. Although both old and new emerging markets are attractive investment sites for various companies, it is important to follow certain steps to minimize the risks involved with investing in emerging markets. It is important to use a less risky channel of entry such as wholesale format or e-commerce and to study the market well before investing. A foreign investor should try to use local partners whenever possible and also employ local talent for their business (Ben-Shabat, Moriarty, and Neary, 2010). By following these steps, the risks of investing in an unknown market are reduced considerably.

CRITICAL THINKING QUESTIONS

1. Why do you think that some emerging markets have been overlooked by foreign investors?
2. Why are Brazil, China, and India compared to the "most popular school girls at the prom"? Do you think it's justified?
3. What factors do you think make the current emerging markets riskier?

Case Study

FUTURE OF THE EMERGING EMERGING MARKET

Although the international economic situation is unpredictable and uncertain, the emerging economy offers sound prospects right now. The middle class in the U.S. and Europe will continue to be pillars of the global economy, however, the world's new consumers and new growth engines will still be found in developing, not developed countries. Some 3 billion people will enter the middle class by 2050, almost all of them in the developing world. In the long run "emerging" would have "emerged" by 2036.

Recent decades have witnessed great changes. The countries at the forefront of these changes have transformed the global dynamics of trade and consumerism. Developing countries are already starting to change the rules. China, India and Russia will be the three biggest contributors to the global economy. How far these emerging markets will influence the economy, and rewrite the rules governing the financial system, will be an intriguing question.

Not every emerging market can achieve "rich" status, however national wealth and influence will be distributed more evenly around the globe. Everyone will buy more products and services from emerging market companies, while the demands of consumers in those markets will shape corporate strategies regardless of location. The big decisions affecting the world won't be made only in the capitals of North America, Western Europe and Japan. It would be reasonable to assume that, in another 20 years, a good number of the consumers will be living in today's developing world.

REFERENCES

Schuman, M. (2015). Emerging Markets Are Still the Future. Retrieved January 27, 2017 from www.bloomberg.com/news/articles/2015–09–03/emerging-markets-are-still-the-future

Young, H (2017). The Future of Emerging Markets. Retrieved January 27, 2017 from www.fnlondon.com/articles/fn-future-of-finance-emerging-markets-hugh-young–20161005

REFERENCES

Ben-Shabat, H., Moriarty, M. & Neary, D. (2010). Expanding Opportunities for Global Retailers. Retrieved December 7, 2010, from www.atkearney.com/images/global/pdf/2010_Global_Retail_Development_Index.pdf

Easier Said Than Done (2010). Retrieved December 7, 2010, from www.economist.com/node/15879299

Schuman, M. (2015). Emerging Markets Are Still the Future. Retrieved January 27, 2017 from www.bloomberg.com/news/articles/2015–09–03/emerging-markets-are-still-the-future

Turner (2010). Retail investors move into emerging markets. Retrieved December 7, 2010, from www.efinancialnews.com/story/2010–12–03/ima-shows-emerging-markets-at-record-high

Young, H (2017). The Future of Emerging Markets. Retrieved January 27, 2017 from www.fnlondon.com/articles/fn-future-of-finance-emerging-markets-hugh-young–20161005

ABOUT THE EDITORS

Jaya Halepete Iyer is an entrepreneur and founder of Svaha USA an online apparel retail business selling STEM themed clothing. She has a Ph.D. in Merchandising from Iowa State University and worked as an Assistant Profession at Marymount University in Arlington, Virginia before joining the retail industry. She has over ten years of experience in apparel manufacturing and apparel buying. She has published research papers in journals such as *Clothing and Textile Research Journal, Journal of Fashion Marketing and Management,* and *International Journal of Retail Distribution and Management.* She currently resides in Oakton, Virginia with her family.

Shubhapriya Bennur is Assistant Professor at University of Nebraska-Lincoln and will soon join as faculty in the Global Fashion Enterprise Graduate program at Kanbar School of Business, Philadelphia University. She did her Ph.D. in Apparel Merchandising from Oklahoma State University. Her research area includes International Retailing and Consumer Behavior. She has peer reviewed publications in journals such as the *Journal of the Textile Institute,* the *Clothing and Textiles Research Journal,* the *Journal of Teaching in International Business* and the *Journal of Fashion Marketing & Management.* She is active member of the International Textiles & Apparel Association and has several research papers in proceedings. She has won the ITAA's Sara Douglas Fellowship for International Study twice for her research papers focusing on comparing apparel consumers of India, China, Korea and USA. She is also an Academic Editorial Board Member of the *British Journal of Applied Science & Technology* and an Editorial Board Member of the *Journal of Textile Science & Engineering.*

ABOUT THE CONTRIBUTORS

Samira Alotaibi is an international Ph.D. student in Apparel Design at the University of Nebraska. Her research interest includes transforming the traditional costumes of Saudi Arabia into contemporary fashion while keeping the identity of Saudi heritage. She also holds a Master of Fine Art degree in Textile Design from East Carolina University. Prior to arriving in the United States, she worked as a teaching assistant at Taif University in Saudi Arabia.

Elida Camille Behar is assistant professor (two-year appointment) at the Fashion Institute of Technology/SUNY, teaching in areas of global merchandising, fashion merchandising, financial planning and assortment, team development, retail math applications at the undergraduate level, and precollege courses. In Summer 2015 and 2016, Elida instructed the global merchandising course with an emphasis on BRICS and MINT markets at Zhejiang Sci-Tech University (ZSTU) in China. She has 25+ years' experience in luxury and off-price retail and merchandising for Saks Fifth Avenue and Daffy's Inc. Elida has done consulting activities both in the shoe industry and the off-price retail sector. She has an MPS (2015) from the Fashion Institute of Technology/SUNY specializing in global fashion management, and a BS in accounting from Fordham University.

Flavia Silveira Cardoso is an assistant professor at Adolfo Ibanez University in Santiago, Chile. She has over 15 years of experience in marketing, focusing on brand management and consumer behavior, with business and academic exposure in Europe, the U.S., and Latin America, where she was brand manager for top multinationals such as General Motors, Prudential, and Chubb.

Yiyue Fan is an international student pursuing a Master's degree in Apparel Merchandising at University of Nebraska-Lincoln. She is also the research assistant currently focusing on early stage entrepreneurship. Her research areas include fast fashion, entrepreneurship in fashion industry, and consumer online buying behaviors. She earned her Bachelor's degree in fashion design and engineering from Xi'an Polytechnic University in China, and a Bachelor's degree in apparel merchandising from California State University, Northridge.

Andrey Gabisov is CMO and co-founder of an emerging IoT startup Oco. Before joining Oco Andrey worked as Digital Director in advertising agencies in the US and Russia where he helped global brands and retailers with their marketing activities. Andrey studied at Marketing Ph.D. program at the St. Petersburg State University, Russia. His research focus was retail and private label. Andrey was a speaker at conferences as well as co-author of several academic publications. One year before the end of the program he dropped out to focus on his entrepreneurial projects.

Yongsoo Ha is the new Assistant Professor of Business Management at Kwangwoon University. Before he started his Ph.D. program, he worked at Lotte Shopping, the largest retailing company in South Korea, as a general manager and financial director. He earned a Ph.D. in Consumer Science at Purdue University in 2016. During his time in Purdue, he participated in several academic conferences, such as Society for Consumer Psychology and American Collegiate Retailing Association, as a presenter and published a research paper in a peer-reviewed journal. He also worked as an Assistant Professor of Business Administration at Saint Joseph's College in Rensselaer, Indiana. Yongsoo Ha's research interest focuses on consumer behavior in the online consumption community. Currently, he is conducting research that investigates the effects of the online brand community on consumers' brand loyalty and community loyalty.

Sowon Hahn is a Project Director at PFIN, which is a trend forecasting agency for fashion industries in Korea. She is also an adjunct professor at the Department of Human Environment and Design at Yonsei University. She has been involved in diverse projects, ranging from analyzing the fashion market to planning brand strategies, seasonal trend and product design. Her research interests include lifestyle and design trend forecasting process. She teaches design trend and fashion trend planning at Yonsei University in Korea. She has a D.E.S.S. from Université Lyon2 and a Ph.D. from Yonsei University.

Sungha Jang is an assistant professor of marketing at Kansas State University. His research areas include choice modeling, consumer search behavior, and advertising by utilizing Bayesian estimation and text mining techniques. He teaches marketing research and business analytics. Prior to his current position, he worked for Experian Korea as a senior consultant in the field of credit risk management. He earned his Ph.D. from the University of Texas at Dallas.

Ji Hye Kang is currently an assistant professor in the department of Textiles, Fashion Merchandizing, and Design at the University of Rhode Island. She has substantial work experience as a fashion market consultant in Korea. As a professional in the field and a researcher in higher education, she has been involved in a variety of projects related to fashion businesses and consumers. Her research interests center on globalization-related issues including cross-cultural consumer behavior, and global fashion business strategies.

Mohammad Ayub Khan is Full-Professor and Director of the Marketing and International Business Department and has remained Director of the International Business Department, Director of the University Honors Program; National Coordinator of International Business Academy and Divisional Coordinator of Internationalization of the Business Faculty, at Tecnológico de Monterrey, campus Monterrey, México. His research interests are cross cultural management, international negotiation and business management education. He has co-authored books titled *The Basics of International Negotiation*, *Diverse Contemporary Issues Facing the Business Management Education in Developing Countries* and has edited a book on *Multinational Enterprises Management Strategies in Developing Countries*. He participates in international conferences and has published articles in various journals in the field of education.

Takeshi KN holds an MBA in Design, Fashion & Luxury Goods Management from the University of Bologna, Bologna Business School in Italy and Design degree from RCDC in Australia and is completing his coursework stage with a Ph.D. in Design at Huddersfield University, UK. His research interests are focused on visual merchandising, consumer behavior and design management. Prior to his academic career conducting classes in India, Malaysia, Vietnam, Italy, and Thailand, he worked in the fashion and retailing industry through positions at United Colors of Benetton and Calvin Klein. Takeshi also has joined several consulting projects focused on branding, visual design and customer-centric research. He is now a full-time professor of fashion design and management in CIDI Chanapatana International Design Institute in Bangkok, Thailand.

Laubie LI is the Academic Dean at SKEMA Business School in China (Suzhou) and Professor of International Business. Laubie holds a Ph.D. from the University of New South Wales, Australia. With a career in management education for over 25 years, he comes to SKEMA Business School with a wealth of experience in teaching, research, business, consulting and academic management. He has had many years of business and industry experience before embarking on an academic career. He was responsible for management training in the Hong Kong Civil Service prior to taking up lecturing and academic management roles at several Australian universities. Laubie's teaching, research and consulting activities focus mainly on internationalization, organizational restructuring, international joint ventures, knowledge management and strategic management. Since spending his sabbatical at Tsinghua University, one of the top universities in China, in 2008, his research interests are Chinese relationship management (guanxi), Chinese expatriates, Chinese managerial roles and strategic congruence in the internationalization process.

Silvio Laban Nato has a Bachelor's degree in Naval Engineering from São Paulo University, a graduate degree in business and a Ph.D. in Marketing from Fundação Getúlio Vargas. He worked for over 19 years as an executive in the following services and retail organizations: Accenture, Carrefour, Pão de Açúcar and Wal-Mart and began his academic activities and professorship at EAESP-FGV, having also served as associate vice-dean of the Center for Excellence in Retailing. Presently he is the Content and Marketing Executive Coordinator at Insper where he also teaches Marketing and IT, having served as Associate Dean Executive MBA Programs at the same institution.

Md. Rashaduzzaman is a graduate research assistant pursuing a Ph.D. in Human Sciences (Merchandising) at the University of Nebraska-Lincoln. His research areas include emerging retail markets, global sourcing and consumer online shopping behavior. Prior to his current position, he worked as Assistant Professor in the Department of Textile Engineering, Green University of Bangladesh. He also worked for DECATHLON as Technical Production Leader and for international magazine *Textile Today* as a Technical Team Member. He earned his Master's degree from Bangladesh University of Textiles.

Junghwa Son is a visiting professor of marketing in the Department of Business Administration at Sejong University, Seoul, S. Korea. She is also an academic coordinator and a director of the international bachelor of business administration (international BBA) program. She teaches global marketing, marketing practices in Asia, services marketing, and international retailing in the undergraduate and MBA level. Her research interests include cross-cultural consumer behavior, international retailing, global brand/product positioning, internationalization of brands, price perception, and luxury consumption. She pursued her Ph.D. from the University of North Carolina at Greensboro, USA.

Monthinee Tricharoenrat has been working in the industry related to consumer studies and research and is based in Thailand. She works for her family business as an assistant to the managing director. She holds an MSc in Economics, Finance and Management from the University of Bristol, UK and was also awarded a degree in Economics from Chulalongkorn University in Thailand and Design Study in Fashion at Chanapatana International Design Institute, Thailand.

John Walsh is the director at SIU Research Center at Shinawatra University in Bangkok, Thailand. He is also an editor for the Southeast Asia, emerging countries network. His books include works on entrepreneurialism and management communications in the Thai context. He received his doctorate from Oxford University in the area of international management, and he has subsequently published widely in the area of social and economic development in Thailand and the Mekong region and related subjects.

Diana Bank Weinberg teaches international business and marketing at the Berlin School of Economics and Law (BSEL) in Berlin. Her main research interests include business diplomacy and DFI in emerging economies. She has worked for the House Subcommittee on Western Hemispheric Affairs and the Mexican Embassy's North American Free Trade Agreement (NAFTA) Office, concentrating on lobbying activities for the passage of the NAFTA, from 1990 to 1995. From 1996 to 2000, Diana worked in the Israeli office of the marketing communications department at BMC, a U.S.-based software company. She has an MBA from Columbia University's Graduate School of Business and a Ph.D. from Israel's Bar Ilan University.

Wlamir Xavier is Assistant Professor of Management at Eastern New Mexico University, United States, with a dual appointment at UNISUL University, Brazil. His research focuses on the business group phenomenon in emerging countries and non-marketing strategies. He has been a visiting scholar at the University of Paris Dauphine, the Wharton School and the Copenhagen Business School. Wlamir's academic work has been recognized on several occasions including the "Emerald Publishing Award for Best Paper on Emerging Markets" in the European International Business Academy Conference—EIBA/2012 and "Best Thematic Paper Award" in the Academy of International Business South East US Chapter Conference—AIB-SE/2012.

Serkan Yalcin is a senior doctoral candidate in the Ph.D. program in marketing and international business at the John Cook School of Business at St Louis University in Missouri. His academic experience has included positions in Turkey, the Republic of Georgia, Kyrgyzstan, and the U.S. His research has appeared in such academic journals as the *Journal of International Entrepreneurship, Multinational Business Review,* the *Journal of Promotion Management,* the *Journal of Developmental Entrepreneurship, Personnel Review,* and *Central Eurasian Studies Review.* Additionally, his work has appeared in the *Handbook of Research on Asian Entrepreneurship* and *Proliferation of the Internet Economy: E-commerce for the Global Adoption, Resistance, and Cultural Evolution.* Focusing on emerging markets such as Turkey, Russia, and the CIS region, Mr. Yalcin's research expertise is in cross-cultural consumer research and international marketing strategy.

Ahmad Youssef is a professor at Humber Institute of Technology and Advanced Learning in Toronto, Canada. He is also a committee member of the Missisauga Board of Trade. His research interests are international business, international knowledge management, and international entrepreneurship. Youssef is a member of the American Academy of Management and has long-term experience in the Brazilian Market as marketing vice president at Web Intelligent Systems S.A. and marketing director at Digitro Technologia Ltd. His Ph.D. is from the Federal University of Santa Catarina in Brazil.

Jun Ying Yu is a lecturer at Glorious-Sun School of Business and Management at Donghua University in Shanghai, China.

GLOSSARY

A

ABAYA: Women in the Arab Gulf states wear a loose over-garment over their street clothes. This is known as the abaya.

ACQUISITION: An existing company purchased by another.

APPAREL WHOLESALE MARKET (CHINA): A retail format that acts as a manufacturer's showroom, wholesale store, and a retail store.

ATACAREJO (BRAZIL): A Brazilian retailing format that combines retailing and wholesaling under one roof with almost no expectations of customer service.

C

CAMELÓDROMOS (BRAZIL): Small-sized and popular street shopping centers that sell low-quality and inexpensive Chinese-made products.

CAMELÔS (BRAZIL): Unregistered street traders that sell in neighborhoods.

CASH-AND-CARRY STORES: A wholesaler that sells to member retailers and other businesses at discounted prices on condition that they pay in cash, collect the goods themselves, and buy in bulk.

CATALOG RETAILING (RUSSIA): Sale of products through the catalog supplied by a retailer or a brand.

COLLECTIVIST SOCIETY: A group of individuals who conform to the goals of a collective, such as the family, tribe, or religious group.

COLOR-CODING OF CLOTHING (THAILAND): Association of colors with political groups; very common in Thailand.

CONFUCIAN CULTURE (KOREA): The cultures most strongly influenced by Confucianism include those of China, Japan, and Korea. Characteristics include respect for old age, and status is important to show power.

CONSIGNMENT SALE: Sale in which the owner transfers possession of goods, but not title of the goods, to a third party. The third party then sells the goods and returns the proceeds to the owner.

CONSUMER AFFLUENCE: The ability of consumers to spend on clothing, calculated based on per capita clothing sales.

COOPERATIVE (MEXICO): A group of small retailers/producers that get together to run a single store so as to reduce cost.

CO-OPERATIVE STORE (CONSUMER CO-OPERATIVE STORE): A store that is owned and controlled by members of the co-operative who use the products. In this retail outlet format, members enjoy not only the benefits of good-quality products at fair prices but also a share of the profits (a dividend) based on the amount of each member's purchases.

D

DESIGNER STORES (CHINA): Single-branded stores that carry merchandise of any one luxury designer label such as Louis Vuitton or Chanel.

DIRECT INVESTMENT: A method of entry in which the foreign company owns 100 percent of the company.

DIRECT SALE: The sale of any consumer product or service by way of personal explanation and demonstrations, done mostly in homes.

DISTRIBUTOR (INDIA): Foreign retailer that sells through local retail chains.

E

EXCLUSIVE MULTIPLE BRAND/NONBRANDED STORES (INDIA): Privately owned single stores that carry branded as well as nonbranded traditional and Western clothing based on the needs of the local consumers. Some beauty stores could also be large chain formats.

F

FACTORY STORES (RUSSIA): Manufacturer-owned stores that are located near the factory and sell new as well as last season's merchandise.

FANILLA COUTURE (QATAR): A scarf and other apparel pieces brand that appeal to a large section of Qatar's Muslim consumers.

FASHION BOUTIQUES (CHINA): Privately owned shops on major commercial streets in big cities that sell high-priced items in limited quantities.

FIRST MOVER'S ADVANTAGE: A sometimes insurmountable advantage gained by the first significant company to move into a new market, or the edge that any company/retailer gains by entering a particular market before any competitors.

FRANCHISING: A license given to a manufacturer, distributor, or trader that enables them to manufacture or sell a named product or service in a particular area for a stated period.

G

GLOBAL TIER: The first of four distinct groups in emerging economies, the global tier consists of consumers who want products and goods to have the same attributes and quality as products in developed countries.

GLOCAL TIER: The second of four distinct groups in emerging economies, the glocal tier consists of consumers who demand customized products of near-**global** standard and are willing to pay a shade less than global consumers do.

GREENFIELD INVESTMENT: When a foreign company invests in a country by starting the construction from the ground up.

GROSS DOMESTIC PRODUCT (GDP): An indicator to measure the economic prosperity of a country that represents the total dollar value of all goods and services produced over a specific time period.

H

HYPERMARKET: Supermarkets and department stores combined together, such as Wal-Mart.

I

INDO-WESTERN CLOTHING (INDIA): Basic Western clothing (like t-shirt or shirts) with an Indian element such as embroidery or traditional print added to it.

INFORMAL ECONOMY: System of trade or economic exchange used outside state controlled or money based transactions, practiced by most of the world's population. It includes barter of goods and services, mutual self-help, odd jobs, street trading, and other such direct sale activities. Income generated by the informal economy is usually not recorded for taxation purposes, and is often unavailable for inclusion in gross domestic product (GDP) computations.

J

JOINT VENTURE: A contract between two companies to conduct business for an agreed upon duration of time.

L

LICENSING: An agreement by which a company (the licensor) permits a foreign company (the licensee) to set up a business in a foreign market using the licensor's manufacturing processes, patents, trademarks, and trade secrets in exchange for payment of a fee or royalty.

LOCAL BAZAAR (TURKEY): Cash-only stores set up by individuals alongside streets, with permission from local authorities, which sell food products, clothing, furniture, jewelry, and antiques.

LOCAL TIER: The set of consumers that follows the glocal tier of consumers in an emerging market economy, these consumers are happy with products of local quality, at local prices.

M

MAIN STREET: The primary street of a town, where most of its shops, banks, and other businesses are located.

MALINCHISTAS (MEXICO): Mexican consumers who prefer foreign products over Mexican products.

MANUFACTURER OUTLET (CHINA): An outlet store owned by the manufacturer of a brand that sells off-season products.

MOM-AND-POP STORE: A small retail business, as a grocery store, owned and operated by members of a family.

N

NAK LENG (THAILAND): A typical Thai tough man who is well dressed and shows off wealth through expensive possessions such as jewelry, cars, and many servants.

NEIGHBORHOOD STORES (BRAZIL): Mom and pop stores converted to neighborhood stores to include grocery, cleaning products, and health and beauty products.

O

OFF-PRICE STORES (BRAZIL): Stores that sell previous season merchandise at substantial discounts.

ONLINE RETAILING (RUSSIA): A nonstore format where consumers buy products through the Internet.

OPEN-AIR MARKETS (CHINA): Markets that sell clothing as well as groceries along major commercial streets or shopping centers during periods of high consumer traffic.

OUTLET STORES (BRAZIL): Stores that are usually bigger than their city counterparts, and offer lower priced merchandise to value conscious consumers.

P

PARTNERSHIP: An agreement between two or more people to work together to carry on a business activity, without local or state filings. Each partner is personally liable for all of the debts of the partnership. Any one partner is able to bind the partnership by entering into a contract on behalf of the partnership.

PHANUNG (THAILAND): A wrap dress traditionally worn by Thai men and women.

PRIVATE LIMITED COMPANY: Type of incorporated firm that (like a public firm) offers limited liability to its shareholders but (unlike a public firm) places certain restrictions on its ownership.

PUBLIC LIMITED COMPANY (PUBLICLY HELD COMPANY): Incorporated, limited liability firm whose securities are traded on a stock exchange and can be bought and sold by anyone. Public companies are strictly regulated, and are required by law to publish their complete and true financial position so that investors can determine the true worth of its their stock (shares).

PULGAS (FLEA MARKET) (MEXICO): Market in Mexico that sells knock-offs of American brands.

R

RETAIL-APPAREL INDEX: An indicator of the rank of a country as an emerging market attractive to foreign investors based on all the important drivers that make a market attractive to foreign investors.

S

SALVAR (TURKEY): Baggy pants worn by Turkish men in villages and the eastern part of Turkey.

SECOND-HAND LUXURY BRAND BOUTIQUE (CHINA): Stores that sell used luxury products.

SPECIALIZED RETAIL NETWORK (BRAZIL): Similar to franchising, a network of stores controlled by a central office that decides the pricing and promotions policies in the stores.

SPECIALIZED SMALL STORES (BRAZIL): Family-owned businesses mainly located on city streets and in shopping centers.

SUPERMARKET: A large, self-service store that carries a wide variety of food, household products, and other goods, which it sells in high volumes at relatively low prices.

T

TIANGUIS (MEXICO): Market on wheels, informal stores located in city centers, near subway stations, inside the malls, at beaches or anywhere with high consumer traffic.

V

VENDING MACHINE (RUSSIA): A self-service retail format where products are stocked in a vending machine and people insert cash or credit card to make a purchase.

W

WAREHOUSE CLUB (WHOLESALE CLUB; MEMBERSHIP WAREHOUSE): A cut-price retailer that sells a limited selection of brand-name grocery items, appliances, clothing, and other goods at substantial discounts to members, who pay an annual membership fee.

WHOLESALE CLUBS (RUSSIA): Stores that offer limited merchandise for members, like Sam's Club or Costco in the United States.

WHOLLY OWNED SUBSIDIARY: A subsidiary in which the parent holding company owns virtually 100 percent of the common stock.

CREDITS

FIGURE 8.7 Michael Luhrenberg / iStock

FIGURE 8.8 John Walsh

FIGURE 8.9 Christophe Archambaul/AFP/Getty Images

FIGURE 9.0A Fairchild Books

FIGURE 9.0B Age Fotostock/Superstock

FIGURE 9.0C Tony Anderson/Getty Images

FIGURE 9.1 Victor Chavez/WireImage/Getty Images

FIGURE 9.2 Jay_Stock / iStock

FIGURE 9.3 nedjelly / iStock

FIGURE 9.4 jmccurley51 / iStock

FIGURE 9.5 Victor Chavez/WireImage/Getty Images

FIGURE 9.6 Gabriel Rossi/LatinContent/Getty Images

FIGURE 9.7 Victor Chavez/WireImage/Getty Images

FIGURE 10.0A Fairchild Books

FIGURE 10.0B Nasreen Shabir Sharif

FIGURE 10.0C Nasreen Shabir Sharif

FIGURE 10.1 Fairchild Books

FIGURE 10.2A Nasreen Shabir Sharif

FIGURE 10.2B Nasreen Shabir Sharif

FIGURE 10.3A Nasreen Shabir Sharif

FIGURE 10.3B Nasreen Shabir Sharif

FIGURE 10.4 Nasreen Shabir Sharif

FIGURE 10.5A Nasreen Shabir Sharif

FIGURE 10.5B Nasreen Shabir Sharif

FIGURE 10.6 Nasreen Shabir Sharif

FIGURE 11.0A Yiyue Fan

FIGURE 11.0B Shubhapriya Bennur

FIGURE 11.0C Sung Ha Jang

FIGURE 11.0D Nasreen Shabir Sharif

INDEX

Page numbers in bold italics refer to figures or tables.